AN IMPERIALIST LOVE STORY

An Imperialist Love Story

Desert Romances and the War on Terror

Amira Jarmakani

NEW YORK UNIVERSITY PRESS

New York and London

NEW YORK UNIVERSITY PRESS
New York and London
www.nyupress.org

References to Internet websites (URLs) were accurate at the time of writing. Neither the author nor New York University Press is responsible for URLs that may have expired or changed since the manuscript was prepared.

Library of Congress Cataloging-in-Publication Data
Jarmakani, Amira, 1974–
An imperialist love story : desert romances and the War on Terror / Amira Jarmakani.
pages cm
Includes bibliographical references and index.
ISBN 978-1-4798-1561-6 (cl : alk. paper) — ISBN 978-1-4798-2086-3 (pb : alk. paper)
1. Love stories, American—History and criticism. 2. Erotic stories, American—History and criticism. 3. Heroes in literature. 4. Masculinity in literature. 5. Desire in literature. 6. Deserts in literature. 7. East and West in literature. 8. Social values in literature.
I. Title. II. Title: Desert romances and the War on Terror.
PS374.L6J36   2015
813'.08509—dc23   2015004666

New York University Press books are printed on acid-free paper, and their binding materials are chosen for strength and durability. We strive to use environmentally responsible suppliers and materials to the greatest extent possible in publishing our books.
Manufactured in the United States of America
10 9 8 7 6 5 4 3 2 1

Also available as an ebook

CONTENTS

PREFACE

In retrospect, Barry Manilow seems like a perfect fit for the 2008 Romance Writers of America (RWA) conference, even if it was not quite what I expected. To the tune of "I Write the Songs," the opening motivational speaker led the conference participants to verbalize their own strengths in song: "We write the books that women love to read / Romance and love is [*sic*] what the whole world needs." Indeed, this sentiment could not fit more perfectly with what seems to be the shared feeling among romance writers and readers alike that romance novels can function as a global salve for any problems occurring worldwide. Since I arrived at the conference eager to investigate a fascinating new development in romance novels—the burgeoning popularity of the sheikh, the alpha-male hero, across category subgenres since 2000—I found the opening inspirational message to be quite intriguing. The upsurge in sheikh-themed romance novels has been widely reported in popular news media.[1] There is even a website, "Sheikhs and Desert Love," devoted specifically to the topic and genre.[2] While the character of the sheikh is certainly not new in U.S. popular culture, the character's resurgence within the genre of romance novels is particularly interesting in a historical moment in which U.S.-led wars in Afghanistan and Iraq provide the political background in which these texts are marketed and consumed.

I attended the 2008 RWA conference eager to explore the contemporaneous boom in popularity of the sheikh as alpha-male hero in mass-market romance novels. What I found was that the desert romance is exceptional in terms of its relationship to the war on terror despite being an unremarkable representation of the romance genre overall. To my disappointment, and as a testament to how much I would learn about the romance novel industry, there was not one workshop presentation title that specifically mentioned sheikhs or desert romances as the main focus. If the romances were mentioned in the sessions I attended, it was as one example of a possible alpha-male character or as an exotic international location in which to possibly set a novel. My online, virtual forays into romancelandia confirmed these initial observations. Though I originally planned to interview fans of the desert romance to learn about the subgenre's rise in popularity, I quickly discovered that fans of the subgenre were exceedingly difficult to locate and even harder to contact. To do so, I created a research blog describing my project, posting on some of the novels I was reading, and inviting comments. I also visited other websites to invite contact with readers. I identified three main websites dedicated to desert romances—two privately created sites and one subsection of the *I [Heart] Harlequin Presents* blog. The first, "Sheikhs and Desert Love," seemed to get a fair amount of traffic but didn't support a blog. I was able to have a short email interview with the creator before Amazon.com took over the site and turned it into a commercial space. On a private blog, *Romancing the Desert*, the creator, blogger, and reviewer Marilyn Shoemaker posted my query, but I did not receive any interested respondents. The commercial blog *I [Heart] Harlequin Presents* provided information from the author's perspective, but not much from readers; my email inquiries about posting a description of my research to readers received no response.

What I did find in relative abundance were discussions about romance readers' dislike of the sheikh-hero. Indeed, the sheikh is a key subject of ridicule on one of the most popular romance novel blogs, *Smart Bitches, Trashy Books*.[3] He often serves as the punchline in witty and sarcastic conversations about romance novels gone wrong. He shows up prominently in the list of books to avoid in a *Smart Bitches, Trashy Books* "What Not to Read" post: "Any romance featuring a sheikh. Or more than one Sheikh. . . . Double that if the Sheikh is also a boardroom tycoon."[4] Though SBSarah (for Smart Bitch Sarah, the screen name for Sarah Wendell), one of the creators and the current webmaster of the site, agrees that sheikhs have recently risen in popularity for the genre as a whole, she declined to post my invitation for readers to talk to me about sheikhs, asserting that her audience did not read those types of novels.[5] She did this despite my asking twice and despite her record of posting other researchers' queries for a range of projects. I was left with the impression that she felt that such a link to the sheikh would somehow compromise the integrity of her blog.

In short, I found a profound ambivalence about the sheikh-hero, and it is this ambivalence that drives both the inquiry and the conclusions of this book. What follows is an exploration both of what is said and what remains unsaid about the sheikh-hero of desert romances. The primary materials for exploring these topics are the desert romances themselves. When I began the project, there were over 100 desert romances; as I write, that number has ballooned to 267, according to "Sheikhs and Desert Love." Of these, I include 40 in my textual analysis. Secondary sources supplementing my interpretation of the novels include interviews with six popular desert romance authors as well as blog entries by the writers themselves in which they discuss the lure of the sheikh. The interviews are admittedly short. I was only able to conduct interactive interviews with two of the authors—one by phone and the other via online chat. The remaining four emailed their responses to my questions about the sheikh, citing their busy schedules for their inability to grant a personal interview.

What remains largely absent from my data are articulations from the readers themselves discussing why they like sheikh novels (except in very few comments on scattered blog posts). When readers do express desire for or interest in sheikhs, they often name it as a "guilty" pleasure. Sheikhs, it seems, remain a guilty pleasure even among romance novel readers who have shed the associations of guilt and shame long attached to romance novels in general. In the rare articulations from readers about why they like desert romances, what comes through most clearly is a disavowal of any connection between these novels and the war on terror, despite the clear engagement with the war on terror in the plot narratives. I read this silence and disavowal through two main lenses. The first is bloggers' and readers' online comments about why they do not like desert romances. As we will see, the main reason offered is that sheikhs cannot be a fantasy hero since they are too close to the perception of terrorists as horrifying. The other main lens I use for interpreting readers' silences about their desire for the sheikh is authors' articulations about his desirability as a character. This expression of the sheikh's desirability is drawn both from interviews with the authors and from a critical analysis of the novels themselves.

Romance novels are often denigrated as silly or trashy fantasies— escape narratives that bear no relation to reality. When accused of being naive and duped by the genre into leading an oppressed existence, avid romance readers often respond by explaining that the (usually feminist) critic is herself the dupe, since she assumes that the readers cannot tell the difference between fantasy and reality.[6] At the same time, romance readers and writers also defend against the accusation that romance novels are trashy fluff by arguing that they learn a lot of historical and geographical facts by reading and/or writing them; indeed, good writers are deemed to be those who have done solid research and who get their historical and geographical details correct. In other words, defenders of the genre use both fantasy and reality as a means of validating the genre and of making it culturally meaningful. In so doing, they demonstrate that fantasy and reality are far from mutually exclusive; they are integrally, and sometimes inexplicably, bound up in one another. Because of the subgenre's imagined (or disavowed) relationship to the war on terror, then, desert romances provide a means of investigating the way that often unacknowledged fantasies guide and shape the realities of the war on terror.

While desert romances have certainly increased in popularity in the last decade, concurrently with the war on terror, they still represent a relatively small proportion of overall romance novels sold.[7] For example, the RWA website lists 8,240 new romance novel titles for 2010, only 16 of which were desert romances (the latter number comes from my own accounting of them). These numbers should be broken down further, though. RWA reports its data according to Simba Information research, which casts an extremely wide net for its categorization of the genre "romance" (including, for example, Nicholas Sparks). When one controls for category romance (and especially Harlequin, the main publisher of both category romance and sheikh or desert romances), the ratio of desert romances is 16 out of 1,375 new titles, or 1.16 percent. Don't let this minuscule percentage fool you, though. It translates to approximately 1.5 million sheikh books sold, not an insignificant number.[8] Indeed, their overall numerical representation within the genre as a whole does not justify the amount of media attention sheikh romances have garnered, a fact that points to their topical intrigue. The shock about their popularity (or the defense of it) centers on the disbelief that an Arab male—overwhelmingly associated with terrorism in the contemporary U.S.-Anglo context—could serve as an object of erotic desire.[9]

The larger frames of exploration of this book circumscribe the war on terror and, even more widely, the question of how contemporary imperialism functions. In that sense, this book both is and is not about desert romance novels. Let me be clear: desert romances are not widely popular in comparison to other subgenres in the industry. Consequently, this book does not argue that desert romances are directly representative of larger cultural associations with the war on terror. Instead, it argues that the whole range of identifications, disavowals, and rejections of the sheikh-hero are broadly reflective of a complex set of cultural associations and identifications with the war on terror.

Rather than directly expressing the U.S. view of the war on terror, desert romances indirectly articulate that which cannot be said: they offer a glimpse into the way that desire motivates contemporary technologies of imperialism as manifested in the war on terror. They do this precisely because of the exemplary ways in which they must negotiate the boundaries between fantasy and reality in representations of the sheikh-hero. Though the sheikh has a long history as romance hero, reaching all the way back to E. M. Hull's 1919 novel *The Sheik*, contemporary desert romances have had to find ways of clearly distinguishing the sheikh-hero from popular associations with the fanatically violent Middle Eastern terrorist. In both the ways that they succeed in casting the sheikh as a hero in spite of powerful and overwhelming images of Arab and/or Muslim terrorists, and the ways they fail to make the sheikh desirable (for romance readers who repudiate the sheikh), the novels reveal a great deal about the imbrication of fantasy in the realities of the war on terror.

Though desert romances are exemplary materials through which to explore the war on terror, they are not the only cultural materials that engage the fantasy-reality relationship. In fact, one advantage of analyzing desert romances in particular is precisely their illumination of how fantasy plays a key role in all sorts of engagements with the Middle East. The following example explores the dialectics of fantasy and reality in popular U.S. investments in the Middle East, demonstrating that while desert romances provide the perfect materials for such an investigation, the phenomenon permeates a much broader set of cultural associations. One of the palpable ways in which this became clear was in the romanticization of what the U.S. media dubbed the Arab Spring.

Protest Like an Egyptian: Tracing Popular Investments in the Middle East through Desert Romances

The rallying cry that emerged from the February 2011 Wisconsin protestors named an affinity that would have been unthinkable, or at least shocking, just a few months earlier. Alternately encouraging supporters to "protest" or "fight like an Egyptian" and calling for Governor Scott Walker to step down (in signs that read "Mubarak—check. Walker _____?" and "Hosni Walker, Elected Dictator"), the protestors in Wisconsin represented just one example of popular U.S. identification with the Middle East that manifested itself during the so-called Arab Spring. The spring 2011 Arab uprisings unsettled some common patterns of representing the Arab world in the United States; instead of the familiar figure of the irrational, aggressive terrorist or the submissive, oppressed veiled woman, mainstream news stories were filled with images of everyday Arab citizens—in Tunisia, Egypt, Yemen, Bahrain, and Syria—protesting oppressive governments and dire conditions. The Wisconsin protests demonstrate that at least some everyday U.S. citizens had been moved to identify with Middle Easterners. As new as these kinds of engagements seem amid a landscape of old, tired stereotypes of the Middle East, they actually bring to the surface long-standing identifications, desires, and investments in the Middle East, which, some may be surprised to discover, have already existed in a subgenre of mass-market romance novels known collectively as desert romances.

Allow me to use another example from the Arab uprisings to outline some key points about desert romances. In the early days of protests in Syria, a post from Syrian American lesbian Amina Abdullah Araf's blog *Gay Girl in Damascus* went viral. In the late April 2011 post, Araf claimed that Syrian secret police had visited her house, that her father had valiantly defended her and sent them away, and (in a later post) that she had been forced to go underground for her own safety. In the larger context of a general U.S. fascination with and investment in the Arab uprisings, it is no surprise that this set of posts—which gave seemingly direct access to the thoughts and experiences of a marginalized subjectivity—was referenced by multiple journalistic sources and accessed by countless individuals. When, a couple of months later, Araf was revealed to be Tom MacMaster, a forty-year-old married white man from Stone Mountain, Georgia, another round of internet frenzy was devoted to him, this time focusing on his insensitivity (to put it mildly) and the damage his hoax would do to "real" Syrian lesbians living under a brutal regime. The controversy and critique centered on a critical tension between reality and fantasy, a tension that is very much alive (and, indeed, a crucial feature) in the romance novel genre.

MacMaster's self-defense was twofold and contradictory. On the one hand, he claimed that he had begun the blog as a creative writing exercise to attempt to inhabit a radically different subjectivity in a believable way. In other words, he used a potent reality to create the fantasy of good fiction. On the other hand, he defended his actions by arguing that he wanted to give voice to a subjugated reality, and he had to do so by ventriloquizing that voice since no one would believe what a white Western heterosexual man would say about Arab lesbians. In other words, he created a fantasy to represent reality. In both instances, fantasy and reality are contingent and dialectical; they are mutually constitutive. One only has to look at the fallout of his hoax for evidence. Unsurprisingly, his antics had the opposite of his intended effect, according to the rescue-narrative (giving voice) version of his defense, since the Syrian government took advantage of the widely publicized hoax to give credence to its claim that protests inside Syria were being fomented (and fabricated) from the outside. In other words, not only did MacMaster's individual fantasy have widely public reverberations, but it also had material effects. It demonstrates the way that identification, desire, and fantasy can operate simultaneously at the individual and the social levels, defying clear distinctions between private and public realms. Even the most generous reading of MacMaster's intentions gives evidence to Diana Fuss's claim that "identification is the point where the psychical/social distinction becomes impossibly confused and finally untenable."[10]

Comparing desert romances with media representations of the Arab Spring is also instructive. Notably, the sheikh-heroes in desert romances closely resemble the leaders who (sometimes brutally) repressed the democratic, nonviolent uprisings in their own countries. As I explore in chapter 1, their countries most closely resemble those in the Persian Gulf in a variety of ways—the countries are typically newly oil-rich, and, consequently, the sheikh-leaders seek alliance with U.S.-Anglo powers as a means of protection against any threat to the often-monarchical regime that controls the country's resources. Though the novels are careful to cast the sheikh-heroes in desert romances as liberal and enlightened when it comes to women's rights (or at least on their way, thanks to the intervention of the usually white heroine in the life of the sheikh), a key marker of the sheikh's civilization is also his strategic alliance with U.S.-Anglo powers—a fact that would align the sheikh-heroes of desert romances more closely with U.S.-allied leaders, like the kings of Bahrain and Jordan. Though the brutal repression of the uprisings in Bahrain received scant attention in U.S. media, King Hamad Al Khalifa, Bahrain's leader was afforded op-ed space in the *Washington Times* to position himself as a progressive leader who wanted to "strike a balance between stability and gradual reform, always adhering to the universal values of human rights, free expression and religious tolerance."[11] He wrote these words even as his government moved to curtail free expression and shut down critique of the religious intolerance perpetrated by his own regime, demonstrating how the language of human rights can function as a way of aligning with the U.S. even while obscuring any actual engagement with human rights abuses.[12]

Though Jordan is not a Gulf country, its allied relationship with the U.S. also mimics some of the key representations of sheikh-heroes in desert romances. Jordan's response to the uprisings related to the Arab Spring is also notable in this regard. Though the monarchy's response to protest in Jordan was much less brutal and repressive than that of Bahrain's monarchy, this simple fact can obscure how the Jordanian regime had successfully contained and diffused protest over the past decade.

One key tactic Jordan deployed was to shift the spatial landscape of the city and simultaneously restrict where people were allowed to hold protests; these two strategies in tandem have ensured both that protests are no longer visible as they once were and that they fail to interrupt commerce as they once did.[13] Instead, the capital city is spatially organized in such a way as to foster international tourism, a key neoliberal industry in the postcolonial context, and one that at best glosses over and at worst represses popular protest in order to present a sanitized vision of a modern, civilized city that nevertheless hosts ancient treasures. Indeed, Jordan's regime can be described in terms that mimic a romance novel narrative: "a romantic, old-style souk environment that will attract tourists and affluent Jordanians, providing Amman with the much-sought combination of a gleaming cosmopolitan city paired with a romantic, exotic old city."[14] Such an image not only is reminiscent of the "new Middle East" represented by gleaming, cosmopolitan cities in the United Arab Emirates (like Dubai and Abu Dhabi, the latter the site of a recent *Sex and the City* film in which the sexy foursome refer to Abu Dhabi by the phrase the "new Middle East"), but also parallels descriptions of sheikh-heroes' cities in contemporary desert romances. For example, Sheikh Zafiq of *Bella and the Merciless Sheikh* "has turned what was once an ancient desert city into an international centre for commerce. The buildings on the waterfront are as modern as anything you would find in Manhattan or Canary Wharf, but only a few streets away is the old city with many wonderful examples of Persian architecture."[15]

Reserving an analysis of the confluence of Arab, Persian, and Turkish markers in desert romances for the introduction, here the example highlights the characteristics that define the successful sheikh-hero. These descriptions of leaders who seek to draw tourists and international commerce to their hybrid cities of gleaming skyscrapers and old-world charm bind sheikh-heroes in desert romances to key U.S.-allied leaders in the Middle East. The remarkable resemblance of romantic desert princes to such leaders therefore suggests that desert romances are particularly rich materials with which to investigate a significantly under-theorized set of figures—those Middle Eastern leaders allied with the U.S. in the war on terror.

Romancing the Sheikh, Desiring the War on Terror

The *Gay Girl in Damascus* example may seem quite distinct from mass-market romance novels—after all, desert romances clearly distinguish themselves as unreal fantasy novels, and readers of the genre must constantly remind critics that they read romances precisely as fantasies that are not necessarily representative of how they would idealize their own real lives. Despite this seeming incongruity (indeed, perhaps because of it), I use it as a framing device here for two reasons: First, it allows me to look at the parallels between popular investments in the Arab uprisings and those fictionalized in desert romances (for far longer). Second, it serves as a key reminder of the messy and blurry distinctions—the dialectical relationship—between fantasy and reality. One of the most interesting things about the contemporary popularity of the sheikh-hero is the vehemence with which many avid readers of romance novels despise him. The most common reason given by those who dislike the sheikh-hero or simply cannot imagine reading a desert romance is that the subject matter is *too close* to reality to succeed in being a good fantasy. Indeed, readers will often explain that they know too much about the violent realities of the Middle East to enjoy these novels. Combining these comments with the commonly cited defense of the genre as trashy fluff—a defense that explains that authors put a lot of research into the writing process to make the contextual and historical details real (believable) enough for the readers to enjoy (and even learn something from) the story—one can immediately realize the delicate tension between reality and fantasy that is at play in romance novels. It is the same kind of tension apparent in the MacMaster hoax, even if the blog and the desert romances have different goals. One of the primary aims of this book is to explore what resides at the edge of this tension—what can be revealed precisely in the way the fantasy and reality grate together, where they collapse, and the ways they perforate one another.

On the *I [Heart] Harlequin Presents* blog, in an entry titled "The Unshakeable Appeal of the Sheikh Hero," an intern blogger for Harlequin poses the question of whether there is any relationship between the popularity of sheikh-themed romance novels and current events in the Middle East.[16] Consistent with the responses to such a suggestion on websites specifically devoted to sheikh-themed romance novels (such as the "Sheikhs and Desert Love" website and the *Romancing the Desert—Sheikh Books* blog), dedicated readers' answers come swift and sure; the popularity of such novels is completely unrelated to the actual events that link the U.S. to the Arab and Muslim worlds, they claim. Instead, these novels have "unshakeable appeal," they explain, because of the electrifying "alpha maleness" of the sheikh-hero; because of the romance of the Orient, which provides a faraway, dreamy setting for fantasy or escape; and because the books provide a forbidden, unknown, and exotic backdrop in which the romantic scene can unfold.

While I do not deny the veracity of such a claim, it is clear that the novels are also intimately engaged with contemporary events, naming, among other things, "weapons of mass destruction," uranium-enriching evil half-brothers, and oil-rich Gulf sheikhs investing in the tourism industry.[17] Coupling this contradiction with a general context within the romance novel industry that casts romance novels as forging new bonds globally, sheikh romance novels are uniquely situated as cultural artifacts that can reveal a great deal about the complex and richly textured ways everyday readers engage with the fact of U.S. intervention in the Middle East. As feminist scholars such as Janet Jakobsen, Jasbir Puar, and Zillah Eisenstein have argued, both implicit and explicit narratives and images of sexuality have informed, and even guided, U.S. engagements with terrorism, war, and militarism, as evinced clearly in the photographs taken by U.S. soldiers at Abu Ghraib.[18] Echoing Gayle Rubin's earlier injunction that "sexuality should be treated with special respect in times of great social stress,"[19] Jakobsen writes that "sex remains at the center of public life because the politics of sexuality and the politics that drive issues like economics or war are fundamentally connected."[20]

In fact, in the recognition of precisely these kinds of connections, romance novels are perhaps ahead of the proverbial curve. Indeed, far from devaluing romance novels as silly or insignificant cultural artifacts, this book argues that they are uniquely useful. Because the genre is free to imagine fictionalized landscapes of the Middle East at the same time that it represents authors' efforts to demonstrate they have done their research, these novels can, ironically, be more direct than other kinds of materials that reference the Middle East. Virtually all of my interviews with romance authors demonstrated this tension—while many of them explained that they created a fictionalized Middle Eastern country for the novel's setting out of anxiety at having to get all the details correct, the writers also described doing research to convincingly represent generalized aspects of the Middle East. The research these writers described—such as searching for Arabic words and names to insert into the dialogue, looking for details about the kinds of scimitars and daggers that are indigenous to the region, and learning about the history of bedouins—itself reveals what can be imagined about the Middle East and what provokes desire. Further, the secondary materials used here— readers' and writers' blogs and comments—offer fresh and honest articulations of the complex associations people have with the (fantasy) figure of the sheikh and with his counterpart, the (real) figure of the terrorist.

Desert romances are by no means a new subgenre; nor have they radically changed in the years following the events of 9/11, which is to say that the main elements of appeal of the sheikh-hero—his exoticism, power, and riches—have remained constant. In this way, desert romances underscore that although 9/11 may have intensified the war on terror, it was very much a continuation of already-existing policies, procedures, and representations vis-à-vis Middle Easterners in the United States. Desert romances therefore refute the claim that 9/11 is a supremely foundational moment for Arabs and Muslims in the United States. Though authors have had to adapt their stories in order to clearly distinguish their heroes from the plethora of Middle Eastern antiheroes that dominate U.S. popular consciousness, the main elements of the stories have remained the same. In fact, readers and writers who reject any relationship between contemporary desert romances and the war on terror argue that these stories have been popular in the larger romance novel industry since long before 9/11. Therefore, what is new about desert romances since 9/11 is the fact that they provoke disavowal from their fans. If disavowal can be taken to mean "an intellectual acceptance of what is repressed, even as the repression is maintained,"[21] these symbolic markers of the war on terror clearly indicate a powerful disavowal functioning in tandem with the recent popularity of desert romances.

Investigating the architecture of this disavowal alongside the comments of sheikh-haters—those who claim to know too much about the brutal realities of the Middle East to fantasize about it—allows me to chart a complex map of U.S.-Anglo investments (both positive and negative) in the Middle East. One might question how a relatively small subgenre of mass-market romance novels can apply to overall mainstream attitudes toward the Middle East. My claim here is not that these novels influence popular perceptions of the Middle East, but that they are in a unique position to reflect these perceptions. Precisely because romance writers must overcome the surfeit of reality—what the general reader thinks she knows—about the Middle East, an investigation of the constructions of, and particularly the silences within, these stories about desert kingdoms provides access to revealing fantasies about the war on terror, and especially to the role of desire in shaping it. In the narratives of what readers do and do not like about the sheikh-heroes in desert romances, we find some of the most honest articulations of desire as an organizing framework of the war on terror and of contemporary U.S. imperialist technologies.

Contemporary U.S. technologies of imperialism operate under the rubrics of benevolence and humanitarianism. These technologies use the frameworks of security and liberation to justify the expansive militaristic project of the war on terror. In its illustration of desire, the cover of this book speaks to the power of this benevolent framework. As an adaptation of one of the original covers of *The Sheik* (1919), the image represents an unfiltered version of the sheikh fantasy. Key elements of this fantasy remain prominent in contemporary desert romances, though these elements could never be represented so starkly today. The sheikh is all-powerful and larger than life; he holds the heroine in the palm of his hand. He is clearly raced; his dark skin and cultural dress signal his exotic difference. Despite his potentially menacing position in relation to his object of desire, not to mention the inexplicable and jarring position of his hand, he wears a softened and benevolent expression on his face. In this way, he demonstrates a fundamental currency of the romantic narrative, which capitalizes on the heroine's desire to be protected by a strong, powerful leader who turns out to have a sensitive, compassionate side.

The trope of the white woman's desire for the dangerous, exotic other is well-covered terrain. As the somewhat quaint and antiquated nature of the image attests, it is embedded in an old, worn story of empire. But what happens if we read this image more broadly—as the liberal-humanist subject's desire for protection and security, which can only be delivered by the suffocating hand of imperialism? Because imperialism on its face contradicts the liberal-democratic ideals of the U.S. nation-state, it must operate under a different guise. It must tell a more nuanced story than the one of violent domination. The image on the cover of the book bluntly represents one of the guises the story may take: do judge the story of imperialism by the cover of this book, but do not believe the shape it has assumed and the figures it has inhabited. The romantic sheikh is contemporary U.S. imperialism personified, now projected onto its most cherished and reviled other. You are, I am, she is, he is, they are the figure in the palm of its hand, half believing and half wanting to believe that the powerful, larger-than-life force can protect us, make us safe, and even, ironically and impossibly, set us free. How did we get here? *An Imperialist Love Story* proposes to answer this question. It argues that contemporary U.S. imperialism adapts the structure of a love story. Cultivating the desire for security and stability so common to classic romantic narratives, the imperialist love story orients us toward willing subjugation to imperialist power, an orientation that enables the war on terror to persevere.

ACKNOWLEDGMENTS

The idea for this book germinated from an email sent to me by a dear friend and colleague, Evelyn Alsultany. The email contained the link to the now-defunct website "Sheikhs and Desert Love" and a short message encouraging me to check it out. I never dreamed that Evelyn's message would develop into a book project, and over time, I admit I have sometimes wished I had never been introduced to the site at all. That email opened onto the complex and fascinating world of romance novels, which one could truly spend a lifetime exploring. Of course, I alone take responsibility for having entered romancelandia, though I am grateful for the introduction and for the encouragement to persevere.

I have subjected a good number of graduate research assistants to the guilty pleasure of sheikh-heroes over the course of my work on this project. Many thanks go to Katie Diebold, Lisa Frazier, Chanel Craft, Nik Ramey, and Kelsey Waninger for their contributions. Three GRAs in particular have both helped to shape the final product and offered wonderful camaraderie along the way. Beyond her incisive research skills, Tahereh Aghdasifar accompanied me on many trips to used bookstores to find the latest desert romances and even to post flyers seeking desert romance readers for interviews. She always found me the novels and authors for which I was (and often wasn't—*A Bed of Sand* comes to mind) searching. Maggie Franz sifted through my underlining in the majority of the novels analyzed here, dedicatedly typing quotes into one master document. It was an onerous and immeasurably important task for the book and one that she met with equal amounts of good humor and precision, an attitude that she brought also to the task of sorting through twenty-two boxes of *National Geographic* magazines to pull out the Middle East–related articles. Finishing the thankless work of typing up quotations from desert romances, Andrea Miller gracefully and brilliantly took on the monumental task of editing the manuscript according to press guidelines and of tidying up all the citations during the first major revision. As I have gone through the final editing process for the manuscript, it is Tahereh's, Maggie's, and Andrea's work that has most clearly allowed me to edit happily ever after. I really can't thank them enough.

Without two internal grants from Georgia State University, I could not have embarked on the ambitious project of interviewing romance writers and attending the Romance Writers of America conference. The first grant was the Advancement of Women Faculty Scholarship Mentoring grant (2007–2008), which enabled me to explore new research methods under the mentorship of Susan Talburt. The second was a Research Initiation Grant (2008–2009), which supported me to attend the Romance Writers of America conference and to develop a research blog about desert romances. Additional thanks go to colleagues at GSU— Andrew Reisinger, Tahereh Aghdasifar, Megan Sinnott, Julie Kubala, Tiffany King, and Lucas Power—for making it an interesting place to work.

Thanks to the anonymous reviewers of my earlier articles appearing in *Signs* and *American Quarterly* for helping me to shape and hone my argument, particularly as I was first beginning to work through the material and sort out what I thought it was doing. I am also indebted to the reviewers for the initial book manuscript, as their insightful comments encouraged me to write a clearer and stronger argument. All the folks at NYU press, and especially Eric Zinner and Alicia Nadkarni, have been wonderfully supportive. Many heartfelt thanks, also, to the copyeditors with whom I have worked— Andrew Mazzaschi at *Signs*, Paula Dragosh at *American Quarterly*, and Patricia E. Boyd—whose careful reading not only sharpened the work itself, but also helped me sharpen my writing more generally. Along these lines, I hold deep gratitude for Mimi Kirk, an amazing editor and scholar, and a dear friend who has edited different stages of my work over the years and whose close and careful readings and incisive suggestions always push me to be a better writer and scholar.

I am grateful to the audiences at the following conferences, where I presented in-progress work on desert romances: Critical Ethnic Studies Association (Chicago, 2013); Popular Culture Association/American Culture Association (Boston, 2011); National Women's Studies Association (Atlanta, 2011); Contemporary Research in Arab American Studies:

New Trends and Critical Perspectives (Dearborn, MI, 2011); American Studies Association (Washington, DC, 2009); Middle East Studies Association (Washington, DC, 2008); National Women's Studies Association (Cincinnati, 2008); Southeast Women's Studies Association (Charlotte, NC, 2008); American Studies Association (Philadelphia, 2007). In particular, many thanks go to my friend and colleague Lara Deeb for inviting me to give a talk for the Core III lecture series at Scripps College and to the attendees for their helpful questions and comments.

I am lucky to have smart friends and colleagues who have graciously taken the time to read and comment on parts of the manuscript, sometimes in a pinch: Susan Talburt, Julie Kubala, Mimi Kirk, Tahereh Aghdasifar, Andrea Miller, Maggie Franz, Dylan McCarthy Blackston, and Bobbi Patterson. Nadine Sinno graciously—and unbelievably—read nearly the entire manuscript and talked me through several drafts of it (not to mention that she screened *Salmon Fishing in the Yemen* with me, which didn't even prove to be fruitful for the book). In these tasks, I can honestly say *ma fi mithlik*! Her encouragement, interest, and fierce readings contributed immeasurably to the final product.

For accompanying me on the journey into an exploration of Deleuze and Guattari, I owe thanks to Susan Talburt, Julie Kubala, Moon Charania, and Claudia Matus. Special accolades go to Sherah Faulkner for enduring the full immersion of both *Anti-Oedipus* and *A Thousand Plateaus* despite an inordinate amount of broken machines. It is hard to learn the lesson that machines work by breaking. More generally, I am grateful for the company of scholars and friends whose work inspires and motivates me. Among these, I include Nadine Naber, Evelyn Alsultany, Carol Fadda-Conrey, Therese Saliba, Sunaina Maira, Steven Salaita, and Sarah Gualtieri.

Thanks to my family for their interest in and support of my work— Jeff Jarmakani, Shadi al-Khatib, Yara al-Khatib, Mama Joyce Hopkins, Cesar Bruno, and Silvia de Titto—and especially to my parents, Jay Moazza Jarmakani and Brenda Hopkins Jarmakani, for enduring the process of my writing another book and for knowing when to ask and when not to ask about how it was coming along. Though none of my parents' title suggestions made the final cut, their thoughtfulness, wit, and interest in my work no doubt framed and supported my own approach to it.

A special kind of acknowledgment goes to those who lived in a house littered with desert romances for several years. Ramona went from fastidiously emptying them from the bookshelves (along with whatever else happened to be shelved next to them) to triumphantly identifying them as "Mami's books" as she first learned to talk. Yara first learned to sit up, then to crawl, and finally to walk alongside scribbled notes toward revision. Both kept me grounded in, and trained on, imagining the kind of story I would like to read and tell, no matter how much of a fantasy it might seem. With Diego Cesar Bruno I have learned which fantasies to take seriously and how to do so with clarity, integrity, and strength. With him, too, I am learning the meaning of *mañana es mejor*.

Introduction

The Romantic Sheikh as Hero of the War on Terror

A finger of fear stroked her spine as he advanced. His look intent, he radiated such masculine force that she doubted she could stop him.
—Bonnie Vanak, *The Sword and the Sheath* (p. 260)

But even without looking directly at him she could feel the effect of the unleashed power and the blatantly sexual aura he radiated lying like a stone fist in her chest.
—Kim Lawrence, *Desert Prince, Defiant Virgin* (p. 30)

His body tightened as if in preparation for attack, his emerald eyes radiating the intent.
—Olivia Gates, *To Touch a Sheikh* (p. 74)

He was full of left-over nervous energy, enough to power his own nuclear weapons.
—Linda Conrad, *Secret Agent Sheik* (p. 66)

A curious figure stalks the pages of a distinct subset of mass-market romance novels, aptly called desert romances. Animalistic yet sensitive, dark and sexy, this desert prince emanates manliness and raw sexual power. Though his aggressive, potent virility is common in the realm of romance novels, what makes him curious is his steady rise in popularity in the intervening years since September 11, 2001, years that have seen a concomitant, and dominant, rise in depictions of Arab masculinity as backward, particularly in relation to what is understood as a violent nature, and therefore as repulsive. In this respect, the figure of the sheikh-hero as a romantic figure demonstrates a set of ambivalent associations that thrive on the mix of violence or danger with the thrill of pleasure and desire. Indeed, this may be why the metaphor of radiation is put to much use in desert romances. Radiation invokes a potent reservoir of seemingly endlessly available and potentially dangerous energy. It is thrilling precisely for its potency; it remains on the exciting side of danger with reassurances (built into the overall plot narrative) that the heroine and the sheikh himself ultimately know how to harness and control his radioactive energy. Despite the "finger of fear [that] stroked [the heroine's] spine" as the sheikh-hero approaches, despite the fear that she might not be able to stop him, even if she wants to—on the contrary, perhaps because of these things—the heroine is irresistibly drawn to the sheikh-hero. In these instances, her fear activates her desire—not because romance novels particularly appeal to duped, naive women, but because the books serve as abundantly fruitful materials for investigating how desire functions, particularly in relation to potent sociopolitical realities. The "nuclear weapons" that Sheikh Tarik in Secret Agent Sheik can power with his "left-over nervous energy," it turns out, do not invoke terror in the heroine, which would be a logical response, given popular associations with Arab/Muslim men and nuclear weapons. She does not fear the sheikh-hero, because by this point in the plot, she has encountered the sheikh's opposition—the real terrorists, who truly do seek nuclear power for evil means. The connection of the sheikh to nuclear weapons therefore serves as a way of highlighting his exceptionality. As a force of good, he has demonstrated himself to be allied with global U.S.-Anglo powers that similarly seek to vanquish the terrorists. Radiation works as a powerful metaphor in this local example because of its ambivalent associations. The sheikh can simultaneously demonstrate his link to the thrill of risk and danger, while assuring the heroine that he has the ability to control the awesome power that radiation can release.

In this way, the novels' invocations of radiation also reference contemporary discursive associations with radiation. If unleashed by the wrong hands, radiation can be globally catastrophic. Conversely, if organized and controlled by responsible, benevolent powers, it can be harvested as an alternative energy source beyond coal and oil, ensure global stability by keeping rogue forces in check, and even function as a palliative force in specific, focused medical contexts. Such narratives suggest that people must learn to subject themselves to the terrible power of radiation, even when they know about its potentially dangerous consequences. This book examines how people learn to submit to power through their own desire for subjugation. Radiation therefore also serves as a powerful metaphor for the larger concern of this book, which is to investigate how desire can serve as a primary engine to consolidate imperialist power, specifically in the power of the (U.S.) nation-state to wage seemingly endless war. How does desire undergird the perpetuation of the war on terror, an operation that by its very name seems to be focused exclusively on fear?

The metaphor of radiation also invokes the realities of resource scarcity (and therefore energy scarcity). Though the Middle East is most commonly associated with oil as a key natural resource, the contemporary political and military focus on nuclear enrichment and on whether the goal of enrichment is to create energy or weapons demonstrates that radiation is at least equally as important. The prospect of resource scarcity seems to operate through the mechanism of fear—energy security is figured as central to national security, which is in turn oriented toward fear through its focus on defense. Security is conceived in terms of defending against those forces that may threaten it. This idea, however, fails to acknowledge that fear cannot function as subtly and effectively as desire in manufacturing consent.[1] Hegemonic power here works by fomenting the desire for security and protection from that which is feared.

In both desert romances and mainstream narratives about the war on terror, the objects of fear are the evil forces who want to do harm to the protagonists because of their own spite, backwardness, or greed. Illuminated by the metaphor of radiation, then, desert romances demonstrate how desire works as a permeating, yet invisible, driving force of the war on terror on both a micropolitical and a macropolitical level. Stimulated by the thrill of danger, the protagonists in these stories learn that to be their own, true selves, they must subject themselves to love. While this basic plot description is characteristic of the romance genre as a whole, desert romances extend the love story to the context of the war on terror. These are love stories that play out on both the individual and the national levels—between both the sheikh-hero and the heroine and their respective countries. As the exceptional leader of his fictionalized Arab (or vaguely Middle Eastern) country, the sheikh-hero learns to love the (usually) U.S.-Anglo heroine precisely because she can help him navigate an alliance with global superpowers; she, in turn, learns that subjecting oneself to the power of love is its own kind of freedom—one not captured by her liberal feminist orientation toward independence and equality. The hero and heroine's love story necessarily also plays out on the world stage; in the narrative arc of the story, their coupling will literally lead toward world peace.

One reason desert romances increased in popularity after 9/11 is that they offer a supreme narrative obstacle—ethnic and cultural differences heightened by the threat of terrorism—that the characters must overcome to achieve a happy ending to their love story. What makes the stories remarkable objects of study is not that they portray a happily-ever-after ending between a sheikh and a U.S.-Anglo heroine, but the way they do so—in the narrative choices the authors make to write successful romance novels. To be believable, the desert romances must engage with popular discourses about the war on terror, shifting the usual orientation of fear into one of desire. In orienting us toward desire, they demonstrate the war on terror, too, to be a classic, if imperialist, love story.

Anatomies of the Sheikh

The character of the sheikh in popular romance novels both borrows from and builds on the history of the figure in U.S. popular culture. Desert romances draw on multiple histories of the sheikh as a noble desert leader, as an oil-rich powerful man, and as a savage and potentially dangerous figure. A key moment of origin for the sheikh in U.S. popular culture is E. M. Hull's popular novel *The Sheik* (1919), itself a precursor of contemporary romance fiction.[2] The novel entered popular U.S. imagination largely through the success of the film adaptation starring Rudolph Valentino. Indeed, the caricature of the sheikh in the U.S. must be contextualized within a tradition of orientalist representations of sheikh characters in Hollywood films, such as *The Sheik, Son of the Sheik, The Thief of Bagdad, Harum Scarum*, and *Lawrence of Arabia*. The Egyptian actor Omar Sharif, who plays a dark, handsome Arab leader in *Lawrence of Arabia*, exemplifies the kind of sheikh-hero readers expect to find in these novels.

Desert romance authors refute the claim that the novels bear a relationship to the war on terror by explaining that they commonly deploy a much more historically based repertoire of orientalist images. The novels often reference *The Arabian Nights*, the poetry of Omar Khayyam, and the film *Lawrence of Arabia*. The film is a clear inspiration for desert romance authors, as evinced by their references to it both on blog postings and in scenes from their novels, in which the authors often use imagery from the film (e.g., a sheikh gallops away on a horse while his white robes billow out behind him).[3] While chapter 4 explores the *Lawrence of Arabia* links more fully, here it is worth noting that both Peter O'Toole (who played Lawrence in the film) and Sharif (who played Lawrence's Arab sidekick, Ali) are invoked as sex symbols for the genre, thereby representing one of the many binaries that define the sheikh.[4] In other words, he is raced as white and marked ethnically to render him palatably exciting, just as he also balances the dichotomies of traditional versus modern, masculine versus feminine, and terrorist versus progressive leader.

In her historical and literary study of desert romances, Hsu-Ming Teo explains how the word *sheik* in English came to signify "irresistible, ruthless, masterful, and over-sexualized" because of its association with the romance genre in both literary and film iterations.[5] Not surprisingly, therefore, the sheikh is an alpha-male hero, as are many other types of contemporary heroes. Probably the most common way of describing the sheikh's appeal is in the phrase "ruler of all he surveys."[6] Indeed, the description of the sheikh as an immensely powerful leader who rules over an exotic and mysterious kingdom somewhere far away is what gives readers' and writers' claims that the novels bear no relationship to the war on terror some validity. These are tropes of popular romance heroes, and the genre has employed the alpha males since long before the war on terror. Sharon Kendrick, a popular writer, puts it this way: "For me, it's the ultimate fantasy. The autocratic ruler leaping onto an enormous stallion and riding it bare-backed across the endlessly baked sands. The arrogant leader who has experienced the harshness of the unforgiving desert terrain, and has survived it. These are Sheikhs we can all recognize."[7]

Kendrick's characterization of the desirable sheikh-hero is broadly representative of the way that other romance writers and readers detail the allure of the sheikh. She overtly describes the two key characteristics of desert sheikhs—their awesome power and its relationship to the desert terrain—while indirectly referencing two others: that the sheikh, as "arrogant leader," can be likened to the royal heroes of historical romances and, closely related, the sheikh's extravagant wealth. Her characterization also illustrates the centrality of the "ruler of all he surveys" formulation, adding that his power is as limitless as the "endlessly baked sands." The sheikh-hero "rules his world with absolute power"; he is "master and commander of all [he] surveys"; and "his word is law."[8] Because he is autocratic, arrogant, and practically all-powerful, he serves as a supreme alpha-male figure who is romanticized both for his power and because of the romantic tension introduced by the heroine's unique ability to "break down all [his] barriers" and even "enslave" him.[9]

Echoing Kendrick's description, a reader comments that her desire for the sheikh has to do with his ability to "command the desert. It takes power, determination and understanding to harness nature's harshest landscape."[10] The reader's comment shows that the desert is itself one of the primary characters of these novels, setting the scene for isolation and captivity as well as exoticism, mystery, and even freedom—associations explored further in chapter 2. The comment also suggests that one of the key features of desert romances, beginning with the progenitor *The Sheik*, is the need to balance an image of the sheikh as a "fierce desert man"[11]—that is, as virile, powerful, and (dangerously) sexy—with the reassurance that through his "understanding," he has a redeemable, softer side, which he can reveal only to the heroine. The sheikh's hard, alpha-male quality therefore gains definition through association with a harsh natural terrain, implying that he is able to conquer both natural and social elements. In this respect, he parallels some of the qualities of a U.S. icon of masculinity, the cowboy, particularly in terms of his association with horses, an association elaborated on in chapter 2. In fact, Liz Fielding refers to the sheikh-hero as a "cowboy in robes," thereby demonstrating how this foreign, exotic hero can nevertheless tap into romanticized notions of rugged, individualistic masculinity so central to U.S. national mythologies.[12] Like the cowboy, the sheikh is a "quintessential male" with the "look of a desert king . . . his sharp angled features, his skin bronzed from the sun and slightly grooved from the elements."[13]

The sheikh is literally carved out and marked by the desert, which is "hot . . . but exciting" and "recklessly wild."[14] He melds with the desert, as observed by the heroine of *Desert Warrior*: "His skin was warm and tasted faintly of the desert."[15] He also embodies the surprising contrasts of the desert landscape, which is characterized as both dangerous and beautiful. In addition to its stark, wild terrain, "the endless desert vista was an unexpected ally, tranquil and beautiful."[16] The desert is a "landscape of barren beauty, so exotic in its fierceness."[17] These descriptions all bear out author Kate Walker's assertion that what romance readers want is "the handsome, stunning, charismatic man, strong, isolated, totally in control, even in the wild and dangerous terrain of the desert."[18] Yet the depictions also indicate more. They demonstrate that the sheikh figure is defined by structuring binaries—he is commanding and powerful, yet uniquely vulnerable to the heroine; he represents both danger and tranquility; he is savage and primal (in bed), yet refined and civilized as a leader. The importance of these dichotomies—and the sheer volume of them—is a defining aspect of the anatomy of the sheikh, a point that will be fleshed out in chapter 4.

The sheikh, no doubt, is eroticized through the idea of his absolute difference. While his civilized nature is always exposed over the course of the romantic narrative, his cultural difference provides a reservoir of mystery and allure. The heroine is drawn to him because "deep in his heart is a cultural darkness she feels she'll never be able to penetrate."[19] Moreover, the sheikh is the only Mediterranean (or European) hero to be "exotic and just down right different. In the end, the Greeks and Venitians [sic] and Londoners and Italians, they are exotic, but still 100% Western, so not a whole lot different."[20] He is therefore "like a Latin or Greek lover squared" since he "alone carries an air of mystery and romance that was once the prerogative of royalty, the rich. He is different. Exotic in manner and dress. Unfathomable."[21]

The increased mainstream U.S.-Anglo perception of Arabs and Muslims (and anyone perceived to be Muslim) as radically different after the events of 9/11, therefore, helps explain the rise in popularity of desert romances. Sheikh-heroes are a stock character in the romance industry, which received a sudden and massive infusion of exposure highlighting some of the very qualities that define these characters as alpha-male exotic heroes—their difference, danger, and impenetrability. As implied by the comment about other Mediterranean (and British) heroes being "100% Western," an important aspect of the sheikh's difference relies on the idea that he is ethnically or racially different, another aspect of his difference that has been highlighted and exaggerated in the aftermath of 9/11 (see chapter 3). If Hull's novel *The Sheik* allayed miscegenation fears by ultimately revealing the sheikh to hail from European ancestry, contemporary desert romances rely on marking the sheikh-hero as ethnically Arab or Middle Eastern, since his otherness is a crucial element of his alpha-male identity, even if he is ethnically mixed.

Indeed, the power of the desert as exotic setting serves to racialize sheikh characters, even when they "look alarmingly Western" or seem to doubt their own authenticity, as is the case with Loreth Anne White's David Rashid.[22] The ethnicity of these sheikh-heroes is sometimes specified: Rashid has an English mother and an "Arabic" father.[23] Penny Jordan's character Xander is half "Zuranese" and half "western."[24] And Emma Darcy's Zageo is, stunningly, Portuguese, Arab, Indian, British, and French.[25] But crucially, the racialization of these characters comes through vague, exoticized markers like the desert itself, cultural dress, or marriage customs. Because most of the novels are set in fictionalized Arabia (like Xander's "Zuran"), desert romances utilize a mix of ethnic and religious markers that tend to get racialized and conflated as "Arabian."[26] Xander, for instance, who is "Zuranese," is eventually named as Tuareg, which would identify him as ethnically Amazigh (Berber) rather than Arab.

The character of the sheikh in desert romances does not represent actual ethnic and religious categories, because the distinctions among these categories do not matter. What matters is that he is redeemable as a believable hero by having enough Western characteristics to balance out his exotic difference, which manifests itself in a way that echoes the fluidity and conflation of ethnic-religious markers in the popular discourse on the war on terror. If the quintessential figure of the terrorist is vaguely Arab, Muslim, Middle Eastern, South Asian, or some mix of popular perceptions of these categories, then the prototypical sheikh-hero is signified as vaguely or abstractly Mediterranean.

According to Linda Conrad, a popular romance writer, the appeal of the sheikh is linked to his ability to evince atavistic qualities. Here again, his ability to straddle the binary is key. As a modern hero, he has "one foot in the old and one in the new," which allows an elaboration of those elements of romantic fantasy that tend to invoke tradition, like notions of chivalry or the dedication to one's family and country.[27] As an important counterpoint to his danger, the sheikh is consistently portrayed as duty- or honor-bound, a characteristic that is normalized through a culturalist (and orientalist) logic, which understands Middle Eastern culture to be defined by its adherence to quaint notions of honor. Sheikh Jamal, for instance, explains to the heroine that "in [his] country [he] would be honor-bound to marry any woman [he] deflowered," and Sheikh Tarik invokes his culture's "code of honor" when railing against a misogynist statement made by a peer.[28] When Molly, the heroine in *Desert Prince, Defiant Virgin*, tells Sheikh Tair that he has a "warped sense of medieval family honour," he shoots back that "though modern society does not acknowledge it, there is such a thing as the right things and duty and service."[29] As these quotes demonstrate, sheikhs are cast as uniquely able to embody medieval notions of chivalry and tradition, while eventually proving to be nostalgically medieval, rather than oppressively, backwardly so.

Indeed, sheikh-heroes are uniquely able to do so in a modern era in which such notions have regrettably fallen out of favor, according to the romance industry. Consider Keira Gillett's blog post, "Kiss Prince Charming Good-Bye: Say Hello to the Sheikh!" in which she explains that "the sheikh is a modern prince in an age when there aren't enough eligible princes to go around."[30] Beginning her blog post with the lament that "Prince William [is] now . . . off the market," she immediately turns to the crown prince of Dubai, Sheikh Hamdan bin Mohammed bin Rashid al Maktoum, whom she credits with "inspiring authors to write sheikh romances as we speak." In another blog, Gillett expresses a similar sentiment:

> Sheik romance like Paranormal romance has risen in the last few years. In an age where chivalrous princes are nearly nonexistent, Sheik romance offers a modern prince to romance readers. He's a little bit wild, more than a little dangerous, but very much in love with his heroine. Combine this irresistible masculine force with the exotic (most times fantastical and fictional) lands of Africa, the Middle East, and the East and it's magic in the making.[31]

Adding to the lure of the sheikh-prince is the idea that contemporary European princes have lost some of their fantasy appeal because they are so "common," as one romance author put it—that is, one sees them getting married and doing everyday things. With a plethora of princes—five thousand in the Saudi kingdom alone, according to *National Geographic*—and a faraway, exotic locale, however, the Gulf region of the Middle East provides fodder for romantic fantasy, especially because "no one really knows what they are doing," as one romance writer told me.[32] While this offhanded remark suggests that the sheikh is defined as mysterious and exotic, the references to the Gulf region of the Middle East invoke a final defining characteristic of the sheikh—his fabulous wealth.

Creating Arabiastan

Desert romances paint a picture of Arabia that incorporates many elements of the Gulf region in the Middle East, probably because of the standard romance trope of the extraordinarily wealthy, elite, debonair hero. As one romance reader explains, the riches are part of the "fun fantasy" of the sheikh: "Private jets, helicopters, fabulous cars, palaces. You can give them anything."[33] Not only are sheikh-heroes largely cast as modern-day princes, but they are also often cast as leaders of newly oil-rich nations, which consequently demonstrate what SBSarah calls the "utter glitz" of places like Dubai.[34]

Significantly, none of the desert romances claim the United Arab Emirates (UAE) as their setting, and very few of them take place in an actual Middle Eastern country. The vast majority of stories take place in a fictionalized Arab country, and those that name an actual existing country are usually historical romances (taking place at least a century ago, and often earlier) or were published before 2001. Some desert romance writers explain that inventing the sheikh's country is part of the fun. Abby Green, for example, explains that she "had so much fun writing *Breaking the Sheikh's Rules* because [she] got to create a fictional land where anything was possible."[35] Indeed, it is because sheikh-heroes exist in a completely distinct world that they have been compared to vampires, werewolves, and other paranormal heroes.[36] During interviews, another reason writers give for creating a fictionalized country is their concern that they "would get something wrong and offend someone or someone's religion" and a sense that it would be impossible to get all the details correct.[37]

While these are undoubtedly compelling reasons, they do not explain the virtual explosive growth of fictionalized Arabia since 2001. Kate Walker gets closer to an explanation for this phenomenon: "As a writer a Sheikh book is a gift—you get to create your own exotic country, a setting with the huge expanse of the desert. . . . And you can invent your own history, customs, traditions. . . . Writers take the best of the culture, avoiding religious or other problems, and they can show that there are Sheikhs to admire and trust, not just the image that the reports of terrorism etc. might show."[38]

Running the gamut of reasons for creating a fictionalized Arabia, Walker nevertheless must acknowledge that desert romances cannot be set in the actual Middle East, because the majority of her audience believes that the realities of the region are incompatible with romantic fantasy. Romance writer Teresa Southwick puts it more bluntly (one is tempted to say, puts it more honestly): "I avoided any hint of 'Arab' as I was concerned that could be a turnoff to readers. And I made up the country so no research was involved. That way it could be anything I wanted and no one could say I'd made a mistake."[39]

Considering that one of the hallmarks of a good romance writer is the ability to get the historical and cultural details of the chosen setting right, it is significant that the majority of contemporary desert romance writers decide to create a fictionalized setting. [40] It suggests that the Middle East is a highly sensitive topic for readers and represents a setting that writers could not possibly get right while maintaining a successful fantasy story. As Marguerite Kaye explains: "The world I've created in my Princes of the Desert trilogy is—hands up—pure fantasy, and of course I've had to tread lightly over some very real cultural conflicts."[41]

In light of the fictionalization of the Arab world in desert romance novels and the fact that the novels combine elements from non-Arab countries in their descriptions (particularly of Iran and Turkey), I use the term *Arabiastan* to refer to the imagined geopolitical territory to which the romances refer. *Arabia* is a fairly antiquated term that now serves mostly as an adjective for a particular breed of horses or for the French and English translations of *One Thousand and One Nights*. Of course, it does also refer to the Arabian Peninsula, of which Saudi Arabia is a part. Though it is the accepted term for the region, it was created in the orientalist spirit. The Arabic term designating the country of Saudi Arabia is simply *al-Saudiyya*, referring to the ruling family's name (for obvious reasons, the adjective *Arabia* is unnecessary). In romancelandia, "Arabia" therefore serves to represent a vague, imagined orientalist landscape, as evinced by the map of "fictional Arabia" on the website "Sheikhs and Desert Love," which includes many of the fabricated countries that appear in desert romances.[42]

My inclusion of the suffix *-stan* is meant to invoke the way that Pakistan and Afghanistan are included in the popular U.S. imagination of the Middle East, as a result of the geopolitics of the war on terror. Etymologically, the suffix means "land" in both Urdu and Persian, rendering it a plausible term that is also meant to signal its own dissonance. My inclusion of the suffix *-stan* is also meant to signal Iran's inclusion in the fictionalized landscape, both in its war-on-terror association and its orientalist (Persian) connotations, an intention materialized by P. T. Barnum's orientalist villa called Iranistan, which was built in the mid-1850s in Connecticut. Therefore, Arabiastan broadly refers to two main phenomena: First, the conflation of Arab and other Islamicate countries in the idea of the Middle East that is invoked by the war on terror (e.g., both the idea that Pakistan and Afghanistan are part of the Middle East, despite the fact that they are Central or South Asian countries, and the conflation of Iranians with Arabs). Second, Arabiastan captures the fantastical, orientalist imagery that helps to shape the fictionalized landscape of the novels. For example, the sheikh's quarters are often lavishly appointed with Persian rugs.[43] As mentioned earlier, the heroines are sometimes reminded of Persian poet Omar Khayyam or of the *Arabian Nights*.[44] Moreover, descriptions of the women's quarters sometimes invoke the imagery of a Turkish (Ottoman) harem.[45] As Annie West explains, the potential settings of "desert strongholds, romantic oases, and sprawling palaces" are part of what makes them fun to write: "For background colour there are silk carpets, souks, glittering jewels and an exotic 'Arabian Nights' aura."[46]

Despite romance writers' likely genuine worries about their ability to get the details of Middle Eastern culture right, this concern is probably not the only—or even the main—reason for the widespread creation of Arabiastan. Were the writers to set their novels in actual Middle Eastern countries, popular perceptions of these countries as war-torn, backward, third-world countries with horrible policies that oppress women and gay people would overwhelm the nostalgic set of orientalist associations. Even the countries associated with oil wealth and "utter glitz," rather than war, nevertheless also stand out as examples of kingdoms defined by their oppression of women. Such an impression would deflate the fantasy and detract from the lush, orientalist setting. The Gulf region of the Middle East nevertheless serves as a point of inspiration for Arabiastan, suggesting that in the world of desert romance, the lines between fictional and actual narratives of the region become blurred.

Indeed, it is especially in the blurry moments that readers' notions of reality can grate against the core of the desert romance fantasy. As one reader quips: "The guy who sells me gyros is exotic? And the power of the attraction of sheikhs left me a long time ago considering the third class citizenship women have in many countries of the middle east. Probably not even third."[47] Responding to a comment asserting that the appeal of the sheikh is his exoticism, this reader considers the image of the sheikh inseparable from that of the oppressive and irredeemable patriarch. She also cuts the desert prince fantasy down to size, tying the image of the sheikh to "the guy who sells [her] gyros," an allusion that sutures Arabiastani masculinity to a working-class immigrant subjectivity inside the U.S.-Anglo context. Even as they discuss the sheikh's characteristics that make them swoon, fans of the desert romance are often careful and quick to note that they "wouldn't want to meet a real one!"[48]

When Fantasy Grates against Reality

In Winstead Jones's *The Sheik and I*, Sheikh Kadin and heroine Cassandra take "one last kiss, before reality returns."[49] One is reminded of both the suffocating presence of too much reality surrounding the topic of desert romances and how desert romance writers must navigate readers' perceptions of the gory realities of Arabiastan—realities that constantly threaten to overwhelm the fantasy of the romance. Because of the realities that make the idea of the sheikh unappealing for some fans of the romance genre, certain story elements must be carefully avoided by the authors and are simply disavowed by fans of the genre. In an online inquiry about the appeal of the sheikh-hero, one fan, Angela, explains on the *All About Romance* blog: "The sheik for me represents mystery and exoticness. He is tall, dark, and dangerous. He is different from me physically and culturally. He is a man's man and knows what he wants and takes it. For me the sheik is pure fantasy and nothing I would want in real life, but then so are most heroes in romanceland."[50]

This reader reaffirms the commonly desired elements of the sheikh (exoticism, aggression, mystery, and, in short, a radically different other) while introducing a key point. Many readers would agree that their preferred heroes—whether in the wealthy Mediterranean category, like Greek and Italian billionaires, or in the paranormal category, like vampires and werewolves, or in the historical category, like rogues and rakes—would not be desirable in real life, and readers would no doubt question the reading of these romances to assess how they portray the reality of the Middle East. Yet what is so interesting about the popularity of desert romances at this particular historical moment is precisely their negotiations of fantasy and reality. In these negotiations, the proximity of desire and disgust—the kind of colonial ambivalence discussed by postcolonial theorist Homi Bhabha—becomes apparent. Two other comments in the *All About Romance* thread will help clarify. Agreeing with Angela, LyndaX writes: "The great thing about Romancelandia is that it rewrites all reality. It's just that the sheik reality is too close to you (which you already knew), plus it's harder these days, with terrorists and because we know too much. . . . As to their appeal, I think Angela nailed it. There is something about a man who is unshackled by convention who is so overwhelmed by a woman that he must have her. In real life, he's a sociopathic rapist, but in romances, he's a hero."[51] Another interlocutor puts it less provocatively to concur that the "flip side and reality of [the fantasy] is obviously very dark."[52]

The nonchalant suggestion that real-life sheikhs—Arabs—are "sociopathic rapists" and "obviously very dark" belies some key differences between the sheikh-hero and other types of alpha-male heroes in the romance genre. Whereas some heroes—like werewolves or rakes—can be objects of fantasy at the same time that readers wouldn't want to encounter them in real life, these figures don't suffer from a surfeit of reality. That is, romance readers don't claim to "know too much" about these characters' real-life attributes, because the characters exist entirely within the fantasy realm—either because they do not actually exist (paranormals), they existed in the distant past (rogues and rakes), or they are still considered Western with an exotic twist (Italians and

Greeks). Precisely for this reason—because desert romances, to operate as fantasy narratives, must combat what the general reader thinks she already knows about the reality of the Middle East—they offer a wealth of information about the collisions of desire, fear, identification, and fantasy in popular U.S.-Anglo engagements with Arabiastani masculinity. Particularly because they engage directly with the theme of the war on terror, the novels demonstrate how desire for and identification with the sheikh can operate as a critical aspect of how the war on terror functions.

A common trope in desert romances is to feature weapons of mass destruction, uranium-enriching villains, and terrorist plots to overthrow sheikh-heroes who foster good relationships with the United States.[53] One of the best examples of this is Loreth Anne White's *The Sheik Who Loved Me* (2005), in which an American spy, Jayde Ashton, falls in love with Sheikh David Rashid. Like Hull's hero in *The Sheik*, Rashid is part English, and this fact of birth functions in the narrative to crucially distinguish him from the prototype of the cruel, savage Arab, namely, his half-brother Tariq. The half-brother is involved in a plot to enrich uranium so that his rebel group can develop nuclear capabilities, which the heroine refers to as "weapons of mass destruction."[54] In just these few details, one can clearly see that the novel is in conversation with contemporaneous mainstream coverage of the war on terror and, more particularly, the Iraq war, with its reference to rogue states attempting to develop nuclear capabilities and its direct mention of WMDs. Significantly, the sheikh-hero becomes a desirable figure precisely because he leads peace negotiations or diplomatic efforts to quell tensions between backward warring tribes or peoples, and he specifically seeks U.S.-Anglo support to do so. Examples of this trope abound. Sheikh Zahid pours a lot of money "into a world peace project," while Sheikh Kazim is involved in international peace talks.[55] Sheikh Xander is even "put forward for the Nobel Peace Prize" as a result of his work setting up a "student exchange between Middle Eastern and European students so that each might better understand the other."[56] Sheikh-heroes in desert romances represent a critically underrepresented figure who nevertheless plays a key role in the war on terror—the figure of the good sheikh, the exceptional ally to U.S.-Anglo imperialist powers.

One reader touches on a defining characteristic of the good-sheikh subjectivity when she suggests that sheikh-heroes are "popular because there's so much to reform."[57] The white heroine is often portrayed as the primary agent of the sheikh's reform, and when she succeeds in capturing his heart, bringing him to his knees and reforming him, she is rewarded with the prize of becoming his "one woman harem."[58] The sheikh-hero is often portrayed as battling regressive elements in his own country in order to bring it in line with the new global economy; aligning his country with the new world order is a critical aspect of his reformation.

Given the common defense of romance novels as feminist—that is, their tendency to feature a strong, independent heroine and to focus on her pleasure—a common subtheme of desert romances focuses on the sheikh's desire for progressive women's rights and his need for a strong heroine to help him achieve such a cultural shift. Though this description of a sheikh may seem atypical in comparison with predominant images of the Arab-Muslim terrorist, it actually quite closely resembles popular nonfiction characterizations of the people of the Arabian Peninsula or the Gulf region of the Middle East. Here again, the boundaries between fantasy and reality begin to blur. Recall the previously mentioned blogger's reference to a real desert prince (the crown prince of Dubai) as a means of delineating the fictional sheikh-hero's desired qualities. While her description of the crown prince is animated by classic (orientalist) associations of the Middle East with opulence and luxury, it notably elides the most popular contemporary association of terrorism with Arab masculinity. Here, the blogger's silences are just as descriptive (if not more so) as her assertions regarding the attractiveness of the sheikh. Romance readers' and writers' online comments about desert romances overwhelmingly insist that the subgenre's popularity in recent years bears no relationship to the contemporaneous war on terror. Instead, the readers and writers point to classic yet vague notions of decadent, exotic oil kingdoms and the powerful masculine rulers as the quintessential heroes of this thriving subgenre of romance novels.[59]

Even if sheikh-heroes are simply updated representations of classic orientalist figures, though, these classic representations were certainly not all positive. While contemporary romance novel sheikhs and sultans do clearly reference the legacy of classic Hollywood film sheikhs, the books are perhaps more immediately linked to the image of the oil sheikh, a U.S.-based concept that appeared in the 1970s and 1980s. Oil

sheikh images emerged in a moment of greatly intensified political conflict between the U.S. and the Middle East, and they reintroduced orientalist stereotypes about the Ottoman Empire, which cast the harem as a
prison-like space for women who were, by nature, at the mercy of brutal
or greedy patriarchal figures. Desert romances that utilize the orientalist trope of the harem as a sexualized setting therefore tend to either
situate the novel historically, during the Ottoman Empire, to play on
the stereotype of the Terrible Turk (as in Nan Ryan's *Burning Love*), or
they invoke the greedy, lascivious oil sheikh stereotype through a villain-
ous character from whom the heroine must be rescued. While contemporary desert romances tend to steer clear of the volatile harem image
since it is understood to be inherently oppressive to women, its framing
of women as sex slaves can be recuperated by authors who choose to
make a point about how the heroine has inspired the sheikh to correct
this practice, as in the previous example about the one-woman harem.
In this case, authors can draw on the edgy fantasy of being a sex slave
while assuring readers that the fantasy will not spill outside the boundaries of civilized, monogamous, bourgeois coupling. Like the use of the
radiation metaphor in the epigraph that begins this chapter, authors can
draw on the power of orientalist stereotypes to create potent, dangerous,
and sexy alpha male sheikh-heroes, even if these heroes will ultimately
be domesticated by the romantic narrative.

Harems play into what Ella Shohat and Robert Stam call the "rape
and rescue fantasy," as the oil sheikh is often represented as particularly
desirous of white women.[60] Thus, the appearance of the oil sheikh character in the 1970s and 1980s primarily signified the increasing antago-
nism between the U.S. and the Middle East. As a symbol that is clearly
tied to the 1973 oil embargo and heralded by globalization scholar David
Harvey as one of the defining events for the shift into late capitalism,
the oil sheikh caricature is a precursor to images of the terrorist figure.[61]
Both are portrayed as hyperpatriarchal, as antagonistic to Western powers, and as the dark or destructive underbelly of globalization, where
globalization is understood in universalized (Eurocentric) ways. Desert romances set in the late 1970s and throughout the 1980s especially
invoke this figure, usually in the character of the villain or antihero, as
exemplified by Nora Roberts's *Sweet Revenge*, in which the villain Abdu
"wanted the money and technology the West would bring, even while

he detested Westerners for providing them."[62] The image of an extremist Islamic regime prominent in the 1980s—an image arising from the Iranian revolution and the concomitant hostage crisis—still holds purchase not only in representations of terrorists but also in the image of the rogue regime that seeks to develop nuclear weapons by enriching uranium. The salient metaphor of oil for Arabiastan therefore morphs into the more potent metaphor of radiation, which permeates popular associations with the region even if it is not explicitly named.

Perhaps because of this representational transition, contemporary desert romances rehabilitate the once-feared or disparaged oil sheikh as a desirable hero. In so doing, the novels use the allied leaders of the Gulf region of the Middle East as their template, reforming the sheikh into an alluring fantasy figure by shaping his gender politics to align with liberal feminist goals and transforming him into a good, liberal, humanist subject. The new, reformed sheikh is characterized by his precarious positioning as a leader who seeks to find the perfect balance between tradition and modernity. As opposed to the greedy, oppressive oil sheikhs of the 1970s and 1980s, these new desert princes are honorable leaders of newly oil-rich countries seeking to use their newfound riches to reform and modernize their countries, while battling the primitive, backward factions of their population who, like Abdu, "detest Westerners."

Importantly, romance writers have not invented the character of the good sheikh; they have a wealth of nonfictional representations on which to draw and which paint the picture of the fraught leader of allied Gulf countries. Consider, for example, a featured spread on Saudi Arabia in *National Geographic*, which includes this lead: "Torn between ancient traditions and the modern world, Saudis search for balance in the post-9/11 glare."[63] The article displays the usual mix of *kufiya*-wearing men wielding swords (e.g., the front-cover image of a sword dance at a camel festival), kufiya-wearing men at a "camel beauty contest," the Prophet's Mosque in Medina filled with praying men, a light-studded Riyadh at night (more specifically of an "ultramodern hotel and complex"), and an aerial view of a sea of cars parked haphazardly in the desert "where camels once trekked." Such juxtaposition of traditional and modern is a common trope in *National Geographic*, and it dominates every aspect of the article. It describes, for example, "the clash between borrowed modernization and threatened traditions," which, it argues, are "the root crisis from which a forest of others has sprung."[64] Though it never explains from whom modernization is "borrowed," the rhetoric of the sentence, as representative of the entire article, invokes the classic clash-of-civilizations argument by continuously associating Islam with backwardness and tradition (e.g., "Today Saudi Arabia is at the center of a cultural and geopolitical maelstrom, where Islam meets the modern world") and by linking modernization with the United States.[65]

While chapter 1 makes the case for the applicability of *National Geographic* magazine to desert romances, the example presented here serves two purposes. It highlights the imbrication of nonfictional discourses about Arabiastan with the fictional desert romance narratives, demonstrating the complex intertextuality between fantasy and reality. Perhaps more importantly, though, the *National Geographic* example helps emphasize the sheikh-hero as a key underrepresented aspect of the war on terror. The war on terror is not only fought in opposition to the violent, backward terrorist, but also fought in alliance with the good sheikh. In other words, the war on terror is constructed not only in terms of fear of the other, but also in terms of desire, where the desire for the other is just one particularly salient manifestation of the way desire works to uphold the architecture of the war on terror. The story of how the heroine comes to desire the desert sheikh turns out to symbolize how desire functions as an engine for contemporary U.S. imperialism as manifested in the war on terror. Her desire for the sheikh-hero leads her to be willingly, rapturously captured and contained by him in ways that are remarkably similar to contemporary technologies of U.S. imperialist power, which have been crafted and honed during the war on terror. The sheikh-hero represents an oasis of security in a chaotic world of danger and terrorism. The heroine desires to be captured and contained by him to feel safe, even ironically referring to her willing submission to her overwhelming love for him as a kind of freedom. Her willingness to stay in Arabiastan with the sheikh is often justified through the logic of the imperialist technology of liberation—she vows to help the sheikh foster women's equality in his modernizing (i.e., civilizing) nation. Moreover, their union is meant to be symbolic of the exceptionalist technology of liberal multiculturalism, where ethnic and cultural differences are commodified and capitalized into spicy details that give the exceptional-universalist power its flavor. The way that romance writers are forced to justify the U.S.-Anglo heroine's desire for an Arabiastani sheikh illustrates a micropolitics of desire that simultaneously resonates at the macropolitical level of imperialism. The heroine's desire for the good sheikh echoes contemporary modes of imperialism, which cast the imperialist project as a benevolent force by cultivating subjects' desires for security, freedom, and liberal multiculturalism. In short, desert romances reveal that contemporary (benevolent) imperialism is a love story, whose primary driving force is desire.

Reading the Desert Romance as an Allegory of U.S. Exceptionalism

In her recent book, *Desert Passions*, Hsu-Ming Teo describes the characterization of sheikh-heroes in desert romances as "ameliorative representations" of Muslim masculinity, which have the potential to "temper negative stereotypes," particularly "given the scarcity of alternative representations of Muslim men in Western popular culture."[66] While she corroborates the assertion that desert romances depict Arabiastani masculinities that are not widely represented in U.S.-Anglo popular culture, Teo nevertheless reads this phenomenon through a liberal multiculturalist lens, where representations coded as positive are understood as the antidote to negative representations. This general sentiment is echoed by Erika Wittlieb, creator of the "Sheikhs and Desert Love" website. In an interview with the *Chicago Tribune*, she argues that desert romances present positive portrayals of Arab masculinity against a sea of negative stereotypes.[67] She makes this claim despite the fact that not only is the sheikh-hero animalistic and aggressive, but his positive, sensitive qualities are manifested only in relation to the prototype of the evil, uranium-enriching half-brother (or another such stereotype).[68] The claim rests on the assumption that while negative stereotypes are bad, they can be combatted by positive images; but this claim elides the fact that stereotypes are strengthened—not weakened—by the binary structure of negative and positive representation.[69]

Perhaps more importantly, though, the valorization of the good sheikh relies on an exceptionalist logic; he is exceptional in the sense of being a uniquely modern and progressive Arabiastani leader. As a civilized leader allied with U.S.-Anglo powers, he is also uniquely situated to uphold the universalizing principles of a liberal multicultural logic, where the assimilation and appropriation of difference becomes the way of demonstrating equality. Teo inadvertently inscribes the good sheikh within an exceptionalist-universalizing discourse when she lauds the recent "ameliorative" depictions of him in contemporary desert romances as "humanizing" representations that "affirm readers' willingness to believe in the power of romantic love to breech cross-cultural, interracial, and interreligious boundaries and to integrate the Arab or Muslim other into modern Western societies."[70] Framing readers' willingness to integrate Arabiastani masculinities into "modern Western societies" through the logic of exceptionalism belies its positive impact; the accolades for integration here are attributed to the U.S.-Anglo societies themselves for their willingness to accept the reformed sheikhs.

Indeed, the narrative of exceptionalism is fundamental to the architecture of U.S. imperialism, where exceptionalism refers both to the idea of the U.S. as uniquely universalist and to the idea that an imperialist state often operates in a state-of-exception mode. The former—unique universalism—functions through the kinds of liberal multiculturalist logics so far described in relation to the good sheikh as well as through the claim of sexual liberation, both of which communicate the idea that the U.S. is constantly progressing toward the ideal of equality for all. This conceit, in turn, provides the moral justification for attacking other countries because of their egregious human-rights records. The state of exception pardons the outwardly hegemonic manifestations of imperialism (like domestic surveillance and the suspension of some civil rights) as necessary precisely because of the uniquely democratic and benevolent nature of U.S. imperialism. This "they hate us for our freedom" attitude asserts that because the U.S. is targeted for its exceptional qualities, the nation must sometimes take extreme measures to protect itself.

Even if some manifestations of imperialism look different in the contemporary U.S. formulations, its ideological structure remains remarkably similar to many of its predecessors, particularly those of the formal colonial era. As Ann Stoler points out, despite the narrative of exceptionalism, the self-creation of the imperialist power as a state of exception operates more obviously as a rule than as a distinguishing characteristic.[71] Indeed, following Edward Said, she argues that "*discourses of exceptionalism are part of the discursive apparatus of empires themselves.*"[72] Discourses of exceptionalism enable the imperial state to manage a set of paradoxes. One paradox is the claim of newness by or on behalf of empires—for example, the claim that the U.S. is only pushed to wield an imperialist form of power because of its altruistic, humanitarian impulses to assist downtrodden peoples and countries. Here, the idea is that even as the appellation of *empire* came to be accepted as a descriptor for the U.S., the term only became acceptable because the U.S. is a reluctant and decidedly *new* form of empire—one that only operates as such because of its unique ability to spread freedom and democracy. As Stoler suggests: "We might step back and ask not only what is new (as many have), but why 'newness' is always a part of imperial narratives."[73] Newness seems to operate as a means of disavowing one's own imperialist formation. While the "new" imperial power may begrudgingly acknowledge that it is, indeed, operating as an empire, it nevertheless claims that it does so with altruistic, rather than hegemonic, aims. Newness becomes the cover under which subtle neo-imperialist forms of power hide.

This paradox is inextricably linked to another—the implication that the exceptional state distinguishes itself from a whole host of other, now universalized (i.e., generalized) states at the same time that the exceptional state claims to uniquely demonstrate true universal (i.e., liberal-humanitarian) values. In his influential essay on U.S. exceptionalism, Daniel Rodgers notes how a narrative of exceptionalism eschews difference, an interesting point given the importance of difference to national U.S. mythologies: "When difference is put in exceptionalist terms, in short, the referent is universalized."[74] Such universalizing of (all) others builds the claim of exception, despite its being a claim of exceptionality based on the imperial state's exemplary embodiment of supposedly universal values. Amy Kaplan concisely describes the paradoxical "claim of the United States to uniqueness and universality at the same time" as "the tenacious paradigm of American exceptionalism."[75] It is a paradox that is neatly embodied by the good sheikh, who is uniquely equipped to reinforce exceptional-universalist ideals through alliance with U.S.-Anglo powers.

Narrating Benevolent Technologies of Imperialism

Through the critical subjectivity of the good sheikh, desert romances provide a means of investigating the ways that contemporary U.S. imperialism operates undercover. Between the lines of desert romances, one can read what Jodi Kim calls a Cold War epistemology—a way of "making sense of the world through the Manichaean logics and grammars of good and evil."[76] The good sheikh-hero and the evil Arabiastani terrorist manifest this sort of logic in the desert romances themselves; the novels concisely illustrate the way that imperialism necessitates the construction of a clearly and simply evil other who must be defeated by the morally righteous exceptional state. The Cold War epistemology functions through new technologies of empire, such as neoliberal economic policies, proxy wars, and the tyranny of humanitarianism. These technologies hide under the cover of humanitarianism and operate through covert and proxy military means.

If the Cold War can be understood as "a genealogy of American empire," as Jodi Kim argues, it marks some critical features in the historical transition of imperialist formations. More than simply signaling a shift away from formal territorial colonization and toward (neocolonial) political, economic, and military hegemony, U.S. imperialist formations after the Cold War refigure the relationship of militarism to empire in key ways.[77] Rather than just providing the forceful means to appropriate new resources, the military and, more broadly, the defense industry operates as a new resource and engine for capitalism through the military-industrial complex.[78] The military also becomes a crucial tool for installing and deploying neoliberal economic policies, as exemplified in Naomi Klein's formulation of the "shock doctrine."[79] Most importantly, the role of the military is refigured so as to (mostly) successfully eclipse the global hegemon—the U.S. imperialist state—as a major aggressive actor. A prime example is the proliferation of proxy wars, the most common kind of warfare during the Cold War, whose legacy can be clearly seen in the current war on terror through the example of Afghanistan. U.S. military engagement in Afghanistan during the height of the Cold War was hidden under the cover of proxy engagement—the funding of *mujahidin* forces—and the covert nature of such proxy engagement later enabled the "why do they hate us" argument. Terrorist actions against the U.S. could then be presented as disengaged from historical and political context and widely construed as the actions of evildoers who simply hated the liberal humanist way of life.

Further, though the action is skillfully obscured, the U.S. does formally (territorially) colonize many parts of the world through its extensive network of military bases.[80] The network provides a concrete example of what Inderpal Grewal and Caren Kaplan call "scattered hegemonies."[81] The sheikh-heroes in desert romances lead Arabiastani countries that remarkably resemble long-standing U.S. allies in the region—Saudi Arabia, Bahrain, Qatar, and the UAE—that host key strategic military bases, as explored in chapter 1. In perhaps the most twisted aspect of the refiguring of militarism in contemporary imperialist formations, militarism has also installed itself as the new form of humanitarianism, particularly through the selective deployment of a human rights framework to force regime change in countries that are strategically important to the United States.[82] A good example of the conflation of militarism and humanitarianism once again takes us to Afghanistan, where, in the early days of the U.S. invasion, the U.S. dropped food aid that was nearly indistinguishable from the cluster bomblets being concurrently dropped.[83]

Though the U.S. has clearly used overt forms of imperialism as a tactic in the war on terror—for example, in the invasion and occupation of Iraq—desert romances perhaps inadvertently chart some of the more covert tactics of the "new" contemporary U.S. imperialism, namely, the tactics coded with positive or humanitarian connotations. As manifested in desert romances, these tactics generally fall into three broad technologies: security, freedom, and liberal multiculturalism (see chapters 1, 2, and 3, respectively). There are several reasons for using the term *technology* as a rubric here—reasons especially clarified for me during a class I taught about contemporary technologies of imperialism.[84] Perhaps most obviously, the term *technology* suggests a mechanism or an apparatus of empire—a way of functioning. In addition, though, the term clearly signals that no direct, unidirectional form of power emanates from a clear intent. Moreover, the technology serves something that is larger than itself, and the subjects (or targets) of technology are bound up in it. As we are intricately bound up in the discourses of security, freedom, and liberal multiculturalism, we can end up contributing to the power of these concepts, even if we do so unwittingly or unwillingly.

Recalling that desire operates as an engine of imperialism through the fundamental mode of provoking desire for one's own repression, the conceptual framework of technologies allows for an exploration of some of the mechanisms through which imperialist desire is maintained and serviced. These technologies are the devices through which imperialism fashions itself as both new and as lamentably necessary, both for the subject-citizens of empire and for those who are subjugated-saved by it. Here again, the epistemology of the Cold War plays a key role in reframing war from a defensive act to a series of preemptive (and endless) acts. The intensification of neoliberalism and nuclear arsenals of the Reagan era wielded the specter of the evil empire as existential threat, whereas George W. Bush called the war on terror a fight against the axis of evil.[85] While the branding of the enemy as evil is certainly not new to war-making, the construction of the evil enemy as an ever-present threat to citizens of the U.S. on their own turf is a distinguishing feature of the Cold War epistemological stance on war and militarism. Nuclear proliferation at the height of the Cold War created the image of an ever-present threat, a condition that facilitated the orientation toward national security as the dominant paradigm, both domestically and internationally. Through the ruse of imminent foreign threat, the Cold War also concealed the social impact of neoliberal economic policies, particularly well illustrated in the shifting of public resources from social services to the defense industry. Under the guise of privatization, personal responsibility, and national security, the defense industry replaced people as the recipients of social welfare. Perhaps the best example of this shift domestically is the expansion of the prison-industrial complex, which criminalized mostly impoverished (and predominantly African American) communities through the war on drugs.[86]

Coinciding with the rise of neoliberalism as a dominant economic policy, the proliferation of metaphorical wars since the 1970s—Nixon's war on crime and Reagan's war on drugs and war on terrorism, both of which have been extended into the contemporary (Bush and Obama) wars on drugs, terror, and immigration—demonstrate less about the purported subjects of these wars (crime, drugs, terror, and immigration) and more about the salience of war as a metaphor. The idea of constant and pervasive threat is cultivated, cementing security as a critical technology of imperialism. Desert romances demonstrate the way citizen-subjects of an empire (represented by the white heroine) come to desire security through a desire for the sheikh-hero, who allies his country with the U.S. war on terror by adopting the logic of securitization.[87]

If the Cold War epistemological construction of the enemy as a pervasive and imminent threat is critical, so too is the Manichaean notion of the threat as evil, insofar as both notions contribute to the construction of freedom as a technology of contemporary imperialism. Christian religious discourse offers a particularly useful way of understanding the technology of freedom. Just as missionary work was shaped by, and helped shape, colonial projects, contemporary Christian evangelical discourses about the Middle East illustrate a neo-imperialist stance crafted through the rubric of saving or liberating the region. In these narratives, the war on terror takes on a moral front, as in an article for *Christianity Today*, titled "The Moral Home Front," which argues that failing to implement the Federal Marriage Amendment (to define marriage as strictly monogamous and heterosexual) is "like handing moral weapons of mass destruction to those who use America's decadence to recruit more snipers and hijackers and suicide bombers."[88] The logic here clearly extends the war on terror to the "home front," essentially implying that (sexual) freedom must be curtailed to win the war on terror. At the same time, the perception of Islam as backward and oppressive, proven through both sexual hyperconservatism and depravity, functions to cast U.S. intervention as a liberating mission. An intriguing set of alliances is suggested here among Christian evangelicals and those with whom the evangelicals politically align, despite sometimes radically different goals or worldviews. One example is Christian Zionism, which has staunchly backed the state of Israel since the nation's founding, because of a belief in biblical prophecy rather than through the support of Jewish people. Another example is the evangelical support of South Sudan. Evangelicals cast their support according to a narrative that identifies South Sudan as Christian and understands the conflict in religious terms; this narrative ironically utilizes a human rights (secular) framework to advance a larger argument about the persecution of Christians by Muslims, an argument that draws on the troubling binary of good Christians and bad Muslims.[89]

Taken to their logical conclusion, these arguments clearly call for saving (i.e., freeing) the territory of the Middle East from the depraved and evil Muslims who inhabit it. In other words, this sort of evangelism argues for liberating Arabiastan from Arabiastanis themselves, and delivering it to Christian Western civilization. Analyzing this movement through the lens of the popular Left Behind series of novels depicting the rapture, Melani McAlister notes that "Left Behind constitutes a literature well fitted for a new era in which the United States defines itself as a frankly imperialist power engaged in a long-term battle for control of the Middle East."[90] The importance of the Middle East in these narratives goes back to nineteenth-century fascinations with the Holy Land but includes a contemporary, imperialist spin. Expanding on the "city upon a hill" narrative, so central to early configurations of U.S. exceptionalism, contemporary Christianity figures the geography of the Middle East to be under the custodianship of the United States. Further, particularly in the Christian evangelical rhetoric about Revelations and the rapture, contemporary sociopolitical events—for example, modern-day warfare, new technologies utilized in the war on terror, and climate change—are read as manifestations of biblical prophecy rather than the catastrophic (and changeable) results of human activity. Here Arabiastan becomes subject to, and an object of, the imperialist technology of freedom, which particularly manifests itself in desert romances through the civilizing of both the sheikh-hero and his Arabiastani country. Significantly, both are commonly civilized through the rubric of women's liberation, echoing the salience of gender equality as a key technology of the actual war on terror. Through this conversion, cast as a project of delivering freedom, Arabiastan is cleansed of its backward, traditional ways, even while the good sheikh learns how to sanitize and capitalize on those customs and traditions considered quaint or colorful.

The process of civilizing the sheikh-hero overlaps with the technology of liberal multiculturalism, a technology that shapes and creates the good sheikh as an exceptional ally to U.S.-Anglo imperialist powers. The sheikh's dependence on benign U.S.-Anglo cooperation echoes the casting of the U.S. by neoconservatives and liberals alike as the only power capable of bringing democracy to the Middle East. In this sense, this image coincides with two suppositions. The first is the historically based national myth of the U.S. as exceptional (i.e., the "city upon a hill," a narrative that clearly embeds the notion of exceptionality with Christianity from the beginning). The second is the contemporary state-of-exception argument deployed to justify increased surveillance regimes and the eroding of civil liberties.[91] As Ashley Dawson and Malini Johar Schueller argue: "Without an understanding of the continuity of American exceptionalism, complexly constituted of religious, economic, cultural, political, and racial elements beginning with Puritan theocracy and continuing with the rhetoric of Manifest Destiny and the Monroe Doctrine, for instance, we cannot make sense of the conviction shared by many contemporary politicians and citizens alike that the United States has been and will always remain the provider and protector of world freedom."[92]

The myth of exceptionalism also proves itself remarkably malleable, operating, for instance, in recent years through various permutations of U.S. sexual exceptionalism.[93] While Jasbir Puar has investigated this phenomenon in relation to the war on terror generally, and more specifically in relation to Abu Ghraib, an example especially well suited for the analysis of desert romances comes in the film *Sex and the City 2*, itself a version of a desert romance.[94] Though the film centers around the antics that the famously sexually liberated foursome get into while visiting Abu Dhabi in the notoriously sexually repressive "new Middle East," the opening scene exudes sexual liberalism par excellence—the gay wedding of close friends of the foursome.[95] In a superb example of what Puar calls homonationalism, the scene economically sets up the key tension around which the film is organized—the exceptional sexual liberalism of the U.S. in contrast to the presumed sexual repression of the Middle East.[96] Desert romances are most successful when they clearly align themselves with the unique universalism of the U.S. through the exceptionally enlightened good sheikh.

The three technologies of security, freedom, and liberal multiculturalism demonstrate that desire is just as important as, if not more important than, fear in the architecture of the war on terror. The novels' resolution with heteronormative marriage demonstrates an organization of desire that is echoed at the social level by the common trope of the sheikh who seeks to work with U.S.-Anglo powers (despite the threats from terrorists in his own country who don't agree with his progressive stance) to bring his country into the modern era.[97] The obligatory HEA (happily ever after) ending—almost always heterosexual marriage—is widely touted as the key element that makes a romance novel successful.[98] Therefore, the resolution of marriage operates as one of the primary technologies for organizing (i.e., containing) desire and orienting it toward hegemonic formations. Though the HEA ending is not a feature unique to desert romances, this subgenre does uniquely illustrate how the larger social field of investment in the war on terror is permeated by these kinds of microinvestments. That is, the organization of desire, illuminated in the narratives of desert romances and existing in myriad cultural formations, propels the war on terror (itself a particular manifestation of contemporary U.S. imperialism) in significant ways. The containment or colonization of desire creates a framework where security, freedom, and liberal multiculturalism can operate as technologies of imperialism.

Mapping Desire

The truth is that sexuality is everywhere: the way a bureaucrat fondles his records, a judge administers justice, a businessman causes money to circulate; the way the bourgeoisie fucks the proletariat; and so on. . . . Flags, nations, armies, banks get a lot of people aroused.
—Gilles Deleuze and Félix Guattari, *Anti-Oedipus* (p. 293)

The primary aim in mapping desire is not to diagnose it or to invent new imperialist pathologies. Rather, as indicated by the focus on technologies, the aim is to figure something out about how desire functions and to map its relationship to other key aspects of imperial power. If the mechanisms of contemporary benevolent imperialism—the technologies of security, freedom, and liberal multiculturalism—are powered by desire, then these technologies (and, by extension, the process of imperialism itself) gain a constant reservoir of justification through the myth of exceptionalism. To recount, the logic goes something like this: As a uniquely multicultural and democratic nation, the empire is obliged to bring freedom to other countries. When backward elements in these countries resist liberation delivered through neoliberal modernization, precautionary state-of-exception measures are required to ensure the security of the empire and its citizen-subjects. In this formulation, the myth of exceptionalism operates according to a paranoid logic. In other words, embedded in the myth are both the potential for grandiosity (in order to truly believe in one's own exceptionality) and the concomitant fear of persecution (presumably by those who are jealous of or desire the exceptional status).[99]

It might be tempting to understand the U.S. as having slid into a state of paranoid power as a result of a radical shift stimulated by the events of September 11, 2001. Hayden White contributes to such a reading when he claims that "the attack on the World Trade Center on September 11, 2001 had the effect of collapsing a particularly triumphalist version of American history."[100] Conversely, Anne McClintock's definition of paranoia as related to empire encourages us to see the continuities across historical constructions of the U.S. empire, rather than understanding 9/11 as a radical break: "I conceive of paranoia as *an inherent contradiction with respect to power*: a double-sided phantasm that oscillates precariously between deliriums of grandeur and nightmares of perpetual threat, a deep and dangerous doubleness with respect to power that is held in unstable tension, but which, if suddenly destabilized (as after 9/11), can produce pyrotechnic displays of violence."[101] Here, she paints a picture of an imperial formation (in the case of the U.S., as exceptional state) that is always inherently unstable and that is held together in many ways by the very duality that causes a suturing tension—the appearance of stability despite its actual precariousness. McClintock leads us away from seeing 9/11 as a radical break while she suggests how 9/11 could have stimulated particularly violent and repressive manifestations of a U.S. empire.

The paradigm of paranoia, in particular, enables a further theorization of the structure of contemporary U.S. imperialism—a theory that connects imperialism to the question of desire. Though McClintock herself does not mention the work of Deleuze and Guattari, her use of paranoia invokes their theories of hegemony.[102] In their schema, paranoia is the "molar" mode of hegemony, a mode that is exemplified in empire (as opposed to a schizophrenic, "molecular" mode, manifested in forms of resistance and potentialities that break free of gridded hegemonic power). In other words, paranoia (the molar mode) represents a hegemonic strategy of organizing, or stratifying, revolutionary energies. Molarization seeks to organize elements toward a coherent whole, while molecularization is attendant to fluidity, flux, and instability. Paul

Elliott describes molarity as "an organising force [that] brings things and people together; it homogenises variety and flattens difference," while he describes the molecular self as "exist[ing] beyond and behind simple structures" and as "evanescent but no less important."[103] Imperialism can be described as paranoid insofar as it relies on a fundamental binary opposition—its own grandiose benevolence and simultaneous fear of existential threat—to organize and consolidate power. As Brian Massumi writes in his *User's Guide to Capitalism and Schizophrenia*, "molarization is as paranoid as it is imperialist."[104] According to this paradigm, one can understand the types of activities carried out by the United States since 9/11—not just literal military violence in Iraq, Afghanistan, Yemen, and Pakistan, but also especially the heightened state of surveillance and biopolitical disciplining through the related networks of immigration detention centers, the prison-industrial complex, military prisons, special registration, and other forms of civil liberty encroachment—as a redoubling of efforts to consolidate, or molarize, biopolitical energies. In other words, the contemporary iteration of U.S. imperialism can be understood as paranoid precisely because of its intensive focus on molarization—because of its efforts to make itself appear whole.

Two key ideas in Deleuze and Guattari's work undergird this assertion. First, desire is not privatized—relegated to the individual or psychic domain as something separate from the functioning of larger social structures: "The most general principle of schizoanalysis is that desire is always constitutive of a social field. In any case desire belongs to the infrastructure, not to ideology."[105] As an integral part of the "infrastructure," desire plays a material role in the construction of the social field. In this sense, desert romances serve as a rich resource for investigation. Insofar as they foreground desire as the main concern of the narrative, they focus on the kinds of microinvestments that animate molarizing technologies of imperialism and they orient us toward exploring collective investments in the war on terror. This is not to say that the novels are proof of an underlying desire; they are rather the route toward exploring often-hidden elements of imperialism. Instead of seeing desire as enclosed within the individual or family unit (i.e., colonized by Oedipus, particularly in the classic psychoanalytic paradigm), Deleuze and Guattari encourage us to explore how it shapes social production.[106] This conceptualization allows me to move away from the much-maligned earlier feminist question about whether romance novels are oppressive (by reinforcing patriarchal norms and values), since this question is focused in the wrong direction—toward the imposition of structural power on a subset of individuals. From the perspective of schizoanalysis, this question misses the point, because it focuses on the impact or outcome of reading the novels rather than exploring how desire functions in them.[107] The latter orientation uses the novels as rich materials for investigating how desire functions on a social or collective level, rather than on a select group of individual readers. More specifically, the schizoanalytic approach notes how the novels repress, rather than oppress, desire, but not repress in a purely psychoanalytic sense.[108] Desert romances offer an exemplary model of how desire can come to be organized—the functional repressing of revolutionary desire and the psychic investment in a repressive (paranoid) social system.[109] Presumably because of the potential for "revolution" to be reterritorialized (think: "the revolution will not be televised," which has been appropriated in countless consumerist ways), Deleuze and Guattari shift from the notion of revolutionary desire, introduced in *Anti-Oedipus*, to that of "lines of flight."[110] The latter term expresses the potential that could be realized when desire is unbound—when it can escape the striating, organizing powers of signifying and postsignifying (capitalist) regimes like the paranoid U.S. empire. As one example of this simultaneously social and psychic repression, desert romances help us explore the imperialist molarization of desire—a process that also occurs in myriad other situations.

Following the focus on the functionality of desire rather than its outcomes, a second key concern of Deleuze and Guattari is to ask how people come to desire their own repression, or how they can be oriented to desire hegemony.[111] Though the answers to this question are multiple, one of the main culprits, according to Deleuze and Guattari, is deterritorialization, which can operate in many guises—from literally divesting people of their territory to figuratively divesting a concept of its meaning. In fact, in its absolute form, deterritorialization can free up lines of flight—it can enable molecular forms of escape from the imperialist-hegemonic molarization of power. Perhaps because of its liberatory potential, deterritorialization is also the process most appropriated by hegemonic capitalist formations.[112]

The war on terror is a brilliant example of the appropriation of deterritorialization, particularly because the war on terror operates in multiple modes of deterritorialization simultaneously. First, it deterritorializes war, where war is understood to be direct military combat against a clearly defined enemy. In the war on terror, the enemy—terrorists everywhere—is vaguely defined and constantly shifting; the ambiguous nature of the definition enables preemptive strikes—that is, the illusion of defending the nation against a constantly imminent attack. Warfare itself is quite literally deterritorialized for the imperialist power through military tactics like drone strikes (which have increased tremendously under the Obama administration, killing many civilians in two countries—Yemen and Pakistan—with which the U.S. is officially allied, much less officially at war). Drone attacks themselves are a particularly alarming evolution of the main mode of U.S. military conflict throughout the past few decades: proxy wars, which signal a clear connection between the current context and the Cold War era.[113]

Closely linked to the form of military action enacted under the war-on-terror rubric is the way the U.S. justifies military intervention. As an aspect of the exceptional-state narrative (in the form of what Melani McAlister has called "benevolent supremacy"), U.S. imperialism deterritorializes colonialism by presenting itself as a liberty-loving nation that was born out of a struggle against the British (colonial) fatherland and which therefore only enacts military intervention for humanitarian reasons—for example, to free states from oppressive dictators, to bring democracy, and to liberate women.[114] Speaking about popular historical romances written at the turn of the nineteenth century, Amy Kaplan notes that "the novels enacted the U.S. fantasy of global conquest without colonial annexation, what Albert Memmi called the ultimate imperial desire for a colony rid of the colonized."[115] A similar sort of fantasy pervades contemporary desert romances through the figure of the progressive-minded sheikh who seeks U.S.-Anglo support to bring his country in line with the global economy (i.e., the new world order). Recalling Deleuze and Guattari's statement that "it is always on the most deterritorialized element that reterritorialization takes place," one can understand the U.S. to be reterritorializing settler colonialism in a vast, scattered, hegemonic network of U.S. military bases, which do effectively function as hundreds of colonies rid of the colonized.[116]

Deterritorialization in the war on terror also takes place on less physical, if not less material, terrains—at the level of signification and subjectification.[117] Regarding signification, a double, negative deterritorialization results from the use of the word *terror*. First, though it gains its force from the reference to a specific, violent attack on the U.S. or its citizens, the term immediately slides into the signifier *terrorism*, which quickly loses contact with any concrete meaning and becomes an empty, floating signifier porous enough to capture any number of activities deemed threatening by the imperialist state.[118] Second, there is a slide from the now slippery term *terrorism* to the even more problematically abstract term *terror*. In this way, the so-called war on terror wages war on everything and nothing at once, with a signifier, *terror*, that is capable of incorporating virtually anything or anyone who may potentially someday provoke fear, with all definitions of these latter terms held under lock and key by the empire itself. Deleuze and Guattari refer to this use of language as a "signifying regime."[119] They describe it as a key mode of the state, which operates by overcoding (a word that is roughly equivalent to reterritorialization). Here, the state overcodes and reterritorializes the war on terror by giving it institutional life (through the new structure of the Department of Homeland Security); through the curtailment of civil liberties in the Patriot Act; and through a network of military prisons (Guantánamo, Abu Ghraib, Bagram). The prisons simultaneously give the impression that there are real terrorist enemies (despite the fact that the vast majority of prisoners are held without charge) and function to constantly symbolize the threat of U.S. terrorist opposition anew.

These discursive constructions of terror and terrorism, in turn, point to the way the war on terror deterritorializes on subjectivity itself. Operating also in the mode of a postsignifying regime, whereby the function of language is subjectification, the war on terror creates a new category of people—terrorists—only a small percentage of whom have committed or planned to commit violent action impacting civilians to directly oppose a state power.[120] The vast majority of people in this new category share the crime of having been in the wrong place at the wrong time while being Muslim.[121]

Though these deterritorializing techniques may not seem to be driven by desire, they nevertheless demonstrate how desire becomes trapped or organized into a social infrastructure permeated by the war on terror. The deterritorializing energies of the war on terror are channeled into the "great danger of Fear," which is animated by desire.[122] Desire is the infrastructure—not a by-product or a separate entity, say Deleuze and Guattari: "Our security, the great molar organization that sustains us, the arborescences we cling to, the binary machines that give us well-defined status, the resonances we enter into, the system of overcoding that dominates us—we desire all that."[123] Sounds a bit like a romance novel. Indeed, at the level of desire, desert romances can be likened to U.S. military bases in terms of their ability to reterritorialize on the impulse toward colonialism.[124]

If U.S. military bases reterritorialize colonialism by instituting a scattered territorial occupation framed in terms of cooperation rather than conquest, desert romances reterritorialize the (Oedipal) colonization of desire by channeling readers' desires (one book at a time) toward heteronormative coupling—the key unit of state biopower. Each book connects to an intricate gridding of desire, all the while claiming a liberatory (feminist) goal of sexual liberation.[125] The romances, and especially the disavowal that they bear no relation to the war on terror, reinscribe the notion of the bourgeoisie, heterosexual family unit as abstract from, or transcendent of, the social field in which it is produced. Further, a careful reading of desert romances within the context of the romance industry reveals key negative deterritorializing and reterritorializing processes of the war on terror. A mapping of the novels' libidinal investments can simultaneously reveal signature aspects of the social infrastructure as permeated by the war on terror. Though they rely heavily on the metaphor of the oasis, portraying heteronormative marriage as the great shelter and bulwark against a sea (or desert) of loneliness, danger, and fear, desert romances are not inured from the impact of the social context in which they are written. When it comes to the potency of the war on terror and its various negative deterritorializations, desert romances certainly do not escape "overcoding by the signifier, irradiation in all directions, unlocalized omnipresence."[126] Though they are fantasy stories and therefore not meant to be real representations of Arabiastan, the structure of fantasy is, in fact, precisely what frees them to more honestly articulate the way that desire functions to uphold the architecture of the war on terror.

Unknown Knowns

At the beginning of the Iraq war, in the lead-up to the U.S. invasion of Iraq, then secretary of state Donald Rumsfeld sought to justify military action by describing, in a mix of corporate and bureaucratic speech, the danger of unknown threats: "There are known knowns. These are things we know that we know. There are known unknowns. That is to say, there are things that we know we don't know. But there are also unknown unknowns. These are things we don't know we don't know."[127] Presumably, it is the last category of (un)knowledge that poses the most threat and plays most forcefully on the fears of the U.S. public, which seemed to experience 9/11 as a previous "unknown unknown" that materialized as a gory, nightmarish reality. The invocation of such an "unknown unknown," even if vaguely or abstractly referenced (after all, we were now engaged in a war on terror, and what is terrifying if not an unknown unknown that doesn't need a direct referent?), could and did justify military aggression against a country that played no role in 9/11.[128] As Slavoj Žižek points out, however, in Rumsfeld's "amateur philosophizing about the relationship between the known and the unknown," he forgot to add the "crucial fourth term [of] 'unknown knowns,' things we don't know that we know."[129] Since fantasy is the prime vehicle for not knowing what one knows, desert romances can also provide a means of exploring the "unknown knowns" of popular U.S. consciousness—the "disavowed beliefs and suppositions we are not even aware of adhering to ourselves, but which nonetheless determine our acts and feelings."[130] Rather than psychoanalyzing a nation-state (the U.S.), this book investigates the unconscious collective psychic investments that animate the war on terror. Recalling that disavowal can be defined as "an intellectual acceptance of what is repressed, even as the repression is maintained," contemporary desert romances enable a "looking awry" at the unknown knowns that shape the structure of the war on terror to shortcut intellectual acceptance and to investigate the workings of desire in animating the war on terror.[131] If the desire for security, freedom, and liberal multiculturalism represents the intellectual acceptance of subjects' attachments to the war on terror, what remains repressed is the way these technologies of security, freedom, and liberal multiculturalism actually orient subject-citizens and allied subjects of empire alike toward desiring their own repression and there-fore toward the perpetuation of the war on terror.

Irradiated by Desire

As indicated in the epigraph to this introduction, sheikh-heroes embody the power of radiation. They radiate sexual energy and raw, masculine power in a way that both thrills and terrifies heroines; they therefore economically communicate how fear can operate as a manifestation of desire. Perhaps more importantly, though, radiation serves as a useful metaphor for desire as a permeating, driving force of the war on terror. If the sheikh-hero is defined by radiation, the potential danger of this force is mitigated both by the heroine's ability to tame him and his ulti-mate emergence as a good sheikh-hero, who seeks to abolish or secure weapons of mass destruction. In those novels that feature a villain coun-terpart to the sheikh-hero, the villain acts as the hero's evil counterpart since the villain is almost always involved in uranium-enriching activi-ties or in seeking nuclear arms in order to seize power from the sheikh and oppose U.S.-Anglo global superpowers.

Beyond mimicking common narratives about rogue Middle Eastern states (e.g., Iraq and Iran), the radiation metaphor speaks to several as-pects of the psychic meanings of desert romances simultaneously. First, the metaphor gives a concrete image to the abstract notion of terror invoked by Rumsfeld's "unknown unknowns." This more literal associa-tion, in turn, slides into the realm of unknown knowns. Writing about Chernobyl, Žižek explains that it is "precisely [the] indifference to its mode of symbolization that locates the radiation in the dimension of the real. No matter what we say about it, it continues to expand, to reduce us to the role of impotent witnesses."[132] Existing powerfully in the realm of the real (the unknown known), in other words, radiation remains nev-ertheless unknown because of its unrepresentability. In this way, radia-tion is also tied metaphorically to globalization, which perhaps explains radiation's common linking to terrorism in desert romances as the sin-ister consequence of the sheikh-hero's efforts to globalize. Globalization is consistently represented as an inevitably expanding process char-acterized by unprecedented fluidities. The optimism of this narrative, however, doesn't allow for the anxieties and horrific realities that the narrative necessarily provokes and that are representationally displaced onto the threat of terrorism, where radiation is a potent weapon in the hands of evil forces.

Radiation also provides a literal and integrative example of the realities of neoliberal globalization, including the primacy of militarism in waging neoliberal imperialism. The effects of radiation are apparent in myriad aftermaths of war and disaster. The recent example of the failed nuclear reactors in Fukushima, Japan, further demonstrates the utility of the metaphor. Insofar as the meltdown was provoked by a natural disaster, the Japanese disaster demonstrates the imbrication of climate change with the politics of violence and war.

The narratives around recent catastrophic environmental events, like Hurricane Katrina; the earthquakes in Haiti and Chile; and the oceanic earthquakes that wreaked havoc in both Aceh, Indonesia, and Thailand in 2004 and in Japan in 2011 emphasized the events' impact as natural disasters and focused on issues of social preparedness and relief efforts for such disasters. However, the realities underlying these events point to a more complex landscape of interrelationships between climate change, resource scarcity, and violence, conflict, and militarization. In short, events that on the surface seem like natural disasters are also embedded in narratives of national security and are therefore inextricably linked to contemporary formations of imperialism and hegemony. Christian Parenti describes this phenomenon as a "catastrophic convergence" of "poverty, violence, and climate change," which is embedded in the convergence of global neoliberal economic restructuring with the lingering framework of Cold War militarism and the contemporary effects of global warming.[133] The actual radiation that emanated from the failed Fukushima nuclear plant, therefore, serves simultaneously as a powerful metaphor for the social invisibility of the "catastrophic convergence" underlying contemporary natural disasters and resource conflicts. While military intervention in the Middle East is sometimes framed in terms of oil as the key resource at the root of the conflict, shifting to the metaphor of radiation helps to illustrate a more complex landscape of imperialist power.

Radiation is silent, intangible, and unrepresentable at the same time that it is uncontainable; it permeates all kinds of material realities, both literal-physical and mental-social. Its impacts can be difficult to trace and are slow to appear. Radiation would seem to affect all people equally, then, regardless of social position, yet the realities of its devastation are socially stratified. Whether the victims of radiation are disenfranchised communities located next to sites of environmental waste, survivors of war dealing with the remnants of chemical warfare, soldiers negotiating the aftermath of contact with depleted uranium, or indigenous peoples grappling with nuclear reactors situated on their land, the devastation of radiation is wrought on those with the least political power. In this respect, radiation reflects the structure of hegemony—the ways power can operate in seemingly invisible, unsuspecting ways while simultaneously having powerful material effects. As the quotes that begin this introduction point out, radiation serves as a potent metaphor in desert romances for good reason; it is thrillingly and terrifyingly tangible and intangible at the same time. In its material and invisible forms, radiation cuts both ways.

Radiation therefore operates as a framing metaphor for how desire animates contemporary technologies of U.S. imperialism. The metaphor is threaded throughout the chapters, each of which addresses a technology of imperialism in relation to the war on terror. In chapter 1, the radiation metaphor takes the form of weapons of mass destruction since they are a clear example of the threat to which the technology of security responds. Investigating the strategies that romance authors use to clearly distance the sheikh-hero from the figure of the terrorist simultaneously reveals the construction of the sheikh-hero as an exceptional leader allied with U.S.-Anglo powers. The authors therefore demonstrate the good-sheikh subjectivity to be a crucially under-theorized one in contemporary investigations of Arabiastani masculinities.

Chapter 2 begins where chapter 1 leaves off, with a consideration of the key word *freedom*. While discourses of terrorism tend to obfuscate any real engagement with the notion of freedom, relegating it to the realm of neoliberal market freedoms, desert romances activate the concept through fantasies of feminist liberation focused on saving the other. The radiation metaphor here takes the form of enriching uranium since the chapter investigates how freedom operates as a primary technology of contemporary imperialism. In other words, at stake here is the question of the politics of uranium enrichment—who has the freedom to enrich uranium, given the process's relationship both to alternative forms of energy and to nuclear weaponry.

The trope of the desert is particularly ripe for exploring these questions. First, the desert operates symbolically as a space in which the heroine loses herself to find herself.[134] The desert therefore enables a kind of exploration that is identified with feminism, where feminism is understood simply as the freedom to choose the life one desires. This individualist notion of freedom further intersects with consumerist ideas of freedom, exemplified by the lavish settings in which the heroines find themselves. Because the usually white heroines are lauded for their strength and independence and, unlike Arab women, can therefore help the sheikh modernize his country, desert romances allow for an exploration of a contemporary iteration of hegemony on the megalomaniacal side of paranoia: the urge to liberate Arabiastani women by reforming their patriarchal societies, one sheikh at a time.

Chapter 3 employs the x-ray mode of the radiation metaphor to explore how race and, in particular, the racialization of Arabs and Muslims after 9/11 operate as a structuring reality in the romance novels precisely because racialization cannot be named or acknowledged. Because race is itself a social fantasy that operates as a social reality, desert romances serve as apropos materials for investigating the unspoken material consequences of race. Since the racialization of actual Arabs and Muslims in western Europe and the U.S. has increased following 9/11 (in conjunction with the rise in popularity of desert romances), authors have had to become more savvy about how they code the sheikh-hero's exoticism without risking his overt racialization. An investigation of these codes reveals the way that ethnicity, religion, and cultural dress operate as key elements around which the racialization of Arabs and Muslims spins. The sheikh-hero is made palatable by ethnicizing him, a move that is based on the liberal multiculturalist notion of tolerance toward difference, while anesthetizing overt raciality. Utilizing "postrace" and "color-blind" logic, the technology of liberal multiculturalism is another mechanism through which the exceptionalist logic of benevolent empire can be communicated. The sheikh-hero serves as an exemplary vehicle through which to deliver the imperialist gift of freedom.[135]

If chapters 1 through 3 investigate particular mechanisms for desiring one's own repression, chapter 4 takes up the overarching narrative of the desire for wholeness that plays out in romance novels. The main idea here is perhaps best exemplified by Omar Sharif (a major sex symbol in the world of desert romances) and his assertion that "to make a woman happy in bed, you've got to be half man and half woman."[136] Indeed, the ideal alpha-male sheikh-hero exudes hypermasculinity externally while revealing a soft, sensitive side only to the heroine. He therefore serves as the perfect figure through which to explore the underlying architecture of one's own desire for repression, which is the desire for wholeness. While the idea of wholeness pervades the larger genre of romance novels, desert romances in particular demonstrate how the desire for wholeness resonates at both the individual level of subjectivity and at the national level of imperialist state formation. Employing the metaphor of radiation in terms of the structural instability of radioactive materials, chapter 4 uses the idea of half-life to demonstrate the importance of complementary binaries in the narrative desire for wholeness. The chapter argues that the romantic narrative of wholeness serves to shore up imperialist power by eliding its actual instabilities.

The imperialist love story of the war on terror does not have a happy ending—neither for the subjects of imperial power nor for its targets—despite the discursive energy expended on resolving the project of benevolent imperialism into a happy ending, or as corporate-bureaucratic speech might have it, a win-win situation. The lack of a happy ending, though, is nothing to lament. Reading the story with this realization can instead be an impetus for seeking an end to the war on terror, for freeing up the desires bounded by contemporary technologies of imperialism, and for spinning them toward truly liberatory aims.

1

"To Catch a Sheikh" in the War on Terror

Remember that *monsters* have the same root as *to demonstrate*; monsters signify.
—Donna Haraway

"They were building something new in the history of the world: not an empire made for plundering by the intruding power, but a modern nation in which American and Arab could work out fair contracts, produce in partnership, and profit mutually by their association."
—Wallace Stegner, quoted in *America's Kingdom*, by Robert Vitalis, 87

Capitalism is defined by a cruelty having no parallel in the primitive system of cruelty, and by a terror having no parallel in the despotic regime of terror.
—Gilles Deleuze and Félix Guattari, *Anti-Oedipus*, 373

Contemporary desert romances offer a distinct interpretation of the famous oil-sheikh caricature that emerged out of the 1970s oil crises.[1] While many popular characterizations of the oil sheikh cast him as greedy and lascivious, desert romances capitalize on his riches to cast him as a desirable and debonair prince. As one of the desert romance novelists, Dana Marton, puts it: "The world was full of beautiful women and there was no shortage of sexy bodies happy to press up against a sheik who owned a couple of oil wells."[2] As we will see with other stereotypes of Arab and Muslim masculinity, this characterization doesn't mean that desert romances categorically dispel the traditional image of the Arab oil sheikh, but rather that they intentionally craft their sheikh-heroes as exemplary figures who responsibly use their country's resources for the greater good.

In my sample of contemporary desert romances, fifteen of them (37.5 percent) mention oil as the primary economy of the sheikh's country. As a significant trope in contemporary desert romances, then, oil provides a sedimented metaphor for the way that security operates as a contemporary technology of imperialism. Not surprisingly, the contemporary desert romances that introduce oil as a key trope follow the mainstream narrative about oil's role in the Middle East as well as in configuring the U.S. relationship to the Middle East. Mimicking the "discovery doctrine" of U.S. settler colonialism, which cast the Americas as a discovered land, oil fields in the Middle East are similarly described as objects of triumphant discovery.[3] In both narratives, the inhabitants of the land are alternately figured as ignorant (if noble) subjects in need of the beneficent help and technology of the discoverer-usurpers or as irrationally violent figures who must be subdued. As evinced by Wallace Stegner's popular account, *Discovery!*, the discovery doctrine as applied to the new oil frontier of the Middle East builds on the basic logic of settler colonialism, though it shifts from expropriating land (outright) to expropriating oil resources.[4]

Desert romances provide some useful examples of the way the logic of the discovery doctrine plays out in popular understandings of the history of oil. In Sharon Kendrick's *Monarch of the Sands*, readers are treated to a classic rendition of the benevolence of discovery. We learn that the heroine is drawn to Arabiastan because of her "brilliant and eccentric geologist father. It had been his unexpected discovery of oil which had lifted Khayarzah out of the crippling debts caused by decades of warfare—and changed its whole future."[5] Here, the discovery is benign not only because it ends "decades of warfare" (presumed to be inherent to a backward Arabiastani country, which hadn't capitalized on its own resources), but also because it is accidental. In other words, outside intervention comes from an altruistic (if eccentric) geologist, not an imperialist state. Though the example is extreme in that it doesn't mention any presence of an outside state, it is nevertheless true to the discovery doctrine, which figures the discovery of oil by U.S.-Anglo powers mostly as a kind of gift to the countries that host it.[6] Parallel to a white-man's-burden logic, the discovery consequently comes with a responsibility, as the story goes, to protect the oil-producing state from would-be plunderers. Crafted in the early days of oil prospecting in the Middle

East—then the Ottoman Empire—this way of conceiving of Arab and Iranian states demonstrated a transitional form of colonialism, which manifested itself in the "mandate" and "protectorate" states of Britain and France.[7] Having dispensed with the quasi-colonial labels for these states, the narrative of protection was nevertheless still deployed to explain the 1991 Gulf Storm attack on Iraq by U.S. forces, for example. As indicated by these examples, the logical conclusion to the narrative of discovery casts the U.S.-Anglo power as the responsible protector of the Arabiastani state; however, the narrative also exploits the idea of cooperation, as indicated by the Stegner epigraph to this chapter.

Exemplified in narratives about the relationship of the U.S. to Saudi Arabia, the basic idea is articulated well by Jarek, the sheikh-hero of *Captive of the Desert King*: "Most of the equipment and materials you see were provided by the United States after we made our tentative agreement to do business with them. Now that we've started production they receive the majority of our crude oil. In return, they give us money and access to certain technology your government is developing."[8] Jarek's use of the vague term "technology" to describe what the U.S. provides in return for access to his country's crude oil implies that the technology has to do with oil production. It therefore replicates mainstream narratives about the benevolence of U.S. involvement in oil-producing states, which tend to gloss over the key form that technological "aid" usually takes—military protection and arms sales. In terms of what it both does and does not explicitly name, Jarek's reference to technological aid exemplifies the centrality of security to the partnership between the U.S. and Arabiastan vis-à-vis oil. Exploring the ideas of cooperation and mutual benefit, this chapter elucidates how security operates as a contemporary technology of imperialism.

As an increasingly important natural resource especially after World War II, oil plays a key role in shaping the strategic importance of the Middle East for global superpowers. The usual narrative describes this importance in terms of national security and specifically in terms of the violent threats actors in the Middle East could pose to the United States and its allies. In its most simplistic form, this violence is portrayed as a natural characteristic of Arab and Muslim peoples, and in its slightly more complicated form, it is portrayed as a consequence of rogue attempts to take over energy supplies or develop nuclear weapons.[9]

A clear focus on the mechanics of oil in terms of capital interests, however, helps to clarify the contradictions underlying the way security operates as a technology of imperialism. U.S. interests in Middle Eastern oil reserves have always been linked to the militarization of these states, but not always for the presumed reasons. As Timothy Mitchell suggests, the arming of Middle Eastern rentier states also originally functioned as a way of recycling petrodollars back to the U.S., and, in fact, officials sought to augment the narrative of the threat these nations faced to encourage an unprecedented scale of arms sales to the region. In other words, the relationship between oil and the doctrine of security began early, but not only because of needing to secure the oil supply. In fact, oil companies at the time were more interested in restricting oil supply (by leaving some oil fields undeveloped) to maintain stable pricing. The point is not that these countries faced no threat to their resources whatsoever, but that the amount and types of arms sold to them did not and could not actually respond to such a threat. Arms sales, then, were "useful for their uselessness," and the "rhetoric of insecurity" about oil-rich regions was produced as a way of justifying the arms sales that ultimately served to return U.S. dollars back to the United States.[10]

While contemporary forms of imperialism share many basic characteristics with earlier colonialist forms of power, then, the example of oil demonstrates some of its novelties. The rhetoric of security uses the tropes of protection and defense as a means of justifying military presence. Moreover, the rhetoric casts this presence as a necessary form of cooperation and mutual benefit. It uses the corporate logic of the win-win situation to move forward with expropriation, described by David Harvey as "accumulation through dispossession."[11] Recast as cooperation, imperialist operations such as manipulating and monopolizing access to crucial natural resources and imposing a strict military presence come to be organized around the anticipation of threat, both to the oil-producing country and to the hegemonic power "protecting" it. In short, security operates as a technology of imperialism by training resources away from basic needs (food, shelter, etc.) and toward the defense industry (at all levels—from gated communities to the military). Further, the emphasis on the necessity of defense obscures its uselessness, recalling Eisenhower's famous critique of the military-industrial complex. At best, the defense industry emerges as an engine of capitalist expansion.[12]

At worst, military expansion produces the conditions for expanded warfare, as is the case with the Middle East, which was heavily militarized as a result of the politics of oil.[13] Either way, the framework of defense displaces the violence of neoliberal capitalism (dispossession) and imperialism (militarized defense) onto racialized others—in this case, the specter of the terrorist.

An important by-product of security as a technology of imperialism, then, is its refiguring of subjectivity. Out of sociopolitical opposition (terrorism), the technology of security creates the categorical construction of personhood—the terrorist—as a reservoir of perpetual threat. From this well of presumed perpetual threat, security as a technology of imperialism feeds. The figure of the terrorist, however, is not the only category of personhood constructed to uphold the rhetoric of security. It also needs a figure of rapprochement—the cooperative sheikh. As we are told in the desert romance *Sheik Seduction*, "they needed someone to take over the company, someone who knew how to lead a large company in the Western way."[14] Though the terrorist certainly exists in desert romances, it is the latter figure on which these novels focus.

Desert romances are full of good sheikhs—those who seek benevolent cooperation with the U.S.-Anglo powers in order to bring their countries into the global economy or, in other words, to catch up. Through the romantic narrative, the sheikh-hero also valorizes hetero-bourgeois companionate marriage and even comes to appreciate liberal notions of gender equality. In short, he embodies liberal humanist forms of subjectivity; he becomes a rational-economic man and affirms the progress narrative. In so doing, he loses the ability to critique the violence of the accumulation-by-dispossession model, and he helps to reify the figure of the terrorist as an irrational, backward, and unintelligible other who serves as the perfect symbol onto which to displace the violence of contemporary neoliberal imperialism. Indeed, in their elaboration of this crucial figure of the good sheikh, desert romances are a most useful set of materials; they subtly demonstrate the way the rhetoric of security demands the formulation of a good sheikh. As is the case with Efraim, the sheikh-hero of *Seized by the Sheikh*, the role of the good sheikh is to "usher his country into the modern age. And part of the pact among the island nations would help develop the infrastructure for such an endeavor, financed by profits from the oil leases off their shores."[15]

No matter which desert romance we consider, the sheikh-heroes usually serve as agents of a particular narrative of globalization, one that disavows the kind of state violence necessary to uphold the economic and social realities (especially the increasing inequalities) that neoliberalism installs. There is the character David Rashid, who wants to bring his (fictional) country Azar into the "global economy," or Xander, who "works tirelessly to promote better relations between his country and the rest of the world."[16] Then there is Sultan Malik Roman Nuri, who needs the white heroine to "teach their sons and daughters to set goals, to dream big, [and] to fight for what one believes," or Zageo, who knows his country must "keep investing to consolidate the wealth we have, ensuring that the future will have no backward steps."[17] In fact, as the above passages demonstrate, desert romance novels combine neoliberal themes of freedom and progress through the means of global free trade and investment with the theme of rapprochement between East and West through heteronormative union. Whether through oil riches or other means, sheikh-heroes are exceptional leaders of exceptional states, and as such, they belie the spirit of cooperative imperialism as a project of scattered hegemonies.

States of Exception

Some of the most crucial work that the rhetoric of security does on behalf of imperialism is precisely the shoring up of particular kinds of personhood—it makes coherent and stable categories out of unruly and chaotic subjectivities. In terms of the terrorist, the rhetoric seeks to consolidate vast and varied forms of violent protest and resistance into one coherent enemy, against whom the wide-ranging war on terror can be fought. The romantic oil sheikhs of desert romances, on the other hand, offer a narrative representation of the cooperative leader, and in so doing, they consolidate complicated and problematic diplomatic relationships with oppressive rulers in the Middle East into the coherent image of the good sheikh.

While the sheikh-heroes of desert romances are clearly fictional, their characterization nevertheless replicates the fantasies of cooperation and humanitarianism—fantasies that implicitly structure the way that security operates as a technology of imperialism. In this scenario, the technology of security protects a particularly exceptional form of imperialism—that of a benevolent U.S. power. It does so, further, by extending the logic of exceptionality to its newly protected, but independent, state. Desert romances make vague references to the kind of partnership the sheikh-heroes seek with the U.S.-Anglo powers. The references are vague so that they do not distract from the romantic plot narrative with an excess of politics; nevertheless, they speak volumes about the kinds of partnership they seek with U.S.-Anglo powers. Sheikh Jarek, for example, explains to the heroine that "we want to be with the U.S. in the forefront of new energy technology. . . . We could not do that with ties to OPEC."[18] His rejection of alliances with other Arabiastani oil-producing countries in favor of an alliance with the U.S. is, of course, quite significant. Under the rubric of progress and advancement, Jarek implies that he wants to collaborate with the U.S. for the greater good of his country and, ultimately, the world. The reference to OPEC serves also to cite the 1973 "oil embargo" to suggest that an alliance of Arabiastani countries would only lead to world economic chaos because it would be led by the greedy capitalist interests of oil-producing nations at the expense of the world economy.[19]

The general sentiment of mistrust regarding a horizontal, democratic alliance with other Arabiastani states is echoed by Sheik Kadir in *The Sheik and I*. Sheik Kadir seeks alliance with the fictional Anglo country of Silvershire (which is, interestingly, a monarchy) to move his country, Kahani, "into the twenty-first century with dignity and strength."[20] We later learn that he therefore opposes affiliation with the (Arabiastani) Union for Democracy because "he could not condone that organization and still ask for an alliance with the monarchy of Silvershire. Besides, there were well substantiated rumors that some factions within the Union for Democracy had begun to advocate violence as a way to meet their goals."[21]

Though most authors I contacted claimed that they set their desert romances in fictional countries to avoid having to worry about getting all the details correct, these examples suggest another possible reason. The sheikh-heroes' kingdoms share many similarities with Saudi Arabia, a country synonymous with the oppression of women in the minds of readers and therefore incompatible with contemporary romance for the vast majority of them. Not the least of these similarities is articulated by Sheikhs Jarek and Kadir quite clearly: they seek to form exceptional states parallel to and in alliance with the United States, and the sheikhs' states use some of the same technologies of imperialism, like security.

A closer look at the alliance between the U.S. and Saudi Arabia elucidates the point. Two main aspects of the relationship—the narrative of exceptionalism and the "deal" of oil for security—highlight the framing of U.S. imperialism both as benevolent and as deployed through the technology of security, which has helped to shroud U.S. state and military violence under the banner of self-defense. As Robert Vitalis points out in *America's Kingdom*, the narrative of U.S. exceptionalism is echoed in Saudi Arabia's own exceptionalist claims, which insist that Saudi Arabia is the only nation in the region to have escaped imperialist rule.[22] (This account, of course, is challenged by the kingdom's opponents, who describe the nation as "a country that imperialism simply invented."[23]) It is the strength of these two narratives together—those of U.S. and Saudi exceptionalism—that leads to the description of the relationship between the two nations as one of "partnership" where the two "profit mutually by their association."[24] Indeed, the "special relationship" between the U.S. and Saudi Arabia, sometimes more cynically described as the "deal," is forged through a key technology of U.S. imperialism— the paradigm of security.[25] The "deal"—oil for security—signals several key shifts in imperial formation—shifts that distinguish the U.S. model from its colonialist predecessors. As exemplified by the phrase *oil frontier*, conquest here shifts from the occupation of an entire territory in order to extract its raw materials to the extraction of raw materials through proxy political and military formations. This sort of indirect domination—through the presence of strategically located military bases, for example—is facilitated by the rhetoric of security and further cemented through the narrative of partnership and cooperation.

Through these very narratives of partnership and cooperation, the U.S. could be described as "concealing imperial ambition in an abstract universalism."[26] The abstract nature of such imperialist universalism obscures how the principle of universalism is exclusively applied to the market. Returning to the sheikh-heroes of desert romances is again instructive. We learn that the sheikh-heroes' efforts to bring their countries into the global economy will essentially be accomplished through a neoliberal valorization of free trade. Upon seeing a Walmart type of

one-stop shop in the U.S., for example, Sheikh Jamal confides that it
is "something [he] plans on building in his country. It will be a place
[his] people can go for their necessities."[27] Perhaps more to the larger
point, Sheikh Tariq, who is incidentally involved in "leading peace talks
between warring Arab states," spearheads a trade agreement that exemplifies the ideology of free trade.[28] As he explains to his beloved Jasmine, "Zulheil [his country] now has a contract with several Western
states that will allow [its] artistic products to cross their borders without
duty. . . . The agreement goes both ways."[29]

Tariq's statement mimics the typical ideology of globalism, which itself adheres to neoliberal principles—it assumes that the benefits of free
trade will equally reach all members involved, including all the citizens
of his country, and that it will therefore achieve a greater good. His assertion overlooks the evidence of the very detrimental effects such arrangements have had on the disenfranchised members of most countries
agreeing to similar kinds of arrangements. Often enacted as a condition
of International Monetary Fund loans, such free-trade agreements most
often benefit those entities most equipped to compete on a large scale—
like multinational corporations—which are then also free to move em-
ployment opportunities from their home countries to regions that have
made labor cheaper often at the expense of workers' rights. The violent
fallout from this process—whether it is through the increased violence
in a criminality of literally disenfranchised communities in the U.S. or
through the violent union-busting in states that seek to make and keep
labor cheap—is no less potent even if it is more diffuse. In this respect,
the sheikh's kingdom as well as his exceptional relationship to the U.S.
demonstrates the concept of scattered hegemonies as a contemporary
formation of imperialist power.[30]

A key paradox of the rhetoric of exceptionality, as demonstrated by
the parallel narrative of Saudi Arabia as an exceptional state, is just how
unexceptional this rhetoric is. The label *exceptional* particularly serves
to obscure the state's own tenuousness. The state-of-exception narrative is nationalistic; it does the ideological work of shoring up the state
as a coherent, sovereign nation-state, despite the many contradictions
and fluidities introduced by globalization. As Daniel Rodgers explains,
regardless of the exceptionalist rhetorical move to shore up the nation-
state, "nations themselves exceed their borders. They have archipela-

gos of presence, power, and vulnerability scattered across the globe. By the same token, the world is now present within virtually every nation's borders in the form of trade, economic investments, satellite communications, and the peoples of the new global cities."[31] Nation-states have varying amounts of power, capital, and influence on private financial interests (including transnational corporations and financial institutions like banks), and in this variation lies a good amount of vulnerability. As with virtually all previous imperial formations, the state seeks to minimize its weaknesses by harnessing the power and volatility of capital often through violent means. The "special relationship" between the U.S. and Saudi Arabia, for example, exemplifies the old imperialist dynamic whereby the imperial power secures access to natural resources through violent means, though these means are framed in terms of benevolence, thanks to the narrative of exceptionalism. Again, rather than a symbol of aggression and violent power, the U.S. military base on Saudi soil is therefore cast in terms of protection and security.

Not only is the violence of the imperialist-protector power obscured, but so too is the violence of the protectorate state. While popular U.S. narratives about Saudi Arabia do tend to focus on its oppressive policies toward women, the rhetoric often obscures one of the key acts of violence that the state enacts through exclusionary citizenship laws, which leave the majority of its population of guest workers unprotected. Adding the UAE to the picture (particularly since the UAE is more closely aligned with the landscape of Arabiastan) emphasizes the point: these states consolidate power through strict, exclusionary citizenship laws, which simultaneously ensure that the oil wealth of the state is only distributed to a small percentage of the population at the same time that the state benefits from vast quantities of migratory exploited labor. Violent resistance to the exploitations that are deeply embedded in the pursuit and protection of capital interests often get labeled as terrorism in a move that effectively displaces state violence onto the specter of terrorism.[32] The rhetoric frames state violence as strictly defensive and never as a preexisting structural violence. Like the "warring Arab states" that sheikh-heroes seek to reconcile through peaceful, diplomatic means, and the violent terrorist elements that threaten the sheikh-heroes' lives at every turn, these mainstream narratives about violent resistance displace the violent acts of both neoliberal globalization and proxy imperialism onto the more simple narrative of terrorism.

Despite the efforts of the exceptionalist narrative to present an image of a solid and stable (imperialist) nation-state, the state's response to violent resistance and terrorism demonstrates its own understanding of the vulnerabilities of contemporary nation-state formations. These vulnerabilities, moreover, are not just the result of violent resistance. The volatility of capital itself—part of what gives capital the power that the state seeks to harness—also poses a threat to the imperialist state by virtue of its unpredictability. The imperialist state therefore shores itself up through the rhetoric of exceptionalism. If, as Rodgers argues, exceptionalism serves as a clear means of dividing "here" and "elsewhere," then the binary of "us" and "them" does not seamlessly map onto neat geographical boundaries of "here" and "elsewhere."[33] Rather, the U.S. has responded to the so-called terrorist threat by intensifying its security apparatus. The primacy of this security apparatus—that is, security used as a technology of imperialism—turns the exceptionalist state into a state of exception. In other words, the idea that the U.S. exhibits the exceptional values of freedom, democracy, and liberal multiculturalism becomes the justification for jettisoning these same ideals in the name of security. The technology of security recasts state-of-emergency measures, which restrict civil liberties and freedoms, as necessary exceptions to the liberal-democratic rule of law.

Though the exceptionalist state and a state of exception are flip sides of the same coin, the latter easily targets both the enemy within (through the heightened surveillances and curtailing of civil liberties enabled by the Patriot Act) and the enemy outside. In this view, terrorists are everywhere, particularly in "rogue" states, and the exceptional state can attack said terrorism (through direct military action in Afghanistan and Iraq and a combination of direct and proxy military action in Yemen, Pakistan, Somalia, and other states). Drawing on Michel Foucault's essay "Society Must be Defended," Ann Stoler identifies the modern logics of such an imperialist binary: "This notion that 'society must be defended' condones the moral right to murder those 'outside,' as it produces not only state-sanctioned disenfranchisements, persecutions, and internments, but a dangerous overproduction of popular seat-of-the-pants profiling by 'good citizens.'"[34] In other words, security operates as a successful technology of imperialism because it enables a supple and flexible targeting of scattered and deterritorialized enemies at the same time that it maintains the image of a stable, exceptionally benevolent, imperialist state. To do so, the rhetoric of security must skillfully craft a clear image of both the enemy and the good citizen—figures represented by the terrorist and the good sheikh-hero in contemporary desert romances.

The Landscape of Arabiastan, Part 1: Securityscapes

The sheikh-heroes' need for a solid security-apparatus in their home countries is either explained in relation to their progressive style of leadership or simply cast as the natural order of things in Arabiastan.[35] We learn, for example, that the sheikh-hero of *Desert Warrior* was "the subject of an assassination attempt by a terrorist organization on his way back from New Zealand."[36] The heroine in *Desert Prince, Defiant Virgin* informs King Malik that his opponents are "dangerous and they're playing for big stakes and they want [him] out of the picture in any way they can."[37] In *The Sheik and I*, we learn that "Kahani [the sheikh's country] wasn't the hotbed of terrorism some of the neighboring countries had become, but neither was it an entirely safe place. Leaders who worked to bring about change were often endangered, and she imagined that Al-Nuri was no exception to the rule."[38] In *Seized by the Sheikh*, the sheikh is part of an international group of leaders meeting in the U.S. for diplomatic reasons, and consequently, he is the target of a terrorist attack.[39] The threat of violence through terrorism in these plots is always irrational; it arises out of hatred for unequivocally good and progressive acts.[40] The sheikh leaders in these novels seek to modernize their countries and educate their people, especially women, raising the standard of living for all. In this framework, violence against the sheikhs can only be backward and illogical, and it therefore calls for an all-encompassing apparatus of security.

Given this prototype of the sheikh-hero as a progressive leader who seeks to align his country with the global economy and to cooperate with U.S.-Anglo powers, here again the implicit landscape of Arabiastan bears much in common with the United Arab Emirates.[41] The commonalities manifested in relatively small plot details like the style of clothing (robes) worn by the sheikh, his hobbies (e.g., falcon hunting and horse racing), and a kingdom often described to have gained wealth and recognition because of a relatively recent oil boom. However, the more important structural similarity resides in the naturalization of an expanding security-military apparatus as a necessity, and symbol, of contemporary middle-class life. Further, the naturalization of this security-military apparatus functions in ways that simultaneously obscure its links to militarization and neoliberalism.

In Dubai, for example, there is a plethora of gated communities, themselves symbols of the normalization of fear in everyday life and the myriad prospects for capitalizing on a generalized climate of imagined threat. Though Sheikh Mohammed al Maktoum, the "CEO" of Dubai, reportedly claims that the introduction of gated communities to "Arabia, the land of nomads and tents" is "one of his proudest achievements," it is less clear what these "safe" communities actually themselves achieve.[42] When questioned about the purpose of the gates for a relatively remote community in Dubai, a real estate agent assured Ahmed Kanna (author of *Dubai: The City as Corporation*), "It's for security." When Kanna pressed the agent, noting that the development was far from any city center and located, in fact, in the middle of the desert, the agent rejoined that it would prevent wild or escaped camels from entering the area before finally admitting that there was "no rational explanation for the fence."[43] There may be no rational explanation for gated communities, but there are clearly compelling, affective reasons and material capital interests that keep these communities proliferating. In this way, they can serve as exemplary discrete examples of the importance of the notion of security to contemporary, globalized, and militarized formations of capital.

Popular narratives about the growth of the security-military industry (from gated communities to airport security to the military itself) would have it that these developments are solely reactionary; they respond to outside, irrational threats like terrorism, the logic goes. In the exceptional-state narrative, a sovereign U.S. nation-state faces the dangerous threat of a deterritorialized enemy (such as al-Qa'ida or ISIS), which operates in remote, hard-to-reach regions of various other nation-states, both allies and foes.[44] In liberal narratives, like Benjamin

Barber's *Jihad vs. McWorld,* terrorists and multinational corporations are posed as equally "anarchic" deterritorialized forces wreaking havoc on democracy.[45] Both of these narratives operate to blame state violence on the specter of terrorism; that is, they elide the state violence necessary to support neoliberal capitalism and thereby perpetuate the notion that terrorism emerges out of a vacuum. When neoliberal capitalism is viewed as an important, violently deterritorializing force, one can see that this form of capitalism itself produces the need for a growing security-military apparatus.[46] One can also see how the state, deeply imbricated with capitalist interests, also becomes intertwined with conservative Islamic regimes—a paradigm that Timothy Mitchell describes as "McJihad."[47]

Flipping the script in this way—or, perhaps more accurately, refusing the false binary of the script—helps refute the idea that security only operates in a defensive mode. In fact, precisely because security can be premised on the conceit of self-defense, it can function as a more subtle technology of contemporary imperialism. Insofar as contemporary imperialism operates through the mode of accumulation through dispossession, security provides the ruse for covertly carrying out this act of accumulation. Mike Davis claims that "the Gulf economies . . . are now capitalized not just on oil production, but also on the fear of its disruption."[48] He goes on to show how this fear spins out into a complex web of lucrative security services. Portraying Dubai as a "paradise of personal security," Davis notes the myriad ways in which capitalizing on security supports Dubai's post-oil economy (oil is currently less than 10 percent of Dubai's GDP).[49] Whether it is "Swiss-style laws governing financial secrecy, armies of concierges, watchmen and bodyguards who protect its sanctums of luxury," or the previously mentioned gated communities, the security industry is at the heart of Dubai's key industries, which are banking, tourism, and real estate.[50] Indeed, the concept of security is at the heart of contemporary finance practices, such as the securitization of mortgages, which played a key role in the 2008 economic crises. Shifting the focus away from the idea that terrorism presents the greatest global threat and toward an investigation of security itself as an apparatus of threat demonstrates the idea that the violent acts of deterritorialization are in many ways produced by the practice of accumulation through dispossession. Despite the common invocation of al-Qa'ida as a violent deterritorialized network with connection to the Gulf, there is perhaps no better example of violent deterritorialization than the corporation formerly known as Blackwater, which is capitalized on the imperialist technology of security.

Tellingly, Abu Dhabi is now home to Erik Prince, founder and former CEO of Blackwater, the private military firm famously contracted by the U.S. government to provide "security services" during the occupations of Iraq and Afghanistan and involved even in the (botched) response to the failed levees in New Orleans after Hurricane Katrina.[51] Indeed, well before relocating to Abu Dhabi (to avoid being charged with war crimes in the U.S. as a result of Blackwater forces' killing of civilians—actions carried out with impunity), Prince had himself learned the financial lessons of a post-oil reality. Blackwater successfully capitalized on the fact that "in Iraq, the postwar business boom is not oil. It is security."[52] With Prince residing now in a "paradise of personal security" that itself exemplifies the deterritorializing impulses of capitalism, his corporate interests are much better examples of violent deterritorialization than is al-Qa'ida.[53] While al-Qa'ida is deterritorialized by virtue of operating as a network that is spatially disparate, Prince's security-focused corporations are deterritorialized both spatially and ideologically. Although Blackwater (which changed its name to Xe Services in 2009 and Academi in 2011) was subcontracted by the U.S. government for military operations, another entity of the corporation called Greystone (which was registered in Barbados to evade taxes) marketed itself as providing "global security" services to such countries as Uzbekistan, Yemen, the Philippines, Romania, Indonesia, Tunisia, Algeria, Hungary, Poland, Croatia, Kenya, Angola, and Jordan.[54] Moreover, the company experimented with advertising strategies, also marketing itself as a resource for "humanitarian aid and peacekeeping."[55] In short, the corporation's holdings exemplify the U.S. empire's key aspects that are obscured in official rhetoric—the primacy of the security-military apparatus, the militarization of humanitarianism, and the vast and violent deterritorializations enacted through the private capital interests infused throughout.[56]

The Landscape of Arabiastan, Part 2: The Sheikh as Gated Community

Romance authors incorporate a fair amount of research into their novels. Even if the love story is a fantasy, readers expect to learn real historical or geographical details.[57] The desert romance authors I interviewed mostly indicated that they did internet and library research to help fill in cultural details (e.g., to find Arabic names or investigate common customs). For example, one author described researching a *khanjar*, a traditional curved dagger, which appears on the flag of Oman.[58] Many writers also said that they set their novels in a fictionalized country specifically so they wouldn't have to worry about getting all the details correct.[59]

Those who did name a particular kind of research often singled out bedouins as something they needed to learn about, though none of them could remember or name any specific titles referenced. Their use of the term *bedouin* is already telling as the term itself seems to have been used more popularly in the 1970s and 1980s, particularly in academic sources, and is now eschewed for more specific terms, like Tuareg. A World-Cat search for sources with "bedouin" in the title reveals that the vast majority of titles are from the 1970s and 1980s, with some of the more recent books either categorized as juvenile (i.e., for young readers) or published by Aramco—the Saudi Arabian Oil Company, an emblem of the partnership between the U.S. and Saudi Arabia. The latter source is important in that the common narrative about nomadic life in Arabiastan is that the discovery of oil fundamentally changed the nomad. The Aramco version unsurprisingly frames the discovery of oil as a positive development that made a physically arduous life easier.[60] On the other hand, anthropological sources tend to lament how the capitalization of oil "sounded the death knell" for bedouin life.[61] Whether one applauds or laments the capitalization of oil in the Gulf region, the process both created a set of states, many of which partnered with the U.S. through security as a technology of imperialism, and literally settled nomadic life, therefore functioning as a kind of settler colonialism.

As a version of the oil-sheikh ruler, the sheikh-hero bears a special relationship to nomadism. While he is often characterized as having the "distinctively Bedouin virtues of courage, generosity and the ability to mediate disputes," it is also clear that he has evolved beyond the "aristocratic simplicity" of the bedouin.[62] He is therefore cast in a protective role of a simple, traditional, noble way of life that nevertheless must be settled if the sheikh is to benefit from progress and modernization. Desiring the oil sheikh, then, is not only about a desire for his riches, but also about craving a particular perception of security. In settling the desert and its dwellers, the sheikh-hero absorbs all of the virtues of its peoples, which he sometimes claims as his own authentic roots, and he simultaneously tames any potential image of them as "dour fanatics who, with their long hair and daggers, are barbarians who appreciate few of the finer things of life."[63] In short, he romanticizes the figure of the bedouin by both absorbing it into his own characterization and by disciplining the bedouin's (threatening) deterritorializing nature through a process of settler colonialism that is framed as benevolent and inevitable.

In this respect, the sheikh-hero can be likened to the metaphor of the gated community; he represents the logic of enclosure, which is justified through the rhetoric of security. Like the gated community in Dubai, which capitalizes on the notion of security despite the lack of a clear referent of danger, the sheikh-as-gated-community naturalizes the need to enclose the commons while obscuring the capitalist interests at the heart of this enclosure. The sheikh is an empty signifier of safety even if he is meaningful as a symbol of the way that security operates as a technology of imperialism. In other words, the danger from which he protects his people and the heroine is the vague and unspecified danger of a deterritorialized way of life that exists outside of the logic of capitalism.

Gated communities gain their appeal, in part, from the presumptive thrill of living in an edgy, dangerous neighborhood. That is, part of what they capitalize on is the promise of security in the midst of the thrill of danger. The sheikh is particularly suited to this aspect of the metaphor since he literally embodies—and therefore contains—the danger of the deterritorialized nomad. While the sheikh-hero may inform the heroine that his "people have barbarian roots," as does Tariq in *Desert Warrior*, they are also likely to drink "Bedouin tea," as does Sheikh Zafiq, leading the heroine Bella to imagine that he is "rediscovering [his] tribal roots."[64] This latter, nostalgic note is the tone most often struck in desert romances, and it is a common take on bedouins and their relationship to the larger Arab cultures. Consider, for example, the following assertion in *The Bedouin*, a scholarly source from the late 1970s: "The Bedouin are not an alien impoverished society, living on the fringe of a stronger sedentary culture in the Middle East; on the contrary, they are the basis of Arabian culture and society; their values are still often the ones which are accepted and admired in the cities today; their language is considered the best Arabic; their poetry the best literature. If they were to vanish from the deserts, it would leave the Arab lands like a garden from which the oldest tree has been uprooted."[65]

This romantic and somewhat bittersweet characterization of nomadic life—lamentably fading from view because of the rapid modernization brought on by the discovery of oil—is still dominant in the Aramco version of the story, one that closely resembles contemporary characterizations in *National Geographic*, both in style and in content. In fact, *National Geographic* could be described as representative of the kinds of sources authors were likely to find in their research about bedouins and the Middle East. Thus, I interweave articles and images from *National Geographic* as an example of popular nonfiction that helps to shape the common U.S. understanding of the Middle East (and many other parts of the world).[66] Rather than looking for evidence of the real or actual Middle East in romantic portrayals of Arabiastan, I am charting here the codes that authors use to navigate readers' preconceived perceptions of reality. Authors must make the setting believable, while steering clear of what I referred to earlier as the surfeit of reality—the plethora of negative characteristics about Arabiastani masculinity that readers perceive to be true. As a widely read popular nonfiction source, *National Geographic* provides a clear and easily accessible account of middle-class nonfictional renderings of the Middle East.

National Geographic is a well-established and well-respected publication that has an impressively wide reach. Even without a subscription, one could encounter the *National Geographic* style through documentaries and TV programs, popular (traveling) images that get anthologized and reprinted, and, most importantly for romance author research, its online articles and images, many of which can be accessed without charge during a quick internet search.[67] It is a widely trusted source because of the successful framing of the magazine as an "unbiased, unmediated" view of the world and as a publication that is, above all, "accurate, balanced, and fair."[68] The organization presents much of its material through a positivist, epistemological lens, tending toward classification and objective truths. Such a classic scientific model helps to balance the entertainment aspect of the *National Geographic* enterprise, enabling the magazine (and the larger industry) to strike a comfortable mix of science and entertainment in its overall sensibility.[69]

National Geographic representations of the Middle East and desert romance portrayals of Arabiastan manifest at least two paradigmatic overlaps that speak to a kind of intertextuality between them. Most importantly, they present the region as another world that is mysterious, yet knowable, and one that is striving (despite its regressive elements) toward modernity, a striving that could be greatly aided by benevolent U.S.-Anglo powers. The two types of publications portray an "American national identity that is rational, generous, and benevolent."[70] Both the *National Geographic* and the romance novel genre date back to the late nineteenth century in terms of their earliest publications, and both experienced huge growth in the post–World War II period (the 1950s and 1960s for *National Geographic* and the 1970s for romance novels). Though this growth probably has to do with advancements in printing technologies, it also highlights a coinciding popular positivist humanism in both genres.[71] While romance novels are often seen as pure fantasy or escapism, the industry as a whole (and particularly internationally focused subgenres and themes) subscribes to a universalizing humanist position, often expressed in the clichés that love is a great leveler and that romance and love are all the world needs to resolve conflicts.

A survey of *National Geographic* issues since 2001 (and up until 2011) reveals a total of twenty-six articles focusing on the Middle East.[72] Of these, the majority focus on the two major themes that appear in desert romances: the desert terrain or nomadism (the two are often conflated) and Gulf states and city-states that share many of the characteristics of Arabiastan (these include Saudi Arabia, Qatar, Dubai, and Abu Dhabi—the latter two being part of the UAE).[73] A favorite topic of *National Geographic* over the years is the Sahara Desert—not surprising, given the Sahara's iconic stature in U.S. associations with the Middle East and its potential for adventure-exploration stories. John Hare's expedition article "Surviving the Sahara" certainly fits the bill while also offering a description of the desert that characterizes many of the images found in desert romances (see chapter 2 for more on this theme): "Desert sand dunes rise and fall like something incarnate, time-bearing, at once peaceful and yet, in their isolated desolation, rather terrifying."[74]

Most importantly, a significant number of the articles focus on nomadism and the romantic figure of the bedouin. Such emphasis makes the interviewed romance writers' naming of bedouin as a key research term that much more salient. The vast majority of desert-related articles profile ethnic minorities living in North Africa—sometimes the Amazigh (Berbers) and, of these, most often the Tuaregs. Consistent with their over-representation in National Geographic (relative to the overall coverage of the Middle East, including North Africa), Tuaregs also tend to be one of the only ethnic groups named or alluded to in desert romances.[75] Though these articles still tend to wax lyrical about the desert (e.g., "To reach this remote corner of the world's largest desert requires traversing a vast primordial landscape,"), they focus on a dying breed of "fierce nomads."[76] Consider, for example, the statement of a Tuareg man, a rebel commander who laments the passing of nomadic traditions at the same time that he pleads for "modern" state provisions: "'My father only knew how to live in the desert,' the commander says. 'He knew how to make the salt caravan to Bilma, how to find grazing in the desert, how to hunt antelope in the canyons and wild sheep in the mountains. And that is what I know, but the life of the desert is ending. Our children need school.'"[77] The commander's bittersweet message is echoed by many sheikh-heroes, who find themselves in just the position to shepherd their people into a new, modern era.[78]

Indeed, the emphasis on bedouin, nomadic, or tribal life carries into the other main set of National Geographic articles, those looking at the Gulf states of Saudi Arabia, Qatar, and the UAE (in two separate articles on Dubai and Abu Dhabi). In a classic article about Abu Dhabi, written through the angle of a beauty pageant for camels, the author explains that the "sand-dusted Bedouin . . . bumpkin . . . image is now giving way to something more romantic: the nomad as quintessential Arab, a symbol of freedom."[79] Reading on, one realizes that this "symbol of freedom" represents the very same characteristics often attributed to the sheikh-hero in desert romances: a nomad by ancestry, he has matured with the boon of oil wealth. This wealth both settled him and enabled him to send his sons to the West to be educated, which, in turn, enabled his country (or sheikhdom) to grow into a financial center of glamor and glitz through the admiration of, and cooperation with, U.S.-Anglo powers.

The intertextuality between contemporary nonfiction representations of the Middle East and Arabiastan (of romancelandia) are further exemplified in the following description of the ruler of Dubai, Sheikh Mohammed bin Rashid al Maktoum, in Ahmed Kanna's *Dubai: City as Corporation*:[80] "Sheikh Muhammad, who calls himself the 'CEO of Dubai,' is a larger-than-life figure in the city. He is frequently depicted, along with his late father and late UAE president, Zayed bin Sultan Al Nahyan, in portraits around the city, often seated atop a white Arabian horse. . . . In this capacity, he has taken it upon himself to will Dubai into the status of a global city."[81] Often described in remarkably similar ways to the description of the ruler of Dubai in the preceding passage, the prototypical sheikh-hero of the desert romance embodies two amalgamations: the common romance-hero blend of virility and (feminine) sensitivity, and a carefully crafted blend of tradition and progress. Both amalgamations simultaneously woo the (usually Western) heroine and assuage any concerns she might have about the hero's violent or backward nature.

The image of Sheikh Mohammed as a regal desert king who can straddle both the traditional image of an Arabian warrior astride a white horse and the picture of a progressive Arab leader striving to bring his country into the new global world order exemplifies the image of the prototypical sheikh-hero in desert romances. Corroborating both romance author Linda Conrad's and scholar Ahmed Kanna's observations, Keira Gillett uses in her blog the image of the crown prince of Dubai to explain what makes the sheikh-hero so "yummy": "The sheikh is a modern prince in an age when there aren't enough eligible princes to go around. His home is the glorious sun-drenched deserts of faraway exotic locales. He's gentlemanly, well educated, disciplined, principled, and honorable. As a hero, the sheikh is powerful, the ruler of his kingdom, and a fine physical specimen. He's proud, dangerous, and very masculine."[82]

These general sentiments are also echoed in a 2003 *National Geographic* article about Qatar. Opening with the familiar trope of contrasting tradition with modernity, the author explains that modern Qatar was formed the "old fashioned way: when a son dethroned his father."[83] Painting a picture of an indulgent and decadent sultan, the article goes on to portray the current sheikh as a progressive leader who struggles to contain the regressive elements of his society, while gently nudging the society forward. It therefore meanders through a description of a falcon market (read: traditional), the oil and natural gas resources that have garnered the country "fabulous wealth," a photo of a child jockey raised for camel racing, and coverage of Qataris' thoughts on whether their nation should host Al Jazeera.[84] Almost always described as "fabulously wealthy," the UAE and wider Gulf region seem to serve as a natural inspiration for desert romances since a main characteristic of sheikh-heroes (and Mediterranean alpha-male heroes in general) is their extravagant wealth.

The *National Geographic* article aptly ends with the scene of young Qataris in the mall riding escalators up and down as a means of surreptitiously socializing with one another. It ends, in other words, on a resoundingly triumphant note about the links of consumerism with progress and freedom, links that have been multiply invoked in the war on terror, most notably by George W. Bush immediately following the events of September 11, 2001. The progress narrative here has these countries moving seamlessly from primitive backwaters into ultramodern globalized cities through their strategic alliance with benevolent Western powers.

Though the vast majority of contemporary desert romances take place in fictionalized Arabiastan, they invoke the context of globalized city-states in the UAE in particular ways. They adopt dress codes from the Arabian Peninsula, especially in references to royal or princely sheikhs who wear garments, called robes in most desert romances, reminiscent of Emirati royal dress. They take place in small countries with significant desert terrain and at least one hypermodern city. Usually, the sheikh must balance the needs of traditional (or tribal) desert-dwellers with a growing city citizenry. And finally, the sheikh's country used to be a little-known desert kingdom until vast quantities of oil were discovered rather recently; the discovery propels him and his nation into a global economy and apparently invites terrorist activity.

The fictional narratives of desert romances and nonfictional accounts of the Gulf region, particularly the UAE, converge here in ways that demonstrate the tenacity of orientalist tropes. As Ahmed Kanna writes (about Dubai): "Thirty years after orientalism was demystified (Said

1978), the Gulf seems a recalcitrant holdout."[85] Indeed, in its reflection and sometimes staging of traditional or tribal culture (in both dress and customs), the imagined Gulf provides the perfect setting for romantic stories that invoke the desert landscape and a proud king rooted in ancient cultural traditions, a "traditional Arab desert democracy" as key elements.[86] So we could say that desert romance authors mobilize orientalist tropes, but not always in ways that are oversimplified or that diverge from popular nonfiction accounts of the Gulf region of the Middle East—the inspiration for Arabiastan.

At the same time, the imagined Gulf could not be a better location for fostering the overly optimistic narrative of neoliberal globalization as a process that has brought prosperity to all, creating the happy and liberated consumer-citizen. That citizenship in the UAE must be rigorously circumscribed and is, in fact, available only to a minority of its inhabitants is a suppressed fact of this narrative, as is the intimate imbrication of a security regime as a necessary consequence of its neoliberalized economy. The dependence of the UAE's fabulous wealth and exotic decadence on the exploitation of the country's large number of guest workers and the normalization of security and surveillance[87] highlights the way this neoliberal narrative gains clarity against the backdrop of a different, darker kind of fantasy—what Wendy Brown calls the "fantasy of a dangerous alien in an increasingly borderless world."[88] In their crafting of romantic fantasies in desert settings, authors necessarily engage with both aspects of the fantasy, shaping their narratives to quell larger fears about the "dangerous alien" (terrorist), while simultaneously drawing on the perception of danger to exoticize their alpha-male sheikhs. The consolidated identity they produce—the sheikh as gated community—serves as a condensed articulation of the intertwining of desire and security in the war on terror. As a native Arabiastani, the sheikh gives credibility to the move of displacing the violence of neoliberal imperialism onto the decontextualized figure of the terrorist while simultaneously providing a safe point of identification. In short, he demonstrates just how sexy security can be.

Ground Zero Tolerance: The Production of the Good Sheikh and the Bad Arabiastani

The gated-community metaphor also serves to domesticate and further naturalize the security regime; it extends to one's own backyard the types of dangers announced by the war on terror. At the same time, it reinforces the idea that the dangers of a borderless world are due to the violence of the "dangerous alien," rather than to the violence of neoliberal imperialism. However, the fortification of borders contemporaneously combined with the idea of a borderless, globalized world belies the kinds of enclosures and violence necessary to sustain economic globalization under recent neoliberal regimes, at both the national and the supranational (e.g., IMF and World Bank) levels.[89] As key manifestations of the security apparatus, enclosures and violence operate both overtly (in the exponential rise of military and civilian prisons and detention centers) and covertly (in the eroding of civil liberties and in increased surveillance tactics), and they depend on a flexible definition of the enemy.[90] While the specter of "terrorists everywhere" certainly fuels many aspects of the war on terror, the particular construction of the enemy-terrorist within amplifies and diversifies the contemporary security-military apparatus. Extending Giorgio Agamben's "state of exception" theory, Mark Salter posits that "the image of the barbarian operates as a portable, fungible state of exception."[91] Using the term *barbarian* to simultaneously reference the clash-of-civilizations discourse and the association of terrorism with backwardness and unintelligibility, he also points to the way the enemy becomes unmoored from nation or territory, thereby allowing for the flexible targeting of that enemy in multiple locations, including within the (U.S.) state itself.[92] This notion of the ever-present threat supports the state-of-exception justification for a heightened security regime just as the myth of U.S. exceptionalism frames military and surveillance actions as the necessary evil of benevolent imperialism.

Extending this logic, the very exceptionalism of the U.S. is what sets the nation up as the potential target of irrational violence and terrorism. As a version of the "they hate our freedom" rhetoric, this argument situates the open, tolerant, multicultural ideals of the U.S. as those that both allow the enemy to infiltrate its borders and make it a key target of closed, intolerant peoples. Though this chapter analytically separates out security as a key contemporary technology of imperialism, desert romances demonstrate how security, freedom, and liberal multiculturalism operate as intersecting technologies of imperialism and depend on the paranoid logic of U.S. exceptionalism.

A brilliant example of the way desert romances uniquely showcase how the narrative of U.S. exceptionalism permeates the framing of the war on terror manifests itself in a seemingly offhanded remark by a desert romance author. Distancing herself from the idea that she represents the real Middle East in her novel, she nevertheless revealed that she "wrote the story during the debate about the mosque that was slated to be built near the World Trade Center site in Manhattan."[93] Testifying to the dialectical relationship between reality and fantasy in the novels, this example demonstrates how mainstream narratives about Arabs and Muslims in the U.S. can help shape the romantic narrative of the desert romance. As part of a sheikh-cowboy crossover series, *Seized by the Sheikh* takes place in Wyoming and is one of the few desert romances set in the U.S. and not in Arabiastan (see chapter 2 for more on sheikh-cowboy crossover). The novel is therefore in a unique position to directly reflect enemy-within anxieties, specifically by engaging with the idea that the U.S. could become a victim of its own exceptional tolerance.

A survey of popular news media coverage about the co-called Ground Zero mosque controversy demonstrates that the coverage did indeed produce the two kinds of narratives that tend to characterize the U.S. state of exception-exceptionality rhetoric.[94] The first is focused on the perpetual threat of the barbarian-terrorist enemy, especially the enemy within. For opponents of the mosque, its construction would symbolize the simultaneous triumph and infiltration of the enemy. As one quoted woman (who had lost her sister in the 9/11 attacks on the World Trade Center) put it: "I presume these people aren't going to be gathering there to plan another attack."[95] The other main narrative about the proposed mosque—originally named Cordoba House and then simply known as Park51—opted to characterize the proposed structure as a "seed of peace" that would "allow moderate Muslims to teach people that not all Muslims are terrorists."[96] In other words, through their characterization of supporters' arguments, these articles chose to stress (and applaud) the distinctly unique U.S. values of religious tolerance and diversity.

The Ground Zero mosque controversy mimics the polarized options available for Arab Americans and Muslim Americans following the attacks of 9/11. As Mahmood Mamdani explains, these two overlapping groups of Americans were to be suspected as bad unless they proved themselves to be good.[97] Given such a powerful rhetorical backdrop, it is not surprising that desert romances reinforce the binary through the continuous triumph of the "good" sheikh-hero over the "bad" terrorist characters in the novels. As Ann Voss Peterson, author of *Seized by the Sheikh*, explains: "The theme I used in my story was one of overcoming prejudice. . . . Instead of giving in to fear and hatred or letting it destroy them, as it did Romeo and Juliet, my characters find love and forgiveness, and inspire their families and communities to do the same."[98] In choosing the universal values of love and forgiveness, the sheikh-hero embodies the triumphant narrative of exceptionalism. Responding to the common disavowal of these novels' relationship to the war on terror, the portrayal of the sheikh demonstrates that desert romances do grapple with the war on terror, but with an emphasis on the redeemable sheikh-hero, who finds the strength to combat terrorism in the arms of the (usually white) heroine. Crucially, in his transformation, he reinforces the inherent goodness of joining the global economy, which is linked to universalized ideas of tolerance and acceptance, while also transferring the culpability of state violence to the specter of terrorism, which is central to the security regime. In other words, desert romances do the important cultural work of crafting the subjectivity of the good sheikh, a necessary purveyor of security as a technology of imperialism.

Good Sheikh, Bad Arabiastani

Focusing here on desert romances that utilize captivity as a central plot device, I explore the transformation of the sheikh from captor to hero to explore the creation of the good-sheikh subjectivity, noting the way that he himself contains (and therefore tames) the potential enemy-terrorist within. In her article "Bound to Love: Captivity in Harlequin Sheikh Novels," Emily Haddad posits a relationship between the Iraq war and sheikh-themed romance novels, though she casts the relationship in mostly negative terms.[99] As actual stories of the abduction (and sometimes killing) of American women in Iraq rose during U.S.

occupation, forced-captivity scenes in sheikh romance novels waned or were diluted and mitigated, she claims. Building on the notion of a dialogical relationship between the Iraq war and romance novels, I expand on Haddad's argument here to explore the productive fantasies vis-à-vis Arabiastan in desert romances. Following Haddad's premise, I concentrate on the sheikh romances that operate through the rubric of captivity (as did the progenitor *The Sheik*), in which the heroine finds herself socially and geographically isolated by the sheikh, dependent upon him for protection, and therefore (usually deliciously) subject to his whims. Rather than avoiding the trope of captivity, several of the novels seem to use the device of forced abduction or isolation precisely to suggest the potential for the bad Arabiastani to be corrected through romantic union. Because the captivity rubric functions through the trope of rescue, these narratives tend to flesh out the image of the evil Arabiastani antagonist (as opposed to the benevolent sheikh-hero) more clearly than some of the other novels and tend to demonstrate how the sheikh proves his good status.

Though the hero-villain dichotomy is a common, long-standing device used in mass-market romances, its use in sheikh-themed stories articulates with orientalist and Islamophobic narratives of the Middle East in important ways. Given the set of Manichaean dualisms that former President George W. Bush used to delineate the so-called war on terror (i.e., "you are either with us or you are with the terrorists"), it is no wonder that Arabiastan replicates such dualisms. In each of the captivity narratives I consider, the sheikh emerges as a hero specifically in terms of his stance against characters who are coded as terrorists. Sometimes this plot device functions to explain the need to hold the heroine captive (so the sheikh can protect her), and in one case (*The Sheik Who Loved Me*), the presence of the heroine herself impels the sheikh to discover the evil machinations of his uranium-enriching half-brother. In each of these cases, the central plot line plays out in a somewhat mundane reiteration of mainstream (and presidential) U.S. discourse about the war on terror, reinforcing a narrative whereby those perceived to be Muslims are coded, to use Mahmood Mamdani's phrase, according to a "good Muslim, bad Muslim" logic: "Unless proved to be 'good,' every Muslim was presumed to be 'bad.' All Muslims were now under obligation to prove their credentials by joining in a war against 'bad Muslims.'"[100] Sheikh romance novels add to this equation by enshrining the importance of the white heroine as the necessary means by which the sheikh can fully actualize his "good Muslim" status. Crucially, "Muslim" must be taken here as a nebulous political-racial-cultural category conflated with Arabiastani ethnicity and not as a religious category, a point more fully explored in chapter 3. Though there are romance genres that deal with religion as a salient category (e.g., Christian inspirational romances), the sheikh subgenre is not one of them.

While the politics of the good Muslim, bad Muslim identities are fleshed out through analytically distinct categories (or characters in the case of the novels), the dichotomy functions most effectively on individuals, both by assuming a default status of bad Muslim and by requiring constant vigilance in proving and maintaining one's good-Muslim status. These characters are, of course, two sides of the same coin. The figure of the sheikh-hero demonstrates how these categories congeal through contemporary discourses of terrorism, in terms of what Jasbir Puar and Amit Rai have called the "monster-terrorist-fag" figure.[101] Focusing on the relationship between the white heroine and the sheikh-hero, I employ Michel Foucault's "Abnormals" lecture to argue that the sheikh-hero emerges as an individual to be corrected, both in contrast to the monstrous figure of the Arab-Muslim villain and despite his own inherent monstrosities. Couched in terms of an individual to be corrected, the sheikh-hero's story of transformation, rendered through the ideal of a heteronormative union with the white heroine, delivers an individualized taxonomy of the normalized sheikh's mind and, by contrast, of the (pathological) villain's mind, thereby suggesting the possibility of disciplining (and therefore modernizing) the figure of the Arab/Muslim/ sheikh/terrorist. That his modernization comes through the form of the companionate, bourgeois ideal of marriage further solidifies the sheikh romance novel as an allegory for the triumph of modern disciplinary forms of power, here exemplified through the technology of security.

The Sheikh as a Primal Specimen of Nature

A key characteristic of sheikh romance novels—and one contiguous with the "fierce desert man" of E. M. Hull's *The Sheik*—is the precarious double-move the stories must make to both portray the character as raw, exotic, and primal, and to "civilize" the character over the course of the unfolding narrative. Significantly, then, most sheikh-heroes are hybrids of some kind, some of which follow the original Hull sheikh formula by having mixed ethnic ancestry, while others seem to transgress the boundaries of the natural world. A case in point is Trish Morey's Tajik, of *The Sheikh's Convenient Virgin*, whom she describes as a "jungle cat," a "hound," a "falcon," a "caged lion," and "wolfish." One might gather from these descriptors that Tajik is too animalistic to be completely human; he prowls; he hunts; he stalks; he growls (the list could go on)—all to make her "purr." This sort of animalism clearly functions as a metaphor for the kind of "primal" or "savage" desire and sexuality that seems to make sheikh romances so appealing to some readers. [102] Nevertheless, the hybridization of human and animal in these novels points to several interrelated strands of my argument. First, it provides a salient link to the concept of monstrosity, particularly as theorized by Foucault and by Donna Haraway and as applied to mainstream discourses of terrorism by Puar and Rai.[103] Second, the hybridization locates sexuality and desire squarely within narratives of monstrosity and terrorism (a positioning that also lies at the core of Puar's main argument in *Terrorist Assemblages*). What follows is a consideration of the sheikh-hero as a figure that signifies the horrors, realities, and possibilities of monstrosity and whose appeal depends on his transformation (i.e., correction) into the "good Muslim" sheikh-hero through romantic coupling with the white heroine.

In "The Promises of Monsters" (as in much of her work), Haraway describes how nature can function as a reductive trope and can be dislodged from overburdened origin stories and recombined in meaningful relation to new ways of being and of thinking. She therefore calls for a cleaving of the concept of nature from highly sedimented tropes: "So, nature is not a physical place to which one can go, nor a treasure to fence in or bank, nor an essence to be saved or violated. Nature is not hidden and so does not need to be unveiled. . . . It is not the 'other' who offers origin, replenishment, and service. Neither mother, nurse, nor slave, nature is not matrix, resource, or tool for the reproduction of man."[104]

She makes this exhortation, of course, because the idea of nature has so often been appropriated in precisely these ways in a stunningly wide range of materials and discourses, including that animalistic specimen of manhood—the sheikh. Through his falcon-like gaze, lion-like prowl, and primal instincts, he signifies a fantastical return-to-an-origin story of virility and a fecund, primordial earth. His very access to such untouched atavism (symbolized by the desert) is what, apparently, gives him such sexual appeal. It is also what categorizes him as a monster, in Foucault's view: "The monster's field of appearance is a juridico-biological domain. The figures of the half-human, half-animal being . . . in turn represented that double violation. . . . The human monster combined the impossible and the forbidden."[105] The "double violation" to which Foucault refers is a violation of both perceived biological norms and juridical categories. It applies to the sheikh's characterization as an amalgamation of human and animal as well as his characterization as an all-powerful figure who creates his own set of laws and codes and who operates according to tribal laws and norms. Most compellingly, he fits the criteria of the monster by virtue of his ability to combine "the impossible and the forbidden"; in fact, these are the very terms through which his desirability is most often described.

While most romance novel heroes could be described as impossible—impossibly handsome, impossibly masculine, and, more to the point, an impossible combination of stereotypically masculine qualities with a shockingly nurturing and caring feminine side—the sheikh-heroes garner fans precisely because they are forbidden. Consider the following description by romance writer Kate Walker: "A true Arabian sheikh is an exciting mass of alluring conflictions, dangerously primitive yet scrumptiously sophisticated, arrogantly cruel yet he can be devastatingly caring and kind. . . . In short, [as Liz Fielding said], there is always something dark in the image of the fantasy sheikh, that hint of the forbidden. In a way that is even stronger and more vivid than any other hero type, he can be everything we would run away from in real life."[106] Leaving aside the question of how "caring" and kindness can be "devastating," this passage demonstrates that the fantasy hero of the sheikh is, in many ways, the figure of the monster *par excellence*. He embodies a hybridity that is not only impossible and forbidden, but also downright frightening; it is the type of monstrosity that one "would run away from in real life."

For all its manifestations as a monstrous figure, though, the sheikh as a narrative couples the idea of the human monster with another figure mentioned in Foucault's "The Abnormals": the individual to be corrected. Like the good Muslim, bad Muslim dichotomy, the human monster and the individual to be corrected operate in importantly linked ways, especially in the case of the sheikh. While Foucault stipulates that the figures are asynchronous (rather than necessarily existing contemporaneously, like good and bad Muslims), both the human monster and the individual to be corrected nevertheless exist in relation to social categories through which individuals are regulated, maintained, and disciplined in a late-modern landscape of power relations. Though the sheikh's appeal lies in his recourse to monstrous origins and ancestry, then, his success as a romance novel hero depends on his ability to function as an individual to be corrected—a figure who does not need to be confined or sanctioned, but who is regulated through the "positive methods of rectification" and who understands the "need to correct, to improve, to lead to repentance, to restore to 'better feelings.'"[107] As the proverbial good Muslim, the sheikh not only embodies and embraces the need to correct and improve the purportedly backward elements in his society, but also imposes these regulations on his country since he is the "supreme ruler" of his land. In novel after novel, the sheikh-hero is revealed to the heroine as just such a reform-minded figure. White's David Rashid fights against his half-brother Tariq and his "fundamentalist ways," which are "compromising global stability."[108] Weston's Kazim al-Saraq is involved in international peace talks.[109] Jordan's Xander, as someone dedicated to "promot[ing] better relations between his country and the rest of the world," fights against Nazir, an evil Zurani.[110] Morey's Sheikh Khaled Al-Ateeq emerges as a "real leader of his people" when he balances the forces of tradition and modernity, all the while quelling "insurgents from neighbouring Jamalbad [who] have been stirring up trouble along the border."[111]

A principal distinction between the monstrous figure and the individual to be corrected occurs in the realm of categorization; the human monster is labeled as such precisely because he or she defies or transgresses categories, while the individual to be corrected is fixed to, and regulated by, such categories. While the sheikh's link to the natural world through descriptions of his character as animalistic and primal has already been established, the arc of the romance story reveals how he is eventually placed into a taxonomy and normalized. As a method of imposing a hierarchical, structured ordering of natural categories, taxonomy provides a useful metaphor for analyzing the construction of the sheikh character; it elucidates the ways he is both located in a (romanticized) natural world and simultaneously disciplined into an intelligible, classifiable creature for the romance novel heroine. The energy spent on rendering the character intelligible itself points to the assumption of his monstrous origins, therefore additionally signifying the ways he occupies both concepts simultaneously.

Key taxonomic texts, like Raphael Patai's *The Arab Mind*, and those that build on Patai, like Jerrold Post's *The Mind of the Terrorist*, bear fascinating resemblance to romance novel descriptions of the sheikh-hero. As indicated by both book titles, these texts seek to classify Arabs, Muslims, or "terrorists" by describing, and producing knowledge about, the mind of such figures, thereby utilizing scientific and medical discourse to create a pathologized image of disparate cultural, religious, and political identities. Following an orientalist logic as theorized by Edward Said, these books depend on and reinforce the idea that Arab and Muslim societies are bound by static traditions.[112] Patai even identifies such elements (for him, bedouin culture is the quintessential living tradition) as a "substratum of Arab personality," giving the sense that one could, in fact, excavate the "Arab mind" and find such a substratum at the core.[113] The generalization does not seem as problematic here as the suggestion that the "Arab mind" can be mapped and catalogued, revealing the solid foundation of ancient tradition.

Nevertheless, characterizations of the sheikh-hero in romance novels notably mimic the kind of taxonomic labeling by Patai and Post. Not only do romance novels replicate the notion that cultural characteristics are hardwired physiologically, but they also seem to borrow Patai's very wording. For example, Xander, in *Possessed by the Sheikh*, laments that he is not "completely desert blood, bone and sinew"; his words recall Patai's description of bedouins as "tense, keen, quick-tempered, a bundle of nerves, sinews, and bones."[114]

More to the point, though, romantic sheikhs are irrevocably rooted in the ways of desert tribal identity (conflated with Arab ethnic identity and Muslim religious identity), which is sometimes named (as in the case of Xander, who is Tuareg), but always simultaneously ancient and timeless. This hardwired layer of the sheikh's mind seems to augment his desirable qualities. According to the "Sheikhs and Desert Love" website, the first two reasons (out of a total of five) that "make a sheikh romance so *hot*" are (1) "having an exotic (and somewhat dangerous) desert kingdom as the backdrop" and (2) "when the sheikh makes a change from wearing Western style clothing to the traditional robes of his country."[115] Like Patai's *The Arab Mind*, the website conflates national with cultural identity, and the romance novel authors follow suit. Jordan presents her character, Xander, for instance, as a "dangerous predator; something, someone who could never be tamed or constrained in the cage of modern urban civilization. This was a man of the desert, a man who had made and then lived by a moral code of his own devising."[116] Likewise, White's David Rashid is "like a wild desert warrior" who "exuded a timelessness, as if the spirit of ancient warrior tribes, the wild and exotic spice of desert leaders, still shaped his thoughts."[117] Morey's Sheikh Al-Ateeq "tasted of intensity and power, of the timeless desert sands, and he tasted so right."[118] These descriptions parallel Patai's description of "the Bedouin," whom he describes as "son and master of the desert, whose way of life has changed very little from the time he domesticated the camel in the eleventh or twelfth century B.C."[119] One is meant to get the message not only that the sheikh is exotic and "primal," but also that these characteristics are built in to his genetic code. They exist as a bedrock layer of his mind.

Recalling romance novelist Kate Walker's statement that the sheikh can be "everything we would run away from in real life," however, sheikh novels clearly must find a way of diffusing the same threatening nature that supposedly makes sheikhs appealing. One prime strategy lies precisely in the kind of classification performed in *The Arab Mind*.[120] Indeed, Post corroborates the claim that classification can help diffuse the sense of threat when he explains the impetus for writing his own tome: "We cannot deter an adversary that we do not understand. An optimal understanding of the psychology and motivations of the terrorists is crucial to developing optimal strategies to deter these violent actors."[121] In this respect, the Arab/Muslim/sheikh/terrorist figure becomes an exemplar of the individual to be corrected. The figure must be studied, understood, classified, and finally disciplined and normalized into polite, civilized, modern society. Despite Post's frequent claims that "hatred is bred in the bones" of terrorists, he takes comfort in the science of pathologizing and categorizing the (collective) mind of such figures as a means of potentially interrupting the "terrorist life cycle," a characterization that quite literally associates terrorists with pathogens.[122] If terrorists can be studied, understood, and classified, he seems to suggest, an antidote can also be developed. He might be surprised to find that the ultimate prescription for taming and inoculating the fiery, primal, and savage Arab/Muslim/sheikh/terrorist lies in the narratives of over two hundred contemporary desert romance novels.

"Standing on the Very Edge of Civilization"

Though Post adamantly argues that individual psychopathology is not adequate to explain terrorist actions (insisting instead upon a collective or social pathology to explain the phenomenon of political terrorism), he does suggest a set of family-of-origin conflicts that could lead to the formation of a "terrorist mind."[123] His recourse to the family unit is quite telling for several linked reasons: it reinforces the idea that terrorism is unintelligible within the bounds of scientifico-rational thought and therefore cannot be understood within the context of historical, political, and social realities. This argument therefore produces a timeless, ahistorical, contemporary "monster" terrorist (as per Puar's and Rai's arguments), who is not only antimodern, but whose very existence demonstrates the boundaries of modernity. This figure provides the acategorical, ahistorical, irrational other that throws the ordered logic of a progress-focused modernity into relief. Finally, it gestures to the primacy of the nuclear family unit in the framework of modern forms of thought and knowledge production. Ironically, despite being construed as backward, the monstrous figure of the Arab/Muslim/sheikh/terrorist is an essential, constitutive part of modernity. As such, the figure is deeply implicated in modern constructions of, and anxieties about, the family structure.

If contemporary mass-market romance novels are based on the sentimental and Gothic novels of the eighteenth century—novels that often address the shifting ideals of marriage, romantic love, and, therefore, the shifting realities of women's isolation in the domestic sphere—then it is not surprising that as a genre, mass-market romances tread in the image of the human monster.[124] In Tania Modleski's estimation, they operate as narrative forms that speak to the anxieties and fears that bourgeois white women faced and that were produced by the women's increased social and domestic isolation and complete dependence. Desert romances corroborate this line of argument insofar as they function as popular narratives of the particular anxieties and fears of late-modern forms of power, but they also extend it by imaginatively promoting contemporary imperialism. Through the neo-orientalist character of the sheikh-hero, they demonstrate the primacy of ameliorative and humanitarian modes of contemporary imperialist power. "Standing on the very edge of civilization," the sheikh-hero can only succeed through a heteronormative and assimilationist union with the white heroine, whose unique qualities can help him "build a bridge between two ways of life," "promote better relations between his country and the rest of the world," and "show snippets of humanity [the heroine] would never have believed him of possessing."[125] Significantly, in each case, the sheikh's ultimate transformation manifests itself either through liberal feminist notions of equality—the sheikh turns away from the "meek manner and accommodating nature" of the Arab woman and toward an independent white woman who wants a relationship in which she is an "equal"—or through neoliberalism, in which the sheikh promotes freedom by bringing his country into the "global economy."[126] This double transformation—in which he is civilized through the romantic ideal of heteronormative union and he, in turn, ushers his country into the realm of civilization through an exceptional alliance with a U.S.-Anglo state—signals the extent to which the civilizing mission here depends on the multilayered discourse of exceptionalism.

Recalling Haraway's observations about monsters, desert romances demonstrate how the construction of the good sheikh as an exceptional leader of his U.S.-Anglo allied state serves to quell contemporary fears and anxieties about the unknowable, mystifying, and pathological figure of the Arabiastani terrorist. In captivity narratives especially, the sheikh actually saves the white heroine from the evil, (purely) monstrous Arabiastani terrorist. Moreover, the hero's ultimate, inevitable union with the white heroine allegorizes the romantic tale of liberal multiculturalism through companionate marriage. Terrorism is relegated to an altogether different landscape—of timeless evil in a Manichaean world—while cultural difference can be appropriated, assimilated, and utilized in the service of circumscribed notions of freedom. As illustrated by the metaphor of the gated community, the figure of the sheikh-hero literally contains the very threat that gives him erotic appeal. In this way, the sheikh-hero exemplifies the logic of security as a contemporary technology of imperialism.

The construction of the sheikh-as-gated-community subjectivity, in turn, raises pressing questions about how the notion of freedom contributes to the logic of the security regime. In particular, desert romances replicate and literally romanticize the slippery and imprecise ways the notion of freedom is deployed in the discourse of the war on terror, where "our freedom" can be offered up as a reason why terrorists "hate us." Like the ambiguities of waging a war on the abstract concept of terror, the idea of freedom here loses its intellectual traction. Perhaps this is one reason the white heroine in *Stolen by the Sheikh*, at the precise moment that she officially breaks free of her sheikh captor, can conceive of asking: "What was it worth to be free, when you were leaving your heart behind? What was the point of freedom, when you had lost the one you loved?"[127] What is striking is not that the denouement of a mass-market romance novel would come through this type of capitulation on the part of the heroine. Remarkable instead is the parallel between her ruminations on the value of freedom and the misconceptions of freedom propagated in the war on terror and in some examples of liberal "global" feminism. The latter two approaches fundamentally disconnect the idea of freedom from that of collective emancipation. Desert romance novels, like the larger U.S. discourses in which they are embedded, refigure freedom through valorization of individual choice as an indicator of women's liberation, through integrating Arabiastan into the global economy, and through the disciplinary mechanism of heteronormative union. As widely read cultural artifacts, mass-market romances may indeed offer an analysis of "what the world needs," to recall the Manilow-styled opening song at the Romance Writers of America "Bridging the World" conference. A close reading of the imbrication of desert romances with the popular discourse on the war on terror suggests that it is not "romance and love" that the world needs, but rather a committed engagement with the notion of freedom. Chapter 2 turns to this notion.

2

Desert Is Just Another Word for Freedom

For the last time the balance of power shifted, away from
both of them. But neither cared. The freedom far outweighed
the risk. They careened toward the edge, exploding over the
precipice, out of control. Each held on to the other as they
plunged into the peaceful abyss beyond . . . where only the
two of them existed.
—Donna Young, *Captive of the Desert King*, 164

[Upon being kidnapped, the heroine] was suddenly acting
with a reckless lack of restraint and a part of her was actually
enjoying it! It was almost liberating.
—Kim Lawrence, *Desert Prince, Defiant Virgin*, 62

Modern individuals are not merely "free to choose," but
obliged to be free.
—Nikolas Rose, *The Powers of Freedom*, 81

The [romance] genre is not silly and empty-headed, as mainstream literary culture would have it. . . . The genre is not
about women's bondage, as the literary critics would have it.
The romance novel is, to the contrary, about women's freedom. The genre is popular because it conveys the pain, up-
lift, and joy that freedom brings.
—Pamela Regis, 2003, xiii

Though the romance novel industry is clearly a market-based capitalist enterprise, the work of writing romance novels is nevertheless often
cast as a kind of altruism, as evinced by the opening remarks of the
president of Romance Writers of America at the 2008 annual conference.[1] In concert with the "Bridging the World" theme, she charged the

largely white female audience with a "profound responsibility to speak to [their] sisters around the world," since, the logic goes, women everywhere crave the healing and educational power of romance novels. The implicit assumption behind her statement shares the conceit of imperialist (global) feminisms; it situates U.S.-Anglo women as the privileged and benevolent benefactors of women living in the so-called global South. Following the logic of this construction, U.S.-Anglo women are positioned as having arrived at, or evolved into, a hierarchically privileged state of equality, one that simultaneously situates them as saviors in relation to their downtrodden sisters. Consider, for example, Trish Morey's *The Sheikh's Convenient Virgin*, in which the heroine Morgan helps her ostensible rival Abir to escape her evil father. Representing the classic image of the young, oppressed Arabiastani girl whose father tries to force her into an arranged marriage (with the hero), Abir escapes a fate of oppression thanks to the white heroine's intervention. The fact that her rescue involves being sent to a college in Australia invokes the common trope of rescue in relation to Arabiastani women, who are viewed as being oppressed principally through sartorial constrictions (e.g., forced veiling) and through being kept ignorant and homebound.

In *The Sheikh's Convenient Virgin*, the trope of rescue is manifested on an individual level, but in the wider subgenre, rescue more often plays out on a national (Arabiastani) level. Because the sheikh-hero is the ruler of his kingdom, the heroine must remain in his country if they are going to be together, and it is therefore commonly implied that she will work to rescue Arabiastani women from the oppressive aspects of their own culture. In sum, the message of female empowerment here is one in which white British, North American, and Australian women either help native women escape the oppressive conditions of their own lives or help the sheikh-hero foster women's equality in his own country.

In conjunction with the romantic fantasy in these novels, then, is a fantasy of feminist liberation, which plays out on multiple levels. The primary mode comes at the level of the heroine's own freedom and is common to romance novels more generally. The heroine finds her own true self and, accordingly, her own sense of freedom, through intimate partnership with the hero. What is interesting about desert romances is the way they extend the conception of freedom crafted in the typical romance narrative by applying it also to the logic of rescue. In desert romances, the fantasy of feminist liberation goes global. As a plot device meant to explain how a U.S.-Anglo woman could conceive of living in Arabiastan, the rescue trope simultaneously exemplifies how freedom can operate as a technology of imperialism. Cast as a gift, the heroine's promise to deliver Arabiastani women to a new reality of liberation therefore obscures both the ongoing state of indebtedness such a gift inscribes and the violence it deploys in its own deliverance.[2]

In the majority of sheikh romances, the white heroine finds herself irresistibly drawn to the powerful and worldly sheikh who, with "one foot in an ancient world and another in a new one," can "build a bridge between two ways of life."[3] As argued in chapter 1, the transformation of his country can only happen through his exceptional leadership, a style that is developed in alliance with U.S.-Anglo powers. Concordantly, he also achieves a good-sheikh subjectivity through romantic coupling; he cannot succeed without the unique qualities and loving support of the white heroine. Sheikh-themed romance novels enact a fantasy of mutual prosperity and peace for the "West" and the "East" (the preferred terms in the novels) through the magical union of the sheikh-hero and the liberal-enlightened white heroine. They also domesticate the notion of freedom by grounding it in a liberal formulation of love. This is not to say that the concept of freedom is circumscribed by the domestic, but rather that it is inscribed by the logics of individualism and privatization, key aspects of liberalism that shape its imperialist mode.

Elizabeth Povinelli describes "the intimate couple [as] a key transfer point within liberalism."[4] Desert romances bear this assertion out, particularly in relation to the crafting of Arabiastani countries as satellite, or proxy, powers of the benevolent U.S.-Anglo empire. In scene after scene, the sheikh-heroes come to realize the unmatchable qualities of the Anglo heroines they encounter, and the readers understand that both he and his country depend on her to impart these qualities to his people. In *Bella and the Merciless Sheikh*, Sheikh Zariq tells Bella: "You're an aggravating, feisty, defiant woman. And I find that unbelievably erotic."[5] He later admits that "it hadn't just been her beauty that had appealed to him—it had been her spirit, her vitality, *her lack of deference*."[6] Sheikh Efraim, in *Seized by the Sheikh*, is described as "a sucker for strong women. Being from a country where women weren't allowed to be strong around men, [he found the heroine's] feistiness . . . novel and [it was] obviously the source of his fascination with Callie."[7] Sheikh Nadim, of *Breaking the Sheikh's Rules*, is cured of his antiquated belief in arranged marriage by the white heroine, Iseult, who overshadows his late wife: "Sara [who died in an accident trying to impress him by riding a horse] died because she wanted me to fall in love with her. My respect and loyalty and affection weren't enough. Yet from the moment *we* [he and the heroine] met you reached right down inside me to a place Sara never could have touched. And the guilt of realizing that has nearly killed me."[8] Perhaps the clearest example comes from Sheikh Azzam in *Sheikh, Children's Doctor . . . Husband*, who proclaims to Alex, the white heroine: "'My country needs women with iron in their souls as leaders of the community, and I'—he kissed her more firmly—'I need a woman with iron in her soul as my consort.'"[9] As intimated in these examples, the sheikh-hero's intimate coupling with the (usually white) heroine secures two key manifestations of freedom as a technology of imperialism.

At the individual, or micro, level of the sheikh, freedom manifests itself as a technology of imperialism in terms of his own personal transformation. As the previous quotes demonstrate, it is only through romantic union with the U.S.-Anglo heroine that the sheikh-hero can complete his transformation into an individualistic, equality-minded progressive and cooperative ruler. In so doing, he demonstrates his inculcation into liberal notions of freedom that serve as the basis of contemporary benevolent imperialism. The particular gift of freedom that the heroine brings manifests itself at the societal, or macro, level of Arabiastani women, who are poised to benefit from the qualities of strength and independence that the heroine promises to bring, as first lady to the sheikh's kingdom. Though the fantasy of feminist liberation is common to the romance genre as a whole, desert romances demonstrate this fantasy to exist simultaneously at a macropolitical level; it operates as a technology of imperialism through the trope of bringing, or gifting, freedom.

The Fantasy of Feminist Liberation

One of the key debates in both scholarly and industry online conversations about romance novels is about the extent to which the books can be considered feminist cultural productions focused positively on female sexual pleasure as opposed to oppressive "trash" books that inure the mostly female readerships to the evils of patriarchy. However exaggerated I have made this dichotomy sound, the debate does seem to play out in terms of these sorts of binaries with stunning regularity. Consider, for example, a 2007 post on the blog *Smart Bitches, Trashy Books*, which takes up this very topic.[10] The occasion is the centennial anniversary of Mills and Boon, the founding press for contemporary mass-market romance novels. The event sparked a spate of newspaper articles covering the anniversary as well as the romance novel industry more generally. The particular subject of this blogger's ire is a piece by Julie Bindel, a famous feminist journalist for *The Guardian*, who made the outdated and well-worn claim that romance novels are "misogynistic hate speech."[11] It is safe to say that most contemporary conversations about romance novels—both among popular bloggers and among academics (not that the two are mutually exclusive—they are far from it) love to hate this classic "feminist" critique, which was a much more common mode of analysis in the late 1970s and into the 1980s.[12] The reigning viewpoint today holds a different perspective on feminism and its relationship to romance novels and can be summed up by SBSarah's final analysis of Bindel's article: "Please. Women harshing on the freedom of other women to read and wank off to whatever fantasy they want is what's Keepin' the Womyn Down."[13]

Scholarly sources concur. In the introduction to her edited collection about romance novels, Sally Goade asks: "Are women readers (and writers) oppressed by their commitment to a narrative with an essentially patriarchal, heterosexual relationship at its center, or are they somehow empowered by their ability to create, escape to, and transform the romance narrative into a vehicle for reimagining women's freedom within relationships?"[14] As indicated by the Pamela Regis epigraph for this chapter, the question of women's "empowerment," "independence," and "freedom" seems to be at the heart of most romance novels and serves as a primary defense of the genre against what many writers see as feminist attacks.[15] Still other scholars suggest a dialectical relationship between the feminist movement and themes of empowerment in romance novels, noting that markers of female strength and independence become more pronounced because of the successes of the women's movement.[16] While this may have truth to it, one of the most crucial and least discussed aspects of the discourse on feminism vis-à-vis romance novels is to specify what readers and writers mean when they refer to feminism.

As might be expected, some romance authors quite clearly distance themselves from popular perceptions of feminism, as in the following example from Teresa Southwick's *To Catch a Sheik*: "Feminists might object, but Penny had the feeling if any of them took one look at Rafiq, bras would go up in flames and not because anyone was protesting."[17] Readers are reassured pages later as to Rafiq's stance on the status of women when he refers to them as a "great natural resource" that has been overlooked as a "vital addition to our workforce [for] far too long."[18] As this example suggests, some romance novels tend to distance themselves from what they perceive to be radical feminist ideals while simultaneously seeking to reassure readers that the sheikh-hero values women's equality. What constitutes equality is another question altogether. As becomes apparent in Lynda Crane's "Romance Novel Readers: In Search of Feminist Change?" though readers largely agree that women's lives have improved over the past few decades (and they can see these changes reflected in the increasing independence of popular heroines), their understanding of feminism seems to boil down to "increased job opportunity and equal pay."[19] In fact, in much of the empowerment-versus-oppression debate, readers and writers alike are clearly engaged with a liberal feminist notion of feminism, which focuses on gender equality and parity (through political and legal channels) and the notion of individual rights. The individual rights are highlighted mostly through the heroine's own story, but possibly also through the stories of other female characters with whom she interacts. As a literary form that valorizes and idealizes the model of a companionate, bourgeois, heterosexual marriage to a hero who (regardless of ethnic "spice") is a member of the propertied elite, the mass-market romance novel is also deeply rooted in some of the key implicit aspects of liberalism. That is, it privileges a discourse of universal equality and freedom ("bridging the world"), despite being rooted in the politics of exclusion, from the overwhelmingly predominant white Anglo heroines in the popular novels, to their royal, rich, elite hero counterparts, to the very industry on which the "new empire" of Harlequin romances are built.[20]

Not only do desert romances incorporate the standard feminist tropes found in most defenses of the genre, but many of them also incorporate the fantasy of liberating Arabiastani women from their patriarchal cultures. For this reason, it is important to first explore the fantasy of feminist liberation: how it is put together and how it functions. An understanding of the micropolitics of freedom as manifested in the debates about romance novels as feminist cultural products can therefore help explain the macropolitics of freedom as they play out in the discourse of the war on terror. Exploring the notion of freedom through the basic lens of governmentality helps show how regimes of discipline, surveillance, and security inculcate themselves on the individual level through the language of freedom and choice. At issue is the crafting of the concept of freedom, its entrenchment (even if unconsciously) in particular political or philosophical systems, and its ultimate deployment in less-than-liberating projects even as, or perhaps because, it claims liberation as its ultimate goal.[21]

SBSarah's resounding statement that, rather than being oppressed by romance novels, women are actually oppressed by "women harshing on the freedom of other women to read and wank off to whatever fantasy they want" seems to be firmly embedded in the notion of negative freedom. In turn, the notion is rooted in the framework of classical liberalism, that is, in "the image of the individualized, autonomous and self-possessed political subject of right, will, and agency."[22] At least two of the comments in response to SBSarah's blog post confirm this view. The first is from Nora Roberts—one of the most famous romance authors, who proclaims that she is free from patriarchal oppression since she is surrounded by men in her life (i.e., her husband, her sons, her father) and none of them would think about oppressing her. While Roberts's comment represents a standard defensive response to the romance-novels-as-misogyny argument, she flips the terms of the argument to reframe popular perceptions of the genre. In her offensive formulation, romance novels simply cannot be oppressive, because they focus on the power of love, which fosters happiness and therefore empowerment.[23] At least one other comment in the thread describes love as a "liberating force," echoing the general sentiment expressed by Roberts.[24] Clearly, one cannot necessarily take Roberts's comments at face value, since her defense of the genre is vital to her livelihood—she wants to continue to sell more books.

More important than the question of intentionality, though, is an examination of the cluster of terms that circle around the concept of freedom. In these discursive circles, romance novels are not just free from patriarchal oppression. They explore women's freedom and advocate empowerment (particularly sexual), fulfillment, happiness, and the ability to choose whatever one desires.[25] Elaborating on two of these terms links the discussion of freedom so far to the contested notion of feminism at stake in the debate. First, the meaning of empowerment in this context tends to adhere to what Patti Lather calls a "reduction of the terms as it is used in the current fashion of individual self-assertion, upward mobility and the psychological experience of feeling powerful."[26] Not only is the concept of empowerment individualized, in other words, but it is oriented to the project of crafting the self, which is its own modern technology of power.[27]

Clarification of this point comes through the much more predominant discussion of choice in the thread that follows SBSarah's post about "women harshing on the freedom of other women." In the sentiments of at least seven respondents on the thread, feminism is (or should be, in the case of their responses to Bindel) about validating the choices of other women, whatever those choices may be. One participant asks: "Isn't that what the feminist movement was all about—having the choice to do what you wanted with your life?"[28] Another participant explains that, instead of focusing on legal rights, "I would feel better if more emphasis was made on the freedom of each individual person to choose whatever makes him/her happy."[29] The focus on choice here is a clear response to the judgment some of these participants feel from a brand of feminism that invalidates and devalues women who choose to be homemakers and caregivers for their own families.[30] Rhetorically, it also functions as a way of atomizing the notions of freedom and feminism and unmooring them from a larger social context. As Nikolas Rose has argued in another context, freedom and empowerment in this sense come through a consistent orientation to the self, and they can be best achieved through shaping the self, insofar as it is a "self freed from all moral obligations but the obligation to construct a life of its own choosing."[31] Though Rose focuses on the arena of psychotherapeutics, including the genre of self-help, his observations about how psychotherapeutics can function as a technology of power through self-management are certainly applicable to the practice of reading romance novels, according to these kinds of (common) conversations among fans of the genre.

One particular comment sums it up: "Romance novels are about the only place I get validation for my choices in life. I consider myself a feminist, because I don't feel inferior or subordinate to men simply because of my gender. But the feminism I subscribe to is about choice—I made the choice to be a wife and homemaker. I made the choice to stay at home with my child. I made the choice to indulge in a submissive sexuality, and I like reading books to which I can relate."[32] Another woman who has worked long-term on the publishing side of the industry explains that "romances are usually by, for and about women. The heroine is the center, it is her story. They are stories of empowerment—stories where women succeed, her values are confirmed, her beliefs are validated."[33] In this schema, in other words, empowerment means having one's choices validated. Freedom is defined as the ability to make choices that will lead to one's own happiness, and feminism is the project of not feeling inferior or oppressed because of the choices one has made. As Rose puts it: "Life is to be measured by the standards of personal fulfillment rather than community welfare or moral fidelity, given purpose through the accumulation of choices and experiences, the accretion of personal pleasures, the triumphs and tragedies of love, sex, and happiness."[34]

This kind of calculation of liberation, which can be measured through the accrual of choices that are validated simply for having been made, demonstrates how freedom can operate as a technology. It functions as a mechanism for training the subject to focus on the neoliberal projects of individual happiness and accumulation. Through a universalizing valuation of the pursuit of happiness, the notion of freedom is radically separated from larger contexts of social realities. Choices are further atomized and abstracted through the universalizing discourse of love as conquering or bridging all obstacles. The point is not that women should not choose to be "a wife and homemaker" or to "indulge in submissive sexuality," but that these choices should be understood as complex and negotiated ones, based in particular realities and histories of oppression. Otherwise, they do not demonstrate the actualization of freedom for women—a triumphant delivery from patriarchy—but rather the way freedom functions as a technology, a mechanism for obscuring the dynamics of power embedded in the choice. As Elizabeth Povinelli reminds us: "If you want to locate the hegemonic home of liberal logics and aspirations, look to love in settler colonies."[35]

If fantasies operate as a screen for reality, here the fantasy of feminist liberation screens the technology of freedom and specifically the way freedom can function as a means of governing.[36] Note that I do not employ the concept of fantasy in its colloquial sense to imply that feminism itself is deluded or mistaken in its pursuit of liberation, but rather to signal how feminism can become invested with abstract or generalized desires (for freedom and equality, for example) that are easily appropriated. In this case, a micropolitics and macropolitics come together insofar as the "power of freedom" operates as a key technology of contemporary U.S. imperialism. In other words, the technology of freedom indicates how self-governing coincides with the larger process of imperialism. I do not mean that romance novels cause their readers to desire their own (patriarchal) oppression or that desert romances must be locked into the binary of oppressive or liberating. Rather, they orient us to a larger question about power, namely, how does one come to desire hegemony? This question drives Deleuze and Guattari's Capitalism and Schizophrenia series, which turns away from the question "Are romance novels oppressive?" and toward other types of questions: How do they striate desire, or, how do they organize (and, in doing so, colonize) desire away from revolutionary possibilities and toward a reproduction of the dominant social registers of power? In this sense, the novels present much larger questions about the intersections between libidinal and social investments in the operation of imperialism.

Submitting to Freedom

In her study of the relationship between historical romances published at the turn of the nineteenth century and contemporaneous formations of U.S. empire, Amy Kaplan notes that in the official rhetoric of President McKinley (speaking specifically about the Philippines), "to be liberated meant, as it does in romance, to submit to being rescued."[37] The presupposition that a nation or a people should submit to being rescued, presumably for their own good, is a particular form of liberal imperialism that Mimi Thy Nguyen formulates as "the gift of freedom." A profound paradox is built into the equation of the gift of freedom (likewise in the idea of submitting to freedom). In this equation, the gift itself actually inscribes a seemingly unlimited relationship of debt. As Nguyen puts it: "As it turns out, the gift of freedom is not the end but another beginning, another bondage."[38]

One can certainly see the echoes of this kind of policy in the contemporary war on terror, in which the will to liberate has served a particularly insidious (and well-critiqued) justification to unleash large-scale military occupations. Consider the monikers given to the U.S.-led military invasions of Iraq and Afghanistan. Dubbed Operation Iraqi Freedom and Operation Enduring Freedom, respectively, both invasions were cast as projects of liberation; moreover, both efforts were partly justified with the claim of freeing women from their oppressive cultures in an appropriation of the fantasy of feminist liberation. Discussions of this co-optation of liberation have mainly focused on a cynical reading of it, implying the government's appropriation of an already-circulating liberal feminist narrative to be a calculated move that departs from the tenets of liberalism. In orienting us toward rescue as a key mode of the fantasy of feminist liberation, however, desert romances demonstrate the logic of submitting oneself to freedom to be rooted in liberalist forms of governing and of being. Further, they allow an exploration of the psychic-libidinal investments that intersect with social-collective investments in empire. Put more simply, the novels allow an exploration of how people come to desire submission to freedom. What could be revealed in taking these desires seriously? Precisely that desire is not merely a private, intimate matter, but is rather integrated into the construction and operation of contemporary liberalist modes of imperialism.

If, as Nguyen offers, "we could say that the gift of freedom aims to perfect the civilizing mission," then one of the main avenues for perfection is at the level of subjectification.[39] Not only does it educate the desires of the colonized, it also colonizes and appropriates the desires of its own subjects, aligning them toward the survival of the imperialist state.[40] The fantasy of feminist liberation is a good example of one such alignment since it demonstrates how the technology of freedom can function at both the micro and the macro levels. The white heroine's freedom can only be realized through submission to the sheikh-hero, a fundamental irony that is then translated and echoed at the level of the

Arabiastani state. By coupling with the Anglo heroine, the sheikh-hero also submits to her fantasy of rescuing Arabiastan from patriarchal oppression and, in doing so, demonstrates his willingness to submit to the gift of freedom.

The Desert as a Symbol for Freedom

As a central trope in desert romances, the desert itself provides a convenient means through which writers can inscribe the symbolic narrative of freedom and self-actualization. Through an intricate interplay of the mythologies of the desert, already common in U.S.-Anglo popular culture, the desert landscape provides the perfect setting for an elaboration of freedom as a technology of imperialism. Echoing the micropolitics of the fantasy of feminist liberation, the desert serves as a space for the heroine's self-actualization; in the process, the macropolitics of freedom as a technology of imperialism are simultaneously elucidated.

In response to a blog posting by author Sharon Kendrick about her latest desert romance novel, a reader explains the lure of the sheikh: "For me it has always been about the man who commands the desert. It takes power, determination and understanding to harness nature's harshest landscape."[41] One of the first associations with the desert that gets clearly communicated in desert romances is its harsh, unforgiving, and isolating qualities. Sarah, the heroine in *Captive of the Desert King*, had "read about the dangers of the desert—scorpions, vipers, raging winds of sand, but didn't think she would ever experience any firsthand."[42] Other heroines are caught in sandstorms either when fleeing their sheikh-captor or while in captivity with him.[43] In these cases, as for the heroine in Penny Jordan's *Possessed by the Sheikh*, "the desert was its own kind of prison—a guard designed by nature to prevent her from escaping him."[44]

Sandstorms prove to be useful plot tactics because they simultaneously communicate the volatility of the desert landscape—sandstorms always emerge out of nowhere and take the characters by surprise—and thereby function as a kind of natural metaphor for the volatile, fearful, and dangerous threat of terrorism, which exists in some form in many of the novels. In *Captive of the Desert King*, the heroine comes to realize that scorpions, vipers, and other dangers of the desert dissolve into metaphors in the face of the terrorist enemy. When Sarah describes the Sahara Desert as a "backyard that has been infested," Sheikh Jarek responds: "That's a good analogy. . . . The Al Asheera [the enemy tribe that is trying to kill him for modernizing the country] have scattered, then hide in the sands, like vermin. It makes it hard to flush them out into the open."[45] It is difficult to miss the echo of President George W. Bush's promise to "smoke [the Taliban or al-Qa'ida] out of their holes." Indeed, in a classic example of author research, the name that Donna Young assigns to the enemy tribe, "Al Asheera," literally means "the tribe" in Arabic.[46] A subtle layer of meaning is thus added to the quite obvious dichotomy drawn between the tribal (i.e., backward) elements of Arabiastan and the individualistic and enlightened sheikh, who transcends this aspect of his culture for the good of his country. In scenes like this, the desert is portrayed as sinister and dangerous. Its sheer breadth and challenging environment become a metaphor for its inscrutability and its role as a refuge for what Bush referred to as evildoers.

The very same qualities, of course, can be flipped to serve as redeeming qualities for the sheikh and his heroine. In fact, in novels in which the desert plays a major role, there is often a moment in which the heroine realizes that "the desert was not as alien and threatening as she imagined," signaling a transition toward a happy desert romance ending.[47] Sometimes this transition comes through the heroine's forced grappling with the isolation of the desert. In *Stolen by the Sheikh*, for example, the heroine is shocked to find herself in *"the middle of nowhere. Never had the phrase been so apt. She gulped down a fortifying lungful of air. Never had she felt so alone."*[48] These kinds of scenes typically highlight the meditative aspects of the desert—the fact that it provides space for self-reflection. Such scenes may also explain the loose orientalism that surfaces in some of the books, as in *Bella and the Merciless Sheikh*, in which Bella's father sends her to the desert for a yoga and meditation retreat. In these scenes, heroines can be found "staring out over the timeless stretch of desert."[49] Once they are awakened to the beauty and mystery of the desert, they can then see for the first time "what a desert looked like. It was like flying over the sea at sunset, something [the heroine had] been lucky enough to do, seeing the ocean turned to red-gold, the row upon row of waves like the dunes beneath them now."[50] Sometimes the heroine simply realizes that "she'd grown to love the desert."[51]

As both a space of transformation and a space through which the heroine mediates the danger and the ecstasy of Arabiastan, the desert plays a key symbolic role in relationship to the notion of freedom. Like in E. M. Hull's *The Sheik*, heroines often demonstrate their headstrong, feisty, and independent spirit by seeking to tame or explore the desert themselves. From this folly (either in the form of a sandstorm or terrorists or other evil bandits), they must be rescued by the sheikh in a scene that inevitably suggests that constraint, rescue, and domination are critical aspects of freedom and liberation. Freedom, these stories assure us, is something to which one must submit.

In this sense, the mythology of the desert shares much in common with that of the frontier, an observation only more overtly highlighted in the few crossover cowboy-sheikh novels.[52] One can see in the appeal of the sheikh the kind of rugged, individualistic masculinity that undergirds some of the founding U.S. national mythologies—the ability to tame or conquer wild terrain and the rendering of indigenous, tribal peoples into either natural elements in the landscape or evil, hostile characters to be eradicated.[53] Perhaps most importantly, paralleling the symbolism of the desert to that of the frontier underscores imperialist connections: conquering territory and the continual displacement of the limit of the frontier (or of Manifest Destiny). In fact, there is a literal connection as well (discussed in chapter 1). The route of U.S. imperialism expanded through displacing the territorial limits of the western U.S. territories onto the material resource of oil, particularly the reserves found in the Gulf region of the Middle East. Mimicking the ability of capitalism to continuously displace its own limit, the frontier is continuously reterritorialized, in this case onto the desert itself.[54] Some of the most powerful elements of the mythology of the frontier are reterritorialized as well, for example, in the figure of rugged masculinity. In *How the Arabian Nights Inspired the American Dream*, Susan Nance notes that entertainment venues at the turn of the twentieth century linked Middle Eastern horsemen performances to the mythology of the Wild West. "Wild Arabs" or "Bedouins" who were billed to perform at venues like the 1893 Chicago World's Fair (the opening of which was the site for Frederick Jackson Turner's famous speech about the end of the frontier), she claims, "crossed over in comprehensible ways as Eastern 'Rough Riders'—an old cowboy term for the men who attempted to ride the most resistant unbroken horses."[55] While Nance concludes that these performances "flattered contemporary male interest in athletic, outdoorsy manhood," she elides the imbrication of such "male interest" in contemporaneous constructions of U.S. expansionism and imperialism, which was itself deeply connected to the mythology of the frontier, the lie of the "virgin land," and the arrogance of Manifest Destiny.

Despite Nance's rather limited definition of the term Rough Riders, it would be difficult to overlook its association with Theodore "Teddy" Roosevelt, who first joined and then led the Rough Riders—the name given to the first U.S. volunteer cavalry, which was deployed during the Spanish-American war. Roosevelt, who went on to become president of the United States from 1901 to 1909, is also famously known for his cultivation of the cowboy-like qualities of rugged masculinity and taming the wilderness through hunting, both of which aligned with his expansionist settler colonialist policies.

If turn-of-the-century entertainment venues staged "Eastern masculinity as a comprehensibly exotic spectacular manhood," contemporary desert romances reterritorialize the image of the rugged, masculine cowboy in the figure of the sheikh, "the man who commands the desert."[56] The cross-association is particularly evident in the novels that portray the sheikh as a modern-day horseman, as in Abby Green's *Breaking the Sheikh's Rules*.[57] These novels reference Hull's *The Sheik* in their allusions to the fact that the sheikh will eventually tame the heroine as he tames his horses.[58] At the same time, they reinforce the rugged masculinity of the sheikh, emphasizing his ability to "harness nature's harshest landscape"—whether that proves to be the desert, the Wild West, or the rebellious heroine herself.

In sum, the desert proves to be a crucial symbol of freedom. On the micropolitical level, it serves as a space through which the dramatic trajectory of the heroine's journey of self-exploration plays out. At the macropolitical level, it blends into the mythology of the frontier to serve as a space through which the imperialist gift of freedom can unfold. Indeed, the gift of freedom itself depends on the image of the frontier as an open space, or a space of exploration, in which the young, liberated United States sowed its national oats. Here, the conquering of the West, the vanquishing of indigenous peoples as a "natural" part of this territory, and the notion of a raw masculinity as distinct from the effete, civilized, and monarchical masculinity of the British motherland amalgamate into the way the U.S. would construct the mythology of its own imperialist formation—as a nation founded on liberation from an oppressive state, a nation forged in the crucible of freedom.

Settling the Desert

In *A Thousand Plateaus*, Gilles Deleuze and Félix Guattari allude to the crossover between frontier and desert imagery: "America . . . put its Orient in the West, as if it were precisely in America that the earth came full circle; its West is the edge of the East."[59] For Deleuze and Guattari, the desert and the figure and movement of the nomad in particular are key symbols of the potentialities of smooth space—namely, the possibilities for new kinds of mapping and becoming that can subvert or refigure hegemonic (capitalist) modes of domination. Yet such smooth spaces are perhaps the most susceptible to striation. They are continuously being *re*territorialized; their fluidities, their potentialities, are precisely what make them ripe for appropriation by the dominant mode of imperialism. This is why, for Deleuze and Guattari, the figure of the (idealized) nomad is paramount—in movement, the nomad eludes reterritorialization.[60]

The nomad, or bedouin, is also dominant in desert romances, but there he is far from idealized in the Deleuze and Guattari sense. As discussed in chapter 1, the term *bedouin* is tied to a constellation of other terms—especially *tribe, nomad,* and *traditional way of life*—that essentially render the whole constellation into a signifier for the receding, quaint, nostalgic, traditional ways that the sheikh must somehow balance against the need to modernize. In the novels, then, bedouins operate as metaphors for the reterritorialization and, literally, settling of Arabiastan. In Abby Green's *Breaking the Sheikh's Rules*, for example, Sheikh Nadim explains to the heroine: "This is al Sahar, the tribal home of my ancestors. These are my people . . . literally. The al Saqrs are descended from the Bedouin warrior people who roamed this land for hundreds of years."[61] This sheikh's ancestors have ceased their traditional nomadic ways to settle in al Sahar (a rough transliteration of the Arabic word meaning "desert"); in this reference, he gains both authenticity and nobility without having to sacrifice his own civilized air. Another example, this time from Linda Conrad's *Secret Agent Sheik*, demonstrates the liminality of the bedouin figure and the way the sheikh must simultaneously reference his ancestral (authentic) connection while distancing himself from its antiquated backwardness. Sheik Tariq's mother's family "comes from a nomadic Bedouin background, same as [his] father's. But unlike the Kadir's [*sic*], her family is still living in the deserts today and surviving on simple trade the way they have for centuries. They exist right on the edge of civilization, only slightly shy of savagery."[62] Though the Middle East does not fit the traditional paradigm of settler colonialism (with the exception of Palestine), the oil frontier did function as a sort of proxy settler colonialism, since it drastically changed nomadic life by settling it (see chapter 1). Desert romances utilize this trope in illustrative ways; the sheikh settles and contains nomadic life through integrating it into his authentic identity and by allowing it a circumscribed existence. Bedouins are clearly marked, though, as "slightly shy of savagery"; in the sheikh-hero's contemporary Arabiastan, liberation can only be fostered through settlement.

The ability of the desert to shift so fluidly from symbolizing captivity and danger to symbolizing freedom makes it a particularly apt setting for playing out one of the major tropes of freedom in romance novels—the ironic twist that the heroine inevitably submits to her own liberation. Avid romance readers will protest that I have glossed over a key feature of romance novels—the fact that the sheikh (or hero, more generally) *also* submits to the heroine; without a dual submission to one another, there would be no happy ending, perhaps the single most important characteristic of a romance novel.[63] Although both hero and heroine must undergo a form of submission, the heroine's submission tends to operate primarily on the individual, micropolitical level while the sheikh-hero's submission plays out on the collective, macropolitical level. The heroine's journey to "choose" her own freedom by submitting to the sheikh demonstrates the micropolitical dimension of the technology of freedom—through self-exploration facilitated by the symbolic space of the desert (she must lose herself in order to find herself), the heroine achieves the fantasy of feminist liberation. The sheikh's own journey toward submission echoes that of the heroine, but in macropolitical dimensions. Through romantic union, the sheikh-hero demonstrates his submission to the sensitive, civilizing, and progressive values that the heroine represents, and he therefore achieves the larger collective fantasy of liberating Arabiastan.

"The Kind of Freedom She Could Only Find in His Arms"

One of the best examples of the (white) heroine's submission to freedom comes in a passage of Nalini Singh's *Desert Warrior*: "His hands were anchors rather than vices forcing her to stay in place. And then she couldn't think. She found the kind of freedom that she could only find in his arms and splintered on the wings of pleasure."[64] Importantly, of course, the sheikh's hands here are "anchors" rather than "vices"; they weigh the heroine down and keep her from floating away, instead of holding her against her will. Yet the author still uses the verb "force" to describe the action of restraining the heroine. Only forced into restraint, the passage implies, can the heroine find freedom.

This example, among others, comes most often in either overt or implicit sex scenes, a fact that shouldn't be glossed over. The classic dismissal of romance novels casts them as meaningless, trashy, soft porn, but this unimaginative dismissal misses the point—it is precisely the way novels frame desire and sex that can reveal the most important and interesting issues. For example, early feminist research on romance novels took seriously the trope of the rape fantasy to complicate the notion that a rape fantasy could solely be about submission or even masochism. These scholars noted, instead, that in a patriarchal context in which women's own experiences of sexual desire were denied (i.e., in a context in which only sluts or whores expressed sexual desire), the rape fantasy functioned in effect to free women up to explore this socially proscribed desire.[65] In the contemporary context, the social or patriarchal injunction against female sexual desire is not as salient, which helps to explain the notable decrease in the rape fantasy trope within the industry as a whole.

Ironically, the social injunction that seems to have taken its place is a particular understanding of feminism outlined earlier—a perception of feminism as a controlling, judgmental ideology that disparages women who choose to be homemakers. Here, a censuring, unforgiving feminism operates as a sort of straw woman against which readers can set their own definition of feminism, one that is all about affirming women's own choices. In both cases, the idea is that the heroine must submit to the hero (who himself takes on the burden of the social injunction) to free herself to pursue what she desires. The problem is that, in this reading, the heroine's desire is presented as if it is a pure thing—as if it could be abstracted from a social context that produces and invests in particular kinds of desires.

Feminist fantasies of liberation never operate solely at the individual level, though popular contemporary discourses about feminism simply being about the freedom to make one's own life choices certainly operate under the assumption that they do. In fact, the famous 1970s feminist slogan "The personal is political" was meant to signal how systemic injustices extend to what were seen as personal and private issues. The slogan, which thereby exploded and politicized the public-private divide, has been neoliberalized (and, to use Deleuze and Guattari's term, reterritorialized) to reinforce the notions of individual responsibility and empowerment.[66] In other words, the idea tends to operate more often through a reversal of the original formulation—the political is personal—to imply that liberation is best achieved by focusing on self-empowerment. The valorization of the freedom to choose, easily routed through a popular notion of feminism, operates here as a technology of power in the way that Nikolas Rose describes it in the epigraph to this chapter; it slides subtly from a freedom to an obligation to choose.

Though Rose analyzes the phenomenon in the specific context of psychotherapy, he refers to other kinds of materials that encourage self-exploration, like memoirs, which have been burgeoning in popularity for some years. Within this genre, popular memoirs like *Reading Lolita in Tehran* deploy their own versions of the fantasy of feminist liberation.[67] A popular example from contemporary TV and film is the hit TV series *Sex and the City*, which spun off into two feature films. Though the second film did not prove to be as financially successful as the first, it parallels and accompanies desert romances in interesting ways (most notably in the fact that the plot revolves around a trip to Abu Dhabi).[68] Indeed, as its own form of desert romance, the movie elucidates the way self-exploration operates as a critical mode of the technology of freedom. It further fleshes out the applications of this micropolitics of freedom to the imperialist aspects of the fantasy of feminist liberation.

One trope strongly shared by both desert romances and *Sex and the City 2* lies in their portrayal of the desert as a liminal space and, as such, a space for self-exploration.[69] As in E. M. Hull's classic *The Sheik*, the white female heroine of this genre goes to the desert in order to lose herself—a prerequisite for the journey back to the self that the narrative arc will enact. For the heroines in desert romances, this is often a framing and somewhat formulaic plot device. For instance, in *Bella and the Merciless Sheikh*, Bella Balfour's father sends her into the desert to participate in a yoga retreat to avoid public family scandal and the paparazzi—basically, to think about what she has done. As a rebellious, headstrong heroine, she escapes into the vast desert, only to get lost and eventually rescued by Sheikh Zafiq. Her process of finding her true self begins once she finds herself in a form of forced captivity as a stable girl at the sheikh's palatial home.

Though *Sex and the City 2* does not use the literal plot twist of getting lost in the desert (it is not the same kind of fantasy genre), the film does use the idea metaphorically, as represented by the principal character's realization about halfway through the film. In classic voiceover narration, Carrie Bradshaw reveals: "I'd never felt so far away from home, or from myself."[70] Not insignificantly, the revelation comes as she heads to dinner with an ex-lover. In the scene, she is clad in a kind of exotic Arabface—thick kohl-lined eyes and a slit black dress reminiscent of "harem pants" (i.e., Western belly-dance style).[71] The scene represents her brush with losing herself and her marriage by committing adultery with her ex-boyfriend. These kinds of scenes, replicated in desert romances, demonstrate the integral role of racism (here, through orientalism) in the fantasy of feminist liberation. In effect, they seem to demonstrate Diana Fuss's claim that "in perhaps its simplest formulation, identification is the detour through the other that defines the self."[72] In so doing, these tropes portray the defining ambivalence undergirding the process of identification that operates here as a micropower of the fantasy of feminist liberation.

Homi Bhabha's "Of Mimicry and Men" and Anne McClintock's "Paranoid Empire" demonstrate the interarticulation of the micro- and macropowers of the fantasy of feminist liberation as I have been theorizing it.[73] Bhabha describes the "ambivalence of colonial authority [as] repeatedly turn[ing] from *mimicry*—a difference that is almost nothing but not quite—to *menace*—a difference that is almost total but not quite," an observation that underscores the violent edge of ambivalence in identification.[74] Indeed, the desert itself—often taking the role of a character in these narratives—seems to symbolize the antinomies of ambivalence. An incarnation of the idea of the blank slate, the desert is represented as a space to be penetrated by the independent, headstrong heroine; it awaits her exploration and discovery and can offer a grand adventure. The moment she sets out to conquer the desert, though, it reveals its menace. It usually happens the same way: the heroine sets out on her own in the desert to escape a captor (or, in the case of Bella, to escape yoga) and becomes utterly lost among an endless landscape of sand dunes. As she trudges on, nearing a dire combination of exhaustion and thirst, a sandstorm inevitably materializes. The sheikh rescues her. What started out as a literal losing of herself transforms into a metaphorical losing of herself. In her detour through the other, she encounters both the lure of what Bhabha calls "mimicry—a difference that is almost nothing but not quite" and what he calls "menace—a difference that is almost total but not quite." She vacillates between the potential violence of consuming (i.e., subsuming) that other and of being obliterated by him on her way to finding her true self.

Within this framework, it is perhaps no surprise that resolution for the desert romance heroine comes in the form of bourgeois heterosexual marriage (a point underscored by several authors who go to some lengths to explain how the heroine ensures that her sheikh will never take another wife).[75] Marriage is, after all, the successful resolution of the process of identification suggested by classic psychoanalytic theory (in Freud, for example), in which the female subject moves through a (same-sex) identification with her mother into an (opposite-sex) desire for her father in the narrative of psychic development.

To stop there, however, would preclude an analysis of the bourgeois couple as a critical unit of biopower—the unit through which the project of optimizing life is often funneled. If romance novels are essentially origin stories about the biopolitical unit of the bourgeois couple (which also explains their genealogical link to sentimental novels), then desert romances demonstrate how such a biopolitical project can be extended to the war on terror.[76] In other words, the war on terror not only (or even primarily) operates through the destructive, violent mode, but also functions through the kinds of productive biopolitical fantasies fleshed out in desert romances, where the sheikh-hero's union with the heroine signals a transition from a (terrorist) politics of death and violence to a (good-sheikh) politics of alliance and cooperation.

Sex and the City is likewise focused on the teleological resolution of marriage, despite its common framing (by both producers and consumers of the TV series and films) as a feminist production valorizing women's choices, whether they be regarding career, family and marriage, or sexuality. *Sex and the City 2*, the film, is no exception as it largely focuses on Carrie's questions about how to keep her marriage lively and strong. Importantly, the film communicates a marriage lesson through a sublimated narrative of homonationalism. The opening, framing scene has the sexy foursome attending the gay marriage of two close friends, a scene focused more on the lavishness of the wedding reception than on the marriage itself. Because the film is centered on the story of four friends traveling together to have an adventure in the "new Middle East" (Abu Dhabi), the opening scene economically communicates the unspoken assumptions that structure much of the film's narrative: despite the economic progress of the "new Middle East," the region is still primitive when it comes to sexuality. Unsurprisingly, then, Abu Dhabi becomes the landscape on which the repressed desires and identifications of the foursome play out. It is also the landscape in which their detour through the other will unfold.

The Detour through the Other on the Way to Liberation

Though the colonialist idea of a detour through the other en route to the self is nothing new, desert romances (as well as *SATC2* as a kind of desert romance) demonstrate the way the idea propels the fantasy of feminist liberation as a contemporary technology of imperialism. In other words, desert romances demonstrate the way the racism of the detour through the other undergirds the fantasy of feminist liberation and structures freedom as a technology of imperialism more generally. Further, both the micropolitical and the macropolitical dimensions of the fantasy of feminist liberation depend on the orientalist detour through the other.

Cynthia Nixon (the actress who plays Miranda, one of the *SATC* foursome) couldn't have invoked the micropolitical version of the fantasy of feminist liberation more succinctly when she explains, in her defense of *SATC2*: "The movie addresses choices for women. And isn't that what the feminist movement is about?"[77] As described in the romance readers' comments discussed above, the anesthetization of feminism through the abstract invocation of choice depends on the "detour through [and violence to] the other" that underlies both the film and the desert romances. In both the film and the novels, the white heroines "try on" submission by going native (usually represented through clothing and fashion) to finally submit themselves to liberation. When creator-director Michael Patrick King says of *SATC2*, "It's a story about looking for love, but of course, mostly looking for love of yourself in this great society," he necessarily obscures the selves or subjects who are effaced in the heroine's route to herself.

One only has to look to fashion to see the evidence. In a series of stories about the "desert chic" turban fashion that was inspired by *SATC2*, the heroine's love of self is clearly manifested through her wearing of the spectral remains of the other. Particularly revealing is the debate in these articles about whether the "Arabian style blowing in from *SATC2*" is political.[78] One article explains that "because turbans have historically been associated with Arab dress, it is tempting to connect them with the conflict in the Middle East. 'They make a strong political statement, like wearing harem pants,' Ms. Ambrose [June Ambrose, a stylist] said. 'We take an element of other cultures and internalize it.'"[79] Ambrose's views are quickly contrasted to those of Harold Koda, a fashion scholar who insists on the apolitical nature of the fashion trend: "It's an exoticism, a sense of the other that is visually compelling." Another fashion expert, Caroline Rennolds Milbank, agrees: "Going back to the turban is a return to the allure and sexiness of a foreign culture."[80] The supposed debate about whether fashion is political turns out to be a ruse—a way of articulating the very same disavowal emphasized by desert romance writers and readers. In insisting that these popular trends are simply cultural entertainment, observers nevertheless emphasize how compelling Middle Eastern culture, in particular, is in these contemporary cultural forms. Fashion here demonstrates the action of "taking an element of another culture and internalizing it," while obscuring the way this action subsumes and obliterates the other.

Since *SATC 2* itself enacts a kind of double mimicry through the trope of fashion, it is a useful film through which to understand the function of mimicry in these contemporary cultural forms. Significantly, it is while fleeing the (Arab male) menace that the foursome has its first point of identification with the female Arab other. As one laudatory review proclaims: "To borrow a phrase from the production notes, it's when the burqa meets the Blahniks on the foursome's trip to Abu Dhabi that the fashion fantasy really begins."[81] While escaping from a hoard of Emirati men who had been enraged by the public display of condoms that Samantha spilled onto the street after a scuffle, the four Americans encounter silent, niqab-clad women who beckon them into their inner harem chambers. Once inside, the foursome encounter Emirati women who go through a series of unveilings to reveal themselves to be just like the New York foursome. First, in order to speak, the Emirati women remove their niqabs and begin to express their gratitude for the foursome's agentic sexual expression since it will keep their men angry for weeks or even months. (The clear implication is that they themselves have no voice or agency, especially in terms of communicating with Emirati men.) Most dramatically and symbolically, though, in a moment of stunning mimicry, the scene culminates in a uniform unveiling of all the Emirati women to reveal their (Western) haute couture underneath. As Carrie puts it: "Halfway around the world, underneath hundreds of years of tradition, was the spring fashion line-up."

The trite lesson of this scene, which seems to imply that everyone is the same underneath, borrows from a well-established stereotypical notion of the veil as a traditional, oppressive garment that hides the liberated (here equated with consumerist) subjects that live "underneath" it. It reifies the presumed denial of agency to Arab (Emirati) or Muslim women unless they adopt Western fashion. Reading this overdetermined trope through a psychoanalytic lens, one cannot avoid the implication that the semiotic function of the veil—its grammar—is to relegate its wearers to the imaginary realm; in other words, they can function as a point of identification for the gazing subject, but they cannot achieve subjectivity. In this logic, veiled women cannot enter the symbolic (linguistic) order; when they do speak (which they can only do once they remove their niqabs), they reveal themselves to be "just like us"—they become a point of identification—a difference that is almost nothing but not quite.

On the level of mimicry, though, one cannot interpret the harem scene without considering the scene that it enables—the moment of double mimicry. If the harem unveiling scene helps the foursome escape the angry hoard of Emirati men, the Americans still have to devise an escape from Abu Dhabi itself. The means they choose to do so are by passing as Emirati women and donning what they call a "burqa."[82] The violence of this type of identification is abundantly clear: the (veiled) Emirati women are annihilated through a consuming identification that displaces their subjectivity. The *SATC* foursome "vampiristically comes to life" through a sartorial exchange—they take a "detour through the other"—a detour that literally enables their return to self.[83]

Desert romance novels enact quite similar sartorial and agentic exchanges, with the exception that the heroine's return to self still leaves her physically in Arabiastan, where, it is implied, she will enact the fantasy of feminist liberation on a larger societal scale. The heroine's version of going native tends to come as a part of her journey toward falling in love with the sheikh and his culture; it is an integral part of her journey toward submitting herself to liberation.[84]

While Arabiastani women themselves seem to be categorically oppressed by their garments, however, the white heroines experience revelatory freedoms in these same garments. Arabiastani women are portrayed as an indistinct mass of shadowy or silly women, as in Jane Porter's *The Sultan's Bought Bride*, in which the heroine finds herself "cornered by a dozen robed ladies."[85] Similarly, Abby Green's *Breaking the Sheikh's Rules* describes "women covered from head to toe, with beautiful flashing kohled eyes, [who] pass [the heroine] in the street" as well as a servant to the heroine portrayed as "a small figure hurrying towards them, covered from head to toe in the traditional *abeyya* and *burka*, with just the most beautiful and enormous dark eyes visible."[86]

The heroine's donning of the hijab, by contrast, is tactical. It presumably allows her to blend in and move freely through the culture, though it often serves as another means of marking the heroine's uniqueness. The heroine in *Vampire Sheikh*, for example, puts on a "big native headscarf to hide her blond hair and fair complexion."[87] In stark contrast to the way the hijab transforms Arabiastani women into a mass of silent and, it is implied, powerless women, the hijab only serves to accentuate the heroine's beauty. In Trish Morey's *Stolen by the Sheikh*, to take another example, the sheikh instructs Arabiastani women to provide the heroine with an impossible amalgamation of clothing—"an *abaya* and *hijab*, a cloak and scarf to cover [her] garments and head, and a *burka* to hide [her] face, as is the custom here in the tribes."[88] Despite the burqa, which covers the wearer's eyes, he further informs her that "all anyone will see of you is your eyes." Though he provides this dress so that the heroine will blend in, we learn that "even covered from head to toe she stood out. There was simply no way Sapphire would blend in by dressing her in the local garb. There was no way she would not be noticed."[89]

Scenes such as these clearly imply that the heroine gains distinction—she develops her own sense of self—through stereotypical flattening of Arabiastani women, the same women she will seek to categorically save. Moreover, these scenes belie the narcissistic intentions of the gift of freedom; the gift turns out to be an extension of the heroine's own fantasy of feminist liberation. It therefore inscribes a debt for a gift that Arabiastani women never sought. This is not to say that Arabiastani women prefer oppression to the freedom that the heroine wants to give them. Rather, the heroine's freedom depends on an uncomplicated assumption of Arabiastani women's oppression, as well as a concomitant assumption of Arabiastani women's ignorance and helplessness in the face of their own oppression. As in wider popular culture, the focus on garments in desert romances provides an easy grammar to articulate the notion of the fantasy of feminist liberation. Arabiastani women hide or are hidden behind their clothing, which dissolves them into an indistinct mass. The white heroine, by contrast, inhabits native Arabiastani dress in a way that demonstrates her capacity to transform her situation into a reality of her own choosing. When Bella is given an abaya, for example, she transforms it into an expression of her unique self: "Somehow she'd turned a modest, shapeless robe into a high-fashion item."[90] Echoing the neoliberal meanings of freedom exhibited by *SATC2*, the heroine demonstrates her independent, feisty spirit through individual style, a marker of consumerist liberation.

The irony that white heroines find freedom in the very garments that constrict and oppress their Arabiastani counterparts further belies the fantasy of feminist liberation as a benevolent gift. As in the exemplary scene from *SATC2*, the white heroines in these stories appropriate Arabiastani dress as a means toward their own self-realization. In doing so, they unwittingly parrot the Arab feminist argument for the way the abaya and hijab can enable freedom of movement through portable seclusion, while reifying the colonialist assumption that it is oppressive for Arabiastani women.[91]

A similar thing happens with the imagery of the harem, which seems to operate as the holding grounds for the silent masses of Arabiastani women. Lacking individuality, Arabiastani women travel in groups, even inside of the harem. In Dana Marton's *Sheik Seduction*, for example, the heroine "woke to the sound of bells. And when she opened her eyes, confused and disoriented, she found herself surrounded by a gaggle of girls, who seemed to range in age from six to sixteen."[92] Nevertheless, the harem provides a predictable trope through which to develop the white heroine's sexual (exotic) awakening. In *The Governess and the Sheikh*, for example, the heroine "dons one of her new outfits for the first time. A pair of loose pantaloons, which Linah told her were called sarwal or harem pants." When she catches a glimpse of herself in the bathroom, the heroine is "confronted by an exotic creature."[93] Through sartorial exchange, the heroine can inhabit the other in a way that leads to her own freedom and awakening, though Arabiastani women do not enjoy this same freedom. Whether it is because they do not choose what they wear or because they lack the individuality of the heroine, Arabiastani women are categorically excluded from this same route to freedom; for the heroine, in contrast, Arabiastani dress is a new frontier of freedom that she discovers through individual choice.

Consider, for example, a scene in Abby Green's *Breaking the Sheikh's Rules*, in which the sartorial reversals described above for *SATC2* repeat in an interaction between the heroine, Iseult, and her appointed servant, Lina:

Lina took off her *burka* . . . revealing that under her long *abeyya* she had been wearing jeans and a t-shirt. . . . She was dressed in silk and chiffon harem pants with ornate ankle bracelets, and her hair was plaited in a shining rope of black against her back. A short sleeved top exposed her belly and hips, and she had gold rings up her arms and a gold chain around her curvaceous waist. A veil was secured at the back of her head, which she pulled across her face above her nose, obscuring her features again. . . . Before Iseult knew what was happening she was being administered to by a dozen women, all intent on getting her dressed exactly as they were . . . and Lina was fastening a gold chain around her waist.

> She felt all at once naked and exhilarated. . . . "Miss Iseult, now you're one of us!"[94]

Like the *SATC2* scene, this scene demonstrates how the white heroine completes her liberating transformation through an identification with the Arabiastani other that simultaneously invokes the logic of universality and that of absolute difference. Underneath her burqa, we are told, Lina is just like a U.S.-Anglo woman—she wears jeans and a T-shirt. When she dresses herself authentically, however, she transforms into the classic U.S.-Anglo fantasy of the exotic harem girl. Iseult is then engulfed by the indistinct mass of harem girls who seek to transform her into one of them. As in the example of the hijab, the same dress that operates for Arabiastani women as a marker of their absolute difference serves as a vehicle for the heroine's own liberation—here, her sexual liberation. Through the universalizing trope of being just like her Arabiastani counterparts, she instead appropriates the vestiges of presumed Arabiastani identity as a means of discovering her own true self. In the process, she inhabits the other in a way that obliterates her, bearing out Diana Fuss's proposition that "all identifications are monstrous assassinations."[95] Becoming "one of them" is, ironically, the move that most distinguishes the white heroine from Arabiastani women.

One is reminded of Frantz Fanon's formulation, in *Black Skin, White Masks*, of the way the colonized subject faces the injunction to "turn White or disappear"—neither option, of course, being possible.[96] Indeed, the impossibility of the Arabiastani female subject position demonstrates the complexity of the relationship between white heroines (including the *SATC2* protagonists) and Arabiastani women. It is not simply a matter of domination; if it were, the Arabiastani subject position would not only be possible, but also be easily defined. Instead, the Arabiastani female subject position is impossible because it vacillates so unstably through ambivalent identification. In his study about blackface minstrelsy in the nineteenth-century United States, Eric Lott argues that the practice exhibited cross-racial desire that "made blackface minstrelsy less a sign of absolute white power and control than of panic, anxiety, terror, and pleasure."[97] Cross-racial desire in desert romances likewise radiates the instability of the project of domination. Upon being transformed into an Arabiastani harem girl—becoming "one of us," in her servant girl's words—the white heroine feels "at once naked and ex-hilarated," demonstrating both the ambivalence and the precariousness of her identification. It is therefore the impossibility of mimicry—the almost but not quite—that can quickly turn to menace, and the response to menace can easily take on paranoid dimensions.

Recalling McClintock's description of the contemporary iteration of U.S. empire as paranoid, particularly noting the way it vacillates between megalomania and the fear of persecution, we can now apply the fantasy of feminist liberation to the macropolitical dimension. While the fear of persecution was obviously animated by the events of 9/11, thereby allowing the U.S. to justify "exceptional" mobilizations of the security state, it is equally important to understand the stated desire to liberate Arabiastani women as a basic operation of imperialist power and one that is mediated through desire. Taken to its logical extreme (and in this framework, the extremity is part of the logic), the idea of liberating Iraqi and Afghan women through invasion and occupation is a megalomania-cal one; it operates as the other, ambivalent pole of paranoia—the fear of persecution. Grounded in the fantasy of feminist liberation, its megalo-maniacal impulse is tamed through the concept of freedom. The basic grammar of freedom as a technology of power demonstrated in the in-dividualized fantasy of feminist liberation operates simultaneously at a collective level as well. It is easily adapted as a technology of imperialism through the fantasy of liberating Arabiastani women by transforming their oppressive, patriarchal society. If popular Muslim women's mem-oirs have tended to stage and valorize the individual woman's ability to escape her own brutal society, desert romances stage a rescue at the societal level; the (usually) white heroine aids (or, in the story's extreme version, teaches) the sheikh to modernize and civilize his country so that women will become equally valued and respected members of so-ciety. The fantasy of feminist liberation, in other words, exemplifies a particular mode of imperialist power—one that operates through the ambivalent registers of love and debt.[98]

Romancing the Revolution

The megalomaniacal dimensions of the gift of freedom are well demon-strated by some novels' references to full-scale revolution, as in Brenda

Jackson's *Delaney's Desert Sheikh*, in which the sheikh imagines that Delaney "would probably cause a women's rights revolution with her way of thinking."[99] Though by the end of the novel this idea is tamed to the more palatable suggestion that Delaney "give some thought to using her medical knowledge to educate the women of Tahran about childhood diseases and what they could do to prevent them," the revolutionary fantasy plays a key role in the development of the plot.[100] As evinced by the way Jackson backs away from the idea that the heroine will cause a women's rights revolution, the idea of implementing a revolution in Arabiastan seems to come too close to readers' fears about the region to operate as a common trope. Alternatively, such a revolution may strike readers as so comical in its implausibility that it ruins the fantasy. Tellingly, only two other novels in my sample allude to revolutionary struggles for women's rights, and they are both historicals, so the revolutionary activity in Arabiastan is safely relegated to the past while grounding it in actual historical events.[101]

Since actual revolution might provoke a surfeit of reality that threatens the fantasy of desert romance novels, a more common strategy is to promise the gift of freedom through the figure of the heroine. In some novels, like Marguerite Kaye's *The Governess and the Sheikh*, the sheikh assures the heroine that "[her] English heritage brings with it modern ideas" and that she will therefore "be an ideal role model for the women of Daar-el-Abbah."[102] Likewise, the white heroine of *The Sheik and I* is "the living, breathing embodiment of what [the sheikh] wished to bring to his country."[103] In other novels, the heroine's role in helping to bring about change is made more clear. In Singh's *Desert Warrior*, the heroine plays an active role in changing the sheikh's own views; the heroine's strength and courage literally transform him: "The autocratic part of him that expected instant obedience bristled at her audacity. But there was a bigger part of him that was awed by her feminine strength. This was a woman with whom he could rule."[104] Likewise, in Sharon Kendrick's *Monarch of the Sands*, the heroine Francesca "makes [the sheikh] see" that implementing changes toward women's equality "would be possible," though it would be a "challenge getting such a traditional male-led society to accept that changes were needed and that they *were* going to be made. The move to allowing women to drive and to attend universities didn't happen overnight, but it *did* happen, albeit very slowly."[105]

The suggestion of a women's rights revolution is certainly tamed through the more sober suggestion of how the heroine will help to bring gradual change by serving as a model for equality and by supporting the sheikh to realize the necessity of it. Nevertheless, the fantasy of feminist liberation operates on the suggestion that she will eventually help realize revolutionary change. Because outright revolution is subdued in desert romances, the megalomaniacal element of this revolutionary fantasy is well demonstrated in a novel from a different genre—Christopher Buckley's comedic *Florence of Arabia*. Described as a "biting satire of how America's good intentions can cause the Shiite to hit the fan," the novel centers around Florence Farfaletti, a high-level State Department official who submits a proposal to the U.S. government titled "Female Emancipation as a Means of Achieving Long-term Political Stability in the Near East: An Operational Proposal."[106] To her surprise, Uncle Sam takes her up on the proposal, which, of course, goes horribly wrong when she tries to implement it. As her U.S. Marine boyfriend tells her: "Don't you understand that since the dawn of time, startin' with the Garden of Eden, *nothing has ever gone right here*? And nothing ever will go right here."[107] The boyfriend's cynicism is underscored by the end of the novel, which reveals Uncle Sam to actually be a panel of investment bankers attempting to protect their oil interests by keeping radical Islamists out of power.

Despite the cynical denouement, the narrative upholds the feminist rescue fantasy in critical ways. While it reveals the capital interests that undergird U.S. intervention in "Arabia," it essentially reinforces the idea that the U.S. state itself is, at best, inept in its efforts to impose equal rights and democracy in the region and, at worst, punished for its "good intentions." Underlying this view is the vacillation between fear of persecution and megalomaniacal (even if benevolently so) impulses that characterize what McClintock refers to as the paranoia of the U.S. empire. The fantasy of feminist liberation is deeply ambivalent, rendering it easily assimilated into various manifestations of paranoid empire.

The fantasies of feminist liberation expressed as the collective desire to save other (colonized) women is not a new phenomenon; in the Middle East alone, it has operated in various geographical and historical contexts to justify imperial rule. Tracing the genealogy of this particular feminist fantasy can therefore elucidate how the rhetoric of recue is tamed and updated through the technology of freedom. While rescue and (enforced) liberation are equally condescending, they are slightly different adaptations of imperialist power. To rescue the Arabiastani woman is to deliver her from her oppressive culture to a new, better reality, one overtly established by the colonial power. In the fantasy of feminist liberation, the direct nature of such a colonial move is obscured by a presumption of empowering Arabiastani women to liberate themselves. In other words, the imperialist move is more subtle; it is better at hiding the debt it seeks to install through the gift of freedom. In short, rather than operating directly through the technology of rescue, the fantasy of feminist liberation operates more indirectly through the technology of freedom, one already well cultivated in neoliberal postfeminist notions of liberation.

An illustration of the genealogy of the fantasy of feminist liberation comes from Mildred Montgomery Logan ("Madam Sam"), the wife of Sam T. Logan, an agricultural consultant to Saudi Arabia in the 1950s.[108] The example is relevant here for a few reasons. As discussed in chapter 1, Saudi Arabia and the Gulf region more broadly constitute the prototypical setting for desert romances. The Gulf region and its oil resources in particular played a significant role in the U.S. rise to global imperial power, particularly important in the decades following World War II, and the United States and Saudi Arabia deploy similar state narratives of exceptionalism. As the wife of a manager whose aim it was to make "Al Kharj again a Garden of Eden for Saudi Arabia," Madam Sam dubbed herself the "Garden of Eden's First Lady." She wrote two articles for the ranching publication *The Cattleman*. What I find fascinating about the two articles—published within three months of one another—is the dramatic shift in tone she demonstrates toward "the Arabs" and particularly toward Arab (Saudi) women. The shift is notable for its increasing hostility in a relatively short time. Whereas her first piece ("I Like Being the Garden of Eden's First Lady") strikes a tone of official, if strained, admiration for the culture in which she finds herself, the second piece ("The Arabs Call Me Madam Sam") articulates a thinly veiled violent, and seemingly repulsed, compassion. A comparison of one passage from each article illustrates the point. From the first:

> [The Arab women's] clothing is both colorful and practical. When the
> women venture outside their homes they put on their head masks and

black cloak. Most all the women carry their baskets and bundles on their heads which promotes good posture and, no doubt, a very strong neck. . . . By visiting with these women I find that women everywhere have many of the same interests, problems, and thoughts, and it is the only really practical way I know of for people of different countries to learn to respect and understand each other.[109]

The conciliatory, if condescending, tone finds a hard edge in the next installment:

I feel compassion when I see the dirt, filth, and ignorance that exists among the bedouin people. . . . The women peer around the corners like Hallowe'en characters. Just two peepholes for their eyes in the stiff black masks—or veils, if you feel like being romantic. The sun beats down on their black robes as the women go scurrying along with their heavy bundles on top of their heads. . . . These things worry me, but the Arabian women don't have the same conception of cleanliness that I have been taught.[110]

The hostility of Madam Sam's "compassion" and "worry" for Arab women is quite alarming in her second installment, particularly given the drastic shift in tone. She marks for us quite clearly a "compassionate" or "benevolent" imperialist ambivalence, one that seems to be a clear precursor to the contemporary formation of paranoid imperialism. The idea is not that Logan actually shifted from strained (fake) admiration to hostile compassion in three months' time, but rather that she probably vacillated back and forth between the two positions (and, no doubt, among a range of others).

This type of ambivalence could easily give way to vacillation between the fear of persecution and a megalomaniacal impulse to rescue or liberate; in this sense, then, the fantasy of feminist liberation, operating through the imperialist technology of freedom, reveals the paranoid structure of contemporary imperialism. Clearly connected to the ambivalent registers of colonial power, contemporary imperialist technologies also update them to account for the contemporary discomfort with direct rule. Like the disavowal of romance readers and writers about the relationship of desert romances to the war on terror, the fantasy of feminist liberation as a technology of imperialism finds a way to "intellectually accept" the fact of the imperialist move at the same time that its "repression is maintained."[111]

Annihilating Freedom

Freedom as a technology of U.S. imperialism further demonstrates the way the concept of freedom is woven into the founding narrative of U.S. exceptionalism and is therefore also shaped by the paradoxes inherent to exceptionalism. The myth of exceptionalism upholds the ability of the U.S. to rule through the paradox of uniquely universalist ideals. In other words, at the same time that the U.S. espouses universalizing ideals, it insists on its own unique ability to uphold these ideals. The contradiction at the heart of this exceptionalist manifesto also appears in Madam Sam's characterization of Saudi Arabian women. She first makes the universalist move, noting that "by visiting these women I find that women everywhere have many of the same interests, problems, and thoughts." This universalizing sentiment, paralleling the romance industry's "bridging the world" discourse, quickly flips to a sentiment of repulsion based on the absolute difference of Saudi women. She notes disparagingly that they "don't have the same conception of cleanliness that [she has] been taught." The classic ambivalent equation of love and hate, attraction and repulsion, here resonates through the narrative of U.S. exceptionalism to manifest in a paranoid imperialism, one that vacillates between the poles of grandiose savior and vulnerable, targeted power.

Here, the pole of love, attraction, and grandiosity—most clearly manifested on the register of desire—is more easily able to obscure the megalomaniacal impulses of the fantasy of feminist liberation. Couched through the trope of universal sisterhood, it glosses over the violent, obliterating impulse that drives the fantasy of feminist liberation as imperialist technique. It works to obscure the implication that the logical conclusion to the megalomaniacal impulse to liberate Arabiastani women is their subjective annihilation.

Indeed, desert romances demonstrate the extent to which the fantasy of feminist liberation operates through the logic of annihilation, as exemplified through the image of the Arabiastani woman, whose main function seems to be to serve as the white heroine's foil. Sometimes, as in Jordan's *Possessed by the Sheikh*, "a group of black-robed and veiled women walking down the alleyway" suffices, while in others, the distinction between "Eastern" and "Western" women is drawn out more explicitly.[112] For example, in Porter's *The Sultan's Bought Bride*, the white heroine finds herself rivaled by the sultan's cousin, Fatima, who had been preparing herself to marry the sultan since her birth. Upon discovering her unarticulated wishes, King Malik Roman Nuri, in true form of the transformed sensitive sheikh, is undone by the hurt he has caused his cousin.[113] However, he makes it clear that he has chosen the heroine, Nicolette, because of the "Western" qualities of independence and self-confidence that she possesses: "He'd assumed that his bride would be loving, loyal, dutiful, and he'd imagined a quiet woman from his own country. But after the attempt on his life, his priorities changed. He needed more than a quiet, obedient bride. He needed a woman who could face the challenges of life with courage, intelligence, and humor."[114]

Intelligence, courage, and humor represent the ideal qualities of the general mass-market romance heroine, so in this respect, desert romances fit the formulaic scheme of others in the wider genre.[115] In the sheikh subgenre, however, the specter of the silent and oppressed Arabiastani woman haunts the novel as a compelling absent presence.[116] She serves as a convenient, nonthreatening foil through which the essential qualities of the white heroine can be emphasized. The defining absence of the Arabiastani woman is even more pronounced in *The Sheik Who Loved Me*, in which the hero's deceased wife, Aisha, fills the role of submissive Arabiastani woman.

> She had been soft and dark, sweet and gentle, raised with a strong religious influence. . . . She'd been a perfect asset. A gentle lover. A wonderful mother. He never thought he could want anything more. Until Sahar [the name the sheikh gives to American spy Jayde Ashton]. This was a shock to his system. She challenged him in a way Aisha never had. She matched him. Her femininity was as strong as it was sensual. Her grace was that of a lioness. Fluid. Powerful. Proud.[117]

For the sheikh to realize the benefits the white heroine can bring—if he is to be "challenged" to liberate the women in his country—his own

Arabiastani wife must be dead. In these novels, coupling with the white heroine requires a clear distancing from Arabiastani women, who are perceived to be passive, obedient, and well meaning, but, well, uninteresting. Even in the most functional of unions, even when the hero grows to love his Arabiastani wife, the union ultimately fails to ignite the sheikh's passions as can the white heroine. One final example, from Jordan's *Possessed by the Sheikh*, will perhaps illustrate the intricacies of the opposition between white heroine and Arabiastani female foil:

> [Xander's] half brother's wife had introduced any number of suitable young women to him as potential brides but none of them had interested him. They had been too sweet, too docile, too lacking in spirit. Soft, tame doves, who would flutter to any man's hand, where something in him craved a little of the proud independence, the desert wildness of the she falcon, who would only allow herself to be tamed by one man—and even then only on her own terms.[118]

Tellingly, the white heroine is more authentically Arabiastani than the Arabiastani woman herself. Only the white heroine can embody the "desert wildness of the she falcon," and only she understands the proper way to submit to freedom, as she would "only allow herself to be tamed by one man." In order to be free, we learn, Arabiastani women must "turn White or disappear," to recall Fanon's formulation. As a key technology of contemporary imperialism, the fantasy of feminist liberation obliterates Arabiastani women in the name of saving them.

As a contemporary technology of imperialism, freedom operates in particularly insidious ways. It dominates precisely by radically obscuring the violence installed in its wake. Just as the good sheikh's orientation toward national security elides the violence that neoliberal alliance with U.S.-Anglo states will bring, the white heroine's attempts to liberate Arabiastani women are designed to ultimately erase them. Taken together, the two technologies discussed so far—security and freedom—demonstrate the central role of desire in animating contemporary modes of imperialism. It is not simply a matter of seeking to dominate others. On the contrary, the imperialist technologies of security and freedom demonstrate how we may come to desire our own repression in a way that recursively serves to dominate others as well. Though the oppression of the colonizer in addition to that of the colonized has long been part of the critical analysis of colonialism, desert romances demonstrate how desire operates as a particularly effective engine of imperialism precisely because of how it subjectifies those on all sides of the imperial power.[119]

Mirroring the irony that the white heroine's freedom only comes through the act of submission, freedom for the sheikh and his country can only be achieved through strategic union and alliance with U.S.-Anglo powers and ideals. The sheikh achieves a negative freedom— freedom from terrorist threat and economic stagnation—only by settling the desert frontier, subordinating his country's energy resources to the supervision of U.S.-Anglo powers, and submitting to a liberal-humanist notion of what gender equality and liberation look like. As in the epigraph to this chapter, the sheikh-hero and his white heroine choose a freedom in which the power shifts elusively away from both of them. They have learned to desire such a denuded freedom—despite its very real risks and violence—because it promises to deliver them to the "peaceful abyss" of subjectification, a phenomenon that will be taken up more fully in chapter 4.

3

Desiring the Big Bad Blade

The Racialization of the Sheikh

Cultural fantasy does not evade but confronts history.
—Geraldine Heng, *Empire of Magic*, 14

Given popular perceptions of the Middle East as a threatening and oppressive place for women, it is perhaps not surprising that the heroine in a popular desert romance, *Burning Love*, characterizes her sheikh thusly: "Sharif was an Arab. To him every woman was a slave, including her. He was a lawless barbarian."[1] Even if expected, though, such uncomfortable facts about her love interest lead the heroine to struggle against her own attraction to him and to subsequently swear: "I'll be damned if [he'll] hoist *me* on [his] big bad blade again!"[2] These revelations, of course, set up the erotic tension that structures the narrative arc of the story; the author will spend the rest of the novel working to convince the heroine and, through her, the reader that her understanding of Sharif had been based on a misunderstanding. Though the notion of Arabs in general as "lawless barbarians" who enslave women will not be dispelled, Sharif, in particular, will be revealed as a powerful and sexy male specimen who can only be tamed by the heroine. Reminiscent of the individual-to-be-corrected from chapter 1, the construction of a good sheikh also orients us to another key technology of contemporary imperialism: liberal multiculturalism. Incorporating some of the language and ideas of antiracist civil rights movements, if not their structural and radical critiques, liberal multiculturalism tends to focus on the framework of individual rights as a means of addressing racial injustice. Leaning toward assimilationist frameworks, it conceives of redress in terms of encouraging diversity and tolerance. Given this background, the existence of representative marginalized or disenfranchised groups in positions of social power are often, not surprisingly, marshaled as de facto evidence that racial justice has been achieved.

As an integral aspect of the narrative of exceptionalism in the United States, liberal multiculturalism also operates as a key technology of contemporary imperialism. Working in tandem with the logic of the gift of freedom, the exceptional claim of racial equity—usually described, simply, in temporal terms as post-racial—situates the U.S. as the teleological example for those subjects it benevolently dominates. Again, imperialism works through the justificatory logic of humanitarianism. As Jodi Melamed puts it: "A language of multiculturalism consistently portrays acts of force required for neoliberal restructuring to be humanitarian: a benevolent multicultural invader (the United States, multinational troops, a multinational corporation) intervenes to save life, 'give' basic goods or jobs, and promote political freedoms."[3]

Desert romances are adept at advancing post-racial logics of neoliberal multiculturalism precisely because they do so through the individualistic and progress-oriented narrative of the love story. If multiculturalism's key accomplice is the myth of American meritocracy (or, commonly, the American Dream and the idea that all have equal opportunity if they work hard enough), romances tap into the myth of universalism (i.e., differences don't matter) through the "love conquers all" trope. In the case of the sheikh, authors must work to situate him as both liberal and neoliberal subject to weave him into the multicultural framework. In other words, he must value both individual rights and free-market ideals. The former can be manifested in several ways, from the sheikhs who assure their heroines that they value women's rights to the sheikhs who speak about wanting to protect the pluralism of their country; importantly, the sheikh seeks to foster these ideals through liberal forms of the rule of law.

Although many desert romances (including Hull's *The Sheik*) restore the sheikh as a viable hero by civilizing him into the narrative domain of universality, his portrayal within a neoliberal framework is a relatively new technique for the contemporary novels. In these novels, the sheikh wants to bring his kingdom into the new "global economy" precisely as a means of making his domain more progressive and liberated.[4] The fact that he unites (usually) with a U.S.-Anglo woman contributes to the typical multicultural logic—not only does their love conquer any obstacle that cultural differences might present, but their cross-cultural union is immensely beneficial to his country. Contemporary desert romances therefore advance what could be called neoliberal multiculturalism; their happily-ever-after endings depend on appropriating the idea of cultural and racial difference for an ultimately profitable end.[5]

Sheikhs are not born as good multicultural subjects, though. Their eligibility for color-blind status must be crafted, particularly during a cultural context in which Arabiastani men are endowed with a racial excess that threatens the sanitary borders of multiculturalism. This chapter charts the way that sheikh-heroes are created as both pre- and postracial subjects amid such a charged racialized landscape, paying special attention to the way that the romance writers manage to both mine and moderate his exoticism. If authors must work hard to make sure their sheikh-hero is not overtly raced, they must work equally hard to preserve an erotic remainder from his exotic difference.

In *Burning Love*, the erotic tension that both draws the heroine to Sharif's masculine magnetism and repels her from his barbarism must persist, even while any cognitive dissonance about why she would couple with a "lawless barbarian" who hates women is resolved. In other words, she must willingly become his love slave, while making it clear that she is not enslaved. Similar to the logic of liberal multiculturalism, the resolution to this seeming paradox comes in the heroine's proclaiming to value difference while demanding assimilation. Using the same strategy as Hull's *The Sheik*, Nan Ryan resolves the question of Sharif's barbarism by giving him European (i.e., civilized) ancestry. While his Arabiastani roots are safely resolved by the novel's end, then, his cultural identity as an Arabiastani sheikh nevertheless serves as a constant reserve for his erotic potential.

Enter the "big, bad blade." As a somewhat clumsy euphemism for his penis, the reference to Sharif's big, bad blade actually illustrates a complex interplay of race and sexuality in the construction of the sheikh as an erotic alpha-male hero. The blade itself evokes a quite literal, if sheathed, reference to a sword or scimitar, props that romance writers often use to simultaneously mark the sheikh as ethnically or racially different as well as aggressive and powerful.[6] Further, the conflation of dark and dangerous, signifying a conflation of race and violence, in the sheikh's eroticized sexuality functions according to long-standing U.S.

racial logics that simultaneously uphold and disavow the links between race and sexuality.[7]

To some extent, these links can be seen in the romance genre as a whole. This is not to say that there is a plethora of nonwhite heroes in mass-market romances; in fact, a common complaint among romance readers is the lack of minorities in romance and, in particular, the lack of multiracial romances.[8] However, because the most common type of hero is an alpha male—that is, a strong, hard, dominant, aggressive, and confident man with a tender spot that the heroine uncovers—authors sometimes use exotic tropes to give the hero his hard edges.[9] In constructing the figure of the Latin lover, for instance, authors can mobilize mainstream assumptions about machismo to signify alpha maleness. In Native American heroes, romance authors can mobilize the fierce-warrior stereotype to make him alpha, and they draw on typical "noble savage" associations to craft his sensitive side for the heroine.[10]

Desert romances fall roughly into this group of exoticized romance heroes, a group that notably excludes the black hero.[11] Far from being part of the racial landscape of mainstream romance novels, black heroes can be found almost exclusively in African American category romance, published by presses like Kimani, an imprint of Harlequin, or Arabesque, also an imprint of Harlequin. The persistence of what seems to be a separate-but-equal clause in mass-market romances speaks powerfully to both the unspoken presence of racial ideologies in the romance genre and the lingering potency of stereotypes about violent black masculinity. The balance between fantasy and reality that romance authors must strike manifests itself tellingly when it comes to race; nonwhite characters are either segregated or contained through various devices, while race appears in phantasmagoric ways. More often than not, authors use the "chromatic associations" of darkness and blackness in describing racially white heroes, thereby incorporating metaphors that are deeply embedded in racial logics of the global North.[12] In romance novels, then, the logic of racialization is often subsumed to that of eroticization since race cannot usually be overtly coded, which is, ironically, what makes the novels such rich objects of study. They speak directly about the construction of race, gender, sexuality, religion, nation, and civilization even as they claim to be universal and color-blind fantasy stories.

In focusing on representations of the sheikh-hero, I chart the discursive construction of race in relation to Arabs and Muslims, or, more generally, Middle Easterners. The figure of the sheikh is, in some ways, perfect for such an inquiry since his characterization mimics the conflation of ethnic (Arab), religious (Muslim), and geographical (Middle Eastern) markers that construct Arabs/Muslims/Middle Easterners as a group in the United States. Since desert romances are overwhelmingly set in fictionalized Arabiastan, the authors tend to confuse and combine references to the Gulf region, North Africa, bedouins, Berbers, Arabic (the language), Iran, and Turkey. Though such conflations have somewhat characterized mainstream U.S. understandings of the Middle East since at least the nineteenth century, the configuration of the Arab/Muslim/Middle Eastern in the particular contexts of the war on terrorism (under Presidents Reagan, Bush Sr., and Clinton) and the war on terror (under Presidents Bush Jr. and Obama) has critically shifted. The configuration highlights religion (Islam) while simultaneously invoking a racial paradigm of cultural and civilizational difference. Put simply, the logic of racialization applies in newly visible ways to Arabs, Muslims, and anyone else perceived as such in the United States.

Following this shift, the field of Arab American studies has taken the movement from discourses of invisibility to hypervisibility as a critical point of inquiry. From Therese Saliba's "Resisting Invisibility" and Nadine Naber's "Ambiguous Insiders: An Investigation of Arab American Invisibility" to Helen Samhan's "Not Quite White," Lisa Suhair Majaj's "Arab Americans and the Meanings of Race," Louise Cainkar's *Homeland Insecurity*, and the collection of essays *Race and Arab Americans Before and After 9/11: From Invisible Citizens to Visible Subjects*, edited by Amaney Jamal and Nadine Naber, scholars have been concerned with a palpable transformation in how Arab and Muslim Americans fit into the landscape of U.S. racial formations. These scholars have noted, in particular, the increasing racialization of Arab and Muslim Americans since at least the 1965 Immigration Act, after which a greater number of Arabs and Muslims were able to immigrate to the United States. While these material considerations are crucial to analyses of Arab and Muslim Americans and race, an equally compelling and relatively unexplored area of inquiry is the role of representation in the racial formations of Arab and Muslim Americans. Scholars such as Evelyn Alsultany and Edward Said have analyzed the shifting racialization of Arabs and Muslims in popular television drama and news media representations.[13] I build on their scholarship by demonstrating the racialization of representational Arabs and Muslims through characteristics that had previously been understood as ethnic, religious, or regional. In doing so, I take aim at the notion of race as a discrete category, sometimes employed even in intersectional analyses, and instead posit race as a partial, diffuse, and porous category, shot through with the residual constructions of ethnicity, sexuality, religion, culture, and civilization (to name a few).

While some scholars have offered alternatives to the intersectionality paradigm, such as "assemblage" and "categorical miscegenation," I offer the metaphor of radiation as a way of thinking about race vis-à-vis Arabs and Muslims in the United States.[14] As several desert romance plots reveal, the Middle East is popularly associated with the radiation involved in nuclear enrichment—the "bad guys" in both contemporary mainstream news media and in many desert romances seek to illegally find ways to enrich uranium and make nuclear weapons.[15] This way of constructing a clear enemy aids in the racialization of that enemy; features that may or may not logically make a group cohere (e.g., geographical location in the case of Iran and Iraq) nevertheless serve to construct that group within the same racial formation for a U.S. audience. On a metaphorical level, radiation suggests how racial logic can silently and invisibly permeate ethnic, religious, and cultural categories in potentially deadly ways (taken to its extreme in the cases of murdered Arabs, Muslims, and Sikhs in the aftermath of 9/11). While radiation can operate silently and invisibly, it nevertheless has material effects. The failure of various nuclear reactors (most recently in Japan), not to mention radioactive remnants of warfare such as depleted uranium, has demonstrated that radiation permeates much larger areas than often admitted or acknowledged. Moreover, though its presence may be very real, the effects of radiation are often not evident until long after the first exposure. Precisely because the effects of exposure can be so hard to chart, I look in what seems to be the unlikeliest of places: fantasy stories that have an invested interest in downplaying the ways they are irradiated by the grammar of race. To use the metaphor differently, then, I give an x-ray reading of desert romances, outlining the skeleton of racial logic on which the flesh of the story hangs.

Figure 3.1. Charlotte Lamb, *Desert Barbarian*.
New York: Harlequin, 1978.

Despite the old adage, the book covers of popular desert romances reveal some interesting things about how the sheikh is coded for popular consumption. Among contemporary mass-market romances, beginning in the late 1960s and continuing to the present, the book covers demonstrate a remarkable inversion of the way that Arab and Muslim men have been racialized in the United States. Whereas early desert romances utilize the exotic marker of the *kufiya* or *ghutrah* and *igal*—colloquially known as a headdress—to adorn the sheikh on the cover, recent romances, particularly since the events of September 11, 2001, are careful to represent the cover sheikh as abstractly Mediterranean with no clear markers of his connection to Arabiastan.[16] The transition to the

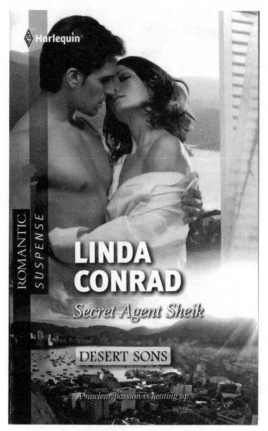

Figure 3.2. Linda Conrad, *Secret Agent Sheik.*
New York: Harlequin, 2011.

unmarked Mediterranean sheikh-hero on the cover highlights a distinctive feature of the romance novel genre; the narratives must negotiate a delicate balance between fantasy and (perceived) reality. By displaying the sheikh-hero in a *ghutrah*, the earlier desert romance novel covers emphasize cultural markers that clearly identify the sheikh as exotic other; at the same time, they reference the filmic representation of Lawrence of Arabia, an object of fantasy for fans of the desert romance.[17]

In the context of the 1970s and 1980s, the Lawrence of Arabia fantasy seems to have been a prominent enough association with the Middle East that there was no danger of readers connecting the sheikh-hero with the unpleasant political realities of U.S. engagement in the region.

However, at least since 2001, when swarthy men in headdresses call up a much more disturbing association with the Middle East for mainstream readers, romance novel covers avoid such overt references to the sheikh-hero's otherness, in what seems to be an effort to protect readers from too much reality. In this complex dialectic between fantasy and reality lies an interesting commentary about the racialization of the sheikh, which, in turn, implies a shift in the racialization of Arabs and Muslims in the United States.

A close analysis of both positive and negative engagements with desert romances on online forums coupled with a textual analysis of some of the novels demonstrates that an inversion in overt ethnic and religious markers for fictional sheikhs ironically signals a shift toward the more overt racialization of actual Arabs and Muslims in the United States. Since (overt) discussions of race are generally irreconcilable with fantasy in romancelandia, the disappearance of the sheikh's headdress on the covers of desert romances suggests its transformation from a widely perceived ethnic marker to a widely perceived racial marker.[18] In short, its representation would preclude the sheikh-hero from embodying the necessary pre- or post-racial identity demanded by liberal multiculturalism.

Interestingly, one of the only book covers to display a sheikh in a *ghutrah* and *igal* after 2001 is *Delaney's Desert Sheikh*, the only desert romance to feature an African American heroine.[19] Like the vast majority of white heroines in desert romances, Delaney is drawn to Sheikh Jamal's "native Arab garb," but she is also attracted to the "rich-caramel coloring of his skin, giving true meaning to the description of tall, dark, and handsome."[20] The attention to a phenotypical description of skin color, replicated in a scene in which Jamal imagines the "dark, copper-colored skin, head of jet-black curls, and dark chocolate colored eyes" of his future son, is virtually nonexistent in most desert romances, particularly in novels from the last decade.[21] This difference highlights the complex relationship between popular notions of race and the fantasy world of the novel. In the racially stratified world of romance novels, the representation of Jamal's headdress on the cover of *Delaney's Desert Sheikh* parallels the interior description of him as a man of color to eroticize him for the intended audience. On the contrary, though the sheikh character has a long history of commodification in the U.S., what

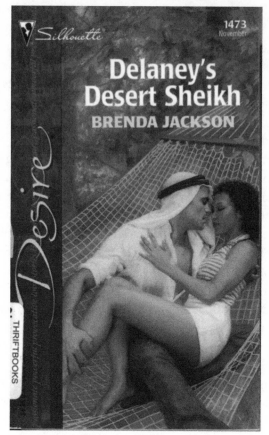

Figure 3.3. Brenda Jackson, *Delaney's Desert Sheikh*.
New York: Silhouette, 2002.

makes him consumable for a mainstream white audience in the post-
9/11 context is a submersion of overt racial markers, precisely because
actual Arabs and Muslims in the U.S. landscape are irradiated with racial
logic in newly intense and legible ways. What were previously employed
as exoticizing ethnic, religious, or cultural markers of the sheikh's desirability now glow with the potential threat of racial overtones.

I do not wish to imply that racialization is a new phenomenon for
Arab and Muslim Americans, as if there has been a clear, distinct switch
from the paradigm of ethnicity to that of race in the last decade. On the
contrary, race has functioned as a submerged logic in the construction
of Arab Americans in particular since the first wave of immigration in

the late 1800s.[22] Nevertheless, I do chart the increased salience of the concept of race to the construction of Arab and Muslim Americans, noting how more recent configurations of the group operate in more overtly racialized ways. Underlying all of this are two basic ideas laid out by Michael Omi and Howard Winant in their hallmark book, *Racial Formations in the United States*: (1) that race presents itself as an immutable and natural characteristic, despite being a sociohistorical concept, and (2) that racialization is a historically specific ideological process that sometimes "extends racial meaning to a previously unclassified relationship, social practice, or group."[23] The first point serves as a reminder of the persistent recourse to the natural, essential, or, especially in scientific iterations, the biological in discourses of race.[24] The second point highlights how organizing elements such as ethnicity, religion, or geopolitics can become racialized and how various political investments generally aid such a process.

There is no easy or shorthand way to refer to the racialization of Arab and Muslim Americans—an observation that further elucidates the above two points. In reality, one must speak of the racialization of Arabs, Muslims, and anyone appearing to be Arab or Muslim in the United States. That last clause, the hardest aspect of this particular racial formation to signify in a neat phrase, suggests, again, that commonsense notions of race fall back on vague assignations of type and descent and tend to (or try to) naturalize a cultural grouping.[25] In this respect, it seems to follow Paul Gilroy's suggestion that race contemporarily functions according to "culture lines rather than color lines."[26] At the same time, one can hardly speak of Arabs, Muslims, South Asians, Iranians, and anyone else appearing to be any of the above as one *cultural* group. Thus, racial notions are rooted in ideological processes, in this case in a political investment that constructs a disparate group formation, which some scholars refer to as Arab/Muslim/Middle Eastern, as enemies of the state.[27] Here, ethnicity and race are clearly not mutually exclusive, as race serves as a means of containing or managing ethnic and religious identities. Race is a famously unstable concept, which often uses a variety of categorizations. Siobhan Somerville has noted, for instance, that "in nineteenth-century scientific usage, [race] might refer to groupings based variously on geography, religion, class, or color."[28] In the Arab/Muslim/Middle Eastern configuration, such groupings are precisely at play—the configuration seems to refer at once to ethnicity, religion, and geopolitical territory—implying that the conflation of these groupings is itself a characteristic of the concept and functioning of race. I refer here to race's fluidity and flexibility, both in terms of space and time. Though I focus on modern notions of race, contemporary constructions of Arabs/Muslims/Middle Easterners seem to incorporate atavistic, proto-racial formations of the Muslim other, rendered through narratives of the Crusades, and especially the Inquisition and the Reconquista in the Iberian Peninsula.[29]

Given its fungibility, I work from a definition of race suggested by Winant in *The New Politics of Race*: "Race is a concept that signifies and symbolizes sociopolitical conflicts and interests in reference to different types of bodies."[30] This definition offers two points of departure—one related to bodies and one related to architecture. Though some phenotypical characteristics, like dark skin or a long beard, certainly play a role in the racialization of Arabs and Muslims in the U.S., one must also take "bodies" to include notions of bodies that understand their embodiment to be shaped by racially marked, habitually worn clothing (like a hijab or turban) as well as habitually performed movements (like *salaat*, the Muslim practice of praying five times a day).[31]

The example of the Sikh turban brings together a number of the elements of racialization I have sought to delineate. Being neither Arab, Muslim, nor Middle Eastern, Sikh men inhabit the often unstated clause of the Arab/Muslim/Middle Eastern formation—they are those appearing to be such (according to mainstream perceptions) partly on the basis of a racially marked, habitually worn item of clothing. With some Sikh clothing probably assigned to the vague term *headdress* by popular U.S. imagination, the racialization of (and violence against) Sikh men in the U.S. after 9/11 also points to the particular architecture of this racial logic—it is designed and built upon U.S. military conflict, the war on terror, and the construction of the enemy of the state par excellence—the terrorist. The term *terrorist* here serves as a means of systematizing a whole set of state policies—classification, surveillance, strategies of punishment and detention, and distribution of resources—that are meted out along racial lines.[32] In this case, it also codifies the Arab/Muslim/Middle Eastern configuration through the specter of the terrorist as a racial formation.

Rather than being entirely new, this racial formation constructs people with ancestry in the South and West Asia and North Africa regions in newly legible ways. As Melani McAlister points out in *Epic Encounters*, the Middle East has variously figured in U.S. national mythologies. These mythologies, in turn, configure race differently from one another. In identifications with the "Holy Land" as an origin of "Western civilization"—a premise popular in the late nineteenth century and into the turn of the century and then again in the post–World War II period (though never fully receding), the peoples of the Middle East tend to be relegated as atavistic elements of the landscape.[33] Insofar as the Middle East has played the representational role of the other in the U.S. progress narrative (e.g., in the belly dance exhibitions at the 1893 Chicago World's Fair, which demonstrated U.S. progress and prowess, in part, against the ethnographic and spectacular exhibits of others), people from the Middle East have often been assigned a quaint, atavistic, or timeless status.[34]

Even in representations that provoke—for example the belly dancing exhibition at the 1893 Fair both attracted and repulsed viewers because of its flouting of Victorian ideals of white femininity—the Middle East appeared distant and containable, able to be inspected and gazed upon, but ultimately controlled. In a third type of U.S. discourse, that of national security, the Middle East figures in both material and representational ways, both of which construct Middle Easterners, and especially Arab and Muslim Americans, as a threatening presence.[35] Though this discourse obviously incorporates the figure of the terrorist as primary enemy of state in the contemporary context, it is also imbricated in the idea that access to natural resources (such as oil) is a primary concern of national security. This configuration turns Arabs and Muslims into a threatening presence, beginning at least with the 1973 oil embargo and accelerating into the Reagan/Bush/Clinton-era war on terrorism as well as the Bush/Obama war on terror. As an object of state regulation and surveillance in newly highlighted ways, particularly after the events of September 11, 2001, the figure of the Arab/Muslim/Middle Eastern/terrorist is therefore more overtly subjected to a political, ideological, and systemic form of racial classification.

The character of the sheikh—broadly conceived—fits into this landscape in multiple ways. As I have argued in earlier chapters, he inhabits both noble savage and violent, primitive other (in the form of the antihero) of the progress narrative. He is the wealthy, dashing sheikh of his own oil-rich kingdom and the rich, greedy oil sheikh of the 1973 oil embargo, both incarnations of the national security discourse.[36] One could even argue that the way the desert is constructed through tropes of freedom in the novels draws on the mythology of the U.S. relationship to the Holy Land. However, the figure of the sheikh has been rendered most overtly through his signification of a particularly aggressive and eroticized sexuality, while, as noted earlier, his sexuality depends on a clear link between eroticism and an ethnicity containing a liminal racial logic.[37] Such liminality, in turn, allows romance writers to negotiate a fine line between fantasy and reality; the sheikh-hero evades the threat of racial identification (as race would destroy the fantasy) through inscription (or escape) into the ethnic and erotic realm and through simultaneous submersion of markers of race.

Ethnic inscription and racial submersion function through an analysis of two discursive realms. In the first realm (posts and discussions on popular romance novel blogs), readers cannot get past the (raced) realities of the sheikh-hero to fall in love with him. Here, then, I chart the failed submersion of racial logic for some potential readers of desert romances, noting in particular how they characterize this racialization as a new phenomenon. In the second realm, I analyze how desert romances themselves submerge race and therefore subordinate it to ethnicity to successfully interpellate readers into the world of fantasy.

The Sheikh: Fantasy or Reality?

Romance novels are widely considered escapist fiction, offering readers reprieve from their own unexciting, everyday realities. Many readers confirm such an assumption on popular blogs and message boards devoted to the genre. Perhaps this is why both readers and writers of the desert romance deny any relationship between its popularity and the resurgence of the war on terror, despite the steady increase in desert romance publications since 2001. As some of the respondents to "The Unshakeable Appeal of the Sheikh Hero" say: "I never even thought about the current problems in the MidEast ("terrorism," theocracy, etc.) in relation to my absolute obsession with Sheikhs. . . . I think my love for Sheikhs is because of their 'alpha maleness' as it is described," and "I don't think about 911 [*sic*] when reading sheikhs."[38] Trish Morey, author of *Stolen by the Sheikh* and *The Sheikh's Convenient Virgin*, puts it perhaps less pointedly, but more helpfully as she contextualizes the claim of distance from current political events: "I just love the escapism and sheer fantasy of the sheikh story. I think EM Hull got it so right when she penned her famous 'The Sheik' about a century ago. Being whisked away by the king of the desert is a theme that resonates with women all over."[39] Here, Morey's point related to "escapism and sheer fantasy" is key to the popular narrative of the sheikh-hero and to romance novels in general.

While romance novel enthusiasts are quick to point out that romance novels are about more than mere escapism, when the novels tread too closely to the real world, readers and writers carefully guard the escapist element of the fiction. After all, they reason, they can (and must) engage with real-world drudgery every day, which is why they turn to fantasy in the first place. Therefore, as Janice Radway has emphasized and as readers will confirm, romance novels actually demonstrate a complex interplay between notions of fantasy and reality.[40] Radway argues that romance readers expect to learn some real historical and geographical facts, even if the romance story itself is fictional.[41]

Indeed, authors' relative success at incorporating historical and cultural research into their novels is often a topic for discussion among readers. The tension between readers' expectations around the balance between fantasy and reality often surfaces in relation to a popular debate among romance readers about the function of rape and rape fantasy (as well as the difference between the two) in romance novels. In one online discussion, to which I will return later, one reader expresses the desire "to talk about issues of historical accuracy and authenticity in ways that allow us to confront the place we want more realism."[42] While this reader is interested in acknowledging the contingencies of reality within romance fiction, her co-respondents seem to reify a vague, commonsense line between fantasy and reality. Most readers in this thread insist that reality in the story doesn't work when it hits too close to home and forecloses the possibility for fantasy, while relatively few are interested in exploring the shared cultural assumptions and sociopolitical realities that make some details more unbearably real than others.

Of course, it is precisely in the unspoken and subtle negotiations between fantasy and reality that romance novels do some of their most important cultural work, since, as Geraldine Heng suggests, the genre of romance can provide a safe venue in which to explore larger cultural transformations.[43] Particularly since desert romances both enjoy a long history and maintain their popularity despite the demonization of Arab/Muslim/Middle Eastern masculinity during the war on terror, they offer a set of materials through which to analyze shifts in the racialization of Arabs and Muslims. As Heng notes: "Race itself, after all, is a fantasy with fully material effects and consequences."[44] Since romance novels are famous for eliding considerations of race, presenting themselves instead as universal love stories, they provide in their very disavowal a complex articulation of the construction of race. Even in the desert romance subgenre, in which the exotic other is the object of fantasy, overt references to race or racialization are hard to find, since, presumably, they would touch too closely on the realities that readers want to leave behind. Rather, covert articulations of race, sometimes coded through the tropes of ethnicity or region, play a vital role in exoticizing and eroticizing the hero.

In online conversations about the popularity of desert romances, readers theorize distance and ignorance as factors that would enable someone to fantasize about the sheikh without allowing reality to get in the way. True to readers' and Morey's claims about the "sheer fantasy" of the sheikh-hero, desert romances almost always animate orientalist representations of Arab masculinity as aggressive and powerful—the sheikh is a "fierce desert man," as E. M. Hull put it.[45] While the novels themselves frequently make reference to *Arabian Nights*, readers commenting in sheikh blog forums mention "berobed desert sheiks" as well as "hot desert winds, cool fountains, slight and slithery silk garments, unusually juicy fruit, attar of roses" as the exotic draw of the sheikh.[46] In other words, one commenter reminded other readers, the imagined distance between the reader and her setting enabled this set of fantasies: "back then [in the 1970s] Arabia was just some mystical place 'out there' where men were dominant and women submissive and the clothes looked nice."[47]

Addressing the question of how these novels could remain popular even in the face of contemporary political events, the commenter suggests that it mimics the original desert fantasy, which invoked a thrilling and exotic "mystical place" far removed from readers' notions of reality. While this comment acknowledges the desert romance setting as one in which writers can develop the alpha male as (dominant) hero to the submissive heroine, it also implies that readers' lack of knowledge about the Middle East is what makes Arabiastan an ideal setting. As a commenter on the *Smart Bitches, Trashy Books* blog explains, "These books only work if you have absolutely no clue whatsoever about the real culture. A 15-year-old Catholic white girl living in Indiana in 1987 just has a vague notion that somewhere way far away, there is a place with lots of sand and camels where people wear long flowing robe-like clothes and men are crazy rich and powerful and oooh it's all so exotic."[48]

Desert romances can operate as the über-escape fantasy, this comment implies, because of the powerful trope of the desert as the ultimate blank slate, an almost otherworldly space, in which the heroine can indulge in erotic and exotic fantasy. The "long flowing robe-like clothes" seem to be just another semiotic marker of the desert trope, which also functions to pull the reader out of her own reality—what one *Smart Bitches, Trashy Books* commenter refers to as "yearning for Calgon."[49] The idea that the reader cannot indulge in the fantasy of the desert trope unless she has "absolutely no clue whatsoever about the real culture" explains the important function of sheikh fans' disavowal of the connection to "real culture." A response to Gwyneth Bolton's blog states it more directly: "I wonder if the physical distance between the U.S. and the Middle East makes sheik romances more acceptable? Perhaps the reader subconsciously thinks she can read about this 'savage' seduction set in the Middle East while she's safe in her suburban home?"[50]

The sense of distance certainly does seem to be a key element of the desert romance fantasy and, indeed, has a major function in all mass-market romance. Tellingly, contributors to the blogs I have been citing continuously reference the late 1970s and the 1980s as a period in which desert romances were more viable because the illusion of absolute distance between the U.S. and the Middle East was still possible. The political context of the 1970s and 1980s was actually precisely the opposite—the 1973 oil embargo helped inaugurate oil sheikh caricatures of greedy, lascivious Arab men, and the 1979 Iranian revolution and 1980s Libyan plane hijackings helped inaugurate the figure of the terrorist, still prominent today. Both of these figures, in their engagement with U.S. notions of national security, helped to develop the notion of the Middle East as a threatening presence. However, according to these commenters' posts, the figures had not yet reached a level of cultural saturation to threaten the sense of distance necessary for the desert fantasy. Instantiating distance (to ultimately overcome it) is one of the main tropes of romance, which makes the question of how to construct a believable distance even more interesting.

Indeed, one comment on the *Smart Bitches, Trashy Books* blog, posted by someone with the screen name Ann Wesley Hardin, notes the contemporary popularity of paranormal romances and muses that cultural, social, physical, and psychic or spiritual boundaries in romance novels operate, at the novel's denouement, to ultimately demonstrate the power of love to overcome any obstacle: "Kinda makes sense when you look at other themes like paranormal, secrets, time travel, etc. All these problems are pretty insurmountable the same way the sociocultural ones used to be. In a sense, the werewolf is the new sheik."[51] While she seems to mean this literally—and without irony—the idea that sheikhs and werewolves are comparable kinds of characters that simply have salience in different political contexts is a revealing one.[52] It demonstrates both the perceived unreality of the sheikh and his simultaneous association with monstrosity, a status that is all too grounded in reality for some readers. Alpha-male heroes must have a (tamable) dangerous edge, but the perceived danger must not tread too closely to the realm of reality for readers, which is why many respondents are vocal about their dislike of the sheikh. As Devon explains: "Sheiks are an area where that suspension of disbelief fails. While I am not saying that all Muslim men or men of M.E. descent are bad, I have difficulty reconciling what I know of the treatment of women in the M.E. with the desert oasis fantasy."[53]

For these readers, it is impossible to engage in a romantic fantasy about the sheikh, because the supposed unpleasant realities of the Middle East are too present and too powerful. Notably, many of these comments display a conceit discussed by Leila Ahmed in her article "Western Ethnocentrism and Perceptions of the Harem."[54] They assume an authority of knowledge about the Middle East, particularly in relation to women's status and women's rights. In "The Unshakeable Appeal of the Sheikh Hero" entry on the *I [Heart] Harlequin Presents* blog, one of the respondents, CT, fills in some of the details regarding such popular "knowledge" about the Middle East: "I have to say that for me, the events of 9/11, plus other issues, among them the horrible kidnapping and abuse of Terry Anderson, the relentless suicide bombers, 'honor' killings and sexual mutilation of young girls, old goats taking a 4th or 5th wife who happens to be 11 or 12 years old, etc. . . . makes it almost impossible for me to think of any sheikh as a hero."[55]

CT's list is illustrative in that it both references popular associations with the war on terror (i.e., "relentless suicide bombers") and it reads like a laundry list of sensationalist stories in the popular press about the backward customs supposedly a part of Arab and Islamicate cultures ("honor killings," sexual mutilation of girls, "old goats" taking prepubescent wives, etc.).[56] If nothing else, these comments demonstrate a clear dialectical relationship between what readers assume they know about the Middle East and their ability to engage with the novels. Moreover, at least one commenter, Stephanie, ties her understanding of the Middle East to the news media: "How is it possible to separate the fantasy from reality—when the reality shows up on the news nightly. Maybe back in 1980—you could overlook it, but today?"[57] Again, the invocation of 1980 underscores my general claim about the shift in overt racialization of Arabs and Muslims in the United States. Stephanie seems to suggest that in the contemporary context of the war on terror, the shady configuration of the Arab/Muslim/Middle Eastern/terrorist shows up on the nightly news as a distinctly identifiable racial formation, one that precludes any kind of fantasy engagement.

Despite these negative associations with the sheikh, he nevertheless seems to maintain a persistent presence within the genre as a whole. In other words, the specter of the sheikh figure is sometimes invoked, even in conversations that have nothing to do with desert romances. In what amounts to a negative presence, where the sheikh only exists as a counterpoint to some larger argument, lie more clues about the racialization of the sheikh, a process that relies heavily on constructing his difference through orientalist perceptions of political events.

Smart Bitches, Ghastly Sheikhs

Another way the sheikh's overt racialization makes him untenable as a hero for many readers is explained through his haunting presence within the genre as a whole. A reader discussion from a wildly popular romance review blog provides some evidence. *Smart Bitches, Trashy Books* has such a large readership that it has been featured on several news programs (including NPR's *All Things Considered*). Moreover, the original authors of the blog—Sarah Wendell and Candy Tan—have published a book, *Beyond Heaving Bosoms*, as a result of the success of their blog.[58] The popularity of *Smart Bitches* seems to be due, at least in part, to the authors' forthright manner in giving negative reviews to romance novels that they consider poor quality. In this way, instead of blindly defending the genre and its worth as a literary form, they lend legitimacy to the genre as a whole by distinguishing good from poor quality.

Interestingly, one of their most popular negative reviews is of a desert romance by Sharon Kendrick, *The Playboy Sheikh's Virgin Stable Girl*.[59] In fact, the blog has little positive to say about sheikhs or desert romances. Given this, I was intrigued to find a veiled conversation about the Middle East and Muslims in the comments section of a long post about rape in romance. In a post called "Alphas in Marriage," SBSarah raises the question of whether "unwilling sex" is problematic or offensive in historical romance novels since it is widely accepted that having sex (even if unwillingly) was a conjugal duty of women during the period in which the novels take place. For the sake of space, I will not go into the debate about rape and coerced sex that followed; however, I do want to focus on the rhetorical strategy that some of the readers employed. In arguing that historical rape was just as problematic as contemporary rape, they use two main strategies. First, the readers compare the historical context in romance novels to contemporary cultural contexts that they view as atavistically still engaging in problematic customs. Second, the readers note other historical practices that are now widely condemned and considered condemnable in their own historical context as well. Both strategies have racialized overtones.

In likening the barbarism of forced sex in historical romance novels to similarly perceived barbaric customs in the contemporary context, the first reference is to some (unspecified) other "modern country where a woman has no right to say 'no.'"[60] However, the examples quickly become more clearly identified with what is commonly referred to as the "Muslim world." When the above comment is misinterpreted, the poster, Angel, specifies: "Women were not the creators of these cultural mores; they were the objects of them. If we accept them, we'd have to retroactively accept the righteousness of the abuses committed against women under them. That's as unappealing a prospect to me as excusing a man who commits an 'honor killing' because that's part of the power his culture has given to him over the women of his family."[61]

Leaving aside a discussion of honor killings and a U.S. fascination with them, what seems clear from this statement is that the very example of honor killings clarifies the popular notion that Muslim "culture" represents the contemporary other who is still engaged in backward, unacceptably misogynist acts in comparison to contemporary enlightened views about women's rights in the U.S.-Anglo culture.[62] This type of assumption seems to undergird much of the blog discussion and is confirmed in a later comment by Najida (who eventually reveals herself to be a white, U.S.-based belly dancer): "I'm a woman who would slap anyone who insulted me with the term 'feminist.' . . . Don't get me wrong, I was and am still very active and vocal in women's issues in Islamic states, etc. They do have it horrible, and we have little to bitch about."[63] In a classic formulation, Najida here employs the common perception of how Muslim women "have it horrible" as a counterpoint to U.S. women's freedom and independence, as discussed in chapter 2. Indeed, these sorts of views about "Islamic states" are precisely what desert romances must overcome to achieve the optimal fantasy-reality balance. Nevertheless, the views remain a key, if submerged, presence in the characterization of the sheikh. As chapter 2 demonstrates, most desert romances speak to these common perceptions by carefully coding the sheikh as a progressive, forward-thinking man who needs the independent, headstrong Western (white) woman to help him modernize his country. Even so, the novels run the risk of remaining unconvincing to some romance readers, like Erin, who explains:

> I'm just too informed on current events and Middle East culture to buy into the world that book tried to set up. . . . The woman had a pretty good life, a good job, decent income, etc. Then she gets kidnapped by sheikh-

dude and after getting brainwashed by his c**k of multiple orgasms, decides that she's going to give it all up to be his little woman out in the middle of the desert? Um, WTF? No mention of the likely multiple wives, her having to convert to Islam or having to wear hijab, and certainly no mention of her being stoned or the husband's right to [do] damn near whatever he wants to do with her, legally.[64]

Incidentally, nearly all of these characteristics appear in Nora Roberts's sheikh antihero novel, *Sweet Revenge*, but Erin's point is well taken in that they don't operate as elements of the sheikh-hero. Her assumption that all unions in the Middle East are both bound by Islam and involve "multiple wives," compulsory veiling, and possible stoning evidences the sheer persistence of such stereotypical notions about the Middle East; it also reinforces the idea that Middle Eastern masculinity is characterized by extreme patriarchal customs. Here, the sheikh is raced through strongly held beliefs about the absolute religiocultural differences of Middle Eastern men. The racialization works through the presence of such negative perceptions, which cast these differences as immutable.

The second strategy readers employ in the rape-in-marriage debate is, perhaps, a clearer articulation of the way common perceptions of Islam fit into the logic of racialization in the United States. In these examples, readers note that historically racist practices directed toward African and African American people are not considered acceptable even in their historical context (and so neither should rape be), *and* they tie these historical examples of racism against black people to contemporary examples of misogyny in Muslim contexts. Snarkhunter argues: "Oooookay . . . so . . . burning heretics alive is not something I should look back and judge? I should be okay with it, because it was just 'part of life'? What about apartheid? Female genital mutilation?"[65] And later, she clarifies and expands: "Is it okay to lynch African-Americans if you're a poor white person who barely scrapes by and who is on the verge of starvation? . . . Is cutting off a little girl's clitoris with a sharp rock okay because it's accepted in her culture?"[66]

Here, she uses clear and powerful examples of racist practices (that are widely understood as such) to lend credence to her overall argument. Importantly, the absolute misogyny of female genital cutting, which is referenced by the more sensationalist term *female genital mutilation* and frequently considered a condoned practice of Islam, is compared to the absolute racism of lynching and apartheid. In this unspoken and unacknowledged way, what are vaguely understood to be Arab and Muslim cultural practices become associated with quintessential racist practices. Though the parallel works to suggest that these alleged Arab and Muslim cultural practices are misogynist on a comparable scale of oppression as the racist practices of lynching and apartheid by white supremacists, the analogy also serves to racialize Arab and Muslim men through the notion of a culturally sanctioned (and even promoted) misogyny. Here, I do not wish to compare the oppressions of Arabs and Muslims with those of African Americans—they are clearly not mutually exclusive categories. Rather, I am interested in popular associations with race, the way that oppression of African Americans and black South Africans is invoked as an absolute and quintessential marker of racism, and the deployment of such markers in parallel with common misperceptions about Arab and Muslim cultural practices.

Delaney's Desert Sheikh, the only desert romance to feature a black heroine, is also one of the only contemporary desert romances in which the sheikh-hero makes an overt reference to Allah, marking him clearly as Muslim.[67] While African Americans comprise approximately 40 percent of the Muslim community in the United States, this is actually not the typical (even if the most obvious) way in which Islam and African Americans tend to be linked within common U.S. racial logics.[68] Rather, as in Delaney's case, Islam seems to operate as a form of racialization that can be coterminous or compatible with blackness. Perhaps through popular notions of Islamism and radicalization, Islam sometimes operates as a marker of radical (racial) difference.

One example of this is President Obama's middle name, Hussein. The name was constantly invoked in the lead-up to the 2008 elections, as a way of overlaying a racialized post-racial candidate with a more radioactive marker of racial difference.[69] This is not to say that Islam is the new black.[70] But Islam is operating in the contemporary U.S. context in particularly racialized ways, some of which manifest themselves through popular linkages to blackness and African American cultural movements, which hold privileged places within the racial logic of the United States.

One final link, or parallel, lies in how sheikhs operate as key ghostly presences in a wider romance genre that is primarily focused on white characters coded as representing universal experience. Here I refer not to desert romances themselves, but to the way the eclipsed figure of the sheikh (in his terrorist incarnation) functions to regulate conversations about what should be deemed acceptable in romances, as in the above-cited conversation about rape in romance. In other words, he operates as a shadowy figure—a racial other—who enables the self-reflective focus on whiteness through the white heroine. He urges us, in Toni Morrison's words, to "realize the obvious" about romance novels, that is, that in them, "the subject of the dream is the dreamer."[71]

Desert romances themselves both utilize and submerge racial notions. The increased salience of race as a category through which Arabs and Muslims are understood today in the U.S. has, as we have seen, shifted some things in the landscape of desert romances: it has made them less believable as fantasy stories for some readers and seems to have stripped the sheikhs of their headdresses on the covers of the books. The latter shift implies a larger one—that is, a shift in popular perceptions of Arab/Muslim as an ethnic or religious identity to a racial one. Within U.S. racial logic, ethnicity has sometimes functioned as a register of inclusion within whiteness, while race has more often functioned as a register of exclusion from hegemonic structures.[72] In actuality, ethnicity itself has a paradox of simultaneous inclusion and exclusion built into the imprecise nature of the category.[73] It operates as a universalist identity category upon which the U.S. founds an argument for tolerance and diversity, at the same time that ethnicity functions as a particularist identity category on the basis of which minoritarian groups struggle for rights and justice; ethnicity often invokes the universal, neutral modality while operating in an exclusionary, boundary-marking manner. Moreover, it has, at least in its origins, a religious valence, as it served as a marker to distinguish Jew and gentile as well as Christian and heathen.[74] These various registers of the ethnic paradigm therefore indicate both the mutability and the permeability of ethnicity, religion, and race as categorical identifiers. Desert romances exploit and manipulate the flexibility among these categories in the careful crafting of a fantasy narrative.

The One-Drop Rule: Mediations between Biological and Cultural Notions of Race

E. M. Hull's original desert romance, *The Sheik*, sets an interesting precedent for questions of race vis-à-vis the sheikh character. Widely known for its miscegenation plot, the novel nevertheless finds an intricate and clever way to negotiate the notion of race. Roughly situating Sheikh Ahmed between black and white, Hull makes the sheikh's racialization clear by having Diana (the white heroine) assume that her brother would consider him black. Referring to him as a "man of different race and colour," Diana goes as far as to imagine that her brother would categorize him in terms of the racial epithet "damned nigger," even as the novel works to position the sheikh as ambiguously raced.[75] At the same time that Hull emphasizes Sheikh Ahmed's racial otherness, she resolves the threat of miscegenation for her readers by revealing the sheikh to have been bred from European ancestry. As Susan Blake notes in "What 'Race' Is the Sheik?" what is particularly interesting about Hull's framing of race is her mediation between biological and cultural understandings of race.[76]

While miscegenation fears are allayed through a biological notion of race (Sheikh Ahmed comes from a Spanish mother and a Scottish—earl—father), Diana's exotic desert romance maintains authenticity by virtue of the fact that she still considers Ahmed culturally Arab, since he has been raised as a future desert sheikh. Such a formulation interestingly parallels Etienne Balibar's discussion of racism in "Is There a Neoracism?" Though the novel predates the period that Balibar discusses, it establishes a framework mimicked by many contemporary desert romances, which do fall within the era of "decolonization" and which therefore operate according to "a racism whose dominant theme is not biological heredity but the insurmountability of cultural differences."[77] In other words, in a context in which colonialism (and the scientific racist projects that helped justify it) is outwardly repudiated, notions of radical difference are instantiated in the liberal-democratic "old metropolis" through the paradigm of cultural difference, a formulation echoed by Rey Chow in her description of "culturalist" or "differentialist" notions of race.[78]

This is not to say that biological notions of race completely recede; rather, they emerge in different ways, such as in reference to ancestry or authenticity. Balibar specifies that the "return of the biological theme" can be neatly contained within the framework of cultural racism, a phenomenon that clearly correlates with conceptions of race in contemporary desert romances.[79] While some contemporary novels (like Nan Ryan's *Burning Love*) mimic Hull's technique of revealing the sheikh-hero to hail completely from European ancestry, most of them bestow authenticity on their heroes by identifying them with some form of desert ancestry.[80] In a move that seems to parallel the logic of the one-drop rule, sheikhs' bloodlines assure their desert status, providing a (biological) foundation on which the culturalist racial markers of civilization and dress can build. In Emma Darcy's *Traded to the Sheikh*, for example, the sheikh-hero Zageo is a mix of Portuguese, Arab, Indian, British, and French. In case this conglomeration seems too diffuse, the author (through her heroine) assures readers: "He might not look like an Arab but he is one at heart."[81] Likewise, the sheikh in Trish Morey's *Stolen by the Sheikh* is half Arab and half French, though the heroine notes that his accent "held touches of English, a trace of American and more besides."[82] Because of his "dark features," the heroine places him as somehow Mediterranean. When she finally discovers his Arab roots, she reveals that "she could see the Arab influence in his features . . . as if he was made for the desert."[83]

Sometimes, as in Loreth Anne White's *The Sheik Who Loved Me*, the Arabic language can provide the authentic link to the primality of the desert. In this novel, the sheikh's "R's rolled in his throat, his Arabic accent swallowing the refined British as his smooth veneer fell away to reveal the rough warrior underneath."[84] Perhaps one reason the recourse to a biologically based notion of race is important is precisely because the stereotype of the priapic sheikh depends on the popular notion that raw sexuality is part of his nature.[85] In turn, the threat of a potentially violent and unbridled nature needs some sort of check or safety valve to assure the heroine (and her identified readers) that her romance will end happily ever after.

In desert romances, the deployment of biological notions of race (again modeled originally in Hull's *The Sheik*) sometimes involves the propensity for the sheikh-hero to have Spanish ancestry. Though it would appear that naming Spanish ancestry would corroborate bio-logical claims to European ancestry (as it did for Hull), its function is actually a bit more ambiguous.[86] Though almost none of the authors who use the Spanish-ancestry technique directly name it, such ancestry implies a possible, or even probable, connection to Moorish ancestry, which simultaneously suggests Muslim ancestry and connects race with religion.[87]

If desert romances harbor strong articulations of race, they do so in part through the ghostly presence of the Moor, a figure through which the amalgamation of race and religion becomes clearer. Though the concept of race is widely understood to be a modern one that draws on biological and cultural characteristics in the social construction of race, several scholars have noted that in fifteenth- and sixteenth-century Spain, religious difference functioned in racialized ways. Regarding the mass displacement and forced conversion of Muslims and Jews dur-ing this period, Anouar Majid argues that "*limpieza de sangre*" statutes served to racialize faith, demonstrating that religious difference (even if regarded in cultural terms) could operate as a foundation for racial-ization.[88] Although the race concept followed a "path toward secular-ization" in the eighteenth and nineteenth centuries and, in its modern form, privileged biological and cultural difference as a way of marking race (through eugenics, scientific racism, and the idea of the civilizing mission), religious difference can still be understood as an integral fac-tor in the construction of race.[89] Neither should religious difference be seen merely as a proto-racial formation. In his book *Semites*, Gil Anidjar explores the way that, regarding the categorization of Arabs and Jews, "race and religion have functioned internally and externally . . . as mark-ers of historical shifts" continuing throughout the modern era.[90] Insofar as modernity can be understood as ideologically linked to the notions of secularism and universality, religious difference has functioned to produce a set of clear, structuring others to the dominant subjects of modernity. Whether it is through the coupling of religion with a sur-passed, traditional past or through the idea that universalism transcends religion, the dominant construction of modernity depends on religious others, who have often been conceived in racialized terms.[91] As Junaid Rana argues: "Race and religion commingled in the formation of mo-dernity."[92] The racialization of the sheikh—just enough to render him an alpha male, but not so much as to make him uncomfortably real—therefore figures in part through his shadowy connection to Spanish Muslim ancestry.

Civilizing Religion

The main deployment of the trope of civilization in desert romances is as a culturalist counterpoint to the biological notions of race that function to prove the sheikh's authentic desert ancestry and therefore lend credibility to his alpha-male nature. This mechanism usually manifests in reference to his careful hygiene and erudite reading collection, probably because these are the markers that Hull originally used in *The Sheik*. There, she coded Sheikh Ahmed as civilized by inserting details about the "fastidious care he took of himself, the frequent bathing, [and] the spotless cleanliness of his robes, the fresh wholesomeness that clung about him" as well as about his collection of French books, which "suggested possibilities that would not have existed in a raw native, or one only superficially coated with a veneer of civilization."[93] These details work to assure the reader that the "raw" and savage nature of the sheikh-hero can be tamed and held in check, and they have been so successful in communicating the point that many contemporary desert romances replicate them almost exactly.[94] This common use of the trope of civilization, then, serves as an overt means of sanitizing the sheikh's absolute difference enough that he can remain an object of reader fantasy.

In a more subtle system of meanings, though, the sheikh is racialized (or sometimes sanitized) through a discursively formed tension around notions of civilization and barbarism, where "civilization" codes a particular ideology of secularism. In other words, in these instances, religiosity serves as a means of racialization. Occasionally, this comes through quite clearly, as in Ryan's *Burning Love*: "The Sheik didn't fall to his knees and face Mecca as his Muslim followers did. But he experienced a great measure of inner peace whenever he was in his beloved desert at sundown."[95] Such overt naming of religion is quite rare because, as I have explained, it borders too closely to what mainstream readers understand to be the uncomfortable realities of Islam. As Janet Jakobsen and Ann Pelligrini remark in their introduction to *Secularisms*, a "network of associations is established between religious-secular opposition and that between bondage and freedom."[96]

Such an opposition can be clearly seen in the passage from *Burning Love*, in which the sheikh's subjects are represented as if in "bondage" to their religion, while the sheikh himself draws on an "inner peace" gained from the desert setting, suggesting his more individual (and liberalized) relationship to religion. Indeed, the passage seems to suggest that he does not adhere to any organized religion at all, regardless of the behaviors of his "Muslim followers." Such rare, but revealing, passages in desert romances demonstrate the complex constellations of meaning that form around the notions of religiosity and secularism and the way these constellations of meaning connect to broader constructions of difference. Though religion remains purposely uncoded (in any overt way) in most desert romances, the sheikh character provides a useful way of understanding how religion operates as an implicit and unmarked signifier of race. Islam is tied to race, in part, through dominant discourses about civilization, such as Samuel Huntington's infamous "clash of civilizations" thesis. One salient example of the connections between notions of race, civilization, and religion is in the 1944 naturalization case for an Arab immigrant. The case held that the immigrant was white because Arabs had "historically served as *transmitters* of western civilization."[97] Here, the concept of Western civilization depends on the image of the (biblical) Holy Land as the (Christian) origins of Western civilization. In other words, though the idea of Western civilization is often presented as a thoroughly secular one, it is best understood as an incarnation of what Jakobsen and Pelligrini have called "Protestant secularism," signaling the co-implication of secularism and religion.[98]

More to the point, perhaps, the notion of civilization works in tandem with that of secularism to produce a set of religious others, quite independently of actual religiosity. Gil Anidjar posits that "secularism is the name Christianity gave itself when it invented 'religion' [and] named its other or others as 'religions.'"[99] The invention of religion—that is, the invention of a particular understanding of religion as provincial, backward, or violent (among other things) and its opposition to a secular formation—clearly manifests itself in the common binary formulation of "Islam and the West," used prominently in the clash-of-civilizations thesis. The use of religious difference as a counterpoint to the secularized (i.e., civilized) West can be seen in Nora Roberts's 1989 novel *Sweet Revenge*, which invokes the image of the greedy and brutal oil sheikh popularized in the U.S. in the 1970s and into the 1980s.

Spinning a tale quite similar to the 1980s hit film *Not Without My Daughter*, the book *Sweet Revenge* chronicles the story of a white U.S. American actress who falls in love with a sheikh and moves to his country, only to be abused and despised by him for giving birth to a girl child. The heroine is sequestered in a harem, while her husband, Abdu, takes other wives in hopes of securing a male heir. As I have argued elsewhere, the image of the harem as evidence of extreme Middle Eastern/Muslim patriarchy and oppression rose in U.S. popular culture in the 1970s and 1980s as the Middle East came to be perceived as a security threat.[100] In this schema, the perception of the harem walls as foreboding and impenetrable becomes crucial to the narrative of brutally oppressive patriarchy steeped in religious fundamentalism. As Roberts puts it in *Sweet Revenge*: "The walls rose high, to prevent a woman who walked there from tempting any man. Such was the way of Islam."[101] Against this oppression, the white heroine in the novel can only hope that Jaquir, her adopted country, will become socially liberalized as it becomes more fiscally liberalized.

Roberts presents Jaquir as a fully primitive and traditional society, with oil as its only real resource; she therefore presents contact with the West as only possible through the lure of oil. Moreover, she adheres to the predominant stereotype of the Arab/Muslim world in the 1970s and 1980s as a place filled with abundant oil and religious (Islamic) fanaticism and simultaneously rooted in atavistic traditions and therefore deeply antagonistic toward the West. Again, as Roberts frames it: "Abdu wanted the money and technology the West would bring, even while he detested Westerners for providing them. With Westerners pouring into Jaquir, there would be progress. In time there might even be liberation."[102] Here, Roberts seems to meld dominant U.S. perceptions of the Middle East emerging from both the 1973 oil embargo and the 1979 Iranian revolution neatly into the character of Abdu, the heartless sheikh antihero of *Sweet Revenge*. He wants to acquire riches from oil, but he sees the West as an "abomination of Allah."[103] In these formulations of the sheikh antihero and his desert kingdom, religion is certainly a crucial aspect of Abdu's otherness, but it is not the only factor. He is set in opposition to a constellation of Western markers—a complex network of associations with secularism, modernity, and civilization— that ultimately serve to mark him as a "racial figure based in notions of universality."[104] Because he is the villain in *Sweet Revenge* and not the heroine's love interest (she falls in love with a fellow spy who helps her seek revenge), his relatively overt racialization within the narrative does not threaten the crucial romantic fantasy.

Berobed or Bedeviled

The most obvious or salient way in which sheikhs are covertly racial- ized through cultural markers are in what amounts to a fetishization of Arabiastani forms of cultural dress. The sheikh's robes and headdress (as they are most often called) serve as exotic markers while simultaneously operating as key signifiers of erotic sexuality. For example, in Sophie Weston's *In the Arms of the Sheikh*, the image of Sheikh Kazim "in full desert robes" and "full desert regalia" provides an erotic teaser for the heroine, Natasha Lambert, until the very last line of the novel, when she is finally able to "[take] off his robe at last."[105] This metaphorical unveil- ing of the sheikh, often at the end of the novel, quite literally signals the taming of his primal/savage/desert nature. While the author must be careful not to rid him of his powerful virility altogether (because in doing so, she would strip him of his alpha-maleness), she does clearly place the power of unveiling in the heroine's hands. Only the heroine has the ability to both excite and tame her desert prince.

Publishers, too, have been clearly attuned to the role of cultural dress in the interplay between reality and fantasy, as evinced by the shift in cover designs over the past decade. In addition to the "money factor" (i.e., the oil-rich Arab sheikh) or the idea that the sheikh has "got crazy money and his own private gas pump," romance readers point to cultural dress as one element that gives him exotic appeal.[106] The "Sheikhs and Desert Love" website lists "when the sheikh makes a change from wear- ing Western style clothing to the traditional robes of his country" as one of the top five things that makes a sheikh hero so "hot."[107]

As demonstrated on another site, in an entry titled "Sheiken and Stirred," at least some fans associate the cultural dress with actors such as Omar Sharif and figures such as T. E. Lawrence (i.e., Lawrence of Arabia), thereby both referencing an orientalist tradition and suggesting a tame, European hero to exist under his exotic garments.[108] As one commenter explains: "The typical romance sheik is a white man wearing a turban, and I agree . . . that this is probably one of the reasons why they sell so well. You have the fantasy of the rich exotic sheik, without dealing with the reality of how a real Middle Eastern man would behave with a female."[109] Several things come together in this quote; the reader's misidentification of the "turban" (an Indian Sikh form of cultural dress) with what might be worn by a sheikh indicates the conflation of multiple ethnic and religious markers in popular perceptions of the sheikh. Further, the comment indicates the tricky balance the novelists try to strike between highlighting exoticized cultural markers and carefully eliding reference to any cultural markers that come too close to uncomfortable realties for readers. The shifting valence of cultural markers becomes apparent, as mentioned earlier, in publishers' decisions about what artwork to include on the book covers.

Prior to 2001, desert romance novels often depicted the sheikh-hero "berobed" on the cover of the book, perhaps as a way of linking to the Sharif/Lawrence fantasy. Since 2001, however, presumably because the events of September 11 in that year reignited popular U.S. association of the *kufiya* or *ghutrah* and *igal* with Arab/Muslim terrorism, the book covers cease to include any cultural markers, depicting instead a generalized image of a Mediterranean (i.e., Greek, Italian, or Arab/Muslim) hero. Nevertheless, the sheikh's cultural dress remains an integral aspect of the romance story itself, making an appearance in many, if not all, desert romances. In this respect, desert robes demonstrate the subtle interplay between overt and covert representations of race, and the way in which the same racial marker (here, robes) can simultaneously operate on various levels, depending on its placement and framing.

One main way in which the robes function is in classic orientalist fashion. Here, Arabiastan usually plays out as the imagined brutal, mysterious, and exotic desert setting, and is clearly informed by popular U.S. orientalist images. In *The Sheikh's Unsuitable Bride*, for example, the heroine Diane Metcalfe finds herself assigned as chauffeur for Sheikh Zahir bin Ali bin Khatib al-Khatib, and when she realizes her assignment, she finds "her head full of snowy robes, the whole Lawrence of

Arabia thing."[110] Other novels also reference memorable scenes from the film *Lawrence of Arabia*, even if they don't name it. In Ryan's *Burning Love*, for example, the author presents sheikh Sharif "riding at tremendous speed, his white robes billowing out behind him, [when he] abruptly gave the reins a powerful jerk that sent the big white horse straight up into the air, spinning high on his hind legs," an image that replicates some of the iconic scenes in the film.[111]

In *Traded to the Sheikh*, the heroine, Emily Ross, makes sense of her surroundings through five separate references to *The Arabian Nights* and one reference to Omar Khayyam.[112] As indicated by the title, Emily finds herself in a potentially dangerous form of captivity at first, so her first encounter with Sheikh Zageo serves to introduce the question of racialization (but not eroticization): "His clothes—a long white undertunic and a sleeveless over-robe in royal purple edged in gold braid—seemed to embrace Arabian culture but he didn't look like an Arab, more aristocratic Spanish."[113] While classic orientalist images, including Lawrence of Arabia, clearly play a role in the novels, the invocation of the sheikh's robes is also connected to race through the exoticization of the sheikh. Although I agree with the commenter who pointed to the Lawrence of Arabia fantasy as one that safely sanitizes the sheikh, the observation ignores the racial dialectics at play in the construction of the sheikh. The white robe sometimes serves as the perfect contrast to highlight the otherness of the Arab character, as in the following scene in *Blue Jasmine*: "His robes fell in sculptured folds around his lean figure and he wore a *shemagh* that was very white against the darkness of his face. He was purely Arabian."[114] Though in this case the character is not the sheikh-hero himself, some desert romances do use the technique for the sheikh-hero. In *A Bed of Sand*, for example, the heroine describes the sheikh as "tall, broad, and desperately gorgeous, his dark skin eating up the paleness of his caftan."[115] In any case, the robes highlight the perceived authenticity of the character as an exotic desert dweller or, as the former author puts it, a "pure Arabian."

The question of what a pure Arabian is points to the curious conflation of religious, tribal, ethnic, and regional conceptions of Arabiastan that seem to meld in the character of the sheikh. The signifier of the sheikh's robes is perhaps a perfect one in the sense that it speaks to the conflated identity of the prototypical sheikh-hero. While the vague references to Arabia quite clearly include popular orientalist representations, they also seem to reflect some amount of research on the authors' part. In other words, fictionalized Arabiastan in desert romancelandia bears some resemblance both to contemporary Saudi Arabia and to a historical notion of the Arabian Peninsula. In these instances, rather than referring to a (modern) ethnic, nation-state notion of Arab (in which the Arabic language is a key aspect of what defines Arabian), the geographical region of the Arabian Peninsula takes on greater importance. Indeed, the sometimes overt and sometimes coded references to "tribal" or "Berber" dress and customs (e.g., "swathed in the blue veils of the Tuareg tribe") seem to get closer to the image of a desert nomadic people, which is the imagined setting from which the sheikh usually hails.[116] Because he is a "desert prince" or even a "desert king," he typically appears in more regal clothing, which may likely be borrowed from the trends of the elite in contemporary Saudi Arabia.

Novelists sometimes include a passage to describe and explain the robe and headdress, and on these occasions, they usually describe contemporary Gulf fashion.[117] When chauffeur Diane Metcalfe finally succeeds in erotic union with her sheikh, she "[finds] herself staring at her fantasy: the desert prince she had expected when she'd dashed to the City Airport. The whole white robes, gold-trimmed cloak, headdress thingy."[118] The robes are almost never directly linked to religion in the novels, though there is some evidence that the clothing references Islam for at least some readers. Roberts's *Sweet Revenge* offers a salient example, since in her novel, the sheikh is the antagonist of the story. He is coded as specifically wearing "the white throbe [*sic*] and headdress of Islam."[119]

From just these cursory examples, it seems clear not only that the sheikh is racialized through the cultural marker of his robes, but also that this marker has no clear ethnic or religious referent for the popular audience. At best, it is tied to a large geographical region, which, in turn, calls up a ready-made set of orientalist images in the readers' minds. The signifier of "desert robes" conflates ethnic, religious, and geographical identities while blurring any direct reference to the Middle East or Islam. It therefore serves to racialize the sheikh-hero in ways that enable desert romance writers to carefully balance the tension of the fantasy tinged with reality that readers demand at the same time that it reflects dominant racial logics of the conflated Arab/Muslim/Middle Eastern/terrorist in the post-9/11 context. As described earlier, the robes always on some level signal a link to Lawrence of Arabia and therefore suggest the whiteness of the hero underneath it all. Usually focusing on the robes and relatively minimizing the "headdress thingy," writers simultaneously reflect and deflect racial anxieties about the Arab/Muslim male, drawing on clothes to eroticize the hero and casting them aside to maintain the aura of fantasy.

For example, since the sheikh is fundamentally an alpha-male hero, his power must be readily apparent, and his cultural dress sometimes operates as an indicator, as in *The Desert Bride of Al Zayed*: "Clad in the *thobe*, the fearsomely muscled body hidden beneath the white folds, he looked foreign, dangerous, and very, very powerful."[120] Contrary to the Lawrence of Arabia image, here the sheikh's foreignness makes him an object of attraction. His dangerous and powerful appearance is a key aspect of what draws the white heroine to him. The process by which he is racialized through cultural dress, though, simultaneously serves to exoticize him. Because of the dialectics between fantasy and reality in romance novels, the sociopolitical realities that his desert robes could potentially cite, or incite, for readers must always be readily submergible to the erotic fantasy around which the narrative arc revolves. For Sheikh Ahmed and his heroine Christa in Connie Mason's *Desert Ecstasy*, the sublimation of race to eroticism comes in one deft move: "With a cry of impatience, his headdress and veil were thrown aside and he captured her lips, kissing her deeply, his tongue pillaging her mouth as his hand continued to work its magic below."[121]

Indeed, the sheikh-heroes in desert romances work various kinds of magic for their (usually white) heroines, but perhaps the most interesting kind of magic is the one they employ for their dedicated readership: an uncanny ability to walk the tightrope between fantasy and reality. If comments from popular romance novel blogs indicate all the reasons romance readers find the sheikh to be undesirable, reasons that imply an intensified racialization of Arabs and Muslims in the contemporary war on terror, the novels themselves speak to the way romance writers have negotiated the shifting racial realities of Arabs and Muslims to keep the desert romance fantasy alive for at least some readers. The grammar of race in desert romances operates on a submerged level, precisely because of the more salient racialization of Arabs and Muslims since 2001. Nevertheless, the authors' use of ethnic, religious, and geographical markers (through mention of the sheikh's ancestry, references to Islam, and eroticized descriptions of his cultural dress) reveals an underlying structure of racialization. It is an adaptable form of racialization, one that shape-shifts into the categories of ethnicity, culture, and religion to appear tamer, hoping to disguise the role of these categories in the racial formation of Arabs and Muslims.

Desert romances are perhaps the ideal texts for reading the lexicon of race vis-à-vis Arabs/Muslims/Middle Easterners in the U.S. Because they must simultaneously subdue and draw on the notion of race while constructing desire for the sheikh-hero, they can offer moments of x-ray clarity about the way markers of ethnicity, religion, and culture can be irradiated with racial logic. In them, the paradox of race as both a social fact and a cultural fantasy throbs in the hot, flickering light of desire: "She could see him now, too, in the ceremonial tribal outfit, his dark hair glowing in the light of the lamp, his dark eyes glowing with untamed desire. He was more than the sheiks of her fantasies—more fierce, more proud, more passionate. And tantalizingly real."[122] Significantly, the sheikh-hero is most real in those private, intimate moments that he shares with the white heroine.

Liberal multiculturalism functions as a technology of imperialism through its crafting of acceptable Arabiastani subjects in the context of the war on terror, relegating those who cannot conform to a realm of social death.[123] Through the logic of liberal multiculturalism—an outward respect for tolerance and diversity at the expense of any meaningful engagement with difference—the sheikh is tamed and domesticated. He is crafted as a good, civilized, secular sheikh who nevertheless maintains the erotic remainder of his "big bad blade" to be unsheathed in the privacy of an intimate moment with the white heroine. In the climactic moment between Sheikh Nadim and Iseult, for example, the heroine becomes "dimly aware of something digging into her belly. Belated realization of what it must be had her pulling back for a moment to look down. Nadim followed her gaze to where his ornate dagger was still tucked into his rope belt." When he pulls it out to discard it, he stops to reconsider, and Iseult "shivers slightly, but with anticipation, not fear."[124] The sheikh has learned to use his dagger appropriately—he wields it to cut through the material of the heroine's top, disrobing her before wantonly discarding the dagger in a dim corner of the room. In other words, his big bad blade is harnessed by the biopolitical power of a romantic coupling designed to bolster the alliance of two exceptional states bound through neoliberal imperialism—Arabiastan and the United States.

In scenes like this, desert romances demonstrate that the technology of liberal multiculturalism does not erase erotic and racial difference; rather, it domesticates the difference. The technology disciplines its subjects to be colorblind, which is a form of racial disavowal. Unsurprisingly, the conceit of this disavowal is necessarily discarded along with the sheikh's hastily flung robes in a moment of climactic passion. Once naked, the heroine cannot help but notice the sheikh's "dark hand [which] cupped the heavy weight of her breast. She had to bite back a moan and couldn't look down, knowing that she might collapse altogether if she saw the darkness of his skin against the paleness of hers."[125] As an erotic remainder par excellence, the sheikh's dark, racialized absolute difference ultimately serves to suggest a kind of complementarity with the heroine's whiteness. Safely domesticated, it can be instrumentalized in shoring up her subjectivity through the logic of classic humanist binaries. When the heroine and hero are stripped down to their elemental differences, she feels "some deeply innate feminine instinct kick."[126] In other words, she comes to know herself as a true woman, and she will seek wholeness in union with the sheikh. Seeking resolution in wholeness, further explored in chapter 4, turns out to be its own exceptionalist myth. Like the technologies of security and freedom explored in chapters 1 and 2, the technology of liberal multiculturalism works by taming and domesticating desire, by putting it in its place, and by orienting subjects toward a desire that contributes to upholding the hegemonic structures in which they live.

Desert romances illustrate the integral role that desire plays in technologies of contemporary imperialism, and the deployment of these technologies in the war on terror further illuminates their expansive nature. Targeting enemy combatants through the flexible category of terrorism, the tactics of the war on terror seek to alternately kill, regulate, surveil, and discipline both from within and outside the state's official boundaries. The illiberal nature of these activities is justified through the covert, submerged rationales (i.e., technologies) of security, freedom, and liberal multiculturalism. Together, these technologies of imperialism demonstrate how subjects can come to desire their own repression, a state that can be described more simply as desiring wholeness.

4

To Make a Woman Happy in Bed . . .

To make a woman happy in bed, you've got to be half man
and half woman.
—Omar Sharif, *The Eternal Male*, 130

The problem of dealing with difference without constituting
an opposition may just be what feminism is all about (might
even be what psychoanalysis is all about). Difference produces great anxiety. Polarization, which is a theatrical representation of difference, tames and binds that anxiety.
—Jane Gallop, *The Daughter's Seduction*, 93

Every loved or desired being serves as a collective agent of
enunciation.
—Gilles Deleuze and Félix Guattari, *Anti-Oedipus*, 353

What is sometimes called the "ceremonial tribal" dress of the sheikh and
other times simply referenced as his "robes" in fact operates as a very
complex signifier in desert romances, embodying a network of hybridities that seem to pulsate through the figure of the sheikh and his erotic
attachment to the heroine.[1] Chapter 3 focused on the eroticized racialization of the sheikh and the way the symbol of the robes reconciles the
eroticized danger of his exotic otherness and the recursive safety of his
(white) civilized origins or socialization. This chapter expands on how
these dichotomies are used in desert romances, particularly in shoring
up subjectivity where the polarization of difference—with regard to
gender (masculine/feminine), race (white/dark), Arabiastani subjectivity (good sheikh/terrorist), and civilization (modern/backward)—serves
to "tame and bind [the] anxiety" of subject formation, to reference the
Gallop epigraph. Romance novels, generally, are allegories about the
benefits of bourgeois heteronormative coupling. But that is not all there

is to say about them. More interesting is the role that binaries play in the process of preparing the hero and heroine for their happily ever after ending. Like Iseult, the heroine from *Breaking the Sheikh's Rules*, the heroines must be awakened to their "deeply innate feminine instinct" to realize the perfect complementarity of coupling with the raw masculinity of the sheikh-hero. Inscribed in the narrative arc of romance novels, in other words, is a conception of subjectivity as striving toward wholeness and toward the lesson that to achieve this wholeness, one must submit to or become tamed by the other. The novels dramatize the paradox that becoming a legible subject requires being subject to the disciplining norms of the categories that describe us.

In desert romances, this desire for wholeness resonates simultaneously at the level of the state and therefore reflects on the architecture of imperialism in the war on terror. As previous chapters have discussed, the myth of exceptionalism seeks to shore up the image of the nation-state as benevolent and reluctant imperialist, while actively glossing over its ambivalent and paranoid mode. In other words, it strives toward a stable presentation despite its own paranoid instability. For this reason, the nation-state installs and magnifies the desire for hegemony, as exemplified through what I have been calling its key technologies. Indeed, the three technologies of imperialism described in earlier chapters obscure their own repressive nature while simultaneously training the characters of desert romances and subjects of the state to desire them. Through the example of the war on terror, the three technologies are alive and well in most desert romances. The first technology, the quest for security, actually cultivates more violence and insecurity. The second technology bills itself as freedom, when it is actually about submission. The third technology masquerades as an exercise in tolerance and respect for differences, when it actually aims to manage, tame, and discipline difference. Rather than introducing a new technology for analysis, this chapter investigates the ambivalent architecture of desire in the imperialist war on terror, focusing on how it shores itself up through the promise of wholeness as exemplified in the framework of the love story. If the three technologies of imperialism reveal how desire can be oriented toward hegemony, the structure of the love story reveals how desire for hegemony can be perpetuated: the narrative drive toward wholeness trains desire to invest in the teleology of the stable, happily-ever-after ending.

The Robes Make the Man

As should be clear by now, the sheikh-hero is structured around a complex network of hybridities. He is both honorably bound by tradition and fiercely modern; he is simultaneously savagely, stunningly male, and vulnerably sensitive in the face of the heroine's inner and outer beauty; he is primitive, primal, and animalistic while demonstrating flashes of his cultured and civilized training and upbringing. He is therefore at once the perfect blend of Eastern and Western, of exotic other and familiar white masculinity. Because the aim of this chapter is to explore what is at stake in these simultaneously structuring and unstable binaries, I employ the metaphor of the half-life of radioactive elements. What essentially makes matter radioactive is its instability; radiation is the energy released in particles or rays from this highly unstable matter, a decay that is measured by the unit of a half-life. While the basic theory behind radioactive decay is the idea that all matter tends toward stability, here the metaphor serves to highlight the sheikh's actual instability, albeit alongside the paradoxical (and stubborn) representations of him as structured by stable binaries. Indeed, the half-life unit of radioactive material suggests that it is infinitely unstable (i.e., releasing half of its energy in constant intervals), even if it is tending toward stability. In the case of the sheikh-hero, the tendency toward stability is manifested in a representation that attempts to fix him in a binary framework and therefore obscure his instability. As suggested by Mahmood Mamdani's "good Muslim, bad Muslim" formulation, the binary also easily maps onto representations of the war on terror. In short, it is an integral binary to the architecture of the war on terror.

That the sheikh-hero's robes are a key desirable element is in itself noteworthy, given the general perception in U.S. popular culture about the feminizing nature of traditional Arab dress. One of the most prominent symbols of this dress in U.S.-Anglo popular culture is that of Peter O'Toole as Lawrence of Arabia, himself an eroticized figure among desert romance fans even if he is simultaneously an ambivalent figure more generally. Steve Caton's anthropological analysis of the film *Lawrence of Arabia* summarizes the ambivalence of Lawrence's sexuality in a way that clarifies the symbolic importance of his "flowing robes that would appear feminine, at moments even bridal."[2] The multiple ways that Lawrence is feminized (through his donning of the "flowing robes"; his eye-lined eyes; and his intellectual, soft-spoken nature) gesture to anxieties about (effete) masculinities at the same time that O'Toole as Lawrence is also considered classically masculine, from his physical square-set jaw and cheek structure to his role as military leader. Nevertheless, in the many popular engagements with the film, the ruminations on the femininity of Lawrence—which sometimes border on obsession—quickly parlay into meditations on, or simply crass references to, the presumed homosexuality of T. E. Lawrence himself. A good example of the latter is *MAD* magazine's parody "Flawrence of Arabia," discussed in Caton's book.[3] While the film is not the focus of my analysis here, it shows that the gender dichotomy central to desert romances actually functions as a complex matrix of intersecting binaries. Desert romances' stubborn focus on Lawrence of Arabia as an erotic and supremely masculine sex symbol despite his ambiguity further demonstrates that the function of the matrix is to render his ambiguous, unstable qualities into a rigid framework. It serves as a (lead) shield from his radioactive instability.

As both a key symbol of the sheikh's virile magnetism and simultaneously a (submerged) indicator of femininity and backwardness, the ceremonial dress, or robes, of the sheikh-hero is actually a perfect symbol for the architecture of ambivalence that defines paranoid imperialism. Like the symbol of the robes, which are continuously reified in desert romances as stable symbols of masculine virility, the mode of imperialism in the war on terror is continually reified as a benevolent, albeit grandiose savior. When the oppositional pole of ambivalence manifests itself—the femininity of the sheikh's robes or the vulnerability of the U.S.-Anglo empire to terrorist attacks—it is quickly transformed into a stable, structuring binary. For the sheikh-hero, this ambivalence is rendered as a complementary quality that makes him whole, and in that way, the radically destabilizing image of fluttering, flowing robes is disarmed.

The symbol of the sheikh's robes here can serve as a sort of synec-doche for the war on terror more generally. The radically destabilizing vulnerability of the imperial power must be constantly recast as complementary to the logic of benevolent imperialism. The imperial power must save the world from the threat of terrorism, even as imperialism constantly fosters an environment in which terrorism will flourish.

In desert romances, the key unit of analysis is a matrix of desire, where the word *matrix* is meant to invoke Judith Butler's *Gender Trouble*, in which she introduces the notion of the heterosexual matrix. To put it in the words of sheikh-hero Zahid in *Monarch of the Sands*, he is "troubled by desire."[4] Butler's use of "trouble" has at least a double valence; gender is trouble for the subject who is subjected to its normalizing influence. At the same time, her theoretical intervention seeks to trouble the category of gender, revealing its precarious and mutable structure. Desire, too, has this double valence. Desire is trouble for the sheikh-hero because it seeks to tame him. However, an engaged theoretical troubling of desire can reveal the radical potential in following what Deleuze and Guattari call desire's "lines of flight," or the aspects of desire that tend toward destabilization rather than shoring up and reinforcing. Understanding desire as a matrix is also meant to signal the network of identity categories that also experience "trouble." An obvious example is W. E. B. DuBois's formulation about the "problem" of the color line with the infamous question: "How does it feel to be a problem?"[5] Perhaps most importantly, the affective focus of the question—how does it *feel* to be a problem?—orients us toward the psychic registers of the "troubling" of identity and subject formation, while simultaneously embedding the psychic in a consideration of the social register. This chapter asks what it means to be "troubled by desire," emphasizing the simultaneous psychic and social registers of the paradigm and therefore flipping the traditional psychoanalytic focus on the (private) individual to the social functions of desire.

The matrix of desire that so troubles Sheikh Zahid, then, is structured by a network of modern binaries that seem to tend or strive toward an idealized wholeness. Constitutive of the liberal-humanist subject, the matrix of desire captures a network of possible identifications and stabilizes them through the rigid rubric of binaries, a rubric that disciplines any excess or excises any subjective remainder to render the subject as whole. For the sheikh-hero and his other half, the white heroine, these complementary binaries are articulated through the tropes of sex or gender (masculinity and femininity) and self or other (especially the racialized and colonialist invocations of this binary, most commonly rendered as white versus black, primitive versus civilized, barbaric versus enlightened, and religious versus secular). Just as the characters will individually strive toward wholeness through a proper embodying or inhabiting of these categories, the desire for wholeness further resonates at the level of romantic coupling—hero and heroine will complete each other. Wholeness here obscures its own reliance on loss. Wholeness cannot be achieved unless the excesses and remainders of subjectivity are lopped off, obscured, or suppressed. Indeed, wholeness itself is given a primordial status that presages the inevitable losses that result from binary differentiation; even if it does so retroactively, wholeness installs itself as an idealized origin. The heroine, for example, must come to realize that her primal, essentialized femininity was there all along—it just needed to be awakened by the equally primal and essentialized masculinity of the sheikh-hero.

This striving toward wholeness, common to most romance novels, takes on an added resonance in desert romances. It demonstrates the way the micropolitics of desire simultaneously reverberates in the macropolitics of desire that propels the war on terror. In *A Thousand Plateaus*, Deleuze and Guattari write: "Our security, the great molar organization that sustains us, the arborescences we cling to, the binary machines that give us well-defined status, the resonances we enter into, the system of overcoding that dominates us—we desire all that."[6] In this articulation of how we come to desire our own repression, Deleuze and Guattari stress the kinds of subjectification—like the use of binary structures to contain a spectrum of possible identifications and the aggressive assignment of identity categories that come to shape and define us ("the system of overcoding that dominates us")—that speak the language of wholeness. The striving toward wholeness that is so exemplified by romance novels echoes in desert romances and demonstrates that these subjectifying processes are integral to the imperialist project as well. The nomad/warrior/terrorist is reterritorialized by the sheikh-hero, who settles the nomadic tribes of Arabiastan to enter into exceptional alliance with U.S.-Anglo powers, a move that echoes the white heroine's recovery of her lost feminine essence when she realizes that she must submit to freedom.

The troubled desires of both sheikh-heroes and feisty heroines in desert romances could certainly be attributed to classic psychoanalytic tropes, such as the loss of parental figures at an early age or the unearthing of a buried authentic femininity in the heroine or the savage and primal masculinity in the sheikh. (Together, these tropes form the semblance of a sexuality made whole.) To stop there, however, would miss the way these narratives index melancholic losses—that is, abstract forms of loss that have no direct referent often because they represent an unattainable ideal—on a social and modern order. The notion of the (exceptional) liberal nation-state and the humanist subject as a critical building block of liberal democracies, for example, are two key modern concepts structured around melancholic loss—they maintain a sense of wholeness that is predicated on striving toward an original state. In this sense, Zahid's troubled desire is not solely indicative of an individual and internal struggle; it is perhaps more illustrative of the way that desire mediates external, social processes. Deleuze and Guattari criticize psychoanalysts for colonizing (one could also say privatizing) social repressions by consistently reading them through the paradigm of sexual difference, especially through the reductive concept of lack as a key modality of desire. Following Deleuze and Guattari, then, I aim to reorient desire toward the social register by using their concept of desiring-machines, which was later formulated into the concept of assemblage.[7] *Desiring-machines* is a phrase that attends to the role of desire in the production of life; the phrase simultaneously emphasizes the imbrication of desire in the social and material realm (think about the Marxist notion of relations of production) and the idea that desire is not predicated on lack but is rather constructive. To put it more simply, desiring-machines articulate how the power inherent in the Freudian concept of libido and in the Marxist concept of labor converge in the Deleuze and Guattarian notion of desire, which is a productive force rather than an aftereffect of lack.[8] Insisting on this expanded understanding of production, Deleuze and Guattari can then argue that just as desire is not simply private or individual, neither is labor under capitalism solely social; the two entities are co-constitutive in crucial ways. The idea is to unlock both the libido and the unconscious from the cage of the privatized individual and to note the many ways that the libido and the unconscious invest the social milieu and therefore participate in multiple kinds of production.

Much more than a theoretical concept meant to invoke a complex grouping or mixing of factors, assemblage is useful because it signals the fluidity of desire: desire can be oriented toward producing new potentialities (deterritorialization) or toward the antiproductive force of fixing and stabilizing (reterritorialization). Deleuze and Guattari's rubric of the "tetravalence of assemblage" argues that the force of desire moves along an axis that can alternately—or even simultaneously—deterritorialize and reterritorialize (see the preceding endnote for a more detailed explanation). Taken together, the concepts of desiring-machines and assemblage chart how, through desire, objects and drives can both become invested with and divested of meanings, symbolic signification, and subjectification to both create and foreclose new kinds of life-giving possibilities.

Sheikh-heroes in desert romances serve as object lessons of how a symbolic figure—the sheikh as a specimen of masculinity—can be brought into being discursively through his characterization as a civilized, cooperative individual to be corrected or as an irrationally backward terrorist. At the same time, they remain theoretically open to the possibility of being either reterritorialized—appropriated by the imperialist machinery of the war on terror—or deterritorialized, escaping the signifying logic of the war on terror. In short, the concept of assemblage is useful because it accounts for the way that desire can both reinforce hegemonic forces and narratives and lead to avenues for disrupting or evading these forces and narratives. It explains how something can be both stable and unstable simultaneously.

First, let us consider the former, reterritorializing, function of desire exemplified in desert romances. The overcoding, or reterritorializing, impulse is so strong in desert romances that the operative binaries (feminine/masculine and civilized/primitive) and the key logic of complementary wholeness are even apparent in gay desert romances. Despite their marginality, then, gay desert romances can be even more exemplary of normativizing impulses than can mainstream examples.[9]

"I've Been Rescued by Lawrence of Bloody Arabia"

So exclaims Russ—the sheikh's British lover—upon his first encounter with Sheikh Ashmit, the troubled future king of Al Nashan in Kitti Bernetti's Desert Nights.[10] As one of the few gay desert romances, it nevertheless proves to be exemplary in both its articulation of orientalist themes and the subtext of its troubled desires. Desert Nights is remarkably similar to mainstream (hetero) romances with respect to several key elements. The sheikh is duty-bound and loyal to his country, something signaled not only by his impending succession to the throne, but also by the very premise of his encounter with his future lover; the sheikh is sent to rescue a visiting English teacher from terrorists to ensure that "big powerful countries [did not] mock his beloved state of Al Nashan and call it backward, third world."[11] He hails from a "newly rich" nation due to a recent oil discovery, and the new wealth creates a strong tension with the traditional, nomadic past of the region.[12] The desert is simultaneously an isolated place as well as a space of creative self-exploration (it is both the place where Ashmit learns how to become a true sheikh and the landscape that greets him with isolating silence after his first sexual encounter with Russ). Even the key symbol of what makes a sheikh so hot makes its appearance—Ashmit gallops to save Russ, his black abaya (i.e., robes) fluttering in the wind. The same robes are then invoked during the first sexual encounter as "the fabrics between them, sheer silk and thin cotton, did little to shield Ashmit from Russ's . . . monstrous, enormous, fabulous erection."[13]

Two other features in *Desert Nights* bridge the important differences in the gay desert romance, though these differences can be resolved through the logic of the gender (matrix) reversal. Perhaps surprisingly, the novel comes to a happily-ever-after resolution with heterosexual marriage, discussed below. Closely related to the marriage resolution is the theme of finding freedom in captivity. Like many of the white heroines in heterosexual desert romances, Ashmit only finds true freedom by submitting to captivity, as he is ultimately only free to be himself in the "prison of the palace."[14] As Ashmit's connection with white heroines of mainstream desert romances suggests, the main differences in the gay desert romance seem to be related to a perceived or implied gender reversal. While Hsu-Ming Teo, building on Joyce Zonana, suggests that typical desert romances exhibit a feminist orientalism, *Desert Nights* also exhibits classical orientalism in several significant ways.[15] First, though the sheikh is a fine physical specimen of manhood, he holds the position of classic heroine in other ways. He is distinctly feminized in his sexual encounters with Russ, playing both the bottom to Russ's top and the demure virgin (a quality that is emphatically not shared by any of his hetero counterparts, but is shared by many white heroines and is even prominently displayed in some desert romance titles).[16] Second, he is eroticized through overt references to his ethnicity in contrast to the covert racialization of the heterosexual desert sheikhs (discussed in chapter 3). He is described as having "deep cappuccino skin, hair as black as [his] robes and eyes the shade of Persian lilac," all of which hint at his exotic "dark cock," which makes its emergence in the primary sex scene of the novel.[17] Finally, in a stark difference from hetero romances, Ashmit is revealed to be illiterate (the result of being heir to a newly oil-rich nation otherwise steeped in backward traditions). In all these ways, he exhibits some key reversals in relation to the sheikh-heroes of hetero desert romances—he is feminized, overtly racialized, and unlearned (though the author is careful to specify that there are other ways of being educated than just book literacy). Taken together, though, these qualities are precisely what allow him to be incorporated into the overall landscape of the desert romance, in which the romantic denouement speaks to the modern melancholic condition of loss through the language of unity, wholeness, and self-realization.

"It Is Good to Know Oneself"

As in mainstream desert romances, *Desert Nights* seems to partly construct its narrative around a set of common assumptions about Arabiastani sexualities, namely, a particularly repressive and punishing stance on sexuality in general and an especially brutal stance on homosexuality. These kinds of orientalist assumptions can be summed up by Russ's observations about his soon-to-be sheikh lover. As the enlightened-liberal white British subject, Russ seems to be in a unique position to diagnose that "the Arab's frigid ways were belied by his eyes that burnt with smouldering passion."[18] The rest of the story both incorporates and validates U.S.-Anglo liberal-progressive constructions of gay identity. Ashmit progresses through a sequence of steps—first moving past denial of his sexuality, then realizing his true gay identity, and finally acknowledging it to himself and his loved ones—that seamlessly fits into the coming-out narrative, even culminating in a creatively rendered gay marriage (through a formal heterosexual marriage). Two of these plot points deserve further elaboration: Ashmit's process of self-realization and the happily-ever-after (marriage) ending.

Desert Nights fits into the general "gay international" framework as explicated by Joseph Massad, insofar as it incorporates normative (U.S.-Anglo) notions of achieving gay identity through the coming-out process.[19] One particularly orientalist aspect of the narrative is especially illustrative. In a move that gestures to the salience of the lascivious and repressive binary in orientalist constructions of Arabiastani sexuality, Russ ushers Ashmit into the realization of his true sexuality by introducing him to the authentic homosexual past of Ashmit's own culture. When they take shelter in an abandoned cave, Russ (intuitively, it seems) illuminates the erotic gay past of Arabiastan by literally shedding light on cave drawings of men engaged in explicit sexual acts (depictions that had somehow escaped Ashmit's gaze in all the years that he had frequented the caves). Ashmit is astonished that "the ancients had not only indulged in such acts but had celebrated them—built a temple dedicated to them, worshipped them."[20] Thus sheltered by Russ's illuminating knowledge, Ashmit can finally let go of his repressive present to embrace his authentic erotic past. As he submits to a passionate bath and massage, which leads to sex, readers are assured that "Ashmit had arrived in a magical kingdom of colour and pleasure and heightened sexuality."[21] Significantly, this physical arrival into an enlightened gay identity is concretized by a rhetorical-redemptive arrival in a later scene in which he comes out to his father. In a deftly written scene, Ashmit's father simultaneously acknowledges that he knows the truth about his son's sexuality while signaling a tacit acceptance. Counseling his son about the creative ways of interpreting marriage, he affirms both Ashmit's sexuality and the coming-out narrative with the sage assurance that "it is good to know oneself."[22] In other words, he implies that self-knowledge leads to liberation, a message that simultaneously invokes the regulatory freedom through captivity discussed in chapter 2 as well as the disciplinary mechanism of self-knowledge through confession, which clearly operates through the hegemony of the coming-out narrative.[23] Thus, Ashmit is ushered into a particular construction of liberal-humanist subjectivity that operates through the regulatory mechanisms of identity politics.

Ashmit's and Russ's happily-ever-after ending further cements them within a homonormative script, which could even be described as homonationalist since it replicates U.S.-Anglo constructions of gay identity as based in the rhetoric of individual (human) rights. In reaching the teleological end point of the coming-out (progress) narrative, Ashmit decides he cannot live a lie and confesses to his betrothed that he is in love with a man. This news turns out to come as a relief to his fiancée, Ashwarya, who has fallen in love with a servant in the palace.[24] With this potentially sticky situation resolved, then, Ashmit proposes the perfect plan: he and Ashwarya will wed as planned, arrange to (permanently) retire to adjoining rooms in the palace with their respective lovers, and they will bear the fruit of offspring through artificial insemination, a process to be facilitated by their respective lovers. The scene in which he suggests the plan to Russ makes it clear that he is in fact making a marriage proposal since Russ responds: "That sounds like a proposal . . . shouldn't you get down on your knees?" before assuredly answering, "I will . . . gladly I will."[25] Enacted through the performative speech act of bourgeois marriage par excellence, Ashmit's story is thus resolved with a (gay) "marriage made in heaven."[26]

Though *Desert Nights* does not appear on the master list of desert romances on the "Sheikhs and Desert Love" website, it is not a unique example of desert romances but rather an exemplary representation of the genre. It demonstrates, further, the constellation of unstable binaries that comprise orientalist discourses and the ways these binaries tend toward stability—that is, the ways their radioactivity is narratively contained. In romance novels, gender and sexuality operate in particularly illuminating ways to explore this tendency toward stability as an effect of late-modern formations, especially in relation to subjectivity. One clear instance of this phenomenon is evident in the language of wholeness, exemplified in a climactic scene between Ashmit and Russ: "[Russ] ran his lips up Ashmit's taut tummy, over his pulsating chest, stilling his thundering heart, kissing his collarbone and finally, he sealed the deal kneeling over Ashmit and taking his lips in one superb, lusty, never-ending kiss which Ashmit felt would suck all the lifeblood out of him if it weren't for the fact that it was breathing life into him, and that it made him feel whole."[27]

This first and, in a way, final moment of realization for Ashmit is what sets the rest of the narrative resolution on its course—his self-confession, his coming out, and his happy union of both hetero- and homonormative marriage. The language of wholeness, in particular, points toward the larger frame of desire that is at work. Ashmit's happy union is a concrete example of how melancholic loss is repetitively and imaginatively resolved through the fantasies of universal/humanist subject formation and the institution of hetero- and homonormative marriage. In desert romances, the melancholic loss further resonates at the level of the imperialist nation-state, which resolves its instabilities through its own set of structuring binaries, often by allying with exceptional Arabiastani rulers. Desert romances exemplify the way the matrix of desire drives the war on terror. Because the matrix functions to reterritorialize desire, tethering it to a stable, binary structure through the fantasy of wholeness, the matrix demonstrates how desire becomes an operative and key element of hegemony. Turning again to the mainstream desert romances and their defining characteristics, the following section explores the architecture of the matrix of desire. Through a consideration of Lawrence of Arabia, a key figure of erotic comparison for sheikh-heroes, the precarious nature of the matrix of desire becomes more apparent, which is why its apparent stability must constantly be refortified.

The Hybridity of Lawrence of Arabia

In his ghostwritten memoir *The Eternal Male*, Omar Sharif (born Michael Shalhoub) quips that "to make a woman happy in bed, you've got to be half man and half woman. The converse is equally true."[28] The statement is quite interesting as it comes from a man who revels in his own hypermasculinity and ultravirility, if we are to take the memoir at its word, and is particularly telling when brought into productive tension with the title of the memoir. In the title *The Eternal Male*, Sharif's manhood is afforded primacy with respect to his self-identification, and it is also described (through the adjective "eternal") in ways that lend it long-term stability and even rigidity. Further, another simultaneous, productive tension operating in the many implied associations of Omar Sharif and Lawrence of Arabia points toward a crucial racial hybridity as well. For example, in the gay romance discussed above, the white British lover imagines himself to be rescued by "Lawrence of bloody Arabia," despite the fact that Lawrence of Arabia is himself a white British subject lionized for his role in saving Arab people from the brutal Turks (or, at least to have critically aided Arabs in saving themselves).

Indeed, in mainstream desert romances, the sheikh-hero is consistently identified with Lawrence of Arabia, which signals his implicit ethnic and racial hybridity (recall from chapter 3 the various ways that whiteness and civilization are coded into the character of the sheikh-hero).[29] In blogs and author posts describing the appeal of the sheikh-hero, both Lawrence of Arabia and Omar Sharif are mentioned (see the section "Anatomies of the Sheikh" in the introduction for numerous examples). Notably, both the character and the actor playing him—Peter O'Toole—are eroticized as Lawrence of Arabia, while in the case of Omar Sharif, only the self-described Westernized actor is eroticized, and not his Arab character.[30] Various characteristics of Lawrence of Arabia and Omar Sharif seem to be melded into the single character of the sheikh-hero. In fact, taken together, Omar Sharif and Lawrence of Arabia represent a set of structuring binaries that define the desert romance genre. These binaries can be organized into three main categories—the gender and sexuality of the virile, aggressive alpha male who reveals feminine qualities of sensitivity and sensuality to the heroine; the ethnic and racially identified exotic Arabiastani man imbued with the markers of civilized whiteness; and the orientalist notion of the traditional Eastern leader who has learned to incorporate Western styles of leadership and rationality.

"Flawrence of Arabia" Redux

Lawrence of Arabia is, then, a key figure in desert romances because he invokes the same set of hybridities that also define the sheikh. The historical figure of T. E. Lawrence is an interestingly fraught one. Lionized in many accounts as a hero of the British empire, he himself seemed to hold an anti-imperialist stance (as argued by Steve Caton in particular) and resented the media attention he received upon returning from World War I.[31] Yet, perhaps even more ink has been spilled on the question of his sexuality, a topic that was taken up in the film that starred O'Toole and that *MAD* magazine then parodied (as "Flawrence of Arabia"). For those hagiographic accounts that see heroism and homosexuality as incompatible, Lawrence is often described as asexual, or else the "accusation" of homosexuality is outright denied.[32] One such account from a British colleague of Lawrence describes him in a way that could map seamlessly onto the prototypical sheikh-hero of a desert romance: "[T. E. Lawrence represents] that curious mingling of women's sensibility with the virility of the male."[33] However curious, it is this very mingling that defines the sheikh-hero (and other hero types) in the contemporary romance novel genre.

One defining characteristic of romance novels is the way they signify the soft, feminine side of the hero at the same time that they emphasize his hypermasculinity. In this respect, the suppressed or latent suggestion of Lawrence's homosexuality makes him an even more compelling figure as an object of erotic attraction and emulation in mainstream (heteronormative) desert romances. One widely discussed scene in the Peter O'Toole film helps to suture the question of gender-sexual hybridity to racial hybridity; the aforementioned scene in which Lawrence tries on his robes for the first time. Rendered in a way that emphasizes Lawrence's femininity—he twirls around to enjoy the free-flowing nature of the dress and even examines his own image in the reflection of his dagger—many scholars comment that the scene seems to enact a symbolic marriage between Lawrence and Sharif Ali (the character played by Omar Sharif) since the abaya is a gift from Ali.[34]

The reading of marriage here clearly depends on a simultaneous mapping of the binary of femininity and masculinity onto the two characters. However, the binary is both fluid and contingent—it exists simultaneously in each character even as it is entwined in the frameworks of race and orientalism. Steve Caton, for example, points out that in the "bridal" scene, Lawrence's dagger serves as a marker of masculinity, even if it is ambivalently and simultaneously rendered as a symbol of (feminine) vanity.[35] Further, Lawrence is especially read as feminine in his new robes because he is white—to be "Easternized" is already feminizing, and the white and flowing nature of the robes reads to a Western audience as feminine with bridal overtones. Sharif Ali, on the other hand, is already feminized by an orientalist framework, which is partly what allows him to be read as masculine in this scene. In other words, because of his hierarchical position relative to Lawrence in this particular scene, he can be read as contingently masculine. At the same time, his eroticization depends on the orientalist notion of hypersexualized masculinity (as Omar Sharif well knows, judging from his memoir), which in turn draws on romanticized ideas about exotic others.

Some particularly modern concerns about masculinity also flutter around the often masked, but usually implied questions about Lawrence's sexuality. Though cast as a war hero by many accounts, he is also often recognized for his slight build and effete manners, details that parallel many of the discourses surrounding Rudolph Valentino, the actor who played the title role in *The Sheik*. Considered by many to demonstrate a polarization of the "increasing effeminacy of men and the masculinity of women," both of these key figures in the world of desert romances were ironically coded as threatening to the gendered social order precisely because of their femininity.[36]

These observations about both the centrality of Lawrence of Arabia to desert romances and the ironic contradictions therein demonstrate a number of related ideas. First, Lawrence of Arabia is a radioactive character, particularly in terms of the half-life metaphor. In observing how the binaries of gender, sex, and sexuality reveal themselves to be fluid and unstable in the discourses surrounding both Lawrence himself and the film *Lawrence of Arabia*, it becomes all the more curious that Lawrence of Arabia is consistently invoked as a stable symbol of masculine sexuality vis-à-vis the sheikh-heroes of desert romances. Indeed, desert romances themselves are a supreme example of the half-life process through which the sheikh character is given a patina of stability. He is enshrined within a heterosexual matrix, a concept described by Judith Butler as a "model of intelligibility that assumes that for bodies to cohere and make sense there must be a stable sex expressed through a stable gender . . . that is oppositionally and hierarchically defined through the compulsory practice of heterosexuality."[37]

This is not to say that the gender/sex/sexuality matrix is primary, but the matrix is a key problematic in romance novels and, as such, it illustrates how the larger matrix of desire works. It demonstrates how the patina of stability should be understood as the overt projection or construction of stability. Despite this consciously projected stability, desert romances are irradiated by the unstable latent and suppressed narratives and questions about Lawrence's sexuality. Rather than revealing something about sexuality per se, though, this invisible irradiation points toward a set of larger conflicts and greater ambivalence situated at the core of desert romances—conflicts that are not directly acknowledged. The troubled desires of the sheikh-hero and his heroine orient us toward the trouble internal to imperialism—its own instabilities. The matrix of desire serves to render the imperial formation as a stable whole and to obscure its unstable, paranoid dimensions.

Deeply Feminine and Primally Male

Most romance novels, especially those featuring alpha-male heroes like desert romances, construct a fairly rigid gender binary between the hero and the heroine, though each character somewhat ironically also replicates the binary within his or her own character development. In other words, though the hero is rendered as an alpha male and the heroine as exemplary of femininity, the hero's (feminine) sensitivity and the heroine's (masculine) independence are crucial to their composition. Given this structural characteristic of romances, they tangibly demonstrate that unstable binaries are reified as stable and whole through the matrix of desire.

The prototype of the heroine's gender sensibility can be found in Hull's *The Sheik*. Published in 1919, the novel has arguably been influential for the romance genre as a whole and certainly as a model for desert romances. In this model, the heroine is a headstrong young woman, wholly uninterested in men's attention (and therefore oblivious to her own beauty), and described in clear terms as a classic tomboy. Throughout the course of the plot, aspects of her biography are revealed to the reader and ostensibly explain the strange anomaly of a beautiful, vibrant young woman who seems to be completely alienated from her own deeply feminine sexuality. These details are usually vaguely related to the heroine's having lost her parents at an early age or, especially, to her having been estranged from her mother because of death or betrayal.

Given the commonality of parental loss and especially mother abandonment or betrayal in romance novels, a psychoanalytic reading almost begs to be made.[38] Keeping in mind the goal of extending what is often seen as a purely internal psychic mode of analysis to foreground its operation in the social, collective domain, we can read these plot details as illustrative of the fundamental architecture of the matrix of desire. Significantly, the descriptions of the heroine's femininity and the hero's masculinity often revert to essentialist or biological notions of the innateness of these qualities. They also strongly suggest that the qualities are complementary—that is, each person needs the other (gendered) opposite to bring out his or her latent innate gender (and sexuality). In other words, the descriptions are allegories that stabilize both gender and sexuality into a rigid binary. If romance novels in general depend on common assumptions about the rigidity of natural biological essences to tame, or at least subdue and repress, the irradiating instability of gender and sexuality, then desert romances demonstrate how this same operation of taming and subduing radical instability plays out at the level of imperial formation as well. Though the notion of a half life in radioactive materials implies the tendency toward stability to be a natural process, the cultural metaphor of radiation reveals the veneer of stability to be an unnatural and fabricated operation of taming and subduing. Such an operation upholds the project of imperialism—not in the outward sense of brutal, visible domination, but rather in the internal, subtle sense of cultivating a desire for one's own repression.[39]

One particularly illustrative passage from Abby Green's *Breaking the Sheikh's Rules* demonstrates some of the key elements of how this phenomenon often functions in desert romances: "And yet . . . some deeply secret and feminine part of her had *thrilled* inside when she'd seen him in the flesh. . . . After losing her mother at the tender age of twelve, she'd never had anyone to encourage her out of her naturally tomboyish state . . . this complete stranger seemed to have unlocked something deeply feminine within her."[40] Crucially, if not entirely "secret," this pure and primal femininity is always located "deep" within the heroine, inaccessible to her unless it is "unlocked" by the impossibly, perfectly male sheikh-hero.[41] Though her tomboyish qualities are described as natural, it is clear from the passage that a tomboyish character, while natural as a developmental stage, must give way to the heroine's innate femininity that is her true essence—which in turn must be nurtured, coaxed out, or unlocked by someone with whom she feels safe. Though it comes as a surprise to her, it is either the sheikh's ultimate masculinity or his culture's preservation of traditional femininity that sparks her to reconnect with this hidden, yet elemental, part of herself.

The orientalist setting of Arabiastan provides the perfect opportunity to emphasize the conceit of the natural stability of the gender-sexuality matrix—a key unit of the matrix of desire. Desert romances use classic elements of the orientalist setting, for example, the heroine's opportunity to "go native" in the harem-like atmosphere of the sheikh's kingdom awakens her femininity, as in the following passage from Trish Morey's *Stolen by the Sheikh*: "Silk slid across her skin at every move, the metal belt shimmying softly over her hips, and tiny bells jangled softly on her ankles. She felt ultra-feminine, exquisitely sensual and sexy in a way she never had before."[42] In a scene that sounds like it might be inspired by a French orientalist painting—Jean-Léon Gérôme's *The Turkish Bath* comes to mind—the heroine is prepared to experience the transformative, unlocking power of the sheikh-hero. Sometimes this can be achieved simply in physical proximity to the very symbol of his "maleness," as in the following rendering: "Kneeling between his legs, she felt primal, powerful, *female*."[43] At other times, she needs him to "strip away the cloak, to find the woman under the full garb, to explore her feminine shape and hidden curves," in a move that is clearly metaphorical as well as physical.[44] Almost always, she needs him to break through her (implied) artificial defenses to get at the feminine essence underneath that is just waiting to emerge. Penny Jordan manages to attribute this unleashing both to the sheikh's masculinity and to his culture in a subtle *Arabian Nights* reference (recall that the Arabic title translates to *One Thousand and One Nights*): "In her dreams she had known of a man like this, a man of fierce, raw passions, untameable and elemental, a man whose merest touch would arouse her senses in a thousand and one ways."[45] In another account, Bonnie Vanak emphasizes the heroine's own barriers to accessing this part of herself, and her need for the sheikh to take control: "But a deep, secret part wanted him to take control, wanted to surrender to desire."[46] The idea of surrendering to desire in particular helps answer the question of why romance novels tend toward and cultivate the idea of the stability of the gender binary; at the same time, it implies that surrender—or submission—is a fundamental orientation of the matrix of desire.

In the typical rendering of the sheikh's (rigid and stable) masculinity, a sense of complementarity is emphasized, which sets up a concomitant, if subtle, notion of wholeness. The authors are first careful to clearly indicate that the hero's maleness is particularly and uniquely coaxed out by the heroine. Delaney's desert sheikh reveals that "around her he always felt primal, needy, lusty," and Olivia Gates assures readers that the sheikh-hero's "maleness only manifested around [the heroine's] manifestation of brazen womanliness."[47] As indicated in the descriptions of the heroine's femininity, the hero's masculinity is unearthed as a "primal" or "elemental" aspect of his being.[48]

It becomes clear that together, the characters' elemental and innate femininity and masculinity form a complementarity that is ultimately transformative for both the hero and the heroine. Though sometimes expressed through the trope of sexuality, as in Ryan's *Burning Love*, in which "unleashed passion made sexual savages of them both," it displays a deeper meaning as well.[49] In *The Sheik Who Loved Me*, the author explains that "it was as if the winds of sand had unleashed something savage in both of them."[50] Coming at the end of the novel, both the unleashing or unlocking of innate gendered qualities and their (implied) inherent complementarity are clearly crucial to the resolution of the narrative. In other words, the typical narrative arc of a desert romance (and of other romances featuring alpha males) depends on a rigidification and stabilization of the gender binary through recourse to essentialist ideas about gender. Further, this stabilization works to subtly submerge the clear evidence of the instability of gender in other aspects of the novels' narratives, demonstrated, for example, in the often-cited observation that successful heroines usually display such characteristics as independence, intelligence, and brazenness, which are often socially constructed as masculine.

"If She Let Him Deny Her Love, Then This Half-Life Would Be All She Ever Had"

Omar Sharif's statement that one must be half man and half woman points ironically to both the stability and the instability of the binary as it functions here, which is why the idea of the radioactivity of gender through the particular notion of a half-life aids in explaining such instability. The notion is echoed by the heroine in *Desert Warrior*. She fights for the sheikh's love so that a "half-life would [not] be all she ever had."[51] If anything is elemental, it is the very instability of gender itself. Romance novels also demonstrate a larger social phenomenon of tending toward stability insofar as they illustrate a consistent social imperative to regulate this instability through the constant iteration of gender norms and heteronormativity as naturalized by the binary. The question then becomes: What is the function of this tending toward stability, so clearly rendered in, but by no means exclusive to, mass-market romance novels?

One answer to this question comes in a reconsideration of the function of complementarity in the match between hero and heroine. To recall the gay desert romance that frames this chapter, the emotional climax of the novel comes when the sheikh-hero's lover "breathed life into him and . . . made him feel whole." The sheikh-hero in *The Sheath and the Sword* puts it (nauseatingly) poetically when he affirms to the heroine in the resolution to the novel that she is "the sheath [he's] hungered for [his] whole life."[52] These formulations reveal the fabricated stability of the gender binary to serve as a framework that can address the primacy of loss in modern constructions of subjectivity. In some desert romances, the way that the idea of wholeness serves as a salve for a primal and unconscious loss is stunningly clear, as in Nalini Singh's *Desert Warrior*, in which the heroine's story resolves with the neat assurance that "the hole inside her heart closed forever."[53] In one final example, this loss can also operate at a foundational and unnameable level: "She kissed him back hungrily, trying to feed an unidentified need deep within."[54]

Romance novels deal with the notion of a constitutive loss as central to the ambivalent process of subject formation by rendering this abstract and unnameable sense of loss into a concrete and actual loss of a loved one. In so doing, the novels enable narrative resolution to an immutable problem—here discussed in terms of the trouble with desire. While sexual difference is clearly a compelling problem in romance novels in general, desert romances demonstrate the resonance of troubled desires at a larger (imperialist) state level as well. In fact, White's *The Sheik Who Loved Me* demonstrates the overlapping reverberations of the constructed need for wholeness through the sheikh's own unacknowledged desire to ally with U.S.-Anglo powers. In this novel, the sheikh's kingdom (Azar) is unstable precisely because it has not found a structuring balance between the romantic residue of tradition and the necessity for Western-defined ways of being modern. Sensing the sheikh's struggle between these two forces, the heroine "had a sense that healing Azar, bridging the divide between the ancient ways and the new, would in a sense make this man whole himself."[55] The wholeness of the good sheikh—the cooperative Arabiastani ruler—serves as a synecdoche for the structural integrity of a particular aspect of U.S. imperial formation: rule by proxy through alliance with strategic states in key regions.

When Joan Wallach Scott claims that "sexual difference is an intractable problem," she simultaneously acknowledges its importance to feminist thought and situates it alongside a set of other modern "problems," most notably secularism, which has its own imbrication in the traditional-modern binary.[56] Though sexual difference, through the psychoanalytic concept of lack or absence holds prominence in many genres of feminist thought, it also resonates with a set of losses invoked by its constituent binaries—the nostalgic loss of tradition or nature (or both) in the traditional-modern binary, the loss of the idea of the universal subject in the racial black-white binary, and the loss of a stable notion of ethno-national identity in transnational neocolonial forms of empire. These few examples indicate that the problem of loss as constitutive of the conceit of wholeness is central not only to liberal-humanist notions of subjectivity, but also to colonialist and neocolonialist imperial formations.

The narrative of becoming whole, so common to romance novels, demonstrates the constitutive element of loss in the architecture of the matrix of desire. The structure of the narrative arc in romance novels further demonstrates that the founding loss must be named and properly mourned if it is to be overcome and if the characters are to become whole. For this reason, many stories name a clear object of loss (usually a family member) to be mourned by the hero or heroine. In this way, the story lines provide an uncannily direct answer to the problem of "gender trouble" as theorized by Judith Butler.[57] If melancholia for an unnameable loss (same-sex desire) is what keeps the heterosexual matrix ultimately unstable, romance novels translate melancholia (an unresolvable feeling because the object of loss is abstract or cannot be named) into mourning, a loss that can be narratively resolved and therefore stabilized.

If love stories between hero and heroine demonstrate the micropolitics of desire, they can also speak to the macropolitics of desire insofar as they spin a narrative of wholeness at the state level as well. They quintessentially illustrate the way the matrix of desire functions simultaneously in both the psychic and the social realms. Extending beyond the question of gender in *The Psychic Life of Power*, Butler's application of Freud's "mourning and melancholia" framework provides some of the theoretical tools necessary to also extend analysis of the matrix of desire beyond questions of gender and sexuality. A complementary theorization also comes in Jonathan Flatley's *Affective Mapping*, in which he situates Freud's "theory of melancholia [as] an allegory for the experience of modernity, an experience . . . that is constitutively linked to loss."[58] Through their shared use of a sometimes overlooked quote in Freud's "Mourning and Melancholia," Butler and Flatley both argue for melancholia as a framework that can account for "how psychic and social domains are produced in relation to one another."[59] Having just claimed that mourning and melancholia are "excited" by the same causes, Freud offers the following description in just the second paragraph of his essay: "Mourning is regularly the reaction to the loss of a loved person, or to the loss of some abstraction which has taken the place of one, such as one's country, liberty, an ideal, and so on."[60] The latter half of the sentence not only explicates the imbrication of the psychic and social realms, but also sets up the notion of loss as foundational to each realm. In addition, it helps set the stage for understanding one of the key Deleuze and Guattarian tenets of desire—that a traditionally psychoanalytic notion of desire misleads us narrowly toward the internal psychic realm, thereby obscuring its crucial role in the social realm.

States of Fantasy

Recall that desert romances can be characterized by disavowal. This characterization holds for fans of the subgenre, who repeatedly deny any connection between the novels and the war on terror. It is also true to some extent for those who repudiate the sheikh as an untenable hero, as the sheikh is simultaneously widely claimed as a founding figure in romance novels through genealogies that situate Hull's *The Sheik* as a progenitor to the genre. Why is disavowal necessary for fans of the sheikh-hero? This query leads to the book's broader questions: What can a consideration of desert romances uncover? What aspects of the war on terror can they access that otherwise remain inaccessible or unable to be directly named? Despite the tendency to frame the war on terror as mobilized by fear of or anger at the (violent) terrorist other, the increased popularity of desert romances immediately following the events of 9/11 suggests that desire also guides the war on terror in palpable, yet unacknowledged ways. Through the staging of fantasy in fictionalized Arabiastan, the war on terror is revealed to center around core late-modern concerns about the saliency of the nation-state, the viability of the liberal-humanist subject as a lasting model of personhood, and the fate of both in the contemporary context. In other words, desire orients us toward foundational questions about subjectivity and power in imperialist formations and the (radioactive) instabilities of each.

In her book *States of Fantasy*, Jacqueline Rose notes that "state" had a psychological meaning long before it denoted the modern-day sense of a polity.[61] She further notes the resonance of mental "states"—as indicating some form of madness or illness—with the sociopolitical notion of a state. Anne McClintock's formulation of the U.S. as a paranoid empire and Rose's observations about the layered meanings of "states" help explain the U.S. as a state of fantasy.[62] What can this formulation reveal about the co-implication of the modern nation-state with a psychic state, and what can that imbrication uncover, specifically, about the war on terror? Asserting that Freud "diagnosed statehood as the symptom of the modern world," Rose argues that "psychoanalysis can help us to understand the symptom of statehood, why there is something inside the very process of upholding the state as a reality which threatens and exceeds it."[63] The paradigm of paranoia implies that whatever "threatens and exceeds" the nation-state is based on its own internally produced fears. As with paranoia, this is not to say that in the war on terror, the threat of terrorism is completely nonexistent. Rather, the threat is a gross exaggeration of an actual threat and finally transforms the real threat into an imagined specter that bears little relation to the very real and particular instances of terrorist violence, including those initiated by states themselves.

In her analysis of the "frenzied building" of walls and the fortification of borders as part of the contemporary political reality of globalization, Wendy Brown notes that walls seem to operate as a means of demarcating and consolidating the clear sovereignty of nation-states in an increasingly transnational (and ostensibly postnational) world.[64] Carefully acknowledging that the prefix *post* here does not denote the end or the "after" of nation-states, she asserts that the proliferation of walls nevertheless coincides with concerns about the declining salience, or "waning sovereignty," of nation-states in a context of the transnational fluidity of capital.[65] In turn, this fluidity intensifies transnational migration and increases threats to nation-states that originate in deterritorialized networks—from nonstate actors to cyber or virtual warfare to the seeming immateriality of threats like bioterrorism and radiation. Against this backdrop, walls seem like particularly antiquated and ineffectual lines of defense unless one considers the metaphorical work they do. Indeed, Brown also uses a psychoanalytic framework to theorize the role of walls and borders in the contemporary context: "Viewed as a form of national psychic defense, walls can be seen as an ideological disavowal of a set of unmanageable appetites, needs, and powers."[66] The fortification of walls and borders acknowledges the unmanageable nature of transnational—and sometimes literally radioactive—threats to the imperialist nation-state at the same time that it purports to address these unmanageable appetites, needs, and powers.[67] Walls and borders operate less as literal solutions to the problem of the instability of imperial power and more as powerful metaphors meant to imaginatively and graphically (not to mention geographically) illustrate the stability of the imperialist nation-state.

If wall-building operates primarily in a defensive register and invokes masculinized notions of protection and (militaristic) security, then romance novels work in an entirely different register—even emphasizing the dissolution of walled states in both the national and the psychic meanings. In desert romances, the psychical need for protective walls is very much seen as a weakness in both the hero and the heroine. The characters' work will be to break down these metaphorical barriers to achieve a universalizing humanistic wholeness built on mutual understanding and complementarity. Here, the argument is not that one response is better than the other, but rather that the heroine and hero are reacting to the same problem: the threatened dissolution of an entity perceived to be unified and stable. Both seek to shore up or reify a primordial unity—in one case, the nation-state, and in the other, the state of liberal subjectivity. The hero and heroine often achieve unity because they are bound together through mourning, and they therefore have a clear objective for resolving a fundamental loss. In one common trope, the heroine has lost her mother at an early age and therefore could not develop her own innate femininity until the sheikh's primal masculinity awakened her to it. In other instances, the hero has experienced a profound loss—here the options are wider, as his loss could be a mother, a younger sibling whom he failed to protect, both parents in a tragic accident (better still if the accident involved terrorism), or even a wife (whom he loved, but in a dutiful rather than passionate way). In most cases, the hero or heroine has repressed feelings about this loss and has crafted a protective emotional wall around the loss. The purpose of the narrative trajectory is then to move toward a mutual breakthrough of the emotional walls and toward a complementary union of the sort described earlier.

Building on the argument that romance novels serve as a localized example of some of the mainstream U.S. emotive engagements with the war on terror, the localized function of mourning in desert romances bears a synecdochic relationship to larger states of mourning, to borrow and build upon Jacqueline Rose's evocative phrase. Keeping in mind the idea that melancholia is a form of mourning that does not have a clear object as its focus, desert romances translate the open-ended, unresolvable melancholia of the modern nation-state into a state of mourning. The sheikh-hero laments the erosion of the country's (and his own) tribal and nomadic roots, so he devises a plan to maintain the romantic image of the bedouin nomad while literally settling the bedouin nomad in his country (as discussed in chapter 1). He mourns a lost object— the historical custom of nomadism—to bring the question of nomadism into a modern notion of wholeness and balance. He maintains (and contains) a sense of tradition while simultaneously introducing a U.S.-Anglo notion of modernity to his country. The translation of melancholia into mourning serves to render his Arabiastani nation-state— exceptional in its alliance with U.S.-Anglo powers—more stable. It seeks to gloss over an actual melancholic attachment of the nation-state to nomadism, since nomadism is precisely that unnameable and unacknowledged thing that threatens to exceed the nation-state itself. The matrix of desire represents both overlapping and mutually informing modern constructions of self and (nation) state, reminding us of the way they incorporate a primordial loss into their architecture. Crucially what is lost here is actually an imagined ideal, rather than a clear object (like a loved one). Desert romances repetitively work on addressing melancholia by translating it into mourning for a clear lost loved one and by achieving unity or "wholeness" again through a stable union, thereby obscuring the actual instability of liberal subjectivity. In this way, the "loved or desired" being in the romance novel actually serves as what Deleuze and Guattari call a "collective agent of enunciation" for modern melancholic loss.[68] Both the stable, universal subject and the stable, exceptional state are recovered through the "loved and desired" good sheikh, a collective agent of enunciation for a benign and lasting imperialist alliance, a happily-ever-after ending.

Let us now consider the paradox of desiring one's own repression. In her recent exploration of the importance of feminist psychoanalytic theory to feminist thought more generally, Joan Wallach Scott observes that "desire is the impossible wish to recover the loss or replenish the lack."[69] Though she is referring particularly to the function of loss in the context of sexual difference, the paradoxes of desire and especially their relationship to loss can be applied more generally to subject formation. Indeed, subject formation is just the process that Judith Butler takes up in *The Psychic Life of Power*. For Butler, subject formation is a fundamentally ambivalent (and, in that ambivalence, paradoxical) operation. The ambivalence can be traced to the conflicting meanings and various modes of the root word *subject* itself. The process of becoming a subject depends both on the power of subjugation and on the agential notion of a subject. As Butler explains, "the subject emerges both as the *effect* of a prior power and as the *condition of possibility* for a radically conditioned form of agency."[70] In other words, subjectivity is dependent upon subjugation insofar as the condition for achieving subjecthood is a radical loss or splitting when one enters into the linguistic (symbolic, according to Lacan) realm. If desire wishes to "recover the loss," then the agency of desire also simultaneously aims at the dissolution of the subject (i.e., to recover the moment before splitting and therefore to return to a state when subjecthood was or is not possible).[71] Butler states: "To desire the conditions of one's own subordination is thus required to persist as oneself."[72]

Such a fundamental (or even elemental, to echo the language of desert romances) ambivalence certainly reverberates through the desert romances on many levels, particularly through the desire for freedom, as discussed in chapter 2. The heroine can only become free through submission; she only finds freedom in captivity. Insofar as the standard resolution of the desert romances also tends to imply the way the heroine will help the sheikh-hero bring his country into the modern era, they powerfully invoke the necessary ambivalence of modern states. Bringing Arabiastan into the modern era requires its own submission to freedom, both at the level of individual subject formation and at the level of nation-statehood and the question of sovereignty.

To ground these assertions in the desert romances themselves, it is useful to recall the quote with which chapter 1 concludes. At the precise moment that the heroine has gained her physical freedom, she revokes it, asking: "What was it worth to be free, when you were leaving your heart behind? What was the point of freedom, when you had lost the one you loved?"[73] As the resolution to the novel, the function of this moment is to clearly signal to the reader that the heroine has freely chosen submission. Further, because the author has done the critical rhetorical work to signal that the sheikh himself is not oppressive (all the more important in desert romances, because of the predominant cultural perceptions of Arabiastanis as hyperpatriarchal), the implicit assurance is also that the heroine has willingly chosen to submit herself to love, rather than to the sheikh per se. She does so because the sheikh has helped her to overcome loss and find her authentic self, making her feel whole.

Though the condition of mourning is therefore theoretically resolved by the end of the novel, it still functions as that which has brought and bound hero and heroine together. Romance novels treat these profound, formative losses (usually of loved ones) as a route toward resolution, but as I have argued, they do so by attempting to elide the notion of melancholia, which would maintain a sense of the radical instability of subjectivity. Mourning is a crucial binding and solidifying operation that serves to shore up subjectivity in romance novels and to shore up the imperialist-aligned nation-state in the context of the war on terror in desert romances. Just as the events of 9/11 galvanized collective mourning, terrorist plots or terrorists themselves in desert romances serve as rallying points around which to solidify the sheikh-hero's vision for Arabiastan. The threat of terrorism does not provoke a serious engagement with the question of what political aim it has and what that implies about the inconsistencies of the sheikh's Arabiastani nation. Rather, it provides a concrete point of counteridentification, a way of reifying the imagined ideal of his country's progress-bound exceptionalism. Sheik Kadir of *The Sheik and I* explains it thoroughly yet succinctly to the heroine when he says that Zahid, the quintessential terrorist, "took an old and precious ideal of tribe and unity and love of ancient culture"— all the things the sheikh-hero presumably has learned how to preserve in his balance of tradition and modernity—"and twisted it into a thing of hate and bloodshed. In the name of taking the people he claims to love back to a simpler yet harsher time, he is willing to kill anyone who disagrees with him. He wraps his own twisted need for power in words of heritage and dignity, and then he destroys both in violence and hate."[74] Echoed in many other desert romances, this general sentiment serves as a key stabilizing technique.[75] In the sheikh-hero's estimation, the terrorist seeks to destroy the very ideals that make Arabiastan exceptional. By using the character of the evil terrorist to concretize the threat to the idealized image of Arabiastan, the sheikh obscures the actual inconsistencies and instabilities of his Arabiastani state. Likewise, the events of public mourning in the U.S. immediately following 9/11 served to concretize the exceptional nation-state by translating the melancholia for the imagined ideal into mourning for the actual literal losses incurred.

At the precise moment that the salience of the nation-state and its usefulness as a construct is most destabilized, it is resolidified through the act of public mourning. As much as the U.S. was attacked as an imperialist state on 9/11, the symbols of transnational capitalism also appeared to be key targets. The attacks on 9/11 could have just as easily been a moment for U.S. citizens to decenter the nation-state and question its role in helping to create the conditions for such an attack (in terms of its earlier alliance with Osama bin Laden, for example), but the results were quite the opposite. Describing this reconstituting power of states, Rose writes: "Mourning was the key. . . . No other condition reveals in the same way a tie which binds most powerfully at the very moment when, objectively speaking at least, it has set you free."[76]

Desert romances connect strongly to the idea of a tie that binds most strongly at the moment it has set the subject free; indeed, they repetitively re-create such a paradoxical moment in the classic scene of resolution. Such a scene is all the more powerfully drawn in those desert romances—such as Hull's *The Sheik*—that center on the theme of captivity. At the very moment that the heroine is physically free to go, she finds herself psychically and emotively bound by her love for the sheikh. The melancholic resonance of this scene is to a particularly modern experience of loss that is foundational to liberal-humanist notions of subjectivity and to liberal-democratic notions of nation-statehood. The unnameable desire in this scenario is the desire for a destabilizing notion of freedom—one that would leave her outside the bounds of heterosexual union and rejecting the happily-ever-after ending between her home country and Arabiastan. It would mean attending to a desire for radical dissolution, through which new modes of subjectivity may form. The language of wholeness, so often deployed in the description of romantic union in romance novels, therefore serves as a metaphor for the way that desire comes to be oriented to its own repression. The individual here is portrayed as having willingly chosen the conditions of his or her own subjugation.[77] The person shores himself or herself up through identification with a unified subject position and through allegiance to the exceptional state as a bulwark against—a way of not seeing (i.e., repressing)—the unnameable loss that is a necessary precondition to the illusion of wholeness.

Becoming-Desert Sheikh: Love Deterritorialized

The narrative of wholeness in desert romances serves as a way of reconstituting—and reterritorializing—key technologies in the war on terror, like freedom and security. Recalling that the concept of assemblage encapsulates both the hegemonic recapturing impulses of reterritorialization and the radical potential of deterritorialization, this concept therefore both exposes the paranoid assumptions of unity that shore up the war on terror and simultaneously proposes a means of destabilizing the conceit of wholeness. Indeed, far from responding to a coherent, stable enemy, the war on terror itself operates at a level of abstraction, which invokes a supreme loss of the defining other/enemy/terrorist. This is, in part, why the war on terror is so keen to produce tangible evidence of "enemy combatants" through the constelled infrastructure of military prisons like Guantánamo, Bagram Air Force Base, and Abu Ghraib, which are filled with subjects captured via "actionable intelligence"; of immigration detention centers; of mandatory registration for racially profiled immigrants; of a heightened surveillance of Muslim communities in the United States; and of the expansion of warfare into drone strikes and extrajudicial killing of U.S. citizens.[78] Faced with the dissolution of the modern (humanist) idea of the rights-bearing subject and its correlative, the sovereign nation-state, the framework of the war on terror works to radically reify them. Thus, freedom can, not surprisingly, be realized only at the moment of captivity, particularly if we understand captivity to signal the reterritorialization of both the bounded subject and the sovereign nation-state. In fact, two related and influential tomes, Francis Fukuyama's *The End of History* and Samuel Huntington's *The Clash of Civilizations*, are organized around the logic of a recapture of this particular modality of freedom, one that is circumscribed by neoliberal democratic nation-states. As Brian Massumi might rejoin: "The liberal nation-state is not repressive as such. It is 'democratic.' It makes the 'right' to vote 'universal'—in other words, it gives every body the 'free' choice to abdicate power."[79] Through their simultaneous portrayal of both the individual liberal subject's and the Arabiastani nation-state's submission to freedom, desert romances offer a keen illustration of this "'free' choice to abdicate power."

Desert romances demonstrate how love can operate as a key analytic category for understanding how imperialism functions by producing the desire for one's own repression. Though it is tempting and familiar to read the love story as a reflection of something about the private, bounded, (feminine) individual, it is perhaps more useful to pay attention to the ways that the war on terror invokes its own love story about the sacrifices we must make to vanquish evil actors who "hate our freedom" if we are to love, cherish, and protect the U.S. as an exceptional state.[80]

"Backlit by Radiating Beams of Silver Light"

The primary image of this chapter—the sheikh's robes—helps illustrate both the coherence of the love story as a stabilizing paradigm and the possibilities of a deterritorialized love. The prominence of the sheikh's robes as an erotic and exotic signifier in desert romances evinces the claim once posted on the "Sheikhs and Desert Love" website that one of the qualities that makes the sheikh so hot is his donning of the traditional dress of his country. This claim situates the robes as an unambiguous marker of a hero's alpha-male status. The robes often serve as a prop that makes the hero "look even more dark and gorgeous. And *dangerous*."[81] As in the gay romance cited earlier, they also serve as a means of accentuating the sheikh's penis and of further conflating his penis with a weapon, usually a scimitar or dagger. In *Bella and the Merciless Sheikh*, for example, "Bella's mouth dried as she watched him slide a dagger into the folds of his robe and her stomach fluttered with nerves."[82] Sometimes the sensation is more direct, as with the heroine Iseult, who "was dimly aware of something hard digging into her belly. Belated realization of what it must be had her pulling back for a moment to look down. Nadim followed her gaze to where his ornate dagger was still tucked into his rope belt."[83] Marguerite Kaye, in *The Governess and the Sheikh*, is more direct when she describes the "scimitar arc of [the sheikh's] erection" after having already established that "the wicked scimitar, with its diamond-and-emerald-encrusted golden hilt that hung at his waist was no mere ceremonial toy."[84] Explored in chapter 3, these types of references seem straightforward enough as hypermasculine attributes identified with the eroticized signifier of the phallus (and the exoticized signifiers of scimitars and daggers), but they are far from the only description of robes that populate the romance novels.

Consistent with the earlier discussion of Lawrence of Arabia and Omar Sharif, the sheikh's robes are often also described in movement, with adjectives that bestow a clear sense of fluidity and femininity upon the sheikh. Western dress (such as a suit) often feels "alien and constricting after the more familiar softness of the Arab robes [the sheikh] wears on formal court occasions."[85] Robes are often described as "swirling," "flowing," "fluttering," and "billowing."[86] In one exaggerated case, the sheikh is even attributed with divine qualities: "She touched his robe above his arm and he felt the heat of her fingers sear through the material . . . the swaying robes making it seem as if he glided just a little above the earth."[87] The combination of these two kinds of attributes—hypermasculine and undeniably feminine—in one key signifier of the sheikh's persona can easily be reconciled with the drive toward wholeness that has been explored throughout the chapter. In this case, femininity and masculinity would parade as a structured opposition that tends toward stability through the logic of complementarity and whole-ness, much as in Omar Sharif's statement that one must be "half man and half woman" to make a woman happy in bed.

A closer focus on the adjectives cited above, however—swirling, flut-tering, billowing, and flowing—suggests a much more fluid and unstable dynamic at work. One final quote from the desert romances solidifies the point: "Dressed in his Bedouin robes, Seth's tall, impressive form was a solid black silhouette backlit by radiating beams of silver light."[88] A shift back to the metaphor of radiation offers a way of understanding a seeming contradiction at work in the primacy of robes as signifier. Put simply, the robes belie the instability of the gender-sexuality matrix and, more importantly, of the matrix of desire as it functions in the novels. The representative focus on robes, in other words, roughly mimics the concept of the half-life of radiation. The symbolization of the sheikh's robes attempts to fix them as stable signifiers—or at least as tending toward stability through their shoring up in the structured binary of femininity and masculinity. Insofar as binaries imply a complementar-ity that constructs a whole, excluding other possibilities that would fall outside the dichotomous framework, this binary works to reify a notion of subjectivity firmly rooted in the idea of the modern, liberal, rights-bearing subject. What these representations seek to keep at bay, then, is precisely the notion of subjectivity (and its identifiers such as gender, sexuality, race, and nation) that riots against such a stable conception. This subjectivity is not disciplined by the overdetermined notion of de-sire as emanating from lack, but is rather radically opened onto the no-tion of desire as a productive force.

In his ruminations on the Capitalism and Schizophrenia series, Brian Massumi describes the "pre-Oedipal body . . . not [as] the debilitating lack of an old unity but a real capacity for new connection."[89] Such a real capacity for new connection may be endlessly tamed and disciplined through the tropes of wholeness (manifested in "modern," "liberal" sub-jectivity) and freedom-through-captivity that have been explored here, but it cannot be completely eradicated. Though one must be careful not to romanticize, the metaphor of radiation enables a recuperation of these stabilized and tamed possibilities. The turn toward possibility through the rehabilitation of instability is the erotic remainder of desert romance narratives. Pointing to the precarious nature of "walled states," it also colors outside the lines of the narrative structure of the love story. Following the cutting edge of deterritorialization that exists in these thoroughly stratified love stories emphasizes the potential for unraveling the notion of U.S. imperialism in the war on terror as inherently stable and infallibly solid. The very repetition of these stories demonstrates the anxious desire to pin down the flowing, fluttering, billowing nature of the war on terror itself.

Conclusion

The Ends

Romance novels are famous for being formulaic, yet this feature also serves as an apt metaphor for the formulaic, structured, and repetitive narratives of empire. Indeed, even the claims of newness and exceptionalism are standard features of imperialism, leading Ann Stoler to propose that it is less useful to ask what is new about U.S. empire and more pertinent to question why the claim of newness is so important to the imperialist narrative.[1] Perhaps the claim is precisely to disguise the fact that it is the same old story with new characters in a novel (in this case Arabiastani) setting. Yet despite the usually disparaging observation that romance novels adhere to a structured narrative formula, potential lines of flight all throughout desert romances at least gesture to other possibilities, even if they are ultimately refastened to the recognizable grid of the imperialist love story. The real revolutionary activity in which the heroines partake, for instance, is ultimately yoked to the image of the sheikh as an enlightened, liberal subject—someone with whom she can willingly submit to freedom (see chapter 2). Rather than focus on this feature as evidence of romance readers' pathologically enjoying their own oppression, however, this book argues that romance novels exemplify the modern mapping of desire onto formulaic and stratifying narratives. Desert romances, in particular, provide a means of exploring how the war on terror itself is framed in terms of the logic and structure of a love story, where the goal is to be made whole through realizing one's own essential and exceptional qualities. In the focus on the figure of the terrorist, analyses of the war on terror have mostly glossed over the romance with the good sheikh, an aspect of the war on terror that desert romances rather remarkably take up.

This book has sought to investigate what desert romances can tell us about the "unknown knowns" of the war on terror—in other words, the unspoken and unacknowledged attachments, beliefs, and identifications that nevertheless guide the war on terror. While the state focuses on fear—fear of a terrorist attack most specifically—to justify increased militarization and surveillance, desert romances suggest that love is (at least) an equally salient lens through which to understand how the war on terror works and persists. The popularity of desert romances during the war on terror has revealed the liberal-enlightened sheikh as a crucial protagonist in this war and has therefore revealed that the war on terror also operates as its own kind of love story. Even for those who do not read desert romances—or romance novels at all, for that matter—desert romances are broadly representative of how popular perceptions about both Arabiastan and the war on terror function insofar as the novels demonstrate which perceived realities about Arabiastan can be transformed into a palatable fantasy. As is customary in the romance industry, romance authors build their narratives on a foundation of research based on popular perceptions of the region and the period in which the story takes place. The novels are therefore supremely representative of the war on terror's unknown knowns—the generally unacknowledged attachments and desires that fuel it. Despite the focus on desert romances, then, this book has not been interested in diagnosing romance readers as uniquely submitting to their own repression, but rather in demonstrating that desiring one's own repression is central to the logic of both modern liberal subjectivity and the imperialist coherence of the nation-state.

It is customary to follow the "so what?" of research on representations of Arabiastan in U.S. popular culture with an equally urgent "so what now?" In other words, insofar as research on popular representations of Arabiastani subjectivities in U.S. popular culture has sought to unpack the problematic assumptions that uphold such representations, it also tends to be the subject of a frustrated, shoulder-shrugging demand that the research conclude with some prescriptions for transforming the representative landscape. Even if unintended, though, such a demand re-inscribes a linear-progressive logic—even if things used to be or have been bad, such logic wants to know how we can correct these things. This book has argued that the answer to the question of how to respond has always been present in potential lines of flight not overtly taken. It is not a matter of writing better stories with more multicultural tolerance—in fact, that would only contribute to the imperialist technology of liberal multiculturalism discussed in chapter 3. The answer, instead, may lie in the possibility of reading the story—whatever story one has been reading or telling about the war on terror—in a different way.

At stake in this new reading is a key tension between stability and instability, particularly in terms of perception. The war on terror is simultaneously waged on two fronts. One front is the constant concretization of a (potential) threat: terror. The other front is the corresponding concretization of the exceptional nation-state's and allies' declared need for security against this threat, even if security necessitates such stretches of logic as preemptive wars and humanitarian militarism. Returning to the metaphor of radiation, this reading of the war on terror focuses on the idea that all radioactive material tends toward stability, therefore emphasizing precisely these sorts of concretizations. It takes a lot of energy—or desire—to interpret radiation as linked to stability since even in its spent form, radioactive material continues to scatter and cause instability (e.g., the uranium waste in the aftermaths of the Gulf War and the Iraq invasions continues to have deleterious effects on both the inhabitants of these regions and the soldiers who fought there).[2]

The focus on fear, and specifically on fear of terrorism or a terrorist attack, serves as one particularly salient means of cementing imperialist state narratives about security and self-defense. As this book has argued, the image of the good sheikh similarly concretizes such narratives. According to Deleuze and Guattari, the "three great strata . . . that directly bind us" are the organism, *signifiance*, and subjectification.[3] The authors refer here to three ways that bodies and subjects are rigidly delimited. Much like the concretizations of terror and nation-state mentioned above, such delimitation partly plays out in the war on terror in the particular ways that the notion of the terrorist is constructed. At the level of organism, he is seen as essentially coherent and recognizable. As described in Jerrold Post's *The Mind of a Terrorist* (see chapter 1), the terrorist's body is organized and understood through psychological and cultural traits that come to be melded to biological or essential notions of the body itself. The terrorist is as bounded by these traits as by his skin, which is imagined (like all other bodies in their schema) not to form hybrid or machinic connections with any other types of bodies (organic or inorganic). In other words, the terrorist is conceived of as an organism motivated by inherent traits rather than as a contingent subject molded by a whole series of interactions—for example, with the abrasive push delivered by an occupying soldier at a checkpoint (organic connection) or with the constant invasive hum of an occupying military aircraft that vibrates through one's body (inorganic connection). To understand these connections as machinic means to be attuned to the ways they *work* on the subject to shape his or her drives, desires, and sense of possibility; it is a reference to the concept of desiring-machines.

Desert romances demonstrate that the good sheikh is also subject to such an organized reading of the body, one that recursively utilizes the trope of a romanticized notion of nature. The heroes of desert romances—and, in a way, heroes of the war on terror—are primal figures etched out of the rough desert environment (see chapter 1). Though desert romance sheikhs are fantasy figures, their characteristics are drawn from popular images of Middle Eastern leaders and from the imagined connection to the primal, elemental desert dweller. Such efforts to stratify central figures of the war on terror at the level of the organism must constantly be redoubled and fortified, however. One of the reasons that the figure of the suicide bomber captures attention is precisely because the idea and the action of the suicide bomber directly contradict the stratification of the body in this way—the action literally blows the body apart. Here again the metaphor of radiation is useful. The actions of the suicide bomber have splintering and lasting effects— the unpredictable impacts of which continue long after the operation is carried out. Perhaps this explains why both those targeted by the attacks and those who claim responsibility for them expend such profound efforts to posthumously restratify the body, either through narratives of psychosis on the one hand or of martyrdom on the other.

Here, the stratifying function of *signifiance*, or the signifying capacity of the suicide bomber, can already be discerned. The act of blowing oneself up provokes a linguistic battle to control and organize the interpretation of the event. One means of control is by attributing a label to the body carrying out the action. For groups targeted by the bomber, the label *suicide bomber* and the attachment of this label to a narrative of cultural pathology reinforces the larger narrative of existential threat for the imperialist nation-state, thereby allowing a justification of disproportional military response. For the groups that claim responsibility for the attack, the label *martyr* validates the death as valuable and necessary to the struggle.[4]

The figure of the good sheikh—the allied Arabiastani leader—also gains coherence through the repetitive assignation of a label or signifier, such as the "CEO of Dubai," where the label serves to inscribe the figure as a familiar protagonist of neoliberal capitalism.[5] In desert romances, the sheikh's robes serve as such an organizing signifier, as discussed in chapter 3. Often, the heroine sees the sheikh-hero from a distance and notices that he is "dressed simply in a white robe, the fabric glaring under the beginnings of the Arabian sun."[6] Through such stark descriptions of the sheikh's traditional dress, the sheikh is simultaneously inscribed in a romantic, natural setting as a regal, composed, and civilized leader.

Finally, there is subjectification—the main type of shoring up of bodies and individuals, discussed in chapter 4. Here, the terrorist or the good sheikh is understood through an assigned identity category, which is presumed to have initial coherence at the level of the body or individual (i.e., as a presupposed or even prefabricated essence and coherent subject—in Butler's parlance, the "doer behind the deed"), rather than understood to be rigidly imposed on the body or individual retroactively. The individual is here subjected to a particular set of attributions. For example, my use of the male gender pronoun in the examples about the figure of the suicide bomber points to the functioning of subjectification since the terrorist (and suicide bomber in particular) is indeed constructed as male. Because the aggressive nature of terrorist action is so incompatible with the popular perception of Arabiastani women as meek and oppressed, female terrorists are literally unintelligible within standard narratives about terrorism, and are therefore subject to a whole different set of explanatory and pathological narratives.[7] In the repetition of themes in desert romances, such as that of the progressive, civilized leader of a newly oil-rich region who seeks to advance his country by allying with key U.S.-Anglo powers, we see a reflection of the way that allied Arabiastani leaders can also become subjectified through a romanticized set of discourses.

Reading past this stratifying logic, a new interpretation of both the horrific and the romantic incarnations of the war on terror might rather attend to these figures as assemblages. The notion of the assemblage specifically works against the rigidifying and organizing ("stratifying" in Deleuze and Guattari terms) tendencies of the three "great strata" discussed above. Therefore, conceptualizing the war on terror through the rubric of assemblages could restore a sense of the actual instabilities of the war itself and help acknowledge the potential "lines of flight" that could disrupt some of its more problematic and disturbing characteristics, such as mass detentions of innocent civilians, extrajudicial killing of innocent civilians and U.S. citizens alike, and racial profiling of Arabs/Muslims/Middle Easterners in the United States. Again, despite their formulaic quality, desert romances also surreptitiously point us to the actual fluidity—the radioactive instability before it is tamed by the notion of a half-life—of the sheikh's fluttering, flowing, swirling, and billowing robes. In so doing, they suggest that a trenchant analysis of the U.S. imperialist romance with the good sheikh is equally as important as the investigation of the figure of the terrorist. Indeed, proliferating studies about the nature of terrorism continually obscure or elide an analysis of those exceptional allies in the region that Arabiastan obliquely references.[8]

The concept of assemblage allows us to see how something—here, the figures of the good sheikh and the terrorist and, ultimately, the war on terror itself—can be simultaneously rigid (stable) and fluid (unstable). Recalling that the concept of assemblage is organized according to two axes demonstrates this idea. The horizontal axis shows how the figure (good sheikh or terrorist) or concept (war on terror) gets constructed, while the vertical axis gives it movement—toward "*territorial sides*, or reterritorialized sides, which stabilize it, and *cutting edges of deterritorialization*, which carry it away."[9] On the horizontal axis, then, one has a fluid and vacillating set of forces and frictions between bodies (both organic and inorganic), and enunciations, signifiers, and speech acts that collide up against and transform the bodies in various ways.

In the world of the desert romance hero, the machinic assemblage of bodies could be the sheikh, his robes, and his scimitar-phallus just as easily as it could be the sheikh-hero and his (white) heroine and their sword-sheath connection. They are incorporeally transformed (i.e., the reality of the assemblage is materially shifted) through the narrative itself, which brings the sheikh into being as a liberal, modern civilized subject and which inscribes the heroine into a notion of freedom as only possible through the confines of captivity. In the novels, one also finds the war-on-terror assemblage of the terrorist alive and well. His machinic assemblage of bodies usually ties him to nuclear weapons or uranium-enriching activities, or both; alternatively, he might simply serve as a physical threat to the sheikh's modern ways. In both instances, he is incorporeally transformed through the collective enunciations that subjectify him as terrorist and evildoer. In the narrative arc, he becomes easily disposable. In both of these examples, the stabilizing force of the assemblage predominates. The assemblage's territorializing or reterritorializing sides are activated as the primary intensities, speeds, or movements.

The standard romantic narrative arc (whether in romance novels or in discourses about the war on terror) implies that the territorializing or reterritorializing move is the only possible one; thus, the narrative relates how we come to be oriented toward desiring our own repression. The framework of the assemblage, however, contextualizes the narrative so as to emphasize that the friction of bodies and enunciation described above collides with a movement, speed, and intensity that can either resolidify the assemblage (reterritorialize it) or carry it away (deterritorialize it to enable a line of flight).

While the romance novel genre is not set up for deterritorializing—on the contrary, it is precisely structured to stratify and organize desire—it does provide an intriguing and radiating set of flashes (or flutters) that gesture to the lines of flight subdued by the narrative arc of the story. In other words, the genre reflects the way that larger discourses about the war on terror tend toward reifying the war as stable at the same time that the novels, if read differently, could reflect a different sensibility. Desert romances therefore also gesture to the destabilizing flashes and flutters in the "actual" war on terror, which, as mentioned earlier, is neither concrete nor inevitable. These novels suggest that pursuing freedom can stimulate a joy and desire that far outweighs the risks of freedom. We recall Donna Young's "For the last time the balance of power shifted, away from both of them. But neither cared. The freedom far outweighed the risk," but read these words in a new way.[10] Rather than reinforce a freedom that is nevertheless contained within the structure of a facile happy ending and oriented toward the relentless drive to narrate wholeness, looking differently at desert romances can cultivate a curiosity about the abyss that opens up if we pay more attention to the deterritorializing lines of flight within the standard narrative arc. Irradiated by this new strategy for reading, common narratives about the war on terror can be illuminated with the desire to write still unimagined ends to the narratives that bind, settle, and securitize us.

NOTES

PREFACE

1. Melissa August, "Sheiks and the Serious Blogger," *Time*, August 22, 2005, www.time.com/time/nation/article/0,8599,1096809,00.html; Glenda Cooper, "A Steamy Centenary," *The Age*, February 17, 2008, www.theage.com.au/news/in-depth/a-steamy-centenary/2008/02/16/1202760669725.html; Samanthi Dissanayake, "All Because the Lady Loves a Foreign Accent," *BBC News*, August 14, 2008, http://news.bbc.co.uk/2/hi/uk_news/magazine/7516672.stm; Christy McCullough, "Desert Hearts: In a New Crop of Romance Novels It's Always Midnight at the Oasis," *Bitch* 36 (2007): 29–31; Patrick T. Reardon, "The Mystery of Sheik Romance Novels," *Chicago Tribune*, April 24, 2006, 1; Francesca Segal, "Who Said Romance Was Dead?" *Observer* (London), January 27, 2008, www.theguardian.com/books/2008/jan/27/fiction.features1; Brian Whitaker, "Those Sexy Arabs," *Guardian* (London and Manchester), March 23, 2006, www.guardian.co.uk/commentisfree/2006/mar/23/thosesexyarabs.

2. The website was privately created by Erika Wittlieb, who describes it this way: "Originally, creating the Sheikhs and Desert Love Web site was simply a way for me to practice my HTML skills in the late 1990s. I had the computer and the software I needed, but had no content to post on my Web pages. I looked around my room and spotted my bookshelf with a growing collection of sheikh romance novels, and the idea of creating an online database that featured these novels, which I have loved reading for years, was born" (email message to author, May 14, 2008). She was surprised to receive a lot of media attention and noted that the site attracted a fairly broad base of fans, most of whom were seeking to purchase the books listed. Perhaps for this reason, Amazon.com appeared to take over operation of the site for a few years beginning sometime around 2010. During the Amazon.com phase, the site functioned mostly as a marketplace and listing of books to buy, and did not include any extra features, like the map of "fictional Arabia" and the list of characteristics that make a sheikh "hot"—all features that had distinguished Wittlieb's site. As of December 2014, the website appears to have been restored to its original form, with all of the original features maintained.

3. *Smart Bitches, Trashy Books* (blog), www.smartbitchestrashybooks.com. The section "The Fantasy of Feminist Liberation" in chapter 2 discusses this blog and its popularity.

4. SBSarah (screen name for Sarah Wendell) (hereafter cited as SBSarah), "What Not to Read," *Smart Bitches, Trashy Books* (blog), October 30, 2006, www.smartbitchestrashybooks.com/index.php/weblog/comments/what_not_to_read/.

5. SBSarah, interview with author, August 25, 2011.

6. Contrary to some early feminist critiques of romance novel readers, which cast them as unwitting cultural dupes vis-à-vis heteronormative patriarchal tales, I follow the work of Janice Radway and others, who argue that readers demonstrate a complex, if ambivalent, engagement with oppressive social realities in romance novels. See Janice Radway, *Reading the Romance: Women, Patriarchy, and Popular Literature* (1984; repr., Chapel Hill: University of North Carolina Press, 1991); Barbara Creed, "The Women's Romance as Sexual Fantasy: 'Mills and Boon,'" in *All Her Labours Two: Embroidering the Framework*, ed. Women and the Labour Publications Collective (Sydney: Hale & Iremonger, 1984), 47–67; Ann Barr Snitow, "Mass Market Romance: Pornography for Women Is Different," in *Powers of Desire: The Politics of Sexuality*, ed. Ann Snitow et al. (1979; repr., New York: Monthly Review Press, 1983); Stephanie Wardrop, "The Heroine Is Being Beaten: Freud, Sadomasochism, and Reading the Romance," *Style* 29, no. 3 (1995): 459–474.

7. Torstar, Inc., the corporation that owns Harlequin and its subsidiaries Mills & Boon and Silhouette, is extremely protective of its sales data and will not release any information about the sales of its books. Searches in *Books in Print* proved fruitless in that I could not isolate desert romances from the rest of the category romance novel titles. The best evidence I found to corroborate claims that desert romances rose in popularity after 2000 was in interviews with romance writers. Three out of six authors interviewed confirmed that they were solicited to write sheikh novels. Significantly, several of these are authors who normally write other types of characters, but were solicited by Harlequin editors (who obviously do have a wealth of marketing research available to them) to specifically write a sheikh-hero novel, signaling that this subgenre was trending up in popularity. Further, five out of six authors said that their sheikh novels were the most lucrative of all the novels they had written (the sixth writes exclusively sheikh novels, so she had no comparison to go by). Finally, from Simba Information data, I can say that from 2001 to 2010, new romance novel titles increased by 35 percent (from 900 to 1,375), while new desert romance titles increased by 87.5 percent (from 2 to 16).

8. Statistics are derived from Michael Norris, Warren Powlowski, and the editors of Simba Information, *Business of Consumer Book Publishing 2010* (Stamford, CT: Simba Information, 2010), 237. The actual number is 1,512,720.

9. I use the term *U.S.-Anglo* throughout the book for several reasons. The first reason is to signal the transnational, yet Anglo-identified, scope of the press that publishes most desert romances. The majority of these novels are category romances published by Torstar, Inc., which owns Harlequin and is based in Canada; Silhouette, based in the United States; and Mills & Boon, based in the United Kingdom and also operating in Australia. The writers of desert romances, then, are primarily (U.S. and Canadian) American and, to a lesser extent, British and Australian. The novels are all originally written in English, and the majority of desert romances feature white heroines. Even the novels sold and marketed in other countries are simply translations of the original English-language version. On the preceding points, see An Goris,

"Romance the World Over," in *Global Cultures*, ed. Frank A. Salamone (Newcastle: Cambridge Scholars Publishing, 2009), 59–72. The second reason for my use of the compound phrase *U.S.-Anglo* is to refer broadly to the colonial and settler-colonial states (the U.S., Canada, Britain, and Australia) that define the publishing landscape of the genre. Like the term *Arabiastan* (explained in the introduction), the term *U.S.-Anglo* both signals a putative focus on the United States in its contemporary imperialist formation and simultaneously gestures to how contemporary imperialism exceeds the boundaries of the nation-state and finds ideological force in the legacies of colonialism (particularly the idea of the white-man's burden) and of settler colonialism.

10. Diana Fuss, *Identification Papers* (New York: Routledge, 1995), 10.

11. Hamad Al Khalifa, "Stability Is Prerequisite for Progress," *Washington Times*, April 19, 2011, www.washingtontimes.com/news/2011/apr/19/ stability-is-prerequisite-for-progress/.

12. See Adam Hanieh, "Bahrain," in *Dispatches from the Arab Spring*, ed. Paul Amar and Vijay Prashad (Minneapolis: University of Minnesota Press, 2013), 63–88, for a good accounting of the uprisings in Bahrain. Hanieh chronicles, for instance, the fact that Karim Fakhrawi, a founder of Bahrain's only independent newspaper, died in police custody in the early days of the uprising.

13. See Jillian Schwedler, "Jordan," in *Dispatches from the Arab Spring*, ed. Paul Amar and Vijay Prashad (Minneapolis: University of Minnesota Press, 2013), 243–265, for an excellent analysis.

14. Ibid., 258.

15. Sarah Morgan, *Bella and the Merciless Sheikh* (New York: Harlequin, 2011), 10. See also these sources, also published by Harlequin in New York: Donna Young, *Captive of the Desert King* (2009), 156; Trish Morey, *Stolen by the Sheikh* (2006), 50; Meredith Webber, *Sheikh, Children's Doctor . . . Husband* (2011), 135; and Abby Green, *Breaking the Sheikh's Rules* (2011), 163.

16. Amy Wilkins, "The Unshakeable Appeal of the Sheikh Hero," *I [Heart] Harlequin Presents* (blog), August 17, 2007, www.iheartpresents.com/2007/08/ the-unshakeable-appeal-of-the-sheikh-hero.

17. Loreth Anne White, *The Sheik Who Loved Me* (New York: Silhouette, 2005); Emma Darcy, *Traded to the Sheikh* (New York: Harlequin, 2005).

18. Janet Jakobsen, "Sex, Secularism, and the 'War on Terrorism,'" in *A Companion to Lesbian, Gay, Bisexual, Transgender, and Queer Studies*, ed. George Haggerty and Molly McGarry (Malden, MA: Blackwell, 2007); Jasbir Puar, *Terrorist Assemblages: Homonationalism in Queer Times* (Durham, NC: Duke University Press, 2007); Zillah Eisenstein, *Sexual Decoys: Gender, Race, and War in Imperial Democracy* (London: Zed, 2007).

19. Gayle Rubin, "Thinking Sex: Notes for a Radical Theory of the Politics of Sexuality," in *Pleasure and Danger: Exploring Female Sexuality*, 2nd ed., ed. Carole Vance (London: Pandora Press, 1992), 267–319.

20. Jakobsen, "Sex, Secularism, and the 'War on Terrorism,'" 17–39.

21. Elizabeth Wright, ed., *Feminism and Psychoanalysis: A Critical Dictionary* (Cambridge, MA: Blackwell, 1992), 70.

INTRODUCTION

1. Antonio Gramsci, *Selections from the Prison Notebooks*, trans. Quintin Hoare and Geoffrey Nowell Smith (New York: International Publishers, 1987); David Harvey, *The New Imperialism* (New York: Oxford University Press, 2005).

2. Patricia Raub, "Issues of Passion and Power in E.M. Hull's *The Sheik*," *Women's Studies* 21, no. 1 (1992): 119–128; Juliet Flesch, *From Australia with Love: A History of Modern Australian Popular Romance Novels* (Fremantle, Australia: Curtin University Books, 2004); jay Dixon, *The Romance Fiction of Mills and Boon, 1909–1990s* (London and Philadelphia: UCL Press, 1999); Pamela Regis, *A Natural History of the Romance Novel* (Philadelphia: University of Pennsylvania Press, 2003).

3. Blog examples are Sharon Kendrick, "Fear and Longing and Desert Sheikhs," *I [Heart] Harlequin Presents*, January 24, 2012, www.iheartpresents.com/2012/01/fear-and-longing-and-desert-sheikhs-by-sharon-kendrick; and Kate Walker, "Sheiken and Stirred," *Pink Heart Society*, October 6, 2006, http://pinkheartsociety.blogspot.com/2006/10/thursday-talk-time-with-kate-walker.html. A few examples from the books themselves are Tessa Radley, *The Desert Bride of Al Zayed* (New York: Silhouette, 2007), 57; and these books published in New York by Harlequin: Dana Marton, *Sheik Seduction* (2008), 25, 45, 161; Liz Fielding, *The Sheikh's Unsuitable Bride* (2008), 12; Trish Morey, *The Sheikh's Convenient Virgin* (2008), 51; and Abby Green, *Breaking the Sheikh's Rules* (2011), 81. See especially: "Riding at tremendous speed, his white robes billowing out behind him, Sharif abruptly gave the reins a powerful jerk that sent the big white horse straight up into the air, spinning high on his hind legs" (Nan Ryan, *Burning Love* [New York: HarperCollins, 1996], 156).

4. See Kendrick, "Fear and Longing," for a Peter O'Toole reference, and Walker, "Sheiken and Stirred," for an Omar Sharif reference.

5. Hsu-Ming Teo, *Desert Passions: Orientalism and Romance Novels* (Austin: University of Texas Press, 2012), 1.

6. Walker, "Sheiken and Stirred."

7. Kendrick, "Fear and Longing."

8. Annie West, "The Lure of the Sheikh Hero," *Down Under Desirabelles* (blog), November 2, 2008, http://desirabelles.wordpress.com/2008/11/02/the-lure-of-the-sheikh-hero-by-annie-west/; Marguerite Kaye, "All Sheikh-en Up," *The Pink Heart Society: Wildcard Weekend* (blog), July 2, 2011, http://pinkheartsociety.blogspot.com/2011/07/wildcard-weekend-all-sheikh-en-up.html; Liz Fielding, email message to author, March 28, 2012.

9. Kaye, "All Sheikh-en Up"; Liz Fielding, "The Sheikh as Hero," *Liz Fielding: Award Winning Romance*, 2009, www.lizfielding.com/onwriting.html#sheikhashero.

10. Pippa Roscoe, January 25, 2012 (2:28 p.m.), comment on Sharon Kendrick, "Fear and Longing."

11. E. M. Hull, *The Sheik* (1919; repr., Holicong, PA: Wildside, 2004), 33.

12. Liz Fielding, "The Sheikh as Hero," *Liz Fielding: Award Winning Romance*, 2009, www.lizfielding.com/onwriting.html#sheikhashero.

13. West, "Lure of the Sheikh Hero"; Donna Young, *Captive of the Desert King* (New York: Harlequin, 2009), 16.

14. Young, *Captive*, 126.

15. Nalini Singh, *Desert Warrior* (New York: Harlequin, 2009), 43.

16. Ibid., 54.

17. Marguerite Kaye, *The Governess and the Sheikh* (New York: Harlequin, 2008), 70.

18. Walker, "Sheiken and Stirred."

19. Kendrick, "Fear and Longing."

20. OVO99, December 5, 2009 (8:03 p.m.), comment on Liz Fielding, "The Appeal of the Sheik," *Harlequin: Entertain, Enrich, Inspire*, December 4, 2009, www.harlequin-films.com/content/appeal-sheikh.

21. Fielding, "Appeal of the Sheik"; Liz Fielding, "The Sheikh as Hero."

22. Jane Porter, *The Sultan's Bought Bride* (New York: Harlequin, 2004), 23.

23. Loreth Anne White, *The Sheik Who Loved Me* (New York: Silhouette, 2005), 60, makes a common mistake here, using the adjective for language (Arabic) rather than the adjective for ethnicity (Arab).

24. Penny Jordan, *Possessed by the Sheikh* (New York: Harlequin, 2005), 14–15.

25. Emma Darcy, *Traded to the Sheikh* (New York: Harlequin, 2005), 100–101.

26. There are real cities or towns named Zuran in Yemen, Iran, and Turkey (obviously, though, it is not the name of an actual country), further suggesting a conflation of ethnicities in desert romances, even when they strive toward accuracy and authenticity. For examples of novels that use the somewhat antiquated adjective "Arabian," see Brenda Jackson, *Delaney's Desert Sheikh* (New York: Silhouette, 2002), 104; Sarah Morgan, *Bella and the Merciless Sheikh* (New York: Harlequin, 2011), 7; Penny Jordan, *A Royal Bride at the Sheikh's Command* (New York: Harlequin, 2007), 13; Olivia Gates, *To Touch a Sheikh* (New York: Harlequin, 2011), 27–30; Darcy, *Traded to the Sheikh*, 18; Singh, *Desert Warrior*, 8; Green, *Breaking the Sheikh's Rules*, 88; Kaye, *The Governess and the Sheikh*, 28.

27. Linda Conrad, telephone interview with author, March 5, 2012.

28. Brenda Jackson, *Delaney's Desert Sheikh*, 100; Bonnie Vanak, *The Sword and the Sheath* (New York: Leisure Books, 2007), 85.

29. Kim Lawrence, *Desert Prince, Defiant Virgin* (New York: Harlequin, 2009),143–144.

30. Keira Gillett, "Kiss Prince Charming Good-bye; Say Hello to a Sheikh!" *Heroes and Heartbreakers* (blog), April 2011, www.heroesandheartbreakers.com/blogs/2011/04/kiss-prince-charming-goodbye-say-hello-to-a-sheikh.

31. Keira Gillett, "Sheik Romance and the Passion of Arabia Nights," *LoveRomancePassion* (blog), May 12, 2011, www.loveromancepassion.com/sheik-romance-and-the-passion-of-arabian-nights/.

32. Frank Viviano, "Saudi Arabia: Kingdom on the Edge," *National Geographic*, October 2003, 10–41, 33; Linda Conrad, telephone interview with author, March 5, 2012.

33. Nancy!, December 5, 2009 (4:28 p.m.), comment on Liz Fielding, "Appeal of the Sheikh."

34. SBSarah, email to author, August 25, 2011.

35. Abby Green, "Sheikhs: Love Them or Loathe Them?" *I [Heart] Harlequin Presents* (blog), April 25, 2011, www.iheartpresents.com/2011/04/sheikhs-love-them-or-loathe-them-by-abby-green/.

36. Nalini Singh, November 5, 2008 (8:26 a.m.), comment on Annie West, "The Lure of the Sheikh Hero"; Gillett, "Sheik Romance and the Passion of Arabian Nights."

37. Dana Marton, email to author, March 19, 2012.

38. Walker, "Sheiken and Stirred."

39. Teresa Southwick, email to author, February 29, 2012.

40. Janice Radway, *Reading the Romance: Women, Patriarchy, and Popular Literature* (1984; repr., Chapel Hill: University of North Carolina Press, 1991), 109; Margaret Ann Jensen, *Love's Sweet Return: The Harlequin Story* (Bowling Green, OH: Bowling Green State University Popular Press, 1984), 148–149; Evelyn Bach, "Sheik Fantasies: Orientalism and Feminine Desire in the Desert Romance," *Hecate* 23, no. 1 (1997): 9–40, 13.

41. Kaye, "All Sheikh-en Up."

42. As noted in the preface the website appears to have been administered by Amazon.com in recent years and therefore did not include the map of "Fictional Arabia" crafted by the website designer, Erika Wittlieb. As of December 2014, the original "Sheikhs and Desert Love" website had been restored. In addition, a reproduction of the map is available online at Anne Galloway, "Hot Desert Nights," *Space and Culture*, September 7, 2007, www.spaceandculture.org/2007/09/07/hot-desert-nights/.

43. Ryan, *Burning*, 61, 181; Marton, *Sheik Seduction*, 21; Nina Bruhns, *Vampire Sheikh* (New York: Harlequin, 2011), 32.

44. Darcy, *Traded*, 35, 53, 66, 97, 110; Bruhns, *Vampire*, 96; Meredith Webber, *Sheikh, Children's Doctor . . . Husband* (New York: Harlequin, 2011), 25; Singh, *Desert Warrior*, 23; Vanak, *Sword*, 210.

45. Green, *Breaking*, 141; Singh, *Desert Warrior* 30; Lawrence, *Defiant Virgin*, 124; Vanak, *Sword*, 220; Ryan, *Burning*, 63, 101, 104, 105, 258, 298, 302, 312. As is probably clear from the number of references in this last novel, it is particularly representative of this phenomenon. Another representative novel in this respect is Beatrice Small *The Kadin* (New York: HarperCollins, 1978), but it is a historical romance set in the Ottoman era, so it differs from most contemporary desert romances in that respect.

46. West, "Lure of the Sheikh Hero."

47. Mingqi, September 19, 2009 (2:52 p. m.), comment on "Hot Desert Nights," www.likesbooks.com/cgi-bin/anthReviewId=232.

48. Green, "Sheikhs: Love Them or Loathe Them?"

49. Laura Winstead Jones, *The Sheik and I* (New York: Silhouette,2006), 69. See also Laura Wright, *A Bed of Sand* (New York: Silhouette, 2004), 132, 149, 162, for more lamentations on the return of reality.

50. Angela, February 15, 2011 (11:56 p.m.), comment on "Someone Explain the Appeal of Sheiks to Me, Please," in "Desert Island Keepers," *All About Romance: The Back Fence for Lovers of Romance Novels*, 2010, www.likesbooks.com/.

51. LyndaX, February 16, 2011 (1:48 p.m.), comment on "Someone Explain."

52. CD, February 21, 2011 (6:46 p.m.), comment on "Someone Explain."

53. See especially Trish Morey, *Stolen by the Sheikh* (New York: Harlequin, 2006); Ann Voss Peterson, *Seized by the Sheikh* (New York: Harlequin, 2008); Linda Conrad, *Secret Agent Sheik* (New York: Harlequin, 2011); Young, *Captive*; White, *Loved*; Marton, *Sheik Seduction*; Jones, *The Sheik and I*.

54. White, *Loved*, 142.

55. Sharon Kendrick, *Monarch of the Sands* (New York: Harlequin, 2011), 22; Sophie Weston, *In the Arms of the Sheikh* (New York: Harlequin, 2006), 12.

56. Jordan, *Possessed*, 48. For more examples, see Peterson, *Seized*, 148, 214, 219; Young, *Captive*, 41, 77, 97.

57. L Susan Meier, December 4, 2009 (10:18 a.m.), comment in Liz Fielding, "Appeal of the Sheikh."

58. Morgan, *Bella and the Merciless Sheikh*, 88.

59. Ironically, though Osama bin Laden hailed from Saudi Arabia, the Gulf region seems to be more popularly associated with oil wealth than terrorism, particularly in relation to the UAE.

60. Ella Shohat and Robert Stam, *Unthinking Eurocentrism: Multiculturalism and the Media* (New York: Routledge, 1994), 156. See the analysis of *Cannonball Run II* in Jack Shaheen, *Reel Bad Arabs: How Hollywood Vilifies a People* (New York: Olive Branch Press, 2009); and the analysis of an oil sheikh cartoon in Ronald Stockton, "Ethnic Archetypes and the Arab Image," in *The Development of Arab-American Identity*, ed. Ernest McCarus (Ann Arbor: University of Michigan Press, 1994), 119–153.

61. David Harvey, *The Condition of Postmodernity: An Enquiry into the Origins of Cultural Change* (Cambridge, MA: Blackwell, 1989).

62. Nora Roberts, *Sweet Revenge* (New York: Bantam Books, 1988), 40.

63. Viviano, "Saudi Arabia," 3.

64. Ibid, 11.

65. Ibid.

66. Hsu-Ming Teo, *Desert Passions*, 302–303.

67. Patrick T. Reardon, "The Mystery of Sheik Romance Novels," *Chicago Tribune*, April 24, 2006, 1.

68. For animalistic characteristics, see the following: Penny Jordan, *A Royal Bride at the Sheikh's Command*, 120 (hawk); Morgan, *Bella*, 24, 63 (purring); Marton, *Sheik Seduction*, 90, 120 (mountain lion); Bruhns, *Vampire*, 76, 139 (predator); 127 (lion); 139 (wild animal); Weston, *In the Arms*, 28 (jungle cat); 67 (the smell of male animal);

Morey, *Convenient Virgin*, 67, 89 (jungle cat); 69 (wolfish); 72 (hound); 144 (falcon); 175 (caged lion); 19 (predatory); Conrad, *Secret Agent*, 17 (roaring); 51 (stalking); 86 (cheetah); 132 (wolf); Young, *Captive*, 84, 85 (panther); 109 (hawkish); Jackson, *Delaney's*, 21, 23, 45, 85, 88, 93, 118 (wolf); Green, *Breaking*, 12 (vulture); 161 (wolf); Olivia Gates, *To Touch a Sheikh*, 46 (hawk); 87, 89, 102, 155, 156, 177, 178 (tiger, leopard, lion, or leonine); 93 (predator); Webber, *Sheikh, Children's Doctor*, 62 (wild leopard); Jones, *The Sheik and I*, 178 (hawk); Sharon Kendrick, *The Playboy Sheikh's Virgin Stable Girl* (New York: Harlequin, 2009), 13 (wolfish); Singh, *Warrior*, 11, 15, 31, 43, 66, 70, 90, 120, 122, 124, 130, 133, 153, 179, 182 (panther); Lawrence, *Defiant Virgin*, 34 (hawklike); 95 (wolfish); 101, 104, 108 (growl/animal groan); Vanak, *Sword*, 19, 95, 104, 151, 164, 203, 204, 209, 261, 262, 275, 280, 286, 287, 288, 297 (jungle cat, lion, growling, and pouncing); Ryan, *Burning*, 89 (sleek, untamed animal); 157 (hawk-faced); 160 (jungle cat); 319 (teeth bared like an animal's). For the aggressive trait usually coded as "primitive," see Morgan, *Bella*, 83; White, *Loved*, 51, 67, 108; Jackson, *Delaney's*, 17, 31, 68; Lawrence, *Defiant Virgin*, 77, 95, 108, 114, 115, 126, 131, 177. For "savage" or "barbaric," see Radley, *Desert Bride*, 93, 95; Jordan, *Royal Bride*, 121, 126; Bruhns, *Vampire*, 105; Jordan, *Possessed*, 83, 110, 123, 155, 70–71, 81; Morey, *Stolen*, 89; Singh, *Warrior*, 16, 18, 32, 39–40, 48, 57, 124; Ryan, *Burning*, 226, 227, 239. The uranium-enriching, evil half-brother is in White, *Loved*, esp. 129, 178. Other examples include Marton, *Sheik Seduction*, 27; Bruhns, *Vampire*, 46; Morey, *Stolen*, 48, 91, 179; Conrad, *Secret Agent*, 8, 10, 13, 21, 26, 37–38, 126, 200; Young, *Captive*, 96, 102; Jones, *Sheik and I*, 12, 19–20, 30, 43, 44, 237; Singh, *Warrior*, 63, 68; Vanak, *Sword*, 230, 330; Ryan, *Burning*, 41, 42, 104, 316.

69. Thanks to Nadine Sinno and Dylan McCarthy Blackston for pushing me to flesh out this point. For a brilliant book-length exploration of this topic, see Evelyn Alsultany, *Arabs and Muslims in the Media: Race and Representation After 9/11* (New York: New York University Press, 2012).

70. Teo, *Desert Passions*, 303.

71. Ann Laura Stoler, "Imperial Formations and the Opacities of Rule," in *Lessons of Empire: Imperial Histories and American Power*, ed. Craig Calhoun, Frederick Cooper, and Kevin W. Moore (New York: New Press, 2006), 48–60, esp. 55.

72. Ibid., 57 (emphasis in original).

73. Ibid., 54.

74. Daniel Rodgers, "Exceptionalism," in *Imagined Histories: American Historians Interpret the Past*, ed. Anthony Molho and Gordon S. Wood (Princeton: Princeton University Press, 1998), 21–40, esp. 23. See also Daniel Rodgers, "American Exceptionalism Revisited," *Raritan* 24, no. 2 (2004): 21–47, esp. 25.

75. Amy Kaplan, "The Tenacious Grasp of American Exceptionalism," *Comparative American Studies: An International Journal* 2, no. 2 (2004): 153–159, esp. 154. See also Donald Pease's discussion of American exceptionalism as being taken to mean "distinctive," "unique," "exemplary," and "exempt." Donald Pease, *The New American Exceptionalism* (Minneapolis: University of Minnesota Press, 2009), 9.

76. Dualisms (between the good hero and his evil counterpart, for example) are, of course, part of the formula of category romances. However, here I refer to tropes used

to demonstrate the respective characters' goodness and evilness. The distinction focuses on what makes the hero good (e.g., wanting to bring his country into the new global order) versus what makes the antagonist evil (e.g., seeking nuclear weapons for use in terrorist activity).

77. Jodi Kim, *Ends of Empire: Asian American Critique and the Cold War* (Minneapolis: University of Minnesota Press, 2010), 8, 29.

78. For a good explication of this idea, see Chris Harman, *Zombie Capitalism* (Chicago: Haymarket Books, 2010).

79. Naomi Klein, *Shock Doctrine* (New York: Picador, 2008).

80. Chalmers Johnson, *Sorrows of Empire: Militarism, Secrecy, and the End of the Republic* (New York: Metropolitan Books, 2004); Catherine Lutz, ed., *The Bases of Empire: The Global Struggle against U.S. Military Posts* (New York: New York University Press, 2009).

81. Inderpal Grewal and Caren Kaplan, eds., *Scattered Hegemonies* (Minneapolis: University of Minnesota Press, 1994).

82. Omar Dahbour, "Hegemony and Rights: On the Liberal Justification for Empire," in *Exceptional State: Contemporary U.S. Culture and the New Imperialism*, ed. Ashley Dawson and Malini Johar Schueller (Durham, NC: Duke University Press, 2007), 105–130; Randall Williams, *The Divided World: Human Rights and Its Violence* (Minneapolis: University of Minnesota Press, 2010); Inderpal Grewal, *Transnational America: Feminisms, Diaspora, Neoliberalisms* (Durham, NC: Duke University Press, 2005).

83. Jennifer Fluri, "'Rallying Public Opinion' and Other Misuses of Feminism," in *Feminism and War: Confronting U.S. Imperialism*, ed. Robin L. Riley, Chandra Talpade Mohanty, and Minnie Bruce Pratt (New York: Zed, 2008), 143–157, esp. 150–151.

84. The class was called New Directions in Feminism: Feminist Exploration of Contemporary Technologies of Imperialism, and I am indebted to the students in that class, who were wonderful interlocutors on this topic: Tahereh Aghdasifar, Sarah Beasley, Siobhan Cooke, Sherah Faulkner, Jennifer Forsthoefel, Maggie Franz, Alex Hutchings, Taryn Jordan, Andrea Miller, Scott Nesbit, Kayleigh Pandolfi, Valerie Pollock, Juliana Ramírez, Jimisha Relerford, Stephanie Rountree, and Jing Zhao.

85. As Jodi Kim brilliantly points out, Bush's naming of North Korea as a part of the "axis of evil" demonstrates both the triangulation of the Cold War throughout Asia and its thriving legacies in the contemporary war on terror despite the reputed end of the Cold War.

86. Linda Evans, "Playing Global Cop," in *Global Lockdown*, ed. Julia Sudbury (New York: Routledge, 2005), 215–227; Julia Sudbury, ed., *Global Lockdown* (New York: Routledge, 2005); Ruth Wilson Gilmore, *Golden Gulag: Prisons, Surplus, Crisis, and Opposition in Globalizing California* (Berkeley: University of California Press, 2007).

87. For more on the rise of securitization in the shift to what he calls "human security states," see Paul Amar, *The Security Archipelago: Human-Security States, Sexuality Politics, and the End of Neoliberalism* (Durham, NC: Duke University Press, 2013).

88. Charles Colson and Anne Morse, "The Moral Home Front," *Christianity Today* 48, no. 10 (October 2004), www.christianitytoday.com/ct/2004/october/18.152.html. Thanks to Andrea Smith, *Native Americans and the Christian Right: The Gendered Politics of Unlikely Alliances* (Durham, NC: Duke University Press, 2008), for leading me to this source.

89. See Mimi Kirk, "The Sudan Split: How U.S. Policy Became Predicated on Secession," *Middle East Report* 262 (spring 2012): 36–42.

90. Melani McAlister, "Left Behind and the Politics of Prophecy Talk," in *Exceptional State: Contemporary U.S. Culture and the New Imperialism*, ed. Ashley Dawson and Malini Johar Schueller (Durham, NC: Duke University Press, 2007), 191–220, esp. 213–214.

91. Giorgio Agamben, *State of Exception*, trans. Kevin Attell (Chicago: University of Chicago Press, 2005).

92. Ashley Dawson and Malini Johar Schueller, introduction to *Exceptional State: Contemporary U.S. Culture and the New Imperialism*, ed. Ashley Dawson and Malini Johar Schueller (Durham, NC: Duke University Press, 2007), 1–33, esp. 15.

93. It also operates through a version of Israeli sexual exceptionalism, seen most clearly in the phenomenon often referenced as "pinkwashing." For an overview, see Gil Z. Hochberg, "Introduction: Israelis, Palestinians, Queers: Points of Departure," *GLQ: A Journal of Lesbian and Gay Studies* 16, no. 4 (2010): 493–516. Also see Jasbir Puar, "Israel's Gay Propaganda War," *Guardian* (London and Manchester), July 1, 2010, www.guardian.co.uk/commentisfree/2010/jul/01/israels-gay-propaganda-war.

94. For Puar's analysis, see Jasbir Puar, *Terrorist Assemblages: Homonationalism in Queer Times* (Durham, NC: Duke University Press, 2007); "On Torture," with Amit Rai, "Monster, Terrorist, Fag: The War on Terrorism and the Production of Docile Patriots," *Social Text* 20, no. 3 (2002): 117–148.

95. "New Middle East" is the term Samantha uses to allay her friends' fears about traveling to the Middle East. The Gulf, particularly the United Arab Emirates, she assures them, is fabulously wealthy and therefore a wonderful place to visit. As such, the logic goes, it caters to tourists and hides its ugly repressions from view.

96. Puar, *Terrorist Assemblages*, is building on Lisa Duggan's conceptualization of homonormativity. See Lisa Duggan, "The New Homonormativity: The Sexual Politics of Neoliberalism," in *Materializing Democracy: Toward a Revitalized Cultural Politics*, ed. Russ Castronova and Dana D. Nelson (Durham, NC: Duke University Press, 2002), 175–194.

97. There is a booming subgenre of romance novels that portray queer and other nonnormative sexualities, but for the most part, the novels do not cross over with desert romances. I have only found two gay sheikh novels (three if one counts erotica as romance, a subject that is hotly debated in the industry), which I discuss further in chapter 4.

98. Regis, *Natural History*, echoed on romance blogs.

99. Thanks to Sam Affholter and the students in my fall 2011 Women, War, and the Middle East class for helpfully engaging with Anne McClintock's "Paranoid Empire:

Specters from Guantánamo and Abu Ghraib," *Small Axe, Number 28* 13, no. 1 (March 2009): 50–74, and for suggesting that paranoia is a useful framework through which to understand exceptionalism.

100. Cited in Teresa de Lauretis, *Freud's Drive: Psychoanalysis, Literature, and Film* (New York: Palgrave Macmillan, 2010), 4.

101. McClintock, "Paranoid Empire," 53 (emphasis in original).

102. Gilles Deleuze and Félix Guattari, *A Thousand Plateaus*, trans. and forward by Brian Massumi (1980; repr., Minneapolis: University of Minnesota Press, 1987); Gilles Deleuze and Félix Guattari, *Anti-Oedipus* (Minneapolis: University of Minnesota Press, 1983).

103. Paul Elliott, *Guattari Reframed* (London: I.B. Tauris, 2012), 26.

104. Brian Massumi, *A User's Guide to Capitalism and Schizophrenia: Deviations from Deleuze and Guattari* (Cambridge, MA: Massachusetts Institute of Technology Publishing, 1992), 115.

105. Deleuze and Guattari, *Anti-Oedipus*, 348. See also "Beneath the conscious investments of economic, political, religious, etc. formations, there are unconscious sexual investments, microinvestments that attest to the way in which desire is present in a social field" (ibid., 183).

106. This is not to say that I eschew all psychoanalytic theory. Indeed, I am influenced by the feminist psychoanalytic theorists who have made similar points about the imbrication of the psychic and social registers. See, for example, Fuss, *Identification Papers*, and Kaja Silverman, *Male Subjectivity at the Margins* (New York: Psychology Press, 1992).

107. This phrasing is a variation on "The question posed by desire is not 'What does it mean?' but rather 'How does it work?'" (Deleuze and Guattari, *Anti-Oedipus*, 109).

108. At its simplest, the distinction they make is that they are discussing social repression rather than psychic repression. A critical interrogation of social repression is constantly displaced onto (and therefore privatized) in the psychoanalytic focus on psychic repression (Deleuze and Guattari, *Anti-Oedipus*, 119).

109. See the discussion of the "fourth and final thesis of schizoanalysis" in Deleuze and Guattari, *Anti-Oedipus*, 366, for an elaboration of this point.

110. The term most often used (and elaborated on) in Deleuze and Guattari, *A Thousand Plateaus*.

111. Deleuze and Guattari, *Anti-Oedipus*, 105, defines answering this question as the primary goal of schizoanalysis. See also ibid., 346; and Deleuze and Guattari, *A Thousand Plateaus*, 215.

112. Deleuze and Guattari, *Anti-Oedipus*, discusses this process in terms of capitalism's ability to displace its own limit. Deleuze and Guattari, *A Thousand Plateaus*, 221, explains that "it is always *on* the most deterritorialized element that reterritorialization takes place," as if to reappropriate (and molarize) it before it takes flight. See also ibid., 134, for an explanation of the different types of deterritorialization.

113. For more on the development of "war waged by labor that is already dead, crystallized into machinery," see Christian Parenti, "Planet America: The Revolution in Military Affairs as Fantasy and Fetish," in *Exceptional State: Contemporary U.S. Culture and the New Imperialism*, ed. Ashley Dawson and Malini Johar Schueller (Durham, NC: Duke University Press, 2007), 88–104, esp. 89.

114. Melani McAlister, *Epic Encounters: Culture, Media, and U.S. Interests in the Middle East 1945–2000* (Berkeley: University of California Press, 2001).

115. Amy Kaplan, "Romancing the Empire," in *The Anarchy of Empire in the Making of U.S. Culture* (Cambridge, MA: Harvard University Press, 2005), 92–120, esp. 116.

116. Deleuze and Guattari, *A Thousand Plateaus*, 221. The framework of settler colonialism is, of course, key here, and points to a burgeoning body of scholarship that seeks to centralize settler colonialism as a key organizing rubric for understanding contemporary imperialism. One influential work in this regard is Scott Lauria Morgensen, *Spaces Between Us: Queer Settler Colonialism and Indigenous Decolonization* (Minneapolis: University of Minnesota Press, 2011), though it is certainly not the only one.

117. These are two of the three "great strata" that "directly bind us," according to Deleuze and Guattari. The third is the "organism" (the strict organization of the body and its functions). See Deleuze and Guattari, *A Thousand Plateaus*, 159.

118. Remember that President Reagan used the phrase "war on terrorism," the precursor to the current "war on terror."

119. Deleuze and Guattari, *A Thousand Plateaus*, 111–148.

120. Though the definition of terrorism is hotly contested, most people can usually agree on the common elements listed here.

121. See, for example, much of the media coverage following the original Wikileaks release about the many Guantánamo detainees who were proven not to be terrorists or enemy combatants and therefore proven not to be a threat to the United States. See especially "Tale of Two Prisons: The Guantanamo Files," *Guardian* (London and Manchester), April 26, 2011; Heidi Blake, Tim Ross, and Conrad Quilty-Harper, "Two-Year Ordeal of an Innocent: Wikileaks Files Children Among the Innocent Captured and Sent to Guantanamo," *Daily Telegraph* (London), April 26, 2011; Stephen Foley, "U.S. Scrambles to Contain Fallout from 'Damaging' Guantanamo Leak," *Independent* (London), April 26, 2011, which reveal both the haphazard means employed to collect suspects as well as the mind-boggling range of prisoners (e.g., the age range, from a fourteen-year-old boy to an eighty-nine-year-old man with dementia). Another clear example is the case of the Uyghurs, many of whom were in detained limbo for many years after having been proven innocent. See Alexandra Poolos, "Reporter's Diary," in "Albania: Getting out of Gitmo," *Frontline/ World: Stories from a Small Planet*, 2011–2012, www.pbs.org/frontlineworld/stories/albania801/interview/poolos.html, for a good account of their story.

122. Fear is one of four "great dangers" identified by Deleuze and Guattari (following Nietzsche and Castaneda). The others are clarity, power, and disgust. See Deleuze and Guattari, *A Thousand Plateaus*, 227–231.

123. Ibid., 227.

124. Thanks to Diego Bruno for this suggestion.

125. Radway, *Reading the Romance*, offers a psychoanalytic reading of romance novels. Mass-market romances themselves perpetuate such an interpretation through the common plot device of inscribing tragedy or betrayal in the mommy-daddy-me triad, which inevitably drives and shapes the love interest between hero and heroine.

126. Deleuze and Guattari, *A Thousand Plateaus*, 115.

127. Donald Rumsfeld, "Secretary Rumsfeld Press Conference at NATO Headquarters, Brussels, Belgium," U.S. Department of Defense, news transcript, June 6, 2002, www.defense.gov/transcripts/transcript.aspx?transcriptid=3490.

128. Not to mention the erosion of civil liberties and heightened surveillance of citizens in the U.S.

129. Slavoj Žižek, *How to Read Lacan* (New York: W.W. Norton & Co, 2007), 52.

130. Ibid.

131. Elizabeth Wright, ed., *Feminism and Psychoanalysis: A Critical Dictionary* (Cambridge, MA: Blackwell, 1992), 70; Slavoj Žižek, *Looking Awry: An Introduction to Jacques Lacan through Popular Culture* (Cambridge, MA: MIT Press,1991).

132. Žižek, *Looking Awry*, 36.

133. Christian Parenti, *Tropic of Chaos: Climate Change and the New Geography of Violence* (New York: Nation Books, 2011), 67.

134. Shohat and Stam, *Unthinking Eurocentrism*, 166–177.

135. Mimi Thy Nguyen, *The Gift of Freedom* (Durham, NC: Duke University Press, 2012).

136. Omar Sharif, with Marie-Thérèse Guinchard, *The Eternal Male*, trans. Martin Sokolinsky (New York: Doubleday and Co., 1977), 130.

CHAPTER 1. "TO CATCH A SHEIKH" IN THE WAR ON TERROR

1. The title of this chapter references Teresa Southwick's desert romance *To Catch a Sheik* (New York: Silhouette, 2003).

2. Dana Marton, *Sheik Seduction* (New York: Harlequin, 2008), 95.

3. Robert Stam and Ella Shohat, *Race in Translation: Culture Wars Around the Postcolonial Atlantic* (New York: NYU Press, 2012), 4.

4. Wallace Stegner, *Discovery! The Search for Arabian Oil* (Beirut: Middle East Export Press, 1971)

5. Sharon Kendrick, *Monarch of the Sands* (New York: Harlequin, 2006), 13.

6. The notion of imperialism as a gift—of democracy, of liberation, or of the discovery of oil resources, for example—builds on Mimi Thy Nguyen's notion of the "gift of freedom" which I discuss further in chapter 2. Mimi Thi Nguyen, *The Gift of Freedom: War, Debt, and Other Refugee Passages* (Durham, NC: Duke University Press, 2012).

7. Timothy Mitchell, *Carbon Democracy: Political Power in the Age of Oil* (New York: Verso, 2011), 78–85.

8. Donna Young, *Captive of the Desert King* (New York: Harlequin, 2009), 18.

9. In fact, nuclear power development in the Middle East is most consistently read as an effort to militarize, while states' claims that they seek to diversify energy are actively denied, reifying the false dichotomy between the two.

10. Mitchell, *Carbon Democracy*, 155–158.

11. David Harvey, *The New Imperialism* (New York: Oxford University Press, 2005).

12. See Chris Harman, *Zombie Capitalism* (Chicago: Haymarket Books, 2010), for more on this.

13. Mitchell, *Carbon Democracy*, 162.

14. Marton, *Sheik Seduction*, 110.

15. Ann Voss Peterson, *Seized by the Sheik* (New York: Harlequin, 2008), 159.

16. Loreth Anne White, *The Sheik Who Loved Me* (New York: Silhouette, 2005); Penny Jordan, *Possessed by the Sheikh* (New York: Harlequin, 2005), 48.

17. Jane Porter, *The Sultan's Bought Bride* (New York, Harlequin, 2004), 72; Emma Darcy, *Traded to the Sheikh* (New York: Harlequin, 2005), 101.

18. Young, *Captive*, 118.

19. See Mitchell, *Carbon Democracy*, 184–185, for a discussion of the misrepresentation of the 1973 crisis as the result of an OPEC oil embargo.

20. Laura Winstead Jones, *The Sheik and I* (New York: Silhouette, 2006), 8.

21. Ibid., 73.

22. Robert Vitalis, *America's Kingdom: Mythmaking on the Saudi Oil Frontier* (Stanford, CA: Stanford University Press, 2007), 2–6.

23. Ibid., 10.

24. Wallace Stegner, quoted in ibid., 87.

25. Vitalis, *America's Kingdom*, xii.

26. Harvey, *New Imperialism*, 50.

27. Brenda Jackson, *Delaney's Desert Sheikh* (New York: Silhouette, 2002), 108.

28. Nalini Singh, *Desert Warrior* (New York: Harlequin, 2009), 8.

29. Ibid., 106.

30. Inderpal Grewal and Caren Kaplan, *Scattered Hegemonies* (Minneapolis: University of Minnesota Press, 1994), 7.

31. Daniel Rodgers, "American Exceptionalism Revisited," *Raritan* 24, no. 2 (2004): 30–31.

32. The Gulf Cooperation Council's support of the oppressive regime in Bahrain during the 2011 Arab uprisings is a case in point; support of the Bahrain regime demonstrates a clear alliance with U.S. military and capital interests, as Bahrain hosts the U.S. Navy's Fifth Fleet.

33. Rodgers, "American Exceptionalism Revisited," 23.

34. Ann Laura Stoler, "Imperial Formations and the Opacities of Rule," in *Lessons of Empire: Imperial Histories and American Power*, ed. Craig Calhoun, Frederick Cooper, and Kevin W. Moore (New York: New Press, 2006), 59.

35. My use of the term *securityscapes* is meant to reference an adaptation of a discussion of ethnoscapes, mediascapes, financescapes, ideoscapes, and technoscapes

in Arjun Appadurai, *Modernity at Large: Cultural Dimension of Globalization* (Minneapolis: University of Minnesota Press, 1996), ch. 2.

36. Singh, *Desert Warrior*, 63.

37. Kim Lawrence, *Desert Prince, Defiant Virgin* (New York: Harlequin, 2009), 171.

38. Jones, *Sheik and I*, 19–20.

39. Peterson, *Seized*, 9.

40. One possible exception to this narrative is Linda Conrad, *Secret Agent Sheik* (New York: Harlequin: 2011), 200, in which the terrorist group the "Taj Jabbar" seeks to force the "U.S. imperialist state to sit up and take notice." Though the book does name imperialism, it does so cynically through the perspective of one-dimensional, evil characters.

41. See also Amy Burge, "Desiring the East: A Comparative Study of Middle English Romance and Modern Popular Sheikh Romance" (PhD diss., University of York, 2012), 54–56, 67, 106, for more on this comparison.

42. For "'CEO' of Dubai," see Ahmed Kanna, *Dubai: The City as Corporation* (Minneapolis: University of Minnesota Press, 2011), 139; Mike Davis, "Fear and Money in Dubai," *New Left Review* 41 (September–October 2006): 47–68; Afshin Molavi, "Sudden City," *National Geographic*, January 2007, 104. For remaining quotes, see Davis, "Fear and Money," 51.

43. Kanna, *Dubai*, 189.

44. Stuart Elden, *Terror and Territory: The Spatial Extent of Sovereignty* (Minneapolis: University of Minnesota Press, 2009), 3, points out that Bush's statement "we will make no distinction between terrorists and those who harbor them" effectively collapses the distinction between those committing an act and their spatial location, thereby at least partly reterritorializing the enemy.

45. Benjamin Barber, *Jihad vs. McWorld* (New York: Ballantine Books, 1996). See also Valentine Moghadam, *Globalizing Women: Transnational Feminist Networks* (Baltimore: Johns Hopkins University Press, 2005).

46. This is, of course, one of Gilles Deleuze and Félix Guattari's key arguments in the Capitalism and Schizophrenia series, which is why I include their quote in the epigraph to this chapter.

47. Mitchell, "McJihad," in *Carbon Democracy*.

48. Davis, "Fear and Money," 60.

49. Quotation from ibid. For oil as percentage of Dubai's GDP, see Molavi, "Sudden City," 105.

50. Davis, "Fear and Money," 60.

51. James Risen, "Blackwater Founder Moves to Abu Dhabi, Records Say," *New York Times*, August 17, 2010.

52. Quoted in Jeremy Scahill, *Blackwater: The Rise of the World's Most Powerful Mercenary Army* (New York: Nation Books, 2007), xx.

53. I realize, of course, that Abu Dhabi and Dubai are not the same, but I am nevertheless relying on their structural economic and historical similarities. In that

spirit, I would add that Dubai has been described as a "nonplace," that is, "like being everywhere and nowhere at the same time" (Kanna, *Dubai*, 199).

54. For Xe Services and Academi name changes, see MSNBC.com Staff and New Services, "Former Blackwater Security Firm Changes Name Again," U.S. News, *NBC News*, December 12, 2011, http://usnews.nbcnews.com/_news/2011/12/12/9393006-former-blackwater-security-firm-changes-name-again?lite. According to promotional materials, the name Greystone was chosen because "in today's grey world . . . the solutions to your security concerns are no longer as simple as black and white" (Scahill, *Blackwater*, 367).

55. Scahill, *Blackwater*, 369.

56. The UAE is reportedly the "financial hub" of "terrorist" money, an interesting territorial-financial link between Prince and al-Qa'ida (Davis, "Fear and Money," 57).

57. Janice Radway, *Reading the Romance: Women, Patriarchy, and Popular Literature* (1984; repr., Chapel Hill: University of North Carolina Press, 1991), 107.

58. Liz Fielding, email message to author, March 28, 2012.

59. Dana Marton, email message to author, March 19, 2012; Ann Voss Peterson, email message to author, March 17, 2012; Teresa Southwick, email message to author, February 29, 2012.

60. Arthur P. Clark et al., *A Land Transformed: The Arabian Peninsula, Saudi Arabia, and Saudi Aramco* (Houston, TX: Aramco Services Company, 2006), 23.

61. Donald Powell Cole, *Nomads of the Nomads: The Al Murrah Bedouin of the Empty Quarter* (Chicago: Aldine Publishing Company, 1975), 22.

62. Clark et al., *Land Transformed*, 21; Cole, *Nomads of the Nomads*, 16.

63. Cole, *Nomads of the Nomads*, 16.

64. Singh, *Desert Warrior*, 142; Sarah Morgan, *Bella and the Merciless Sheikh* (New York, Harlequin, 2011), 53.

65. Shirley Kay, *The Bedouin* (New York: Crane, Russak, 1978), 128–129.

66. For an extensive analysis of *National Geographic* representations of the Arab world, see Linda Steet, *Veils and Daggers: A Century of* National Geographic's *Representation of the Arab World* (Philadelphia: Temple University Press, 2000). I will be using examples from more recent issues of the magazine, as they coincide with the publication of the novels I investigate.

67. The "Afghan girl" image is a good example—see Amira Jarmakani, *Imagining Arab Womanhood* (New York: Palgrave, 2008), ch. 4, and Wendy Hesford and Wendy Kozol, eds., *Just Advocacy? Women's Human Rights, Transnational Feminisms, and the Politics of Representation* (New Brunswick, NJ: Rutgers University Press, 2005), for more.

68. Catherine Lutz and Jane Lou Collins, *Reading National Geographic* (Chicago: University of Chicago Press, 1993), 28.

69. Ibid., 16. There is an interesting overlap here with the *Arabian Nights*, which was valued both for educational and entertainment purposes. See Susan Nance, *How the Arabian Nights Inspired the American Dream* (Chapel Hill: University of North Carolina Press, 2009), 178.

70. Lutz and Collins, *Reading National Geographic*, 46.

71. See ibid., 37, for *National Geographic*; and Radway, *Reading the Romance*, ch. 1, "The Institutional Matrix," for romance novels.

72. See the following *National Geographic* articles: "A Middle East Atlas, Just in Time," June 2003; Jeffrey Bartholet, "Young, Angry, and Wired-In: The Middle East a Generation in Waiting Can Wait No More," July 2011; Don Belt, "The Forgotten Faithful: Arab Christians," June 2009; Don Belt, "Shadowland: Poised to Play a Pivotal New Role in the Middle East, Syria Struggles to Escape Its Dark Past," November 2009; Charles Bowden, "Unseen Sahara," October 2009; Evan Dale Santos, "Among the Berbers," May 2005; Winona Dimeo-Ediger, "Dubai's Rotating Skyscraper," February 2009; Robert Draper, "The Black Pharaohs," February 2008; "Ground Truths," February 2005; Peter Gwin, "Lost Lords of the Sahara," September 2011; John Hare, "Surviving the Sahara," December 2002; Jennifer S. Holland, "The Tortoise and the Bedouin," April 2007; Dylan Humphries, "Dubai: The Sudden City," May 2007; Karen M. Kostyal, "Alaa Al Aswany: Voice of Reason," September 2006; Karen E. Lange and Stephen Ferry, "Sahara Occidental," June 2007; Afshin Molavi, "Sudden City," January 2007; Virginia Morrell, "The Cruelest Place on Earth," October 2005; "Repeat Performance," June 2003; Frank Viviano, "Saudi Arabia on Edge: Tribal Traditions and Modern Wealth Clash in the Birthplace of Islam," October 2003; Nancy Roberts-Moneir, "Unseen Sahara," February 2010; Jeffrey Taylor, "Among the Berbers," January 2005; Matthew Teague, "Isn't She Lovely," August 2009; Matthew Teague, "The Sinai," March 2009; "United Arab Emirates," April 2009; Mary Ann Weaver, "Qatar: Revolution from the Top Down" March 2003; Donovan Webster, "Empty Quarter," February 2005; Margaret G. Zackowitz, "Worlds Away," December 2009.

73. The remaining five articles either focus on a tourist-environmental aspect of the nation (here, famous caves in Oman), appealing to the adventure and exploration aspects of *National Geographic*, or they focus on war and conflict—a relatively new topic for the magazine (Lutz and Collins, *Reading National Geographic*, 41–46). *National Geographic* featured three articles on Iraq in the wake of the U.S. invasion (two in 2003 and one in 2004), and one article on the occupied Palestinian territories (the West Bank and Gaza).

74. John Hare, "Surviving the Sahara," *National Geographic*, December 2002, 66.

75. See, for example, White, *Loved*, which names the sheikh as Tuareg, while Jordan, *Possessed by the Sheikh*, and Jackson, *Delaney's Desert Sheikh*, describe the characteristic blue clothing worn by Tuaregs without naming this group specifically.

76. Peter Gwin, "Lost Lords of the Sahara," *National Geographic*, September 2011, 143, 140. Andrew Cockburn, "Yemen United," *National Geographic*, April 2000, 30–53, also roughly fits into this category, as one of its main sidebars reads: "Yemenis have been wandering ever since the Queen of Sheba set off to visit King Solomon."

77. Gwin, "Lost Lords," 142.

78. See, for example, Morgan, *Bella*, 10; Marton, *Sheik Seduction*, 164, 168, 240; Porter, *Bought Bride*, 122; White, *Loved*, 124, 212; Trish Morey, *Stolen by the Sheikh*

(New York: Harlequin, 2006), 114; Conrad, *Secret Agent*, 37; Young, *Captive*, 119; Jones, *Sheik and I*, 33, 74; Lawrence, *Defiant Virgin*, 12, 45.

79. Matthew Teague, "Isn't She Lovely?" *National Geographic*, August 2009, 123.

80. Though "Mohammed" is an Anglicized transliteration of the Arabic name Muhammad, I follow the spelling given on Sheikh Mohammed's official English-language Web page (sheikhmohammed.ae).

81. Kanna, *Dubai*, 40. As should be obvious by now, I do not mean this as a critique of Kanna's wonderful book.

82. Keira Gillett, "Kiss Prince Charming Good-bye; Say Hello to a Sheikh!" *Heroes and Heartbreakers* (blog), April 2011, www.heroesandheartbreakers.com/blogs/2011/04/kiss-prince-charming-goodbye-say-hello-to-a-sheikh.

83. Mary Anne Weaver, "Revolution from the Top Down," *National Geographic*, March 2003, 89.

84. See Sharon Kendrick, *The Playboy Sheikh and the Virgin Stable Girl* (New York: Harlequin, 2009), for a good example of a preponderance of falcon references in desert romances.

85. Kanna, *Dubai*, 3.

86. For staging, see Sulayman Khalaf, "Poetics and Politics of Newly Invented Traditions in the Gulf: Camel Racing in the United Arab Emirates," *Ethnology* 39, no. 3 (summer 2000): 243–261. For "traditional Arab desert democracy," see Kanna, *Dubai*, 86.

87. Davis, "Fear and Money," 64–68; Kanna, *Dubai*, 171–204.

88. Wendy Brown, *Walled States, Waning Sovereignty* (New York: Zone Books, 2010), 115.

89. See ibid., and Mike Davis, "The Great Wall of Capital," in *Against the Wall: Israel's Barrier to Peace*, ed. Michael Sorkin (New York: New Press, 2005), 88–99, for elaboration of this point.

90. For the growth of prisons and detention centers, see Julia Sudbury, ed., *Global Lockdown: Race, Gender, and the Prison-Industrial Complex* (New York: Routledge, 2005).

91. Mark Salter, "Not Waiting for the Barbarians," in *Civilizational Identity: The Production and Reproduction of 'Civilizations' in International Relations*, ed. Martin Hall and Patrick Thaddeus Jackson (New York: Palgrave, 2007), 81–93, esp. 85.

92. See Elden, *Terror and Territory*, for a complication of the idea that terrorism completely deterritorializes.

93. Ann Voss Peterson, email message to author, March 17, 2012.

94. Thanks to Andrea Miller for collecting these sources. See Cristian Salazar, "Mosque Going up in NYC Building Damaged on 9/11," *Associated Press*, May 7, 2010; "Ground Zero to Have Mosque," *Evening Standard*, May 26, 2010; "New York Board OKs 'Ground Zero' Mosque Plan," *The Nation* (Thailand), May 27, 2010; Pamela Geller, "Unindicted Co-Conspirator CAIR Crawls Out from Under Their Rock at Ground Zero Mosque Hearing," *Atlas Shrugs*, July 14, 2010, http://atlasshrugs2000.typepad.com/atlas_shrugs/2010/07/

unindicted-coconspirator-crawls-out-from-under-their-rock-at-ground-zero-mosque-hearing.html; Hamdan Azhar, "'Ground Zero Mosque': Islamophobic Extremists Are Fueling the Controversy," *Christian Science Monitor*, August 4, 2010; Bill O'Reilly, "Factor Follow-Up," Fox News Network, August 4, 2010, www.lexisnexis.com.ezproxy.gsu.edu/lnacui2api/api/version1/getDocCui?lni=803K-07F0-Y8Y1-72S6&csi=174179&hl=t&hv=t&hnsd=f&hns=t&hgn=t&oc=00240&perma=true; Anne Barnard, "Calling to Allah, from Lower Manhattan," *New York Times*, August 14, 2010, www.lexisnexis.com/lnacui2api/api/version1/getDocCui?lni=805G-YVX0-Y8TC-S40K&csi=6742&hl=t&hv=t&hnsd=f&hns=t&hgn=t&oc=00240&perma=true; Rush Limbaugh, "Ground Zero Terrorist Recruitment Center Imam: Build Mosque or Else," *Rush Limbaugh Show*, September 9, 2010. www.rushlimbaugh.com/daily/2010/09/09/ground_zero_terrorist_recruitment_center_imam_build_mosque_or_else.

95. Salazar, "Mosque Going up in NYC."

96. "Ground Zero to Have Mosque"; "New York Board OKs 'Ground Zero' Mosque Plan."

97. Mahmood Mamdani, *Good Muslim, Bad Muslim: America, the Cold War, and the Roots of Terror* (New York: Pantheon, 2004).

98. Ann Voss Peterson, email message to author, March 17, 2012.

99. Emily Haddad, "Bound to Love: Captivity in Harlequin Sheikh Novels," in *Empowerment versus Oppression: Twenty First Century Views of Popular Romance Novels*, ed. Sally Goade (Newcastle, England: Cambridge Scholars, 2007), 42–64.

100. Mamdani, *Good Muslim, Bad Muslim*, 15.

101. Jasbir Puar and Amit Rai, "Monster, Terrorist, Fag: The War on Terrorism and the Production of Docile Patriots," *Social Text* 20, no. 3 (2002): 117–148.

102. For "primal," see White, *Loved*, 13, 86, 153, 182, 224, 229, 231, 233. See also Tessa Radley, *The Desert Bride of Al Zayed* (New York: Silhouette, 2007), 116; Penny Jordan, *A Royal Bride at the Sheikh's Command* (New York: Harlequin, 2007), 126; Jordan, *Possessed*, 83; Darcy, *Traded*, 19; Morey, *Stolen*, 77; Morgan, *Bella*, 83; Nina Bruhns, *Vampire Sheikh* (New York: Harlequin, 2011), 143; Abby Green, *Breaking the Sheikh's Rules* (New York: Harlequin, 2011), 84, 91, 94, 98; Meredith Webber, *Sheikh, Children's Doctor . . . Husband* (New York: Harlequin, 2011), 146; Lawrence, *Defiant Virgin*, 109; Bonnie Vanak, *The Sword and the Sheath* (New York: Leisure Books, 2007), 205; Marguerite Kaye, *The Governess and the Sheikh* (New York: Harlequin, 2011), 160. For "savage," see Jordan, *Possessed*, 37, 48, 110, 111, 123, 155. See also Radley, *Desert Bride*, 36, 93; Jordan, *Royal Bride*, 121, 126; Bruhns, *Vampire*, 128; Olivia Gates, *To Touch a Sheikh* (New York: Harlequin, 2011), 77; Singh, *Warrior*, 18, 32; Lawrence, *Defiant Virgin*, 131; Ryan, *Burning*, 68, 118, 177, 181, 226, 239; Kate Hewitt, *The Sheikh's Forbidden Virgin* (New York: Harlequin, 2009), 83, 101, 122; Kendrick, *Monarch*, 174, 178.

103. Michel Foucault, *Society Must Be Defended: Lectures at the College de France, 1975–76*, trans. David Macey (New York: Picador, 2003); Haraway, "Promises of Monsters," 295–337; Puar and Rai, "Monster, Terrorist, Fag."

104. Haraway, "Promises of Monsters," 296.

105. Foucault, *Society Must Be Defended*, 51.

106. Kate Walker, "Sheiken and Stirred," *Pink Heart Society* (blog), October 6, 2006, http://pinkheartsociety.blogspot.com/2006/10/thursday-talk-time-with-kate-walker. html.

107. Foucault, *Society Must Be Defended*, 53.

108. White, *Loved*, 125, 178.

109. Sophie Weston, *In the Arms of the Sheikh* (New York: Harlequin, 2006), 12.

110. Jordan, *Possessed*, 48.

111. Morey, *Stolen*, 114, 91.

112. Edward Said, *Orientalism* (New York: Pantheon, 1978).

113. Raphael Patai, *The Arab Mind* (1973; repr., Long Island City, NY: Hatherleigh Press, 2007), 78.

114. Jordan, *Possessed*, 46; Patai, *The Arab Mind*, 81.

115. "What Makes a Sheikh Romance So *Hot*?" "Sheikhs and Desert Love" website, accessed June 6, 2008, www.sheikhs-and-desert-love.com/allfeatures.html.

116. Jordan, *Possessed*, 5–6.

117. White, *Loved*, 48, 118.

118. Morey, *Stolen*, 77.

119. Patai, 81.

120. For Said's critique of Patai, see Said, *Orientalism*, 309.

121. Jerrold Post, *The Mind of the Terrorist: The Psychology of Terrorism from the IRA to al-Qa'ida* (New York: Palgrave, 2007), 9.

122. Ibid., 8, 9, 12, 15, 37.

123. He wants to argue against the idea that terrorists act independently as "crazy" individuals, because he does not want them to have recourse to the claim of insanity during a criminal trial.

124. Tania Modleski, *Loving with a Vengeance: Mass-Produced Fantasies for Women* (1982; repr., New York: Routledge, 2008), 5, 11, 28; Pamela Regis, *A Natural History of the Romance Novel* (Philadelphia: University of Pennsylvania Press, 2003); Juliet Flesch, *From Australia with Love: A History of Modern Australian Popular Romance Novels* (Fremantle, Australia: Curtin University Books, 2004).

125. White, *Loved*, 212; ibid.; Jordan, *Possessed*, 48; Trish Morey, *The Sheikh's Convenient Virgin* 143.

126. Morey, *Convenient Virgin*, 97; Porter, *Bought Bride*, 64, 181, 182; White, *Loved*, 124.

127. Morey, *Stolen*, 173.

CHAPTER 2. *DESERT* IS JUST ANOTHER WORD FOR FREEDOM

1. According the Romance Writers of America (RWA) website, "Romance fiction was the largest share of the U.S. consumer market in 2012 at 16.7 percent." Romance novels generated $1.438 billion in sales in 2012 and an estimated $1.350 billion in sales in 2013. To better understand how lucrative the romance fiction industry is, it is helpful to compare these figures to sales in other genres in 2012: Religion/inspirational: $717.9 million; mystery: $728.2 million; science fiction/fantasy: $590.2 million; classic literary fiction: $470.5 million. Romance Writers of America, "Romance Industry Statistics," Romance Writers of America, accessed August 22, 2014, www.rwa.org/p/cm/ld/ fid=580.

2. Mimi Thi Nguyen, *The Gift of Freedom: War, Debt, and Other Refugee Passages* (Durham, NC: Duke University Press, 2012).

3. Loreth Anne White, *The Sheik Who Loved Me* (New York: Silhouette, 2005), 213.

4. Elizabeth Povinelli, *The Empire of Love: Toward a Theory of Intimacy, Genealogy, and Carnality* (Durham, NC: Duke University Press, 2006), 17.

5. Sarah Morgan, *Bella and the Merciless Sheikh* (New York: Harlequin, 2011), 83.

6. Ibid., 115 (emphasis in original).

7. Ann Voss Peterson, *Seized by the Sheikh* (New York: Harlequin, 2011), 10.

8. Abby Green, *Breaking the Sheikh's Rules* (New York: Harlequin, 2011), 183.

9. Meredith Webber, *Sheikh, Children's Doctor* (New York: Harlequin, 2011), 183–184.

10. As is obvious from my consistent references to the *Smart Bitches, Trashy Books* website and blog, I take it as exemplary of the mainstream online romance novel community. A survey of the traffic statistics for other romance novel websites that seem to enjoy a wide readership demonstrates just how exemplary *Smart Bitches* is. While the U.S. ranking for *Smart Bitches, Trashy Books* is 42,828, the U.S. ranking for *Romantic Times* (another common romance website and blog) is 70,390. Compare also the global rankings: *Smart Bitches, Trashy Books* 162,220; *I [Heart] Harlequin Presents* (a category of Harlequin romances with a blog) 2,694,532; *Pink Heart Society* 293,215; and *Romancing the Blog* 10,126,456. Alexa.com: The Web Information Company, accessed September 24, 2012, www.alexa.com/.

11. Daisy Cummins and Julie Bindel, "Mills & Boon: 100 Years of Heaven or Hell?" *The Guardian* (London and Manchester), December 4, 2007, www.guardian.co.uk/ lifeandstyle/2007/dec/05/women.fiction.

12. See, for example, Dixon, *The Romance Fiction of Mills and Boon, 1909–1990's* (London and Philadelphia: UCL Press, 1999); Juliet Flesch, *From Australia with Love: A History of Modern Australian Popular Romance Novels* (Fremantle, Australia: Curtin University Books, 2004); Pamela Regis, *A Natural History of the Romance Novel* (Philadelphia: University of Pennsylvania Press, 2003).

13. SBSarah, "Mills and Boon: Heaven, Hell, or Just People Hyperventilating," *Smart Bitches, Trashy Books* (blog), December 6, 2007, http://smartbitchestrashybooks.com/ blog/mills_boon_heaven_hell_or_just_people_hyperventilating/. Interestingly, one of the arguments against Bindel is the fact that she quotes from some of the most egregious examples of books, according to *Smart Bitches*, one of which is a sheikh romance novel.

14. Sally Goade, *Empowerment versus Oppression: Twenty First Century Views on Popular Romance Novels* (Newcastle, UK: Cambridge Scholars Publishing, 2007), 1.

15. Margaret Ann Jensen, *Love's Sweet Return: The Harlequin Story* (Bowling Green, OH: Bowling Green State University Popular Press, 1984), 122–139; Regis, *A Natural History*, 9–16; Candice Proctor, "The Romance Genre Blues or Why We Don't Get No Respect," in *Empowerment versus Oppression: Twenty First Century Views of Popular*

Romance Novels, ed. Sally Goade (Newcastle, UK: Cambridge Scholars, 2007), 12–19; Susan Elizabeth Phillips, "The Romance and the Empowerment of Women," in *Dangerous Men and Adventurous Women: Romance Writers on the Appeal of the Romance*, ed. Jayne Ann Krentz (Philadelphia: University of Pennsylvania Press, 1992), 53–60; Flesch; Dixon, *Mills and Boon*, 9, 179–195.

16. Ann Rosalind Jones, "Mills and Boon Meets Feminism" in *The Progress of Romance: the Politics of Popular Fiction*, ed. Jean Radford (London and New York: Routledge & Kegan Paul, 1986), 195–218; Lynda L. Crane, "Romance Novel Readers: In Search of Feminist Change?" *Women Studies* 23 (1994): 257–269.

17. Teresa Southwick, *To Catch a Sheik* (New York: Silhouette, 2003), 33.

18. Ibid., 39.

19. Crane, "In Search of Feminist Change?" 266.

20. Joseph McAleer, *Passion's Fortune: The Story of Mills and Boon* (Oxford: Oxford University Press, 1999), 290.

21. I am not arguing against the utility of freedom as a concept, but rather about its particular use in these contexts. I tend to agree with Nikolas Rose's assertion that "we can distinguish freedom as a formula of resistance from freedom as a formula of power." Nikolas Rose, *Powers of Freedom: Reframing Political Thought* (New York: Cambridge University Press, 1999), 65.

22. Ibid., 1.

23. Nora Roberts, December 7, 2007 (2:27 a.m.), comment on SBSarah, "Mills and Boon."

24. Robin, December 6, 2007 (10:22 a.m.) comment on SBSarah, "Mills and Boon." (This commenter has a nuanced view of power and oppression.)

25. See also TracyS, December 6, 2007 (2:49 p.m.); Miranda, December 7, 2007 (3:54 a.m.); Xandra, December 7, 2007 (12:57 p.m.), comments on SBSarah, "Mills and Boon."

26. Patricia Lather, *Getting Smart: Feminist Research and Pedagogy with/in the Postmodern* (New York: Routledge, 1991), 3. As is probably apparent from the quote, Lather does not herself subscribe to this definition, instead favoring a more structural, community-oriented definition.

27. Nikolas Rose, *Governing the Soul: The Shaping of the Private Self* (New York: Routledge, 1990).

28. TracyS, December 6, 2007 (2:49 p.m.), comment on SBSarah, "Mills and Boon."

29. Azteclady, December 6, 2007 (2:29 p.m.), comment on SBSarah, "Mills and Boon."

30. See, for example, Baconsmom, December 6, 2007 (1:13 p.m.); and SamG, December 6, 2007 (10:10 a.m.), comments on SBSarah, "Mills and Boon." Interestingly, Janice Radway, *Reading the Romance: Women, Patriarchy, and Popular Literature* (1984; repr., Chapel Hill: University of North Carolina Press, 1991), 208, commented on this kind of defense in her conclusion: "Therefore, while the act of romance reading is used by women as a means of partial protest against the role prescribed for them by the culture, the discourse itself actively insists on the desirability, naturalness, and benefits

of that role by portraying it not as the imposed necessity that it is but as a freely designed, personally controlled, individual choice."

31. Rose, *Governing*, 258.

32. Baconsmom, December 6, 2007 (1:13 p.m.), comment on SBSarah, "Mills and Boon."

33. Isabel Swift, "The 'R' Word . . . by Isabel Swift," *Isabel Swift . . . Wouldn't You Like to Know?* (blog), May 23, 2011, http://isabelswift.blogspot.com/2011/05/r-word-by-isabel-swift.html.

34. Rose, *Governing*, 258.

35. Povinelli, *Empire of Love*, 17.

36. Slavoj Žižek, *How to Read Lacan* (New York: W.W. Norton & Co., 2007), 57.

37. Amy Kaplan, "Romancing the Empire," in *The Anarchy of Empire in the Making of U.S. Culture* (Cambridge, MA: Harvard University Press, 2005), 92–120, esp. 110.

38. Nguyen, *Gift of Freedom*, 20.

39. Ibid., 17.

40. Ann Laura Stoler, *Race and the Education of Desire: Foucault's History of Sexuality and the Colonial Order of Things* (Durham, NC: Duke University Press, 1995).

41. Pippa Roscoe, January 25, 2012, comment on Sharon Kendrick, "Fear and Longing and Desert Sheikhs," *I [Heart] Harlequin Presents* (blog), January 24, 2012, www.iheartpresents.com/2012/01/fear-and-longing-and-desert-sheikhs-by-sharon-kendrick.

42. Donna Young, *Captive of the Desert King* (New York: Harlequin, 2009) .

43. See, for example, Olivia Gates, *To Touch a Sheikh* (New York: Harlequin, 2011).

44. Penny Jordan, *Possessed by the Sheikh* (New York: Harlequin, 2005), 40.

45. Young, *Captive*, 47.

46. Thanks to Nadine Sinno for pointing this out.

47. Tessa Radley, *The Desert Bride of Al Zayed* (New York: Silhouette, 2007), 67.

48. Trish Morey, *Stolen by the Sheikh* (New York: Harlequin, 2006), 43.

49. Radley, *Desert Bride*, 86.

50. Webber, *Sheikh, Children's Doctor*, 45.

51. Young, *Captive*, 203.

52. An excellent example is Peterson, *Seized by the Sheikh*, which features a Native American sheriff with whom the sheikh identifies as he recognizes him as a person of color. Efraim, the sheikh, says of the sheriff: "Obviously he wasn't of Middle Eastern descent, but Native American. However, Efraim had to admit the resemblance in coloring made him feel a little more at ease. A little less the enemy" (58).

53. For more on comparisons between Middle Eastern and Native American imagery in the U.S., see Steven Salaita, *The Holy Land in Transit: Colonialism and the Quest for Canaan* (Syracuse, NY: Syracuse University Press, 2006); and Amira Jarmakani, "Veiled Intentions: The Cultural Mythology of Veils, Harems, and Belly Dancers in the Service of Empire, Security, and Globalization," in *Imagining Arab Womanhood: The Cultural Mythology of Veils, Harems, and Belly Dancers in the U.S.* (New York: Palgrave Macmillan, 2008).

54. This is one of the primary ways Gilles Deleuze and Félix Guattari, *Anti-Oedipus* (Minneapolis: University of Minnesota Press, 1983), describes the hegemonic quality of capitalism.

55. Susan Nance, *How the Arabian Nights Inspired the American Dream* (Chapel Hill: University of North Carolina Press, 2009), 177.

56. Ibid., 118; Pippa Roscoe, comment on Sharon Kendrick, "Fear and Longing."

57. Green, *Breaking*. See also Sharon Kendrick, *The Playboy Sheikh's Virgin Stable Girl* (New York: Harlequin, 2009); Bonnie Vanak, *The Sword and the Sheath* (New York: Leisure Books, 2007); Nan Ryan, *Burning Love* (New York: HarperCollins, 1996).

58. A good example is in Kendrick, *Playboy Sheikh*: "[The heroine] was like an unbroken horse, he realized. All fire and spirit—with an innate need to be conquered" (105).

59. Gilles Deleuze and Félix Guattari, *A Thousand Plateaus*, trans. and forward by Brian Massumi (1980; repr., Minneapolis: University of Minnesota Press, 1987), 19.

60. "If the nomad can be called the Deterritorialized par excellence, it is precisely because there is no reterritorialization *afterward*" (Deleuze and Guattari, *A Thousand Plateaus*, 381).

61. Green, *Breaking*, 104.

62. Linda Conrad, *Secret Agent Sheik* (New York: Harlequin, 2011), 95.

63. See Regis, *A Natural History*, 9, 16, 22; Radway, *Reading the Romance*, 66–67, 170.

64. Nalini Singh, *Desert Warrior* (New York: Harlequin, 2009), 105. See also Morgan, *Bella*, 94; Morey, *Stolen*, 173; Gates, *Touch*, 94; Young, *Captive*, 164.

65. Snitow, "Mass Market Romance : Pornography for Women is Different," in *Powers of Desire: The Politics of Sexuality*, ed. Ann Snitow et al. (1979; repr., New York: Monthly Review Press, 1983), 245–263; Barbara Creed, "The Women's Romance as Sexual Fantasy: 'Mills and Boon,'" in *All Her Labours Two: Embroidering the Framework*, ed. Women and the Labour Publications Collective (Sydney: Hale & Iremonger, 1984), 47–67.

66. For a concrete example, see Shahrzad Mojab, "'Post-War Reconstruction,' Imperialism and Kurdish Women's NGOs," in *Women and War in the Middle East*, ed. Nadje Al-Ali and Nicola Pratt (London: Zed, 2009), 99–128.

67. Many scholars discuss this genre of memoirs. See, for example, Saba Mahmood, "Feminism, Democracy, and Empire: Islam and the War of Terror" in *Women's Studies on the Edge*, ed. Joan Wallach Scott (Durham, NC: Duke University Press, 2008), 81–114; Sunaina Maira, "'Good' and 'Bad' Muslim Citizens: Feminists, Terrorists, and U.S. Orientalisms," *Feminist Studies* 35, no. 3 (2009): 631–656; Hamid Dabashi, *Brown Skin, White Masks* (London: Pluto, 2011); Dohra Ahmad, "Not Yet Beyond the Veil: Muslim Women in American Popular Literature," *Social Text 99* 27, no. 2 (summer 2009): 105–131; Ali Behdad and Juliet Williams, "Neo-Orientalism" in *Globalizing American Studies*, ed. Brian T. Edwards and Dilip Parameshwar Gaonkar (Chicago: University of Chicago Press, 2010), 283–299.

68. Nevertheless, it still earned $401 million at the box office. See "Might the Harem Scare 'Em?" *New Zealand Herald*, May 28, 2010.

69. Ella Shohat and Robert Stam, *Unthinking Eurocentrism: Multiculturalism and the Media* (New York: Routledge, 1994), 166–170, esp. 169.

70. Note the similarity in the previously quoted passage in Morey, *Stolen*, 43.

71. Sunaina Maira, "Belly Dancing: Arab-Face, Orientalist Feminism, and U.S. Empire," *American Quarterly* 60, no. 2 (2008): 317–345.

72. Diana Fuss, *Identification Papers* (New York: Routledge, 1995), 2.

73. Homi Bhabha, "Of Mimicry and Men," in *The Location of Culture* (New York: Routledge, 1994), 121–131; Anne McClintock, "Paranoid Empire: Specters from Guantánamo and Abu Ghraib," *Small Axe, Number 28* 13, no. 1 (2009): 50–74.

74. Ibid., 131.

75. Singh, *Warrior*, 111, 183; Radley, *Desert Bride*, 36; Morgan, *Bella*, 10, 116; Marton, *Sheik Seduction*, 104–105, 126.

76. For romance novels as origin stories, see Hsu-Ming Teo, *Desert Passions: Orientalism and Romance Novels* (Austin: University of Texas Press, 2012), 49.

77. "Might the Harem Scare 'Em?" *Sex and the City* is the subject of some debate among feminist scholars regarding the extent to which it can be considered a feminist program. I tend to agree with Angela McRobbie's reading of *SATC* as a containment of feminism through an appropriation that ultimately transforms feminism into a vacuous kind of commodity feminism. In McRobbie's comment on the way that *SATC* invokes second-wave feminism, one can also see a clear connection to the function of feminism in contemporary romance novels: "*SATC* works as a provocation to second-wave feminism [because] it enacts a kind of gender re-stabilization by summoning the ghost of the old disappearing feminist (did she ever really exist?)" (541). See Angela McRobbie, "Young Women and Consumer Culture: An Intervention," *Cultural Studies* 22, no. 5 (September 2008): 531–550.

78. Rachel Wells, "Desert Storm," *Sydney Morning Herald*, June 12, 2010.

79. Simone S. Oliver, "Head Over Heels Over Turbans: The Exotic Headdress of a Bygone Era Catches On with a Younger Crowd," *International Herald Tribune*, November 16, 2010. Turbans have undoubtedly been historically associated with Arab dress, though they are not actually a culturally Arab form of dress. They are generally worn by (Indian) Sikhs, who have been conflated with Arabs and Muslims in the U.S. in the post-9/11 context, as tragically demonstrated with the mass shooting carried out by a white supremacist at a Sikh temple in Wisconsin on August 5, 2012, among multiple other incidents.

80. Ibid.

81. Eva Friede, "*Sex and the City 2* Dazzles in the Desert: Ball Gowns, Blazers and Burqas That Meet Blahniks Make for a Fashion Fantasy in Abu Dhabi for the Fab Foursome," *Montreal Gazette*, May 27, 2010.

82. Emirati women do not wear burqas—they typically wear a hijab and/or a niqab and an abaya. The *Sex and the City 2* materials all adopt the term *burqa*, though, probably because it is the style of dress worn in Afghanistan under the Taliban and was popularized in the U.S. after 9/11. Since both the abaya and burqa are long garments that cover the wearer's body, there would be no reason to wear them simultaneously.

Further, the abaya is mostly a Middle Eastern cultural garment while the burqa can be more culturally linked to Central Asia.

83. Fuss, *Identification Papers*, 1.

84. Submission does not always mean a lack of agency, as Saba Mahmood skillfully demonstrates in her study of the women's mosque movement in Egypt. However, agency can be co-opted in the service of biopower, which doesn't mean it is monolithic.

85. Porter, *Bought Bride*, 71.

86. Green, *Breaking*, 61, 88. As mentioned in a previous endnote, it would be ridiculous (and redundant) to wear both an abaya and a burqa. See Morey, *Stolen*, 119, for another example.

87. Nina Bruhns, *Vampire Sheikh* (New York: Harlequin, 2011), 46.

88. Morey, *Stolen*, 119.

89. Ibid.

90. Marton, *Sheik Seduction*, 62.

91. Lila Abu-Lughod, "Do Muslim Women Really Need Saving? Anthropological Reflections on Cultural Relativism and Its Others," *American Anthropologist* 104, no. 3 (2002): 783–790.

92. Marton, *Sheik Seduction*, 173.

93. Marguerite Kaye, *The Governess and the Sheikh* (New York: Harlequin, 2011), 182.

94. Green, *Breaking*, 116–117. See also Bruhns, *Vampire*, 46, 62; Morey, *Stolen*, 121; Young, *Captive*, 27; Lawrence, *Defiant Virgin*, 173.

95. Fuss, *Identification Papers*, 34.

96. Frantz Fanon, *Black Skin, White Masks*, trans. Charles Lam Markmann (New York: Grove Press, 1967, 100).

97. Eric Lott, *Love and Theft: Blackface Minstrelsy and the American Working Class* (New York: Oxford University Press, 1993), 6.

98. Here I am adapting Lott's title (ibid.).

99. Brenda Jackson, *Delaney's Desert Sheikh* (New York, Silhouette, 2002), 29.

100. Ibid., 183.

101. Also of note is the fact that neither of these novels are category Harlequin romances, though most desert romances are. Both mention actual feminist leaders. In Vanak, *Sword*, 281, the heroine is Arab, and she participates in a march for women's rights with Huda Sha'arawi (misspelled in the novel as Sah'rawi), a famous feminist activist in early twentieth-century Egypt. In Nan Ryan, *Burning Love* (New York: HarperCollins, 1996), 209, the white heroine is "jailed with Susan B. Antony [the famous U.S. feminist who struggled for women's suffrage] for leading a suffrage march in the capital."

102. Kaye, *Governess*, 205.

103. Linda Winstead Jones, *The Sheik and I* (New York: Silhouette, 2006), 194.

104. Singh, *Warrior*, 132.

105. Sharon Kendrick, *Monarch of the Sands* (New York: Harlequin, 2011), 180, 183.

106. Christopher Buckley, *Florence of Arabia* (New York: Random House, 2004), back cover, 18.

107. Ibid., 113.

108. Thanks to Robert Vitalis's wonderful book *America's Kingdom* for leading me to this source.

109. Mildred Montgomery Logan, "I Like Being the Garden of Eden's First Lady," *Cattleman* 38, no. 5 (October 1951): 30–31, 107–117, 110.

110. Mildred Montgomery Logan, "They Call Me Madam Sam," *Cattleman* 38, no. 8 (January 1952): 22, 62–65.

111. Elizabeth Wright, ed., *Feminism and Psychoanalysis: A Critical Dictionary* (Cambridge, MA: Blackwell, 1992), 70. In the preface, I define *disavowal*, using similar wording from Wright.

112. Jordan, *Possessed*, 7.

113. Romance novels are much heralded and defended on the basis of the "accurate" historical and cultural information they provide to readers. The example of King Nuri lends both credence and doubt to this claim. While Porter researched aspects of Arab culture and Arabic language, her use of "King Malik" clearly demonstrates the limitations of such research, since she seems not to recognize the redundancy of such a name: *malik* means "king" in Arabic.

114. Porter, *Bought Bride*, 54.

115. Radway, *Reading the Romance*, 77, 101, 123, 125.

116. For examples, see the following: Radley, *Desert Bride*, 74, 99; Marton, *Sheik Seduction*, 14, 104–105; Porter, *Bought Bride*, 28; Trish Morey, *The Sheikh's Convenient Virgin* (New York: Harlequin, 2008), 31; Liz Fielding, *The Sheikh's Unsuitable Bride* (New York: Harlequin, 2008), 53; Peterson, *Seized*, 96; Jackson, *Delaney's*, 13, 49; Jones, *The Sheik and I*, 26; Singh, *Warrior*, 56; Lawrence, *Defiant Virgin*, 84; Vanak, *Sword*, 20, 45, 180.

117. White, *Loved*, 90–91.

118. Jordan, *Possessed*, 49.

119. The oppression of the colonizer is addressed most famously in Albert Memmi, *The Colonizer and the Colonized*, trans. Howard Greenfield (Boston: Beacon Press, 1965).

CHAPTER 3. DESIRING THE BIG BAD BLADE

1. Nan Ryan, *Burning Love* (New York: HarperCollins, 1996), 213.

2. Ibid.

3. Jodi Melamed, "The Spirit of Neoliberalism: From Racial Liberalism to Neoliberal Multiculturalism," *Social Text 89*, 24, no. 4 (winter 2006): 1–24.

4. Loreth Anne White, *The Sheik Who Loved Me* (New York: Silhouette, 2005), 124.

5. We could understand liberal and neoliberal multiculturalism to be somewhat coterminous, where *neoliberal* signals more of a temporal shift than anything else. In other words, if *liberal* here signals some of its own key political and philosophical

ideals—individualism, freedom as rooted in the humanist subject, a focus on rights (and especially property rights) as a key mode of the individual subject, and an idea of universalism that belies its own specificity—then we can understand how the term *liberal multiculturalism* refers to the way that notions of tolerance and diversity (to name a few) operate to individualize structural inequalities and oppressions in a way that leads to tokenizing and minimizing the very thing (racial diversity and justice) it purports to care about. In her book *Arab America: Gender, Cultural Politics, and Activism* (New York: New York University Press, 2012), Nadine Naber seems to use the term "neoliberal multiculturalism" in this way—as coterminous with liberal multiculturalism while also referencing a temporal shift to the rise of neoliberal policies and frameworks beginning in the 1970s, burgeoning in the 1980s, and continuing to the current context. While this context may add some of neoliberalism's key features— flexibility and an emphasis on market freedoms as core to the idea of freedom—the idea as a whole (vis-à-vis tolerance and diversity, but perhaps now in the language of color-blindness and post-racial politics) lives on. A shift from *liberal* to *neoliberal* could also signal a shift in conceptualizations of the nation-state. If liberalism is rooted in a concept of the bounded nation-state as sovereign power, the era of neoliberalism has certainly witnessed a sense of the decreasing salience of the nation-state. The flexibility and suppleness of capital (as organized through corporations, usually) seems to undercut the salience of the nation-state in many ways (hence the rise of the idea of global cities, which are also major financial centers), and so the shift to neoliberal multiculturalism would likely signal some of this as well. Mimi Thi Nguyen's formulation of "transnational multiculturalism" (*The Gift of Freedom: War, Debt, and Other Refugee Passages* [Durham, NC: Duke University Press, 2012], 142–143) could help here. She seems to be using a "scattered hegemonies" approach (Inderpal Grewal and Caren Kaplan, *Scattered Hegemonies* [Minneapolis: University of Minnesota Press, 1994]). That is, she may be referencing the way that imperialist state power operates in "scattered" kinds of formations—not necessarily in monolithic ways that are bounded by the nation-state. Put simply, the "global North" is not all power and privilege and the "global South" is not all "development" and destitution. Transnational multiculturalism would be able to capture how these pockets could connect with one another and form networks across national boundaries.

6. A good example can be found on the cover of Bonnie Vanak, *The Sword and the Sheath* (New York: Leisure Books, 2007).

7. Siobhan Somerville, *Queering the Color Line: Race and the Invention of Homosexuality in American Culture* (Durham, NC: Duke University Press, 2000).

8. Sarah Wendell and Candy Tan, *Beyond Heaving Bosoms: The Smart Bitches' Guide to Romance Novels* (New York: Simon & Schuster, 2009), 190; SBSarah, "Trend Spotting," *Smart Bitches Trashy Books: All of the Romance, None of the Bullshit* (blog), June 21, 2011, http://smartbitchestrashybooks.com/blog/trend-spotting/.

9. Wendell and Tan, *Beyond Heaving Bosoms*, 77.

10. Stephanie Wardrop, "Last of the Red Hot Mohicans: Miscegenation in the Popular American Romance," *MELUS* 22, no. 2 (summer 1997): 61–74.

11. On the link between the Latin lover and the sheikh, see Gaylyn Studlar, "Discourses of Gender and Ethnicity: The Construction and De(con)struction of Rudolph Valentino as Other," *Film Criticism*, 13, no. 2 (winter 1989): 18–35.

12. Stephanie Burley, "Shadows and Silhouettes: The Racial Politics of Category Romance," *Paradoxa*, 5, nos. 13–14 (2000): 324–343, esp. 324.

13. Evelyn Alsultany, *Arabs and Muslims in the Media: Race and Representation after 9/11* (New York: New York University Press, 2012); Edward Said, *Covering Islam: How the Media and the Experts Determine How We See the Rest of the World* (New York: Pantheon Books, 1981).

14. For "assemblage," see Jasbir Puar, *Terrorist Assemblages: Homonationalism in Queer Times* (Durham, NC: Duke University Press, 2007). For "categorical miscegenation," see Rey Chow, *The Protestant Ethnic and the Spirit of Capitalism* (New York: Columbia University Press, 2002), 7.

15. See, for example, Loreth Anne White, *The Sheik Who Loved Me* (New York: Silhouette, 2005), 8, 129; Olivia Gates, *To Touch a Sheikh* (New York: Harlequin, 2011), 35; Donna Young, *Captive of the Desert King* (New York: Harlequin, 2009), 102; Linda Conrad, *Secret Agent Sheik* (New York: Harlequin, 2011), 170–200.

16. A *kufiya* is a garment of triangularly folded cloth, often with a checkered pattern, worn (usually) by Arab or Kurdish men to protect the head from heat and cold. It became known in the U.S. mostly through the late Palestinian leader Yasser Arafat, though it has recently been popularized as both a (Palestinian) resistance and solidarity symbol and a "global chic" fashion symbol. See Ted Swedenburg, "Bad Rap for a Neck Scarf?" *International Journal of Middle East Studies* 41 (2009): 184–185. The term for the similar item of clothing (usually white), worn mostly in the Gulf region of the Middle East, is *ghutrah*, and the term for the rope cord that holds the *kufiya* or *ghutrah* in place on the head is *igal*.

17. For more on Lawrence of Arabia as an object of desire, see Ella Shohat and Robert Stam, *Unthinking Eurocentrism: Multiculturalism and the Media* (New York: Routledge, 1994). See also Steve Caton's discussion of the racial politics of the original movie poster for *Lawrence of Arabia* (the 1962 film). Because the shadowed figure of T. E. Lawrence could be read as black, the poster was quickly rescinded and revised. Steven Caton, *Lawrence of Arabia: A Film's Anthropology* (Berkeley: University of California Press, 1999).

18. For an analysis of the racial politics of sheikh romance covers with a focus on the shifts in skin color, see Amy Burge, "Disappearing Difference," *Teach Me Tonight: Musings on Romance Fiction from an Academic Perspective* (blog), August 24, 2011, http://teachmetonight.blogspot.com/. See also Amy Burge, "Desiring the East: A Comparative Study of Middle English Romance and Modern Popular Sheikh Romance" (PhD diss., University of York, 2012), 163–170.

19. Nine out of sixty-five desert romances published between 2002 and 2010 (less than 15 percent) feature a sheikh wearing a headdress on the cover, whereas thirty-seven out of eighty-two published before 2002 (nearly 50 percent) feature such a cover.

20. Brenda Jackson, *Delaney's Desert Sheikh* (New York: Silhouette, 2002), 158, 10.

21. Ibid., 139.

22. Melanie McAlister, *Epic Encounters: Culture, Media, and U.S. Interests in the Middle East 1945–2000* (Berkeley: University of California Press, 2001), 37; Sarah Gualtieri, *Between Arab and White: Race and Ethnicity in the Early Syrian American Diaspora* (Berkeley: University of California Press, 2009).

23. Michael Omi and Howard Winant, *Racial Formation in the United States*, 2nd ed. (Philadelphia: Temple University Press, 1994), 64.

24. Paul Gilroy, *Against Race: Imagining Political Culture Beyond the Color Line* (Cambridge, MA: Harvard University Press, 2000), 29.

25. Ibid., 31.

26. Ibid., 1.

27. Nadine Naber, "'Look, Mohammed the Terrorist Is Coming!': Cultural Racism, Nation-Based Racism, and the Intersectionality of Oppressions after 9/11," in *Race and Arab Americans Before and After 9/11*, ed. Amaney Jamal and Nadine Naber (New York: Syracuse University Press, 2008), 276–304.

28. Somerville, *Queering the Color Line*, 21.

29. Howard Winant, *The New Politics of Race: Globalism, Difference, Justice* (Minneapolis: University of Minnesota Press, 2004), 85, 123–124, 139.

30. Ibid., x.

31. On the racialization of muhajabaat, or women who wear hijab, see Louise Cainkar, *Homeland Insecurity: The Arab American and Muslim American Experience after 9/11* (New York: Russell Sage, 2009).

32. Winant, *New Politics of Race*, 3.

33. Burke Long, *Imagining the Holy Land: Maps, Models, and Fantasy Travels* (Bloomington: Indiana University Press, 2003); McAlister, *Epic Encounters*, 45–83; Steven Salaita, *The Holy Land in Transit: Colonialism and the Quest for Canaan* (Syracuse, NY: Syracuse University Press, 2006); Amira Jarmakani, *Imagining Arab Womanhood: The Cultural Mythology of Veils, Harems, and Belly Dancers in the U.S.* (New York: Palgrave Macmillan, 2008).

34. Robert Rydell, *All the World's a Fair: Visions of Empire at American International Expositions, 1976–1916* (Chicago: University of Chicago Press, 1984).

35. A similar shift can be charted with reference to Chinese Americans, whose racial construction as distant and exotic shifted into one understood as "present and threatening," though they clearly bear a different relationship to the discourse of national security. See Robert G. Lee, *Orientals: Asian Americans in Popular Culture* (Philadelphia: Temple University Press, 1999), 28.

36. For examples of the greedy oil sheikh, see McAlister, *Epic Encounters*, 137.

37. Somerville, *Queering the Color Line*, 154–156.

38. Mitchy, August 17, 2007 (6:23 p.m.), comment on Amy Wilkins, "The Unshakeable Appeal of the Sheikh Hero," *I [Heart] Harlequin Presents* (blog), August 17, 2007, www.iheartpresents.com/?p=96; Marilyn S, August 20, 2007 (3:18 p.m.), comment on Wilkins, "Unshakeable Appeal."

39. Trish Morey, March 30, 2007 (8:21 a.m.), comment on Kimberly Young, "Kimberly Young Is a Love-Slave to the Sheikh!" *I [Heart] Harlequin Presents* (blog), March 28, 2008, www.iheartpresents.com/?p=40.

40. Radway, *Reading the Romance: Women, Patriarchy, and Popular Literature* (1984; repr., Chapel Hill: University of North Carolina Press, 1991).

41. Ibid, 107.

42. Robin, August 19, 2007 (11:19 p.m.), comment on SBSarah, "Alphas in Marriage," *Smart Bitches, Trashy Books* (blog), August 16, 2007, http://smartbitchestrashybooks. com/index.php/weblog/comments/alphas_in_marriage/.

43. Geraldine Heng, *Empire of Magic: Medieval Romance and the Politics of Cultural Fantasy* (New York: Columbia University Press, 2003), 18.

44. Ibid., 14.

45. E. M. Hull, *The Sheik* (1919; repr., Holicong, PA: Wildside, 2004), 133.

46. Dalia, June 12, 2007 (5:51 p.m.), comment on Gwyneth Bolton, "*Bitch* Magazine Does Romance," *Gwyneth Bolton's Blog*, June 12, 2007, http://gwynethbolton.blogspot. com/2007/06/bitch-magazine-does-romance.html; Cyranetta, May 22, 2007 (11:01 a.m.), comment on SBSarah, "Meg Cabot, Comfort Reads, and Sheikh Romance," *Smart Bitches Trashy Books* (blog), May 22, 2007, http://smartbitchestrashybooks.com/ index.php/weblog/comments/meg_cabot_comfort_reads_and_sheikh_romance/.

47. Charlene, May 22, 2007 (4:06 p.m.), comment on SBSarah, "Meg Cabot, Comfort Reads."

48. Beth, May 22, 2007 (6:16 p.m.), comment on SBSarah, "Meg Cabot, Comfort Reads."

49. Ostensibly, she is referring to a set of commercials for Calgon bubble bath, which used the popular slogan "Calgon, take me away."

50. patricia sargeant, June 12, 2007 (4:12 p.m.), comment on Bolton, "*Bitch* Magazine Does Romance."

51. Ann Wesley Hardin, May 22, 2007 (8:41 a.m.), comment on SBSarah, "Meg Cabot, Comfort Reads."

52. Desert romances and paranormal romances are not necessarily mutually exclusive categories, as demonstrated by Nina Bruhns's Vampire Sheikh series, but the crossover is limited.

53. Devon, June 12, 2007 (10:21 a.m.), comment on Bolton, "*Bitch* Magazine Does Romance."

54. Leila Ahmed, "Western Ethnocentrism and Perceptions of the Harem," *Feminist Studies* 8, no. 3 (1982): 521–534.

55. CT, August 18, 2007 (11:40 a.m.), comment on Wilkins, "The Unshakeable Appeal."

56. The term *Islamicate* refers to countries or cultures in which Islam is part of the governing or dominant structure of the society. Coined by Marshall G. S. Hodgson, the term acknowledges the variety of religions and ethnicities that may be represented in such a society, and the complexities of Islam as both a religious and a cultural influence in such societies.

57. Stephanie, May 22, 2007 (7:26 a.m.), comment on SBSarah, "Meg Cabot, Comfort Reads."

58. The original "Smart Bitches" were Sarah Wendell (screen name SBSarah) and Candy Tan. Since then, Tan has mostly left the site (since she enrolled in law school and presumably couldn't keep up with the volume of responses), leaving Wendell to author and manage the site. Wendell seems to have turned it into a successful business and has authored a second book: Sarah Wendell, *Everything I Know About Love, I Learned from Romance Novels* (Naperville, IL: Sourcebooks Casablanca, 2011).

59. SBSarah, "The Playboy Sheikh's Virgin Stable Girl by Sharon Kendrick," *Smart Bitches Trashy Books* (blog), September 10, 2009, www.smartbitchestrashybooks.com/index.php/weblog/comments/
the-playbot-sheikhs-virgin-stable-girl-by-Sharon-Kendrick/.

60. Angel, August 16, 2007 (9:44 p.m.), comment on SBSarah, "Alphas in Marriage," *Smart Bitches, Trashy Books* (blog), August 16, 2007, http://smartbitchestrashybooks.com/index.php/weblog/comments/alphas_in_marriage/.

61. Ibid. (11:41 p.m.).

62. The major sites of romance novel production are the U.S., the U.K., Canada, and Australia, and these regions also tend to be the homes of the mostly white heroines.

63. Najida, August 19, 2007 (6:51 a.m.), comment on SBSarah, "Alphas in Marriage."

64. Erin, May 22, 2007 (8:43 a.m.), comment on SBSarah, "Meg Cabot, Comfort Reads."

65. snarkhunter, August 17, 2007 (9:55 a.m.), comment on SBSarah, "Alphas in Marriage."

66. Ibid. (2:45 p.m.).

67. Jackson, *Delaney's*, 84, 150, 160. Another example is Dana Marton, *Sheik Seduction* (New York: Harlequin, 2008), 223, in which the sheikh concludes that if "he was a good Muslim, he should be able to accept Allah's will. But he could not submit to death, not yet." Even though Allah is mentioned here, the author makes it clear that the sheikh does not fully subscribe to Muslim beliefs, in contradistinction to Jackson, *Delaney's*, 84, in which the hero "inwardly prays for Allah's intervention."

68. Jane Smith, *Islam in America* (New York: Columbia University Press, 1999), xiii.

69. Another interesting moment in the campaign was the spectacular, decontextualized coverage of Jeremiah Wright's comment about September 11 as an example of "America's chickens coming home to roost." Despite his standing as a prominent member of the black church, the coverage seemed to cast him as a Farrakhan-like figure, a conflation that was especially interesting given Malcolm X's famous comment about JFK's assassination "representing a case of chickens coming home to roost" (ibid., 88).

70. For further ruminations on the comparison of Arabs and Muslims to African Americans, and "Arabs as the new Blacks," see Moustafa Bayoumi, "The Race Is On: Muslims and Arabs in the American Imagination," *Middle East Report Online*, March 2010, www.merip.org/mero/interventions/bayoumi_interv.html.

71. Toni Morrison, *Playing in the Dark: Whiteness and the Literary Imagination* (Cambridge, MA: Harvard University Press, 1992), 17.

72. Karen Brodkin, *How Jews Became White Folks: And What That Says About Race in America* (New Brunswick, NJ: Rutgers University Press, 1998).

73. Chow, *Protestant Ethnic*, 23–30.

74. Ibid., 25.

75. Hull, *Sheik*, 133.

76. Susan Blake, "What 'Race' Is the Sheik: Rereading a Desert Romance," in *Doubled Plots: Romance and History*, ed. Susan Strenle and Mary Paniccia Carden (Jackson: University of Mississippi Press, 2003), 67–85, esp. 76–78.

77. Etienne Balibar, "Is There a 'Neo-Racism'?" in *Race, Nation, Class: Ambiguous Identities*, ed. Etienne Balibar and Immanuel Wallerstein (London: Verso, 1991), 17–28, esp. 21.

78. Chow, *Protestant Ethnic*, 13–14.

79. Balibar, "Neo-Racism," 26.

80. I use the somewhat awkward formulation "desert ancestry" here because of the construction of Arabiastan as a fictionalized region characterized by its location in a desert climate.

81. Emma Darcy, *Traded to the Sheikh* (New York: Harlequin, 2005), 111.

82. Trish Morey, *Stolen by the Sheikh* (New York: Harlequin, 2006), 9.

83. Ibid., 19.

84. White, *Loved*, 155.

85. Indeed, this is what the term *sheik* came to mean after the 1921 Rudolph Valentino film. See Patricia Raub, "Issues of Passion and Power in E.M. Hull's *The Sheik*," *Women's Studies* 21, no. 1 (1992): 119–128; and Billie Melman, *Women and the Popular Imagination in the Twenties* (New York: Palgrave Macmillan, 1988).

86. See, for example, Marguerite Kaye, *The Governess and the Sheikh* (New York: Harlequin, 2008), 13; Darcy, *Traded*, 18; Ryan, *Burning Love*, 325; and Violet Winspear, *Blue Jasmine* (New York: Harlequin, 1970), 50.

87. For an exception among authors who fail to mention Moorish roots, see Ryan, *Burning Love*, 325, which curiously names Moorish ancestry in connection with the sheikh's Irish mother. See also Annie West, *For the Sheikh's Pleasure* (New York: Harlequin, 2007), 10, for mention of "the Moorish fantasy." "Who would dare deny that religious distinctions . . . hide the most persistent remnants of the history of racism?" Gil Anidjar, *Semites: Race, Religion, Literature* (Stanford, CA: Stanford University Press, 2008), 20.

88. Anouar Majid, *We Are All Moors: Ending Centuries of Crusades against Muslims and Other Enemies* (Minneapolis: University of Minnesota Press, 2009), 53.

89. Junaid Rana, "The Story of Islamophobia," *Souls: A Critical Journal of Black Politics, Culture, and Society* 9, no. 2 (April 2007): 148–161, esp. 152. See also the discussion in his more recent book: Junaid Rana, *Terrifying Muslims: Race and Labor in the South Asian Diaspora* (Durham, NC: Duke University Press, 2011), 57–65.

90. Anidjar, *Semites*, 18.

91. See Janet Jakobsen and Ann Pelligrini, eds., *Secularisms* (Durham, NC: Duke University Press, 2008), for an exploration of these as main elements of the dominant narrative of secularization, a process deeply embedded in the project of modernity.

92. Rana, "Story of Islamophobia," 150.

93. Hull, *Sheik*, 223, 68.

94. See, for example, Ryan, *Burning*, 84; Kim Lawrence, *Defiant Virgin* (New York: Harlequin, 2009), 77, 86; Penny Jordan, *Possessed by the Sheikh* (New York: Harlequin, 2005), 7; Violet Winspear, *Blue Jasmine* (New York: Harlequin, 1970), 32.

95. Ryan, *Burning*, 65.

96. Jakobsen and Pelligrini, *Secularisms*, 6.

97. Lisa Suhair Majaj, "Arab Americans and the Meaning of Race," in *Postcolonial Theory and the United States: Race, Ethnicity, and Literature*, ed. Amaritjit Singh and Peter Schmidt (Jackson: University of Mississippi Press, 2000), 320–337, esp. 324. See also Gualtieri, *Between Arab and White*, 56–57, for an immigration case that made the argument for Syrian compatibility with whiteness and Western civilization, in light of Syria's inclusion in the "Christian fold."

98. Jakobsen and Pelligrini, *Secularisms*, 3.

99. Anidjar, *Semites*, 48. For more on the social construction of religion and secularism, see Talal Asad, *Formations of the Secular: Christianity, Islam, Modernity* (Stanford, CA: Stanford University Press, 2003), 21–66.

100. Jarmakani, *Imagining Arab Womanhood*.

101. Nora Roberts, *Sweet Revenge* (New York: Bantam Books, 1988), 30.

102. Ibid., 40.

103. Ibid., 41.

104. Rana, "Story of Islamophobia," 150.

105. Sophie Weston, *In the Arms of the Sheikh* (New York: Harlequin, 2006), 92, 127, 188.

106. Ann Aguirre, June 12, 2007 (1:02 p.m.), comment on Bolton, "*Bitch* Magazine Does Romance"; Kaite, May 22, 2007 (7:23 a.m.), comment on SBSarah, "Meg Cabot, Comfort Reads."

107. "What Makes a Sheikh Romance *Hot?*" "Sheikhs and Desert Romance" website, accessed June 3, 2008, http://sheikhs-and-desert-love.com/presentation02.html.

108. Kate Walker, "Sheiken and Stirred," *Pink Heart Society* (blog), October 6, 2006, http://pinkheartsociety.blogspot.com/2006/10/thursday-talk-time-with-kate-walker.html.

109. Karen Scott, June 12, 2007 (7:50 a.m.), comment on Bolton, "*Bitch* Magazine Does Romance."

110. Liz Fielding, *The Sheikh's Unsuitable Bride* (New York: Harlequin, 2008), 12.

111. Ryan, *Burning*, 156. See also Sara Wood, *Desert Hostage* (New York: Harlequin, 1991), 51.

112. Darcy, *Traded* (*Arabian Nights* references are on 35, 53, 66, 97, 110, and Omar Khayyam on 53).

113. Ibid., 18.

114. Winspear, *Blue Jasmine*, 113.

115. Laura Wright, *A Bed of Sand* (New York: Silhouette, 2004), 14. On page 52, she describes his skin as "so dark and threaded with sinewy muscle." See also Wood, *Desert Hostage*, 152, for another example.

116. Connie Mason, *Desert Ecstasy* (New York: Dorchester, 1988), 136.

117. Jane Porter, *The Sheikh's Chosen Queen* (New York: Harlequin, 2008), 10; Tessa Radley, *The Desert Bride of Al Zayed* (New York: Harlequin, 2007), 51, 64, 66.

118. Fielding, *Unsuitable Bride*, 171.

119. Roberts, *Sweet Revenge*, 345.

120. Radley, *Desert Bride*, 34.

121. Mason, *Desert Ecstasy*, 158.

122. Marton, *Sheik Seduction*.

123. For more on the concept of social death, see Lisa Marie Cacho, *Social Death: Racialized Rightlessness and the Criminalization of the Unprotected* (New York: New York University Press, 2012).

124. Abby Green, *Breaking the Sheikh's Rules* (New York: Harlequin, 2011), 123.

125. Ibid., 124.

126. Ibid.

CHAPTER 4. TO MAKE A WOMAN HAPPY IN BED . . .

1. Dana Marton, *Sheik Seduction* (New York: Harlequin, 2008), 203.

2. Steven Caton, *Lawrence of Arabia: A Film's Anthropology* (Berkeley: University of California Press, 1999), 208.

3. Ibid. See the chapter "Maskulinities," 200–238, for a discussion of gender and sexuality in the film.

4. Sharon Kendrick, *Monarch of the Sands* (New York: Harlequin, 2011), 87.

5. W.E.B. DuBois, *The Souls of Black Folk* (1903; repr., New York: Bantam, 1989), 1, 10. Moustafa Bayoumi's invocation of DuBois's famous question in his book about how Arab and Muslim identifications have shifted in the post-9/11 U.S. context extends the notion of the color line to Arab and Muslim Americans. See Moustafa Bayoumi, *How Does It Feel to Be a Problem? Being Young and Arab in America* (New York: Penguin Books, 2009).

6. Gilles Deleuze and Félix Guattari, *A Thousand Plateaus*, trans. and forward by Brian Massumi (1980; repr., Minneapolis: University of Minnesota Press, 1987), 227.

7. Gilles Deleuze and Félix Guattari, *Anti-Oedipus* (Minneapolis: University of Minnesota Press, 1983), describe the notion of "desiring-machines," which link the psychic or libidinal realm ("desiring-production," in their terms) to the social realm ("social production," in their terms). See, in particular, pages 28–29, and Eugene Holland, *Deleuze and Guattari's "Anti-Oedipus": Introduction to Schizoanalysis* (New York: Routledge, 1999), 61, for more on this. Deleuze and Guattari's use of the word "machine" also underscores that they focus on the question of how desire works, rather than what it means. In *A Thousand Plateaus*, 89, they develop the notion of the

assemblage through a rather mathematical description of what they call the "tetrava-lence of the assemblage." The tetravalence consists of two axes—a horizontal axis composed of the two vacillating poles described as the "hand-tool" pole and the "face-image" pole, and a vertical axis, which comprises both *territorial sides,* or reterritorialized sides, which stabilize it, and *cutting edges of deterritorialization,* which carry it away" (*ATP*, 88). On the horizontal axis, one finds a complex interaction between objects, things, or signifieds (though none of these words completely captures what Deleuze and Guattari mean by "hand-tool") and the language and discourses that express (and therefore shape) these things. The "hand-tool" pole is also described as the "lesson of things" (*ATP*, 85) and is associated with the "machinic assemblage of bodies," with the body, and with content, though "content" is not to be taken for the simple notion of the signified. The "face-language pole" is also described as the "lesson of signs" and is associated with the "collective assemblage of enunciation," with incorporeal transformations, and with expression, though "expression" is not to be taken for the simple notion of the signifier. Summing up some key ideas about these two poles, they say: "Content is not a signified nor expression a signifier; rather, both are variables of the assemblage" (*ATP*, 91). Both the concept of desiring-machines and the concept of assemblage dramatize how desire is simultaneously libidinal and social. In her explanation of the concept of assemblage (and its use for feminist understand-ings of intersectionality), Jasbir Puar interestingly relates an example from Brian Massumi's *Parables for the Virtual.* In both pieces, which focus on reports of increased domestic violence during the Super Bowl, a curiously relevant event is highlighted—the specific event of domestic violence as manifested in an act of physical violence: the strike or movement of "hand against face." Though neither Massumi nor Puar specifically mentions the tetravalence of assemblage, the friction of hand against face not coincidentally invokes the horizontal axis described here. The event both demon-strates how the "lesson of things" (hand) and the "lesson of signs" (face) collide and that they cannot be conflated. At the same time that the materiality and the signifi-cance of the event overlap, its meanings and interpretations also exceed such an overlapping. See Jasbir Puar, "'I Would Rather Be a Cyborg Than a Goddess': Intersectionality, Assemblage, and Affective Politics," *EIPCP: European Institute for Progressive Cultural Policies*, January 2011, http://eipcp.net/transversal/0811/puar/en; and Brian Massumi, *Parables for the Virtual: Movement, Affect, Sensation* (Durham, NC: Duke University Press, 2002). The horizontal axis, which accounts for the constant interaction between objects, things, and signifieds and the ways they are materialized through language and expression, is simultaneously intersected by the vertical axis, which demonstrates how objects and concepts constantly vacillate from being used in the service of reterritorializing oppressive forms of power to escaping these uses.

   8. See Eugene Holland, *Deleuze and Guattari's "Anti-Oedipus": Introduction to Schizoanalysis*; and Eugene Holland, "Capitalism + Universal History," in *The Deleuze Dictionary*, ed. Adrian Parr (New York: Columbia University Press, 2005), 42–43, for more on this.

9. Many thanks to Maggie Franz for locating two gay desert romances, which were the only examples of desert romances that we could find among queer romances. A second round of searching by Andrea Miller turned up a third title that could fit in this category. They are Kitty Bernetti, *Desert Nights* (n.p.: Xcite Books, 2012), Kindle edition (analyzed here); Alcamia Payne, "The Egyptian Slave," (London: Xcite Books, 2012) (a short story); and Sonja Spencer, *The Sheikh and the Servant* (Tallahassee, FL: Dreamspinner Press, 2009). All are labeled as "gay erotica," which further complicates the search. There is a debate within the romance industry as to whether erotica qualifies as part of the genre. These novels' blurring of the line between romance and erotica is itself indicative of the status of gay romance in the industry at large.

10. Bernetti, *Desert Nights*, ch. 1, 84/808.

11. Ibid., ch. 1, 55/808.

12. Ibid., ch. 2, 462/808.

13. Ibid., ch. 1, 182/808.

14. Ibid., ch. 3, 788/808.

15. Joyce Zonana, "The Sultan and the Slave: Feminist Orientalism and the Structure of 'Jane Eyre'" *Signs*, 18 (1993): 592–617, uses the term "feminist orientalism" to describe the displacement of patriarchal oppression onto the Orient to argue for equality in the West. In other words, gender inequality is understood to be an Oriental practice and therefore becomes a way to excoriate the existence of gender inequality in the West. Hsu-Ming Teo, *Desert Passions: Orientalism and Romance Novels* (Austin: University of Texas Press, 2012), 232–233, builds on this understanding to argue that the sheikhs in desert romances must learn how to "de-orientalize" themselves to successfully couple with the white heroine. In Teo's estimation, desert romances are consistent also with Zonana's formulation of feminist orientalism, as is clear by Teo's statement that "the modern sheik novel is nothing if not a vehicle for liberal feminist concerns" (267).

16. See, for example, Kate Hewitt, *The Sheikh's Forbidden Virgin* (New York: Harlequin, 2009); Sharon Kendrick, *The Playboy Sheikh's Virgin Stable Girl* (New York: Harlequin, 2009); Trish Morey, *The Sheikh's Convenient Virgin* (New York: Harlequin, 2006).

17. Bernetti, *Desert Nights*, ch. 1, 99/808, 197/808.

18. Ibid., ch. 1, 117/808.

19. Joseph Massad, "Re-orienting Desire: The Gay International and the Arab World," in *Desiring Arabs* (Chicago: Chicago University Press, 2008), 160–190.

20. Bernetti, *Desert Nights*, ch. 2, 352/808.

21. Ibid., ch. 2, 360/808.

22. The passage continues: "We all have layers so deep inside us, some of which we keep hidden and some of which we display to the world" (ibid., ch. 3, 605/808).

23. Biddy Martin, *Femininity Played Straight: The Significance of Being Lesbian* (New York: Routledge, 1996); Judith Roof, *Come as You Are: Sexuality and Narrative* (New York, Columbia University Press, 1996); Susan Talburt, "Intelligibility and Narrating Queer Youth," in *Youth and Sexualities: Pleasure, Subversion, and Insubordination In and Out of Schools*, ed. Mary Lou Rasmussen, Eric Rofes, and Susan Talburt (New

York: Palgrave, 2004), 17–39. Building on Amy Kaplan, Jasbir Puar notes in her introduction to *Terrorist Assemblages: Homonationalism in Queer Times* (Durham, NC: Duke University Press, 2007), that the coming-out narrative has also been applied to the increasing ease with which U.S. officials describe the United States as an empire.

24. Through this move, the author invokes a common theme from the stories of *One Thousand and One Nights*, and she embeds multiple layers of a *Romeo and Juliet* type of story, a very common trope in romance novels. Both the hero's and his fiancée's names replicate another common aspect of mainstream desert romances—the evidence that authors have done research to find "authentic" names, but might miss the mark a bit. As far as I can tell, both Ashmit and Ashwarya are made-up names, but they are very close to the popular Indian (Hindi) names Amit and Aishwarya.

25. Bernetti, *Desert Nights*, ch. 3, 792/808.

26. Ibid., ch. 3, 800/808.

27. Ibid., ch. 2, 396/808.

28. Omar Sharif, with Marie Thérèse Guinchard, *The Eternal Male*, trans. Martin Sokolinsky (New York: Doubleday and Co., 1977), 8, 15, 130.

29. See, for example, Liz Fielding, *The Sheikh's Unsuitable Bride* (New York: Harlequin, 2008), 12; Nan Ryan, *Burning Love* (New York: HarperCollins, 1996), 95.

30. Sharif actually describes himself in an almost universalized way, which of course implies a kind of Westernization: "I spoke [David Lean's] language with a slight and undefinable accent, just as I spoke French, Greek, Italian, Spanish, and even Arabic. I spoke those six languages in the same way, with an accent that enabled me to play the role of a foreigner without anyone knowing exactly where I came from, something that has proved highly useful throughout my career" (Sharif, *Eternal Male*, 12).

31. Caton, *Lawrence of Arabia*, 3.

32. For a classic denial, see Don Belt, "Lawrence of Arabia," *National Geographic*, January 1999, 52. For an overview of how his biographers handled the issue, see Abdullah AlMaaini, "'You Are an Interesting Man': Gender, Empire, and Desire in David Lean's *Lawrence of Arabia*," in *Swinging Single: Representing Sexuality in the 1960s*, ed. Hilary Radner and Moya Luckett (Minneapolis: University of Minnesota Press, 1999), 77–102, esp. 83.

33. AlMaaini, "'You Are an Interesting Man,'" 85.

34. Ibid., 95–97; Ella Shohat and Robert Stam, *Unthinking Eurocentrism: Multiculturalism and the Media* (New York: Routledge, 1994), 168; Caton, *Lawrence of Arabia*, 208–209; Marjorie Garber, *Vested Interests: Cross-Dressing and Cultural Anxiety* (New York: Routledge, 1992), 304–305; Murray Pomerance, "Baghdad Bad," *Film International* 7, no. 5 (2009): 27–49, 41.

35. Caton, *Lawrence of Arabia*, 208–209.

36. Gaylyn Studlar, "Discourses of Gender and Ethnicity: The Construction and De(con)struction of Rudolph Valentino as Other," *Film Criticism*, 13, no. 2 (winter 1989): 25. See also Garber, *Vested Interests*, 310: "Valentino's clean-shaven, boyish face, like his cigarette holder, became objects of defensive scorn for many self-identified 'red-blooded-American-males.'"

37. Judith Butler, *Gender Trouble* (New York: Routledge, 1990), 194n6.

38. Indeed, psychoanalytic theory is the cornerstone of much feminist analysis of romance novels, particularly the early work. The most famous example is Radway, *Reading the Romance* (employing Chodorow). See also Stephanie Wardrop, "'The Heroine Is Being Beaten: Freud, Sadomasochism, and Reading the Romance," *Style* 29, no. 3 (1995): 459–474.

39. I emphasize this point because of the potential for misreading how I use the metaphor of radioactivity; because it is, above all, a scientific concept, it would be easy to assume that I consider the tendency toward stability a natural process, when my argument is actually quite the opposite.

40. Abby Green, *Breaking the Sheikh's Rules* (New York: Harlequin, 2011), 28.

41. In case it is not clear from the already-cited passage, the author reiterates the point in two other passages: "That deep secret inner part of her was unfurling like a bud in the sun . . . obeying some primal urge from deep within her" (ibid., 84). And: "She felt some deeply innate feminine instinct kick . . . if she saw the darkness of his skin against the paleness of hers" (ibid., 124).

42. Trish Morey, *Stolen by the Sheikh* (New York: Harlequin, 2006), 121. See also Laura Wright, *A Bed of Sand* (New York, Silhouette, 2004), 147, in which the heroine's "ultrafeminine genes . . . spring to life."

43. Jane Porter, *The Sultan's Bought Bride* (New York: Harlequin, 2004), 170.

44. Morey, *Stolen*, 120.

45. Penny Jordan, *Possessed by the Sheikh* (New York: Harlequin, 2005), 114.

46. Bonnie Vanak, *The Sword and the Sheath* (New York: Leisure Books, 2007), 153.

47. Brenda Jackson, *Delaney's Desert Sheikh* (New York: Silhouette, 2002), 139; Olivia Gates, *To Touch a Sheikh* (New York: Harlequin, 2011), 16.

48. See, for example, the following descriptions: There was an "innate arrogant *maleness* to him that kicked a stream of primal fear through her" (Emma Darcy, *Traded to the Sheikh* [New York: Harlequin, 2005], 19); "There was an elemental primitive strength about him that made her shiver" (Sarah Morgan, *Bella and the Merciless Sheikh* [New York: Harlequin, 2011], 83); "The ache he had thought controlled had become a raging, savage, primal male call he couldn't silence or ignore" (Penny Jordan, *A Royal Bride at the Sheikh's Command* [New York: Silhouette, 2007], 126); "In his eyes she saw the pure rawness of primal male hunger. It was as if the winds of sand had unleashed something savage in both of them" (Loreth Anne White, *The Sheik Who Loved Me* [New York: Silhouette, 2005], 231).

49. Ryan, *Burning*, 177.

50. White, *Loved*, 231.

51. Nalini Singh, *Desert Warrior* (New York: Harlequin, 2009), 87.

52. Vanak, *Sword*, 315. The sheath metaphor seems to be particularly conducive to historical romances. See, for example, Marguerite Kaye, *The Governess and the Sheikh* (New York: Harlequin, 2011), 273.

53. Singh, *Warrior*, 181.

54. White, *Loved*, 86.

55. Ibid., 124.

56. Joan Wallach Scott, *The Fantasy of Feminist History* (Durham, NC: Duke University Press, 2011), 5, 113.

57. Butler, *Gender Trouble*, 63–64.

58. Jonathan Flatley, *Affective Mapping: Melancholia and the Politics of Modernism* (Cambridge, MA: Harvard University Press, 2008), 2.

59. Judith Butler, *The Psychic Life of Power: Theories in Subjection* (Stanford, CA: Stanford University Press, 1997), 167.

60. Sigmund Freud, "Mourning and Melancholia," in *The Standard Edition of the Complete Psychological Works of Sigmund Freud*, vol. 14, trans. James Strachey (London: Hogarth Press, 1915), 243. See Flatley, *Affective Mapping*, 43; and Butler, *Psychic Life of Power*, 172, for their discussions of the quote.

61. Jacqueline Rose, *States of Fantasy* (New York: Oxford University Press, 1994), 6.

62. For a cogent analysis of the concept of U.S. exceptionalism through the lens of fantasy, see Donald Pease, *The New American Exceptionalism*. I owe thanks to this book for leading me to Rose, *States of Fantasy*.

63. Rose, *States of Fantasy*, 12, 10.

64. Wendy Brown, *Walled States, Waning Sovereignty* (New York: Zone Books, 2010), 8. See also Mike Davis, "The Great Wall of Capital," in *Against the Wall: Israel's Barrier to Peace*, ed. Michael Sorkin (New York: New Press, 2005), 88–99.

65. Brown, *Walled States*, 21.

66. Ibid., 130.

67. See ibid., 126–131, for a discussion of the psychoanalytic theory of defense as applied to wall building.

68. Deleuze and Guattari, *Anti-Oedipus*, 353.

69. Scott, *Fantasy of Feminist History*, 113.

70. Butler, *Psychic Life of Power*, 14–15.

71. Deleuze and Guattari's concept of the BwO (body without organs) can be understood as an effort to maximize the potentialities of "aiming toward dissolution," rather than simply seeing it as destructive or negative.

72. Butler, *Psychic Life of Power*, 9.

73. Morey, *Stolen*, 173.

74. Linda Winstead Jones, *The Sheik and I* (New York: Silhouette, 2006), 44.

75. See, for example, Jordan, *Royal Bride*, 15; Morgan, *Bella*, 10; Morey, *Stolen*, 114; Young, *Captive*, 119; Gates, *Touch*, 142, 182; Jones, *The Sheik and I*, 74, 126; Kaye, *Governess*, 11–13, 121; White, *Loved*, 200; Kim Lawrence, *Defiant Virgin* (New York: Harlequin, 2009), 171.

76. Rose, *States of Fantasy*, 3.

77. See the conclusion to Louis Althusser, "Ideology and Ideological State Apparatuses," in *Essays on Ideology* (1977; repr., New York: Verso, 1984), in which he notes the way that ideology most effectively works through the implication of its being willingly chosen; closely connected to this idea is his overall argument about the imbrication of ideology in subject formation itself.

78. On drone warfare and extrajudicial killing, see Jeremy Scahill, *Dirty Wars: The World Is a Battlefield* (New York: Nation Books, 2013). For more on the production of the enemy-target in relation to the war on terror and drone warfare, see Andrea Miller, "Performing Specters of Imperialism: Affect, Terror, and the Body in Naveed Mir's *The Cinco Sanders Show*" (master's thesis, Georgia State University, 2014); and Ian Graham Ronald Shaw and Majed Akhter, "The Unbearable Humanness of Drone Warfare in FATA, Pakistan," *Antipode* 44, no. 4 (2012): 1490–1509. An endnote in the "Mapping Desire" section of the introduction discusses the media coverage following the original Wikileaks release about Guantánamo prisoners erroneously labeled "terrorists" and "enemy combatants."

79. Brian Massumi, *A User's Guide to Capitalism and Schizophrenia: Deviations from Deleuze and Guattari* (Cambridge, MA: Massachusetts Institute of Technology Publishing, 1992), 123.

80. See Maggie Franz, "Mexican/Migrant Mothers and 'Anchor Babies' in Anti-Immigration Discourses: Meanings of Citizenship and Illegality in the United States" (master's thesis, Georgia State University, 2013), for an excellent analysis of discourses of love in relation to the United States.

81. Green, *Breaking*, 118. Or they "emphasize his dark, hawklike features and make him appear more imposing than ever" (Tessa Radley, *The Desert Bride of Al Zayed* [New York: Harlequin, 2007], 29).

82. Morgan, *Bella*, 31.

83. Green, *Breaking*, 123.

84. Kaye, *Governess*, 189, 8.

85. Jordan, *Royal Bride*, 81.

86. "Swirling": Radley, *Desert Bride*, 51; Webber, *Sheikh, Children's Doctor*, 20; Marton, *Sheik*, 20. "Flowing": Morey, *Convenient Virgin*, 75; Jackson, *Delaney's*, 83; Marton, *Sheik*, 21, 69; Green, *Breaking*, 81; Kendrick, *Playboy Sheikh*, 11, 87; Kendrick, *Monarch*, 9, 96; Lawrence, *Defiant Virgin*, 45; Ryan, *Burning*, 73; Singh, *Warrior*, 8, 29. "Fluttering": Marton, *Sheik*, 161; Vanak, *Sword*, 143; Kaye, *Governess*, 97. "Billowing": Green, *Breaking*, 138; Radley, *Desert Bride*, 57; Ryan, *Burning*, 166.

87. Meredith Webber, *Sheikh, Children's Doctor* (New York: Harlequin, 2011), 31.

88. Nina Bruhns, *Vampire Sheikh* (New York: Harlequin, 2011), 263.

89. Massumi, *User's Guide*, 85.

CONCLUSION

1. Ann Laura Stoler, "Imperial Formations and the Opacities of Rule," in *Lessons of Empire: Imperial Histories and American Power*, ed. Craig Calhoun, Frederick Cooper, and Kevin W. Moore (New York: New Press, 2006), 54.

2. Though there is debate about whether depleted uranium (DU) can be conclusively linked to birth defects in Iraq and Gulf War syndrome afflicting about a third of the U.S. veterans from that war, the debate ultimately strengthens the claim that depleted uranium is a poisonous and otherwise detrimental by-product of military action for all actors involved. Even studies that argue that DU has not been proven to

be the sole cause of birth defects and veterans' illnesses admit that DU is poisonous, very easily spread, and present in the bodies of exposed Gulf War veterans and Iraqis living in DU-rich regions. Though the detrimental impacts of war come from a wide range of sources (including, for example, stress, carcinogenic by-products from burning oil fields, and chemical weapons), that doesn't negate the deleterious role of DU. See, for example, Rosalie Bertell, "Depleted Uranium: All the Questions about DU and Gulf War Syndrome Are Not Yet Answered," *International Journal of Health Services: Planning, Administration, Evaluation* 36, no. 3 (2006): 503–520; Tariq Al-Hadithi et al., "Birth Defects in Iraq and the Plausibility of Environmental Exposure: A Review," *Conflict and Health* 6, no. 3 (January 2012): 1–7; "Iraq Veterans Poisoned by Depleted Uranium," *Ecologist* 35, no. 8 (October 2005): 9; Toby Jones, "Toxic War and the Politics of Uncertainty in Iraq," *International Journal of Middle East Studies* 46, no. 4 (November 2014): 797–799.

3. *Organism* is the strict organization of the body and its functions. *Significance,* a French term retained by the translator, could be translated as "signifying capacity." See Gilles Deleuze and Félix Guattari, *A Thousand Plateaus,* trans. and forward by Brian Massumi (1980; repr., Minneapolis: University of Minnesota Press, 1987), xviii and 159.

4. On occasion, a speech act can also effect what Deleuze and Guattari (ibid., 80) call an "incorporeal transformation"; that is, it materially shifts the reality of a body. Defining a person as an "enemy combatant," for example, makes the person eligible either for detention in a military prison without due process or for extrajudicial assassination by a drone attack.

5. As cited also in chapter 1, for the label "'CEO' of Dubai," see Ahmed Kanna, *Dubai: The City as Corporation* (Minneapolis: University of Minnesota Press, 2011), 139; Mike Davis, "Fear and Money in Dubai," *New Left Review* 41 (September–October 2006): 47–68; Afshin Molavi, "Sudden City," *National Geographic,* January 2007, 104.

6. Sara Morgan, *Bella and the Merciless Sheikh* (New York: Harlequin, 2011), 7. See also Tessa Radley, *The Desert Bride of Al Zayed* (New York: Silhouette, 2007), 29, 34, 43, 51, 57, 66, 89; Dana Marton, *Sheik Seduction* (New York: Harlequin, 2008), 21, 129, 161; Nina Bruhns, *Vampire Sheikh* (New York: Harlequin, 2011), 99; Trish Morey, *The Sheikh's Convenient Virgin* (New York: Harlequin, 2008), 51; Liz Fielding, *The Sheikh's Unsuitable Bride* (New York: Harlequin, 2008), 145, 171; Emma Darcy, *Traded to the Sheikh* (New York: Harlequin, 2005), 124; Trish Morey, *Stolen by the Sheikh* (New York: Harlequin, 2006), 120; Brenda Jackson, *Delaney's Desert Sheikh* (New York: Silhouette, 2006), 45, 83; Abby Green, *Breaking the Sheikh's Rules* (New York: Harlequin, 2011), 81, 82, 103, 112; Meredith Webber, *Sheikh, Children's Doctor . . . Husband* (New York: Harlequin, 2011), 13, 20, 31, 99; Jane Porter, *The Sheikh's Chosen Queen* (New York: Harlequin, 2008), 10; Sharon Kendrick, *The Playboy Sheikh's Virgin Stable Girl* (New York: Harlequin, 2009), 10, 11, 38, 60, 87; Kim Lawrence, *Desert Prince, Defiant Virgin* (New York: Harlequin, 2009), 45, 77, 161; Bonnie Vanak, *The Sword and the Sheath* (New York: Leisure Books, 2007), 97; Nan Ryan, *Burning Love* (New York: HarperCollins, 1996), 119, 166; Kate Hewitt, *The Sheikh's Forbidden Virgin* (New York: Harlequin, 2009), 59; Sharon Kendrick, *Monarch of the Sands* (New York: Harlequin,

2011), 96, 108; Marguerite Kaye, *The Governess and the Sheikh* (New York: Harlequin, 2011), 42, 84, 202.

7. On this subject in relation to female "suicide bombers," see Amal Amireh, "Palestinian Women's Disappearing Act: The Suicide Bomber through Western Feminist Eyes," in *Arab & Arab American Feminisms: Gender, Violence, and Belonging,* ed. Rabab Abdulhadi, Evelyn Alsultany, and Nadine Naber (Syracuse, NY: Syracuse University Press, 2011), 29–45.

8. One recent example is Clark McCauley and Sophia Moskalenko, *Friction: How Radicalization Happens to Them and Us* (New York: Oxford University Press, 2011), 4, which seeks to diagnose the "psychological trajectory" of radicalization and to explain how it can happen to apparently normal people. See Jasbir Puar, *Terrorist Assemblages: Homonationalism in Queer Times* (Durham, NC: Duke University Press, 2007), 52–56, for a critique of counterterrorism studies.

9. Gilles Deleuze and Félix Guattari, *A Thousand Plateaus*, trans. and forward by Brian Massumi (1980; repr., Minneapolis: University of Minnesota Press, 1987), 88.

10. Donna Young, *Captive of the Desert King* (New York: Harlequin, 2009), 164.

BIBLIOGRAPHY

PRIMARY SOURCES

Bruhns, Nina. *Vampire Sheikh*. New York: Harlequin, 2011.

Buckley, Christopher. *Florence of Arabia*. New York: Random House, 2004.

Conrad, Linda. *Secret Agent Sheik*. New York: Harlequin, 2011.

Darcy, Emma. *Traded to the Sheikh*. New York: Harlequin, 2005.

Fielding, Liz. *The Sheikh's Unsuitable Bride*. New York: Harlequin, 2008.

Gates, Olivia. *To Touch a Sheikh*. New York: Harlequin, 2011.

Green, Abby. *Breaking the Sheikh's Rules*. New York: Harlequin, 2011.

Hewitt, Kate. *The Sheikh's Forbidden Virgin*. New York: Harlequin, 2009.

Hull, E. M. *The Sheik*. 1919. Reprint, Holicong, PA: Wildside, 2004.

Jackson, Brenda. *Delaney's Desert Sheikh*. New York: Silhouette, 2002.

Jones, Linda Winstead. *The Sheik and I*. New York: Silhouette, 2006.

Jordan, Penny. *Possessed by the Sheikh*. New York: Harlequin, 2005.

———. *A Royal Bride at the Sheikh's Command*. New York: Harlequin, 2007.

Kaye, Marguerite. *The Governess and the Sheikh*. New York: Harlequin, 2011.

Kendrick, Sharon. *Monarch of the Sands*. New York: Harlequin, 2011.

———. *The Playboy Sheikh's Virgin Stable Girl*. New York: Harlequin, 2009.

Lawrence, Kim. *Desert Prince, Defiant Virgin*. New York: Harlequin, 2009.

Marton, Dana *Sheik Seduction*. New York: Harlequin, 2008.

Mason, Connie. *Desert Ecstasy*. New York: Dorchester, 1988.

Morey, Trish. *The Sheikh's Convenient Virgin*. New York: Harlequin, 2008.

———. *Stolen by the Sheikh*. New York: Harlequin, 2006.

Morgan, Sarah. *Bella and the Merciless Sheikh*. New York: Harlequin, 2011.

Payne, Alcamia. *The Egyptian Slave*. London: Xcite Books, 2012.

Peterson, Ann Voss. *Seized by the Sheikh*. New York: Harlequin, 2011.

Porter, Jane. *The Sheikh's Chosen Queen*. New York: Harlequin, 2008.

———. *The Sultan's Bought Bride*. New York: Harlequin, 2004.

Radley, Tessa. *The Desert Bride of Al Zayed*. New York: Silhouette, 2007.

Roberts, Nora. *Sweet Revenge*. New York: Bantam Books, 1988.

Ryan, Nan. *Burning Love*. New York: HarperCollins, 1996.

Sex and the City 2. Directed by Michael Patrick King. Burbank, CA: Warner Home Video, 2010.

Singh, Nalini. *Desert Warrior*. New York: Harlequin, 2009.

Small, Beatrice. *The Kadin*. New York: HarperCollins, 1978.

Southwick, Teresa. *To Catch a Sheik*. New York: Silhouette, 2003.

Spencer, Sonja. *The Sheikh and the Servant*. Tallahassee, FL: Dreamspinner Press, 2009.

Vanak, Bonnie. *The Sword and the Sheath*. New York: Leisure Books, 2007.

Webber, Meredith. *Sheikh, Children's Doctor . . . Husband*. New York: Harlequin, 2011.

West, Annie. *For the Sheikh's Pleasure*. New York: Harlequin, 2007.

Weston, Sophie. *In the Arms of the Sheikh*. New York: Harlequin, 2006.

White, Loreth Anne. *The Sheik Who Loved Me*. New York: Silhouette, 2005.

Winspear, Violet. *Blue Jasmine*. New York: Harlequin, 1970.

Wood, Sara. *Desert Hostage*. New York: Harlequin, 1991.

Wright, Laura. *A Bed of Sand*. New York: Silhouette Books, 2004.

Young, Donna. *Captive of the Desert King*. New York: Harlequin, 2009.

SECONDARY SOURCES

Abu-Lughod, Lila. "Do Muslim Women Really Need Saving? Anthropological Reflections on Cultural Relativism and Its Others." *American Anthropologist* 104, no. 3 (2002): 783–790.

Agamben, Giorgio. *State of Exception*. Translated by Kevin Attell. Chicago: University of Chicago Press, 2005.

Ahmad, Dohra. "Not Yet Beyond the Veil: Muslim Women in American Popular Literature." *Social Text 99* 27, no. 2 (summer 2009): 105–131.

Ahmed, Leila. "Western Ethnocentrism and Perceptions of the Harem." *Feminist Studies* 8, no. 3 (1982): 521–534.

AlMaaini, Abdullah Habib. "'You Are an Interesting Man': Gender, Empire, and Desire in David Lean's *Lawrence of Arabia*." In *Swinging Single: Representing Sexuality in the 1960s*, edited by Hilary Radner and Moya Luckett, 77–102. Minneapolis: University of Minnesota Press, 1999.

Alsultany, Evelyn. *Arabs and Muslims in the Media: Race and Representation after 9/11*. New York: New York University Press, 2012.

Althusser, Louis. "Ideology and Ideological State Apparatuses." In *Essays on Ideology*. 1977. Reprint. New York: Verso, 1984.

Amar, Paul. *The Security Archipelago: Human-Security States, Sexuality Politics, and the End of Neoliberalism*. Durham, NC: Duke University Press, 2013.

Amireh, Amal. "Palestinian Women's Disappearing Act: The Suicide Bomber through Western Feminist Eyes." In *Arab & Arab American Feminisms: Gender, Violence, and Belonging*, edited by Rabab Abdulhadi, Evelyn Alsultany, and Nadine Naber, 29–45. Syracuse, NY: Syracuse University Press, 2011.

Anidjar, Gil. *Semites: Race, Religion, Literature*. Stanford, CA: Stanford University Press, 2008.

Appadurai, Arjun. *Modernity at Large: Cultural Dimensions of Globalization*. Minneapolis: University of Minnesota Press, 1996.

Asad, Talal. *Formations of the Secular: Christianity, Islam, Modernity*. Stanford, CA: Stanford University Press, 2003.

August, Melissa. "Sheikhs and the Serious Blogger." *Time*, August 22, 2005. www.time. com/time/nation/article/0,8599,1096809,00.html.

Bach, Evelyn. "Sheik Fantasies: Orientalism and Feminine Desire in the Desert Romance." *Hecate* 23, no. 1 (1997): 9–40.

Balibar, Etienne. "Is There a 'Neo-Racism'?" In *Race, Nation, Class: Ambiguous Identities*, edited by Etienne Balibar and Immanuel Wallerstein, 17–28. London: Verso, 1991.

Barber, Benjamin. *Jihad Vs. McWorld*. New York: Ballantine Books, 1996.

Barnard, Anne. "Calling to Allah, from Lower Manhattan." *New York Times*, August 14, 2010. www.lexisnexis.com/lnacui2api/api/version1/getDocCui?lni=805G-YVX0-Y8TC-S40K&csi=6742&hl=t&hv=t&hnsd=f&hns=t&hgn=t&oc=00240&perma=true.

Bartholet, Jeffrey. "Young, Angry, and Wired-in: The Middle East: A Generation in Waiting Can Wait No More." *National Geographic*, July 2011.

Bayoumi, Moustafa. *How Does It Feel to Be a Problem? Being Young and Arab in America*. New York: Penguin Books, 2009.

——. "The Race Is On: Muslims and Arabs in the American Imagination." *Middle East Report Online*, March 2010. www.merip.org/mero/interventions/bayoumi_interv.html.

Behdad, Ali, and Juliet Williams. "Neo-Orientalism." In *Globalizing American Studies*, edited by Brian T. Edwards and Dilip Parameshwar Gaonkar, 283–299. Chicago: University of Chicago Press, 2010.

Belt, Don. "The Forgotten Faithful: Arab Christians." *National Geographic*, June 2009.

——. "Lawrence of Arabia." *National Geographic*, January 1999.

——. "Shadowland: Poised to Play a Pivotal New Role in the Middle East, Syria Struggles to Escape its Dark Past." National Geographic, November 2009.

Bhabha, Homi. "Of Mimicry and Men." In *The Location of Culture*, 121–131. New York: Routledge, 1994.

Blake, Heidi, Tim Ross, and Conrad Quilty-Harper. "Two-Year Ordeal of an Innocent: Wikileaks Files Children Among the Innocent Captured and Sent to Guantanamo." *Daily Telegraph*, April, 26, 2011.

Blake, Susan. "What 'Race' Is the Sheik: Rereading a Desert Romance." In *Doubled Plots: Romance and History*, edited by Susan Strenle and Mary Paniccia Carden, 67–85. Jackson: University of Mississippi Press, 2003.

Bolton, Gwyneth. "*Bitch* Magazine Does Romance." *Gwyneth Bolton's Blog*. June 12, 2007. http://gwynethbolton.blogspot.com/2007/06/bitch-magazine-does-romance.html.

Bowden, Charles. "Unseen Sahara." *National Geographic*. October 2009.

Brodkin, Karen. *How Jews Became White Folks: And What That Says about Race in America*. New Brunswick, NJ: Rutgers University Press, 1998.

Brown, Wendy. *Walled States, Waning Sovereignty*. New York: Zone Books, 2010.

Burge, Amy. "Desiring the East: A Comparative Study of Middle English Romance and Modern Popular Sheikh Romance." PhD diss., University of York, 2012.

————. "Disappearing Difference." *Teach Me Tonight: Musings on Romance Fiction from an Academic Perspective* (blog), August 24, 2011. http://teachmetonight.blogspot. com/.

Burley, Stephanie. "Shadows and Silhouettes: The Racial Politics of Category Romance." *Paradoxa* 5, nos. 13–14 (2000): 324–343.

Butler, Judith. *Gender Trouble*. New York: Routledge, 1990.

————. *The Psychic Life of Power: Theories in Subjection*. Stanford, CA: Stanford University Press, 1997.

Cacho, Lisa Marie. *Social Death: Racialized Rightlessness and the Criminalization of the Unprotected*. New York: New York University Press, 2012.

Cainkar, Louise. *Homeland Insecurity: The Arab American and Muslim American Experience After 9/11*. New York: Russell Sage, 2009.

Caton, Steven. *Lawrence of Arabia: A Film's Anthropology*. Berkeley: University of California Press, 1999.

Chen, Eva Y. I. "Forms of Pleasure in the Reading of Popular Romance: Psychic and Cultural Dimensions." In *Empowerment versus Oppression: Twenty First Century Views of Popular Romance Novels*, edited by Sally Goade, 30–41. Newcastle, England: Cambridge Scholars, 2007.

Chow, Rey. *The Protestant Ethnic and the Spirit of Capitalism*. New York: Columbia University Press, 2002.

Clark, Arthur P., Muhammed A. Tahlawi, William Facey, Thomas A. Pledge, and Saudi Aramco. *A Land Transformed: The Arabian Peninsula, Saudi Arabia, and Saudi Aramco*. Houston: Aramco Services, 2006.

Cockburn, Andrew. "Yemen United." *National Geographic*, April 2000.

Cole, Donald Powell. *Nomads of the Nomads: The Al Murrah Bedouin of the Empty Quarter*. Chicago: Aldine Publishing Company, 1975.

Colson, Charles, and Anne Morse. "The Moral Home Front," *Christianity Today* 48, no. 10 (1995). www.christianitytoday.com/ct/2004/october/18.152.html.

Cooper, Glenda. "A Steamy Centenary." *The Age*, February 17, 2008. www.theage.com. au/news/in-depth/a-steamy-centenary/2008/02/16/1202760669725.html.

Crane, Lynda L. "Romance Novel Readers: In Search of Feminist Change?" *Women Studies* 23 (1994): 257–269.

Creed, Barbara. "The Women's Romance as Sexual Fantasy: 'Mills and Boon.'" In *All Her Labours Two: Embroidering the Framework*, edited by Women and the Labour Publications Collective, 47–67. Sydney: Hale & Iremonger, 1984.

Cummins, Daisy, and Julie Bindel. "Mills & Boon: 100 Years of Heaven or Hell?" *Guardian* (London), December 4, 2007. www.guardian.co.uk/lifeandstyle/2007/ dec/05/women.fiction.

Dabashi, Hamid. *Brown Skin, White Masks*. London: Pluto, 2011.

Dahbour, Omar. "Hegemony and Rights: On the Liberal Justification for Empire." In *Exceptional State: Contemporary U.S. Culture and the New Imperialism*, edited by Ashley Dawson and Malini Johar Schueller, 105–130. Durham, NC: Duke University Press, 2007.

Davis, Mike. "Fear and Money in Dubai." *New Left Review* 41 (2006): 47–68.

——. "The Great Wall of Capital." In *Against the Wall: Israel's Barrier to Peace*, edited Michael Sorkin, 88–99. New York: New Press, 2005.

Dawson, Ashley, and Malini Johar Schueller. Introduction to *Exceptional State: Contemporary U.S. Culture and the New Imperialism*, edited by Ashley Dawson and Malini Johar Schueller, 1–33. Durham, NC: Duke University Press, 2007.

Deleuze, Gilles, and Félix Guattari. *Anti-Oedipus*. Minneapolis: University of Minnesota Press, 1983.

——. *A Thousand Plateaus*. Translated and forward by Brian Massumi. 1980. Reprint, Minneapolis: University of Minnesota Press, 1987.

Dimeo-Ediger, Winona. "Dubai's Rotating Skyscraper." *National Geographic*, February 2009.

Dissanayake, Samanthi. "All Because the Lady Loves a Foreign Accent." *BBC News*, August 14, 2008. http://news.bbc.co.uk/2/hi/uk_news/magazine/7516672.stm.

Dixon, jay. *The Romance Fiction of Mills and Boon, 1909–1990's*. London and Philadelphia: UCL Press, 1999.

Draper, Robert. "The Black Pharaohs." *National Geographic*, February 2008.

DuBois, W. E. B. *The Souls of Black Folk*. 1903. Reprint. New York: Bantam, 1989.

Duggan, Lisa. "The New Homonormativity: The Sexual Politics of Neoliberalism." In *Materializing Democracy: Toward a Revitalized Cultural Politics*, edited by Russ Castronova and Dana D. Nelson, 175–194. Durham, NC: Duke University Press, 2002.

Elden, Stuart. *Terror and Territory: The Spatial Extent of Sovereignty*. Minneapolis: University of Minnesota Press, 2009.

Elliott, Paul. *Guattari Reframed*. London: I.B. Tauris, 2012.

Evans, Linda. "Playing Global Cop: U.S. Militarism and the Prison-Industrial Complex." In *Global Lockdown: Race, Gender, and the Prison-Industrial Complex*, ed. Julia Sudbury, 215–227. New York: Routledge, 2005.

Evening Standard (London). "Ground Zero to Have Mosque." May 26, 2010.

Fanon, Frantz. *Black Skin, White Masks*. Translated by Charles Lam Markmann. New York: Grove Press, 1967.

Fielding, Liz. "The Appeal of the Sheikh." *Harlequin: Entertain, Enrich, Inspire*, December 4, 2009. www.harlequinfilms.com/content/appeal-sheikh.

——. "The Sheikh as Hero." *Liz Fielding: Award Winning Romance*. 2009. www.lizfielding.com/onwriting.html#sheikhashero.

Flatley, Jonathan. *Affective Mapping: Melancholia and the Politics of Modernism*. Cambridge, MA: Harvard University Press, 2008.

Flesch, Juliet. *From Australia with Love: A History of Modern Australian Popular Romance Novels*. Fremantle, Australia: Curtin University Books, 2004.

Fluri, Jennifer. "'Rallying Public Opinion' and Other Misuses of Feminism." In *Feminism and War: Confronting U.S. Imperialism*, edited by Robin L. Riley, Chandra Talpade Mohanty, and Minnie Bruce Pratt, 143–157. New York: Zed, 2008.

Foley, Stephen. "U.S. Scrambles to Contain Fallout from 'Damaging' Guantanamo Leak." *Independent* (London), April 26, 2011.

U.S. News on NBC News. "Former Blackwater Security Firm Changes Name Again," December 12, 2011. http://usnews.nbcnews.com/_news/2011/12/12/9393006-former-blackwater-security-firm-changes-name-again?lite.

Foucault, Michel. *Society Must Be Defended: Lectures at the College de France, 1975–76.* Translated by David Macey. New York: Picador, 2003.

Franz, Margaret. "Mexican/Migrant Mothers and 'Anchor Babies' in Anti-Immigration Discourses: Meanings of Citizenship and Illegality in the United States." Master's thesis, Georgia State University, 2013.

Freud, Sigmund. "Mourning and Melancholia." In *The Standard Edition of the Complete Psychological Works of Sigmund Freud,* vol. 14. Translated by James Strachey. London: Hogarth Press, 1915.

Friede, Eva. "*Sex and the City 2* Dazzles in the Desert: Ball Gowns, Blazers and Burqas That Meet Blahnicks Make for a Fashion Fantasy in Abu Dhabi for the Fab Foursome." *Gazette* (Montreal). May 27, 2010.

Fukuyama, Francis. *The End of History and the Last Man.* New York: Free Press, 1992.

Fuss, Diana. *Identification Papers.* New York: Routledge, 1995.

Gallop, Jane. *The Daughter's Seduction: Feminism and Psychoanalysis.* Ithaca, NY: Cornell University Press, 1982.

Galloway, Anne. "Hot Desert Nights." *Space and Culture* (blog), September 7, 2007. www.spaceandculture.org/2007/09/07/hot-desert-nights/.

Garber, Marjorie. *Vested Interests: Cross-Dressing and Cultural Anxiety.* New York: Routledge, 1992.

Gibson-Graham, J. K. *The End of Capitalism (As We Knew It): A Feminist Critique of Political Economy.* Minneapolis: University of Minnesota Press, 2006.

Gillett, Keira. "Kiss Prince Charming Good-Bye; Say Hello to a Sheikh!" *Heroes and Heartbreakers* (blog), April 2011. www.heroesandheartbreakers.com/blogs/2011/04/kiss-prince-charming-goodbye-say-hello-to-a-sheikh.

———. "Sheik Romance and the Passion of Arabia Nights." *LoveRomancePassion* (blog). May 12, 2011. www.loveromancepassion.com/sheik-romance-and-the-passion-of-arabian-nights/.

Gilmore, Ruth Wilson. *Golden Gulag: Prisons, Surplus, Crisis, and Opposition in Globalizing California.* Berkeley: University of California Press, 2007.

Gilroy, Paul. *Against Race: Imagining Political Culture Beyond the Color Line.* Cambridge, MA: Harvard University Press, 2000.

Goade, Sally. *Empowerment versus Oppression: Twenty First Century Views on Popular Romance Novels.* Newcastle, UK: Cambridge Scholars Publishing, 2007.

Goris, An. "Romance the World Over." In *Global Cultures,* edited by Frank A. Salamone, 59–72. Newcastle: Cambridge Scholars Publishing, 2009.

Gramsci, Antonio. *Selections from the Prison Notebooks.* Translated by Quintin Hoare and Geoffrey Nowell Smith. New York: International Publishers, 1987.

Green, Abby. "Sheikhs: Love Them or Loathe Them?" *I [Heart] Harlequin Presents* (blog), April 25, 2011. www.iheartpresents.com/2011/04/sheikhs-love-them-or-loathe-them-by-abby-green/.

Grescoe, Paul. *The Merchants of Venice: Inside Harlequin and the Empire of Romance.* Vancouver: Raincoast Books, 1996.

Grewal, Inderpal. *Transnational America: Feminisms, Diaspora, Neoliberalisms.* Durham, NC: Duke University Press, 2005.

Grewal, Inderpal, and Caren Kaplan, eds. *Scattered Hegemonies.* Minneapolis: University of Minnesota Press, 1994.

Gualtieri, Sarah. *Between Arab and White: Race and Ethnicity in the Early Syrian American Diaspora.* Berkeley: University of California Press, 2009.

Gwin, Peter. "Lost Lords of the Sahara." *National Geographic,* September 2011.

Haddad, Emily. "Bound to Love: Captivity in Harlequin Sheikh Novels." In *Empowerment versus Oppression: Twenty First Century Views of Popular Romance Novels,* edited by Sally Goade, 42–64. Newcastle, UK: Cambridge Scholars, 2007.

Hanieh, Adam. "Bahrain." In *Dispatches from the Arab Spring,* edited by Paul Amar and Vijay Prashad, 63–88. Minneapolis: University of Minnesota Press, 2013.

Haraway, Donna. "The Promises of Monsters: A Regenerative Politics for Inappropriate/d Others." In *Cultural Studies,* edited by Lawrence Grossberg et al., 295–337. New York: Routledge, 1992.

Hare, John. "Surviving the Sahara." *National Geographic,* December 2002.

Harman, Chris. *Zombie Capitalism.* Chicago: Haymarket Books, 2010.

Harvey, David. *The Condition of Postmodernity: An Enquiry into the Origins of Cultural Change.* Cambridge, MA: Blackwell, 1989.

———. *The New Imperialism.* New York: Oxford University Press, 2005.

Heng, Geraldine. *Empire of Magic: Medieval Romance and the Politics of Cultural Fantasy.* New York: Columbia University Press, 2003.

Hesford, Wendy, and Wendy Kozol, eds. *Just Advocacy? Women's Human Rights, Transnational Feminisms, and the Politics of Representation.* New Brunswick, NJ: Rutgers University Press, 2005.

Hochberg, Gil Z. "Introduction: Israelis, Palestinians, Queers: Points of Departure." *GLQ: A Journal of Lesbian and Gay Studies* 16, no. 4 (2010): 493–516.

Hodgson, Marshall G. S. *The Venture of Islam: Conscience and History in a World Civilization.* Vol. 1. Chicago: University of Chicago Press, 1974.

Holland, Eugene. "Capitalism + Universal History" in *The Deleuze Dictionary,* edited by Adrian Parr, 42–43, New York: Columbia University Press, 2005.

———. *Deleuze and Guattari's "Anti-Oedipus": Introduction to Schizoanalysis.* New York: Routledge, 1999.

Holland, Jennifer S. "The Tortoise and the Bedouin." *National Geographic.* April 2007.

Humphries, Dylan. "Dubai: The Sudden City." *National Geographic.* May 2007.

Huntington, Samuel. *The Clash of Civilizations and the Remaking of World Order.* New York: Simon & Schuster, 1996.

I [Heart] Harlequin Presents. "Category Archives: Sheikh." *I [Heart] Harlequin Presents* (blog). 2012. www.iheartpresents.com/category/sheikh/.

Jakobsen, Janet. "Sex, Secularism, and the 'War on Terrorism.'" In *A Companion to Lesbian, Gay, Bisexual, Transgender, and Queer Studies*, edited by George Haggerty and Molly McGarry, 17–39. Malden, MA: Blackwell, 2007.

Jakobsen, Janet, and Ann Pelligrini, eds. *Secularisms*. Durham, NC: Duke University Press, 2008.

Jameson, Fredric. "Postmodernism, or the Cultural Logic of Late Capitalism." *New Left Review* 146 (1984): 53–92.

Jarmakani, Amira. *Imagining Arab Womanhood: The Cultural Mythology of Veils, Harems, and Belly Dancers in the U.S.* New York: Palgrave Macmillan, 2008.

———. "Romance Literature: US, Canada, UK, Australia." *Encyclopedia of Women & Islamic Cultures*, edited by Suad Joseph. Brill, 2010. www.paulyonline.brill.nl/subscriber/uid=2026/title_home?title_id=ewic_ewic.

———. "'The Sheik Who Loved Me': Romancing the War on Terror." *Signs: Journal of Women in Culture and Society* 35, no. 4 (summer 2010): 993–1017.

Jenn. "Another Great Interview with Dana Marton." *Coffee Time Romance & More*, accessed January 28, 2013. www.coffeetimeromance.com/Interviews/DanaMarton.html#.UPwOZ7b7mpI.

Jensen, Margaret Ann. *Love's Sweet Return: The Harlequin Story*. Bowling Green, OH: Bowling Green State University Popular Press, 1984.

Johnson, Chalmers. *Sorrows of Empire: Militarism, Secrecy, and the End of the Republic*. New York: Metropolitan Books, 2004.

Jones, Ann Rosalind. "Mills and Boon Meets Feminism." In *The Progress of Romance: the Politics of Popular Fiction*, edited by Jean Radford, 195–218. London and New York: Routledge & Kegan Paul, 1986.

Kanna, Ahmed. *Dubai: The City as Corporation*. Minneapolis: University of Minnesota Press, 2011.

Kaplan, Amy. "Romancing the Empire." In *The Anarchy of Empire in the Making of U.S. Culture*, 92–120. Cambridge, MA: Harvard University Press, 2005.

———. "The Tenacious Grasp of American Exceptionalism." *Comparative American Studies: An International Journal* 2, no. 2 (2004): 153–159.

Kay, Shirley. *The Bedouin*. New York: Crane, Russak, 1978.

Kaye, Marguerite. "All Sheikh-en Up." *The Pink Heart Society: Wildcard Weekend* (blog), July 2, 2011. http://pinkheartsociety.blogspot.com/2011/07/wildcard-weekend-all-sheikh-en-up.html.

Kendrick, Sharon. "Fear and Longing and Desert Sheikhs." *I [Heart] Harlequin Presents* (blog), January 24, 2012. www.iheartpresents.com/2012/01/fear-and-longing-and-desert-sheikhs-by-sharon-kendrick.

Khalaf, Sulayman. "Poetics and Politics of Newly Invented Traditions in the Gulf: Camel Racing in the United Arab Emirates." *Ethnology* 39, no. 3 (summer 2000): 243–261.

Khalifa, Hamad bin Isa bin Salman Al. "Stability Is Prerequisite for Progress." *Washington Times*, April 19, 2011. www.washingtontimes.com/news/2011/apr/19/stability-is-prerequisite-for-progress/.

Kim, Jodi. *Ends of Empire: Asian American Critique and the Cold War*. Minneapolis: University of Minnesota Press, 2010.

Kirk, Mimi. "The Sudan Split: How U.S. Policy Became Predicated on Secession." *Middle East Report*, no. 262 (2012): 36–42.

Klein, Naomi. *Shock Doctrine*. New York: Picador, 2008.

Kostyal, Karen M. "Alaa Al Aswany: Voice of Reason." *National Geographic*, September 2006.

Lather, Patricia. *Getting Smart: Feminist Research and Pedagogy with/in the Postmodern*. New York: Routledge, 1991.

Lauretis, Teresa de. *Freud's Drive: Psychoanalysis, Literature, and Film*. New York: Palgrave Macmillan, 2010.

Lee, Robert G. *Orientals: Asian Americans in Popular Culture*. Philadelphia: Temple University Press, 1999.

Limbaugh, Rush. "Ground Zero Terrorist Recruitment Center Imam: Build Mosque or Else." *The Rush Limbaugh Show*, September 9, 2010. www.rushlimbaugh.com/daily/2010/09/09/ground_zero_terrorist_recruitment_center_imam_build_mosque_or_else.

Logan, Mildred Montgomery. "I Like Being the Garden of Eden's First Lady." *The Cattleman* 38, no. 5 (October 1951): 30–31, 107–117.

———. "They Call Me Madam Sam." *The Cattleman* 38, no. 8 (January 1952): 22, 62–65.

Long, Burke. *Imagining the Holy Land: Maps, Models, and Fantasy Travels*. Bloomington: Indiana University Press, 2003.

Lott, Eric. *Love and Theft: Blackface Minstrelsy and the American Working Class*. New York: Oxford University Press, 1993.

Lutz, Catherine, ed. *The Bases of Empire: The Global Struggle against U.S. Military Posts*. New York: New York University Press, 2009.

Lutz, Catherine, and Jane Lou Collins. *Reading National Geographic*. Chicago: University of Chicago Press, 1993.

Mahmood, Saba. "Feminism, Democracy, and Empire: Islam and the War of Terror." In *Women's Studies on the Edge*, edited by Joan Wallach Scott, 81–114. Durham, NC: Duke University Press, 2008.

Maira, Sunaina. "Belly Dancing: Arab-Face, Orientalist Feminism, and U.S. Empire." *American Quarterly* 60, no. 2 (2008): 317–345.

———. "'Good' and 'Bad' Muslim Citizens: Feminists, Terrorists, and U.S. Orientalisms." *Feminist Studies* 35, no. 3 (2009): 631–656.

Majaj, Lisa Suhair. "Arab Americans and the Meaning of Race." In *Postcolonial Theory and the United States: Race, Ethnicity, and Literature*, edited by Amaritjit Singh and Peter Schmidt, 320–37. Jackson: University of Mississippi Press, 2000.

Majid, Anouar. *We Are All Moors: Ending Centuries of Crusades Against Muslims and Other Enemies*. Minneapolis: University of Minnesota Press, 2009.

Mamdani, Mahmood. *Good Muslim, Bad Muslim: America, the Cold War, and the Roots of Terror*. New York: Pantheon, 2004.

Margolis, Judy. "Romancing the East." *Report on Business Magazine*, December 1991.

Martin, Biddy. *Femininity Played Straight: The Significance of Being Lesbian*. New York: Routledge, 1996.

Massad, Joseph. "Re-orienting Desire: The Gay International and the Arab World." In *Desiring Arabs*, 160–190. Chicago: Chicago University Press, 2008.

Massumi, Brian. *Parables for the Virtual: Movement, Affect, Sensation*. Durham, NC: Duke University Press, 2002.

———. *A User's Guide to Capitalism and Schizophrenia: Deviations from Deleuze and Guattari*. Cambridge, MA: Massachusetts Institute of Technology Publishing, 1992.

McAleer, Joseph. *Passion's Fortune: The Story of Mills and Boon*. Oxford: Oxford University Press, 1999.

McAlister, Melani. *Epic Encounters: Culture, Media, and U.S. Interests in the Middle East 1945–2000*. Berkeley: University of California Press, 2001.

———. "Left Behind and the Politics of Prophecy Talk." In *Exceptional State: Contemporary U.S. Culture and the New Imperialism*, edited by Ashley Dawson and Malini Johar Schueller, 191–220. Durham, NC: Duke University Press, 2007.

McCauley, Clark, and Sophia Moskalenko. *Friction: How Radicalization Happens to Them and Us*. New York: Oxford University Press, 2011.

McClintock, Anne. "Paranoid Empire: Specters from Guantánamo and Abu Ghraib." *Small Axe, Number 28* 13, no. 1 (2009): 50–74.

McCullough, Christy. "Desert Hearts: In a New Crop of Romance Novels It's Always Midnight at the Oasis." *Bitch* 36 (2007): 29–31.

McRobbie, Angela. "Young Women and Consumer Culture: An Intervention." *Cultural Studies* 22, no. 5 (September 2008): 531–550.

Melamed, Jodi. "The Spirit of Neoliberalism: From Racial Liberalism to Neoliberal Multiculturalism." *Social Text 89* 24, no. 4 (winter 2006): 1–24.

Melman, Billie. *Women and the Popular Imagination in the Twenties*. New York: Palgrave Macmillan, 1988.

Memmi, Albert. *The Colonizer and the Colonized*. Translated by Howard Greenfield. Boston: Beacon Press, 1965.

"Might the Harem Scare 'Em?" *New Zealand Herald*, May 28, 2010.

Miller, Andrea. "Performing Specters of Imperialism: Affect, Terror, and the Body in Naveed Mir's *The Cinco Sanders Show*." Master's thesis, Georgia State University, 2014. http://scholarworks.gsu.edu/wsi_theses/39.

Mitchell, Timothy. *Carbon Democracy: Political Power in the Age of Oil*. New York: Verso, 2011.

Modleski, Tania. *Loving with a Vengeance: Mass-Produced Fantasies for Women*. 1982. Reprint, New York: Routledge, 2008.

Moghadam, Valentine. *Globalizing Women: Transnational Feminist Networks*. Baltimore: Johns Hopkins University Press, 2005.

Mojab, Shahrzad. "'Post-War Reconstruction,' Imperialism and Kurdish Women's NGOs." In *Women and War in the Middle East*, edited by Nadje Al-Ali and Nicola Pratt, 99–128. London: Zed, 2009.

Molavi, Afshin. "Sudden City." *National Geographic*, January 2007.

Morgensen, Scott Lauria. *Spaces between Us: Queer Settler Colonialism and Indigenous Decolonization.* Minneapolis: University of Minnesota Press, 2011.

Morrell, Virginia. "The Cruelest Place on Earth." *National Geographic,* October 2005.

Morrison, Toni. *Playing in the Dark: Whiteness and the Literary Imagination.* Cambridge, MA: Harvard University Press, 1992.

Naber, Nadine. "Ambiguous Insiders: An Investigation of Arab American Invisibility." *Ethnic and Racial Studies* 23, no. 1 (January 2000): 37–61.

——. *Arab America: Gender, Cultural Politics, and Activism.* New York: New York University Press, 2012.

——. "'Look, Mohammed the Terrorist Is Coming!' Cultural Racism, Nation-Based Racism, and the Intersectionality of Oppressions after 9/11." In *Race and Arab Americans Before and After 9/11: From Invisible Citizens to Visible Subjects,* edited by Amaney Jamal and Nadine Naber, 276–304. New York: Syracuse University Press, 2008.

Nance, Susan. *How the Arabian Nights Inspired the American Dream.* Chapel Hill: University of North Carolina Press, 2009.

National Geographic. "Ground Truths." February 2005.

——. "A Middle East Atlas, Just in Time." June 2003.

——. "Repeat Performance." June 2003.

——. "United Arab Emirates." April 2009.

"New York Board OKs 'Ground Zero' Mosque Plan." *Nation* (Thailand), May 27, 2010.

Nguyen, Mimi Thi. *The Gift of Freedom: War, Debt, and Other Refugee Passages.* Durham, NC: Duke University Press, 2012.

Norris, Michael, Warren Powlowski, and the editors of Simba Information. *Business of Consumer Book Publishing 2010.* Stamford, CT: Simba Information, 2010.

Oliver, Simone S. "Head over Heels over Turbans: The Exotic Headdress of a Bygone Era Catches On with a Younger Crowd." *International Herald Tribune,* November 16, 2010.

Omi, Michael, and Howard Winant. *Racial Formation in the United States,* 2nd ed. Philadelphia: Temple University Press, 1994.

O'Reilly, Bill. "Factor Follow-Up." Fox News Network, August 4, 2010. www.lexisnexis. com.ezproxy.gsu.edu/lnacui2api/api/version1/getDocCui?lni=803K-07F0-Y8Y1–72S6&csi=174179&hl=t&hv=t&hnsd=f&hns=t&hgn=t&oc=00240&perma=true.

Parameswaran, Radhika. "Reading Fictions of Romance: Gender, Sexuality, and Nationalism in Postcolonial India." *Journal of Communication* 52, no. 4 (2002): 832–851.

Parenti, Christian. "Planet America: The Revolution in Military Affairs as Fantasy and Fetish." In *Exceptional State: Contemporary U.S. Culture and the New Imperialism,* edited by Ashley Dawson and Malini Johar Schueller, 88–104. Durham, NC: Duke University Press, 2007.

——. *Tropic of Chaos: Climate Change and the New Geography of Violence.* New York: Nation Books, 2011.

Patai, Raphael. *The Arab Mind.* 1973. Reprint, Long Island City, NY: Hatherleigh Press, 2007.

Paula. "The Lure of the Sheikh Hero by Annie West." *Welcome to . . . Down Under Desirabelles* (blog), November 2, 2008. http://desirabelles.wordpress.com/2008/11/02/the-lure-of-the-sheikh-hero-by-annie-west/.

Pease, Donald. *The New American Exceptionalism*. Minneapolis: University of Minnesota Press, 2009.

Phillips, Susan Elizabeth. "The Romance and the Empowerment of Women." In *Dangerous Men and Adventurous Women: Romance Writers on the Appeal of the Romance*, edited by Jayne Ann Krentz, 53–60. Philadelphia: University of Pennsylvania Press, 1992.

Pomerance, Murray. "Baghdad Bad." *Film International* 7, no. 5 (2009): 27–49.

Poolos, Alexandra. "Reporter's Diary." In "Albania: Getting Out of Gitmo." *Frontline/World: Stories from a Small Planet*, 2011–2012. www.pbs.org/frontlineworld/stories/albania801/interview/poolos.html.

Post, Jerrold. *The Mind of the Terrorist: The Psychology of Terrorism from the IRA to al-Qa'ida*. New York: Palgrave, 2007.

Povinelli, Elizabeth A. *The Empire of Love: Toward a Theory of Intimacy, Genealogy, and Carnality*. Durham, NC: Duke University Press, 2006.

Proctor, Candice. "The Romance Genre Blues or Why We Don't Get No Respect." In *Empowerment versus Oppression: Twenty First Century Views of Popular Romance Novels*, edited by Sally Goade, 12–19. Newcastle, UK: Cambridge Scholars, 2007.

Puar, Jasbir. "'I Would Rather Be a Cyborg than a Goddess': Intersectionality, Assemblage, and Affective Politics." *EIPCP: European Institute for Progressive Cultural Policies*, January 2011. http://eipcp.net/transversal/0811/puar/en.

———. "Israel's Gay Propaganda War." *Guardian* (London and Manchester), July 1, 2010. www.guardian.co.uk/commentisfree/2010/jul/01/israels-gay-propaganda-war.

———. "On Torture: Abu Ghraib." *Radical History Review* 93 (2005): 13–38.

———. *Terrorist Assemblages: Homonationalism in Queer Times*. Durham, NC: Duke University Press, 2007.

Puar, Jasbir, and Amit Rai. "Monster, Terrorist, Fag: The War on Terrorism and the Production of Docile Patriots." *Social Text* 20, no. 3 (2002): 117–148.

Radway, Janice. *Reading the Romance: Women, Patriarchy, and Popular Literature*. 1984. Reprint, Chapel Hill: University of North Carolina Press, 1991.

Rana, Junaid. "The Story of Islamophobia." *Souls: A Critical Journal of Black Politics, Culture, and Society* 9, no. 2 (April 2007): 148–161.

———. *Terrifying Muslims: Race and Labor in the South Asian Diaspora*. Durham, NC: Duke University Press, 2011.

Raub, Patricia. "Issues of Passion and Power in E.M. Hull's The Sheik." *Women's Studies* 21, no. 1 (March 1992): 119–128.

Reardon, Patrick T. "The Mystery of Sheik Romance Novels." *Chicago Tribune*, April 24, 2006.

Regis, Pamela. *A Natural History of the Romance Novel*. Philadelphia: University of Pennsylvania Press, 2003.

Risen, James. "Blackwater Founder Moves to Abu Dhabi, Records Say." *New York Times*, August 17, 2010.

Roberts-Moneir, Nancy. "Unseen Sahara." *National Geographic*, February 2010.

Rodgers, Daniel. "American Exceptionalism Revisited." *Raritan* 24, no. 2 (2004): 21–47.

———. "Exceptionalism." In *Imagined Histories: American Historians Interpret the Past*, edited by Anthony Molho and Gordon S. Wood, 21–40. Princeton, NJ: Princeton University Press, 1998.

Romance Writers of America. 2012. www.rwa.org.

Romancing the Desert—Sheikh Books (blog). 2012. http://romancing-the-desert—sheikh-books.blogspot.com.

Roof, Judith. *Come as You Are: Sexuality and Narrative*. New York: Columbia University Press, 1996.

Rose, Jacqueline. *States of Fantasy*. New York: Oxford University Press, 1994.

Rose, Nikolas. *Governing the Soul: The Shaping of the Private Self*. New York: Routledge, 1990.

———. *Powers of Freedom: Reframing Political Thought*. New York: Cambridge University Press, 1999.

Rubin, Gayle. "Thinking Sex: Notes for a Radical Theory of the Politics of Sexuality." In *Pleasure and Danger: Exploring Female Sexuality*, edited by Carole Vance, 2nd ed., 267–319. London: Pandora Press, 1992.

Rumsfeld, Donald. "Secretary Rumsfeld Press Conference at NATO Headquarters, Brussels, Belgium," U.S. Department of Defense, News Transcript, June 6, 2002. www.defense.gov/transcripts/transcript.aspx?transcriptid=3490.

Rydell, Robert. *All the World's a Fair: Visions of Empire at American International Expositions, 1976–1916*. Chicago: University of Chicago Press, 1984.

Said, Edward. *Covering Islam: How the Media and the Experts Determine How We See the Rest of the World*. New York: Pantheon Books, 1981.

———. *Orientalism*. New York: Pantheon Books, 1978.

Salaita, Steven. *The Holy Land in Transit: Colonialism and the Quest for Canaan*. Syracuse, NY: Syracuse University Press, 2006.

Salazar, Cristian. "Mosque Going Up in NYC Building Damaged on 9/11." *Associated Press*, May 7, 2010.

Saliba, Therese. "Resisting Invisibility: Arab Americans in Academia and Activism." In *Arabs in the Americas: Building a New Future*, ed. Michael Suleiman, 304–19. Philadelphia: Temple University Press, 1999.

Salter, Mark. "Not Waiting for the Barbarians." In *Civilizational Identity: The Production and Reproduction of 'Civilizations' in International Relations*, edited by Martin Hall and Patrick Thaddeus Jackson, 81–93. New York: Palgrave, 2007.

Samhan, Helen. "Not Quite White: Race Classification and the Arab-American Experience." In *Arabs in the Americas: Building A New Future*, ed. Michael Suleiman, 209–26. Philadelphia: Temple University Press, 1999.

Santos, Evan Dale. "Among the Berbers." *National Geographic*, May 2005

Scahill, Jeremy. *Blackwater: The Rise of the World's Most Powerful Mercenary Army*. New York: Nation Books, 2007.

———. *Dirty Wars: The World Is a Battlefield*. New York: Nation Books, 2013.

Schwedler, Jillian. "Jordan." In *Dispatches from the Arab Spring*, edited by Paul Amar and Vijay Prashad, 243–65. Minneapolis: University of Minnesota Press, 2013.

Scott, Joan Wallach. *The Fantasy of Feminist History*. Durham, NC: Duke University Press, 2011.

Segal, Francesca. "Who Said Romance Was Dead?" *Observer* (London), January 27, 2008. www.theguardian.com/books/2008/jan/27/fiction.features1.

Shaheen, Jack. *Reel Bad Arabs: How Hollywood Vilifies a People*. New York: Olive Branch Press, 2009.

Sharif, Omar, with Marie-Thérèse Guinchard. *The Eternal Male*. Translated by Martin Sokolinsky. New York: Doubleday and Co., 1977.

Shaw, Ian Graham Ronald, and Majed Akhter, "The Unbearable Humanness of Drone Warfare in FATA, Pakistan," *Antipode* 44, no. 4 (2012): 1490–1509.

"Sheikhs and Desert Love" website. Amazon.com, 2012. www.sheikhs-and-desert-love.com/index.htm.

Shohat, Ella, and Robert Stam. *Unthinking Eurocentrism: Multiculturalism and the Media*. New York: Routledge, 1994.

Silverman, Kaja. *Male Subjectivity at the Margins*. New York: Psychology Press, 1992.

Smith, Andrea. *Native Americans and the Christian Right: The Gendered Politics of Unlikely Alliances*. Durham, NC: Duke University Press, 2008.

Smith, Jane. *Islam in America*. New York: Columbia University Press, 1999.

Snitow, Ann Barr. "Mass Market Romance: Pornography for Women is Different." In *Powers of Desire: The Politics of Sexuality*, edited Ann Snitow et al., 245–263. 1979. Reprint, New York: Monthly Review Press, 1983.

"Someone Explain the Appeal of Sheiks to Me, Please." *All About Romance: The Back Fence for Lovers of Romance Novels*. Desert Island Keepers. 2010. www.likesbooks.com.

Somerville, Siobhan. *Queering the Color Line: Race and the Invention of Homosexuality in American Culture*. Durham, NC: Duke University Press, 2000.

Stam, Robert, and Ella Shohat. *Race in Translation: Culture Wars Around the Postcolonial Atlantic*. New York: New York University Press, 2012.

Steet, Linda. *Veils and Daggers: A Century of* National Geographic's *Representation of the Arab World*. Philadelphia: Temple University Press, 2000.

Stegner, Wallace. *Discovery! The Search for Arabian Oil*. Beirut, Lebanon: Middle East Export Press, 1971.

Stockton, Ronald. "Ethnic Archetypes and the Arab Image." In *The Development of Arab-American Identity*, edited by Ernest McCarus, 119–153. Ann Arbor: University of Michigan Press, 1994.

Stoler, Ann Laura. "Imperial Formations and the Opacities of Rule." In *Lessons of Empire: Imperial Histories and American Power*, edited by Craig Calhoun, Frederick Cooper, and Kevin W. Moore, 48–60. New York: New Press, 2006.

———. *Race and the Education of Desire: Foucault's* History of Sexuality *and the Colonial Order of Things*. Durham, NC: Duke University Press, 1995.

Studlar, Gaylyn. "Discourses of Gender and Ethnicity: The Construction and De(con)struction of Rudolph Valentino as Other." *Film Criticism* 13, no. 2 (winter 1989): 18–35.

Sudbury, Julia, ed. *Global Lockdown: Gender, Race and the Rise of the Prison Industrial Complex around the World*. New York: Routledge, 2005.

Swedenburg, Ted. "Bad Rap for a Neck Scarf?" *International Journal of Middle East Studies* 41 (2009): 184–185.

Swift, Isabel. "The 'R' Word . . . by Isabel Swift." *Isabel Swift . . . Wouldn't You Like to Know?* (blog), May 23, 2011. http://isabelswift.blogspot.com/2011/05/r-word-by-isabel-swift.html.

Talburt, Susan. "Intelligibility and Narrating Queer Youth." In *Youth and Sexualities: Pleasure, Subversion, and Insubordination in and out of Schools*, edited by Mary Lou Rasmussen, Eric Rofes, and Susan Talburt, 17–39. New York: Palgrave, 2004.

"Tale of Two Prisons: The Guantanamo Files." *Guardian* (London and Manchester), April 26, 2011.

Taylor, Jeffrey. "Among the Berbers." *National Geographic*, January 2005.

Taylor, Jessica. "And You Can Be My Sheikh: Gender, Race, and Orientalism in Contemporary Romance Novels." *Journal of Popular Culture* 40, no. 6 (2007): 1032–1051.

Teague, Matthew. "Isn't She Lovely?" *National Geographic*, August 2009.

———. "The Sinai." *National Geographic*, March 2009.

Teo, Hsu-Ming. *Desert Passions: Orientalism and Romance Novels*. Austin: University of Texas Press, 2012.

———. "Shanghaied by Sheiks: Orientalism and Hybridity in Women's Romance Writing." *Olive Pink Society Bulletin* 11, no. 1 (1999): 12–21.

Vitalis, Robert. *America's Kingdom: Mythmaking on the Saudi Oil Frontier*. Stanford, CA: Stanford University Press, 2007.

Viviano, Frank. "Saudi Arabia: Kingdom on the Edge." *National Geographic*, October 2003.

Volpp, Leti. "The Citizen and the Terrorist." In *September 11 in History: A Watershed Moment?*, edited by Mary L. Dudziak, 147–162. Durham, NC: Duke University Press, 2003.

Walker, Kate. "Sheiken and Stirred." *Pink Heart Society* (blog), October 6, 2006. http://pinkheartsociety.blogspot.com/2006/10/thursday-talk-time-with-kate-walker.html.

Wardrop, Stephanie. "The Heroine Is Being Beaten: Freud, Sadomasochism, and Reading the Romance." *Style* 29, no. 3 (1995): 459–474.

———. "Last of the Red Hot Mohicans: Miscegenation in the Popular American Romance." *MELUS* 22, no. 2 (summer 1997): 61–74.

Weaver, Mary Anne. "Qatar: Revolution from the Top Down." *National Geographic*, March 2003.

Webster, Donovan. "Empty Quarter." *National Geographic*, February 2005.

Wells, Rachel. "Desert Storm." *Sydney Morning Herald*, June 12, 2010.

Wendell, Sarah. *Everything I Know about Love, I Learned from Romance Novels*. Naperville, IL: Sourcebooks Casablanca, 2011.

Wendell, Sarah [screen name SBSarah]. "Alphas in Marriage." *Smart Bitches, Trashy Books* (blog), August 16, 2007. http://smartbitchestrashybooks.com/index.php/weblog/comments/alphas_in_marriage/.

———. "Meg Cabot, Comfort Reads, and Sheikh Romance." *Smart Bitches Trashy Books* (blog), May 22, 2007. http://smartbitchestrashybooks.com/index.php/weblog/comments/meg_cabot_comfort_reads_and_sheikh_romance/.

———. "Mills and Boon: Heaven, Hell, or Just People Hyperventilating." *Smart Bitches, Trashy Books* (blog), December 6, 2007. http://smartbitchestrashybooks.com/blog/mills_boon_heaven_hell_or_just_people_hyperventilating/.

———. "The Playboy Sheikh's Virgin Stable Girl by Sharon Kendrick." *Smart Bitches Trashy Books* (blog), September 10, 2009. www.smartbitchestrashybooks.com/index.php/weblog/comments/the-playbot-sheikhs-virgin-stable-girl-by-Sharon-Kendrick/.

———. "Trend Spotting." *Smart Bitches Trashy Books: All of the Romance, None of the Bullshit* (blog), June 21, 2011. http://smartbitchestrashybooks.com/blog/trend-spotting/.

———. "What Not to Read." *Smart Bitches, Trashy Books* (blog), October 30, 2006. *www.smartbitchestrashybooks.com/index.php/weblog/comments/what_not_to_read/*.

Wendell, Sarah, and Candy Tan. *Beyond Heaving Bosoms: The Smart Bitches' Guide to Romance Novels*. New York: Simon & Schuster, 2009.

West, Annie. "The Lure of the Sheikh Hero." *Down Under Desirabelles* (blog), November 2, 2008. http://desirabelles.wordpress.com/2008/11/02/the-lure-of-the-sheikh-hero-by-annie-west/.

"What Makes a Sheikh Romance Hot?" In "Sheikhs and Desert Love" website. Amazon.com, 2012. Accessed June 3, 2008. http://sheikhs-and-desert-love.com/presentation02.html.

Whitaker, Brian. "Those Sexy Arabs." *Guardian* (London and Manchester), March 23, 2006. www.guardian.co.uk/commentisfree/2006/mar/23/thosesexyarabs.

Wilkins, Amy. "The Unshakeable Appeal of the Sheikh Hero." *I [Heart] Harlequin Presents* (blog), August 17, 2007. www.iheartpresents.com/2007/08/the-unshakeable-appeal-of-the-sheikh-hero.

Williams, Randall. *The Divided World: Human Rights and Its Violence*. Minneapolis: University of Minnesota Press, 2010.

Winant, Howard. *The New Politics of Race: Globalism, Difference, Justice*. Minneapolis: University of Minnesota Press, 2004.

Wright, Elizabeth, ed. *Feminism and Psychoanalysis: A Critical Dictionary*. Cambridge, MA: Blackwell, 1992.

Young, Kimberly. "Kimberly Young Is a Love-Slave to the Sheikh!" *I [Heart] Harlequin Presents* (blog), March 28, 2007. www.iheartpresents.com/?p=40.

Zackowitz, Margaret G. "Worlds Away." *National Geographic*, December 2009.

Žižek, Slavoj. *How to Read Lacan*. New York: W.W. Norton & Co., 2007.

———. *Looking Awry: An Introduction to Jacques Lacan through Popular Culture*. Cambridge, MA: MIT Press, 1991.

Zonana, Joyce. "The Sultan and the Slave: Feminist Orientalism and the Structure of 'Jane Eyre'" *Signs* 18 (1993): 592–617.

INDEX

Numbers in italics refer to figures.

ABOUT THE AUTHOR

Amira Jarmakani is Associate Professor and Director of the Institute for Women's, Gender, and Sexuality Studies at Georgia State University. Also the author of *Imagining Arab Womanhood: The Cultural Mythology of Veils, Harems, and Belly Dancers in the U.S.* (2008), which won the National Women's Studies Association Gloria E. Anzaldúa book prize, she works in the fields of women's, gender, and sexuality studies; Arab American studies; and cultural studies.